OCEAN *of* MILK,
OCEAN *of* BLOOD

A Mongolian Monk in the
Ruins of the Qing Empire

MATTHEW W. KING

COLUMBIA UNIVERSITY PRESS *NEW YORK*

Columbia University Press
Publishers Since 1893
New York   Chichester, West Sussex
cup.columbia.edu
Copyright © 2019 Columbia University Press
All rights reserved
Library of Congress Cataloging-in-Publication Data

Names: King, Matthew W. (Matthew William), author.
Title: Ocean of milk, ocean of blood : a Mongolian monk in the ruins of the
Qing Empire / Matthew King.
Description: New York : Columbia University Press, [2019] | Includes
bibliographical references and index.
Identifiers: LCCN 2018040266 (print) | LCCN 2018051372 (ebook) |
ISBN 9780231549226 (electronic) | ISBN 9780231191067 (cloth : alk. paper)
Subjects: LCSH: Blo-bzang-rta-mgrin, 1867-1937. | Buddhism—Asia—History.
Classification: LCC BQ942.L5825 (ebook) | LCC BQ942.L5825 K56 2019 (print) |
DDC 294.3/923092 [B]—dc23
LC record available at https://lccn.loc.gov/2018040266

Columbia University Press books are printed on permanent and durable acid-free paper.
Printed in the United States of America
Cover design: Noah Arlow

To my family

Contents

CONTENTS

Acknowledgments

The completion of the research and writing for this book was made possible through the financial assistance of several programs and institutions. I would like to acknowledge the generosity of the American Council of Learned Societies, the Social Science and Humanities Research Council of Canada, the Association for Asian Studies, the Khyentse Foundation, the Sheng-Yen Lu Foundation, the UC Riverside Regent's Faculty Fellowship, UC Riverside's Center for Ideas and Society, and the Mellon Advancing Intercultural Studies Workshop series at CIS.

I am especially grateful to the Social Science Research Council for their generous support. Many of the ideas in this book were solidified while I was participating in the 2016–17 SSRC Transregional Research Junior Scholar Fellowship program. In addition to supporting leave from teaching and other responsibilities to write and research abroad, the SSRC convened fellows for extended interdisciplinary workshops on our projects at Duke University, in Chiang Mai, and in Phnom Penh. The feedback, critique, and conversation that occurred at those events on this project (and the next!) was rich and challenging and is widely represented in many of these pages. I am particularly grateful for the insights and generosity of our senior faculty mentors, especially Prasenjit Duara and Engseng Ho.

I have been fortunate to work out some of the ideas explored in this book at several meetings, workshops, and invited talks in the last two or three years. Delivered across conference rooms, beer halls, train cars, and dinner tables, the insights of colleagues at these events have been invaluable in the final stretches of this writing. Thank you to the funders, organizers, and participants at UC Berkeley's Mongolia Initiative conferences, the Buddhist Studies Program Fund of UC Santa Barbara's Department of Religious Studies & the XIVth Dalai Lama Endowment, the Yale MacMillan Center's Inter-Asia Initiative, Eötvös Loránd University's Mongolian Buddhism Workshop Series in Budapest, the Oriental Studies Conference at the University of Warsaw, the Käte Hamburger Kolleg Dynamics in the History of Religions Between Asia and Europe in Bochum, and the Oriental Studies Colloquium at Oxford University. I would also like to thank the many friends, colleagues, co-panelists, and audience members at recent meetings of the American Academy of Religion, the Association for Asian Studies, and the International Association for Buddhist Studies whose questions, challenges, and suggestions have made this a stronger project.

I wish to specifically acknowledge the invaluable suggestions received on aspects of this project from colleagues and former teachers and supervisors. Represented in these pages are insights and historical facts received in recent years from conversations with Christopher Atwood, Agata Bareja-Starczyńska, Brian Baumann, David Brophy, José Cabezón, Isabelle Charleux, Johan Elverskog, Frances Garrett, Holly Gayley, Amanda Goodman, Matthew Kapstein, Pamela Klassen, Rongdao Lai, Max Oidtmann, Natalie Rothman, Ivan Sablin, Tsering Shakya, Michael Sheehy, Brenton Sullivan, Uranchimeg Tsultem, Nikolay Tsyrempilov, Sangseraima Ujeed, and Stacey Van Vleet. In Warsaw I had the chance to discuss the organization of this book with Elliot Sperling not long before his untimely passing. I am immensely grateful for his generosity and attention. Professor Vesna Wallace had been, since I was a master's student, an endlessly knowledgeable and generous friend, mentor, and colleague during my long odyssey with Zava Damdin's works.

I would like to thank my lively and always interesting colleagues and students at the University of California, Riverside. For insightful conversation on aspects of this project and for solidarity while it was written, profound thanks are due to Professors Amanda Lucia, Adam Harmer, Andreja Novakovic, Pashaura Singh, Michael Alexander, Lisa Raphals, Melissa Wilcox, Paul Chang, Muhamad Ali, and Eugene Anderson. I would also like to thank current and former students for conversations that have helped me think in new ways about questions explored in these pages, especially Sierra Lapoint, Steven Quach, Elizabeth Miller, Uudam Borjigin, Shou-Jen Kuo, and Agatha Tesmer. I have been grateful to present and explore some of this material in semiregular conversation with the Buddhist Studies graduate students at UC Santa Barbara. Thank you to Daigengna Duoer, Erdenebaatar Erdene-Ochir, Jed Forman, Michael Ium, Christine Murphy, Jake Nagasawa, and Patrick Lambelet for perceptive suggestions and questions during my visits to UCSB.

This project owes a tremendous debt to Khenpo Kunga Sherab, my kind friend and expert on all things Inner Asian and Buddhist. I consider myself extremely fortunate to have had the chance for twice-weekly conversations with Khenpo-la for many years now, to speak and read Tibetan and discuss matters historical and doctrinal in Inner Asia. Many of the primary sources treated in this book were discussed with Khenpo-la in one way or another, and I am extremely appreciative. Early in my graduate career, Thubten Champa graciously helped me begin working on *The Dharma Conch* by Zava Damdin outside of his seminars on Classical Tibetan, and so I also wish to thank him.

Many Mongolian friends and colleagues, more than I can properly acknowledge in these few lines, supported this project despite the unpredictability that often accompanies research and travel in their homeland. For overwhelming hospitality and encouragement (and for helping me recover from many illnesses, providing food and housing, showing me strange caves and magical stones, arranging meetings, pointing out ruins, rescuing me from broken-down vans deep in the Gobi, and seeing me through countless other "obstacle blessings"), I wish to thank: Boldbaatar Nyemsuren, his wife Nomon, his brothers and their families, and his mother; Damdin Gerlee and her extended family; Ven. B. Tushikhbayar; Gombo Lam; the abbot and monks of Amarbayasgalant Monastery; and the centenarian Guru Dewa Rinpoche and his staff, with whom I stayed several times before Rinpoche's passing. A most sincere thanks to Munkchimeg Tserendorj, a colleague and friend formerly of the National Library of Mongolia, who very generously helped me locate contemporary Mongolian scholarship on Zava Damdin. I express my most sincere thanks to the current incarnation of Zava Damdin, Zava Renbüchi Luvsandarjaa, his entire family (especially Ama-la and Bilguun), and all the monks at Delgeruun Choira Monastery in

Dungov Aimag. Finally, a magical midnight meeting with Dr. L. Terbish in his enchanted study many years ago continues to inspire, and I am grateful that he took the time to clarify issues with this research early on.

Lastly, I would like to sincerely thank Wendy Lochner, Lowell Frye, Leslie Kriesel, and the staff at Columbia University Press for their support and guidance. I would like to thank the anonymous reviewers of my manuscript, whose insights, critique, and perspectives were extremely helpful in seeing this project to completion. I am grateful to Liz Harmer for taking the time to edit a draft of this book with such attention and discernment. Finally, I must thank Jody Butterworth, curator of the British Library's Endangered Archives Programme, for permission to reproduce many of the glass plate negatives found in these pages, all of which are physically housed at Mon-sound and Vision foundation in Ulaanbaatar under the supervision of Mr. Bayasgalan Bayanbat.

In 2005, I had just returned to Vancouver from my first trip to Mongolia. I was twenty-four, not in school, and barely employed. I had been acting as attendant for Ācārya Zasep Rinpoché as he did a teaching tour of Ulaan-baatar and in monasteries, town halls, and hillsides in Central and South Gobi provinces. Just moments before we parted company after eating, sleeping, and driving within a few feet of each other for many weeks (and for months prior while in India), I asked with the urgency and earnestness of confused young people: What should I do with my life? He suggested without hesitation that I should do a master's thesis on Zava Damdin's histories and see where it would lead.

Many months later, while doing labor on a stonemasonry job in the middle of the Canadian winter, I learned I had been accepted into a graduate program in Buddhist Studies. I told my boss that I was thinking about quitting and going to school. He sighed and said that this was a good idea, since if I went his route the inevitable injured back or rock dust in lungs would mean not feeding a family. He insisted I quit and allowed me to do so on the required day when he didn't have to, as long as I thanked him at the start of my first book.

Thank you, Rinpoche and B.M. This is the very overdue result of your generosity and encouragement.

Conventions

Tibetan

The transcription of Tibetan words in this book follows the Tibetan and Himalayan Library (THL)'s Simplified Phonetic Transcription of Standard Tibetan. The Wylie transliteration is given on first usage, either as a note or in parentheses in the text as appropriate.

Mongolian

Keeping the spelling of Mongolian words consistent and not overly technical for the sake of non-specialists has been challenging. The primary sources I treat here are mostly in Tibetan and use Tibetan letters and conventions erratically to transcribe literary and Khalkha vernacular Mongolian. In addition, contemporaneous Mongolian sources used the vertical (Uyghur-Mongolian) script while the Mongolian secondary scholarship I reference uses a Cyrillic script that was instituted years after Zava Damdin's death. For the sake of historical accuracy, I transliterate the vertical script for all persons, places, and equivalents for Sanskrit and Tibetan Buddhist technical terms and canonical works (marked in notes and parentheses as "Mong."). For Cyrillic I follow the Tibetan and Himalayan Library (THL)'s simplified Mongolian transcription system, developed by Christopher Atwood (marked in notes and parentheses as "Kh. Mong."), except that I keep "v" for в on the Library of Congress model. For the older vertical script I also use the Atwood system, except that I keep γ instead of ġ or gh on the old Mostaert and Lessing models.

Tibetan Capitalization

This book capitalizes the first letter of all Tibetan text titles, personal names, and place names, regardless of whether it is the root letter.

Foreign Terminology in Parenthesis

Certain English terms, Buddhist technical language, and proper nouns are followed by transliterated equivalents in Tibetanand, as the case may be, Mongolian, Sanskrit, Chinese, French, German, or Russian. In each case, transliterated equivalents are given in parentheses or as notes with the respective language clearly marked, separated by a semicolon: for example, "Buddhist logic (Skt. *pramāṇa*; Tib. *tshad ma*; Mong. *kemjiy-e*)."

Ocean of Milk, Ocean of Blood

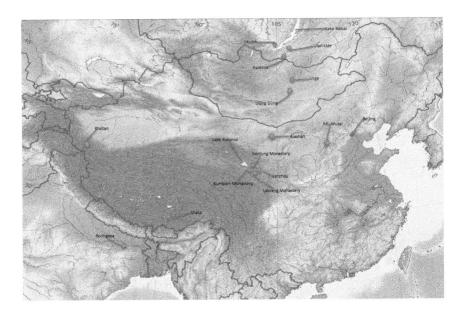

FIGURE I.1 Map of Inner Asia, c. 1900.

Introduction

To be anybody in Mongolia you must be the reincarnation of somebody.

—*THE WASHINGTON POST*, 1914[1]

ONE SUMMER'S DAY, an elderly monk known as "the spiritual friend who pleases Mañjughoṣa" took his seat at the head of a large assembly at the monastic college of Dashichoijurling. Nestled within the patchwork of Urga city's markets, yurt residences, and temples, Dashichoijurling braided intellectual and religious life on the northerly Khalkha Mongol steppes with Tibetan, Chinese, Siberian, Manchu, and Russian spheres of influence and routes of exchange.[2] An unnamed scribe recorded events, preserved in a short work titled *Notes Clarifying the Meaning of Some of the Holy Emperor's Secret Prophecies* (Tib. *Dam pa gong ma'i gsang ba'i lung bstan 'ga' zhig gi don mchan bus gsal bar byas pa*). "All Mongolian monks, lamas, gods, and protectors" had congregated to listen, "undifferentiated in their devotion, here at the edge of time and place."[3] They came to hear about a prophecy once given by the enlightened bodhisattva Mañjuśrī in his most prominent human incarnation, the Manchu emperor of the mighty Qing Empire. The emperor as Mañjuśrī, noted the scribe, was the singular object of the assembly's reverence that day.

Adding his own interpretations to the original prophecy in great doses, the appropriately named "spiritual friend who pleases Mañjughoṣa" first reminded his audience that long ago Mañjuśrī had chosen China as his primary field of enlightened activity.[4] This was a land "in the direction of the rising sun, to the east of Tibet" and northeast of the Indian kingdom of Magadha, where the Buddha Śākyamuni had been born thousands of years prior.[5] In this telling, Mañjuśrī had first manifested in Chinese territory not in human form but as great swaths of the rural and urban landscape: cliffs, trees, and rivers spontaneously enacting enlightened wisdom and benevolence. The holy pilgrimage site of Mount Wutai in Shanxi—long considered by Chinese, Mongolian, and Tibetan devotees to be the pure land of Mañjuśrī here on earth—was an especially noteworthy example. So too was the "exceedingly beautiful, great city called Beijing." In the center of Mañjuśrī's materialized maṇḍala—within the Forbidden City in the center of the imperial capital, in the center of the great multiethnic Qing Empire, in the center of the world—dwelled the enlightened Manchu emperor and entourage.[6]

The "spiritual friend who pleases Mañjughoṣa" then explained how, after enchanting physical geographies such as these, Mañjuśrī began to more actively intervene in human affairs by taking on the flesh of prominent men. These always-masculine bodies had been draped in the robes of monks and emperors and sat upon thrones at the center of imperial and monastic complexes. They managed complementary spheres of authority across the world, which they knew as the southern continent of Jambudvīpa (Tib. 'Dzam bu gling; Mong. Jambu-tib). Ancient and medieval India, desert cities dotting the old Silk Road, imperial Tibet, the courts of the Mongol Empire, the grassy abodes of the old Turkic kaγans, the sandy throughways of pre-Islamic Mecca, and the domes of distant Saint Petersburg were all once Mañjuśrī's dominion.

The assembly then heard that, over the longue durée, Mañjuśrī had channeled the current of his human manifestations into two streams. The first was "that great chief of the gods, the Mañjuśrī [i.e., the Manchu] emperor." The other was successive manifestations of Tibetan, Uyghur, and Mongolian "living buddhas." Many were lamas whose incarnation lineages had become officially recognized within the Qing imperial order. They were called trülku in Tibetan (Tib. sprul sku), khubilγan or khutuγtu in Mongolian, and huofo (活佛). Since the dawn of time, courtly and monastic incarnations such as these had publicly recognized one another. These many Mañjuśrīs then set into motion an enlightened drama that became the wellspring of civilization. Seated upon thrones in monastic assemblies or imperial courts and wrapped in silk or saffron, they had exchanged precepts and titles, introduced literacy and medicine, and established the complementary "yokes" of legal, political, and soteriological infrastructure in Indian, Chinese, Manchu, Mongolian, Turkic, Russian, and Tibetan societies.

While he manifested Chinese landscapes, so much rock and mortar, and enchanted the bones and flesh of emperors and eminent monks since a time before time was recorded, Mañjuśrī's intent had ever remained singular: to unify the "Two Systems of the [Buddhist] teachings and politics."[7] The packed temple courtyards of Dashichoijurling, the surrounding monastic city of Urga teeming with saffron-robed monks and pilgrims, and the multiethnic Qing Empire itself were the clearest testimony of Mañjuśrī's success. In his principal guise as successive Manchu emperors, he had become "like a full moon on the crowns of the nine types of beings of China, Tibet, and Mongolia."[8] From that celestial position, he had "gathered like a cloud in the sky of fortunate sentient beings and uninterruptedly rained very white virtue and goodness."[9] The message to the men and gods assembled that summer's day was this: all Eurasian historical events were details in the total order of Mañjuśrī's holy biography.

However, this prophetic commentary at Dashichoijurling was given not only to affirm the enlightened identity of the Manchu emperor, a "lord" who "directly perceives all phenomena associated with the Two Systems" in "the mirror of his heart-mind."[10] The "spiritual friend who pleases Mañjughoṣa" intended also to clarify how the Qing imperial project had been completed by merging with the reformed Géluk school, founded in Central Tibet in the fifteenth century:

> The stainless Yellow Hat Dharma tradition
> joined together with the mighty dominion of the Manchu emperor,
> was long sustained over many centuries,
> and endured in Chinese, Tibetan, and Mongol lands.[11]

Ever since, generations of Buddhist scholars and meditators had transmitted the Buddhadharma in its perfected form as the "Yellow Religion" (Mong. *sira yin shasin*), the Géluk (Tib. *Dge lugs pa*) or Ganden (Tib. *Dga' ldan pa*) tradition shared across Tibetan, Mongol, Manchu, Siberian, and Han communities.[12] Vast webs of Géluk monastic colleges such as Dashichoijurling thus wove together regional courses of lineage transmission, mass monasticism, the ritual cosmologies of tantrism, discourses of Qing imperial sovereignty, and globalized (and globalizing) imperial history.

The "spiritual friend who pleases Mañjughoṣa" then shifted from a laudatory to a cautionary tone as he closed his commentary on the holy emperor's secret prophecies. Just as it is natural for the wind sweeping across the slopes of Mount Mālaya to absorb the fragrant odor of its sandalwood forests,

> So too, it is natural for those higher lamas and political leaders,
> those endowed with the good quality of knowledge about the Two Systems,
> to follow Mañjughoṣa in his consecutive manifestations
> as both lama and emperor.[13]

"Demonic armies" who had opposed the Qing and its favored Géluk tradition, recorded the scribe, long suffered only abysmal defeat and perpetual incarceration in a "house of mourning." Those who refused to recognize the enlightened presence driving forward the Qing-Géluk formation had

FIGURE I.2 The spiritual friend who pleases Mañjughoṣa.
Image from Blo-bzaṅ-rta-mgrin, *Zhongguo Xi Bei Wen Xian Cong Shu / v. 143-157*. 西北少数民族文字文献; *Byaṅ Phyogs Hor Gyi Yul Du Dam Pa'i Chos Rin Po Che 'Byuṅ Tshul Gyi Gtam Rgyud Bkra Śis Chos Duṅ Dźad Pa'i Sgra Dbyaṅs*, vol. 150 (Lanzhou: Zhongguo Lanzhou: Lanzhou gu ji shu dian, 1990), 25.

suffered, were suffering, and would suffer again "a rain of activity [that] banishes them from our land to the far shore of an endless ocean."[14]

This scene of public prophetic commentary opens this book not because of its content but because of its timing. A public ode to a thriving Qing political and religious formation—to histories, territories, and communities ordered and enchanted by enlightened presence and imperial sovereignty—would not have been out of place at the height of Qing imperial power and influence in the late seventeenth or eighteenth century, or even as imperial control over Inner Asian frontiers waned in the nineteenth. But these men and gods gathered on the eighth day of the seventh month of the Wood Rat year in the fifteenth *rapjung*, or August 8, 1924.

By that summer, more than a decade had passed since the political collapse of the Qing Empire. The "enlightened" ruling elite had long since been displaced. On the very day when the "spiritual friend who pleases Mañjughoṣa" took his seat at Dashichoijurling, the last Qing emperor, Puyi, lay in hiding in the Japanese legation in Beijing, having been given three

FIGURE I.3 A view of Ganden monastery and its surrounding area, Ulaanbaatar. Notice prayer wheel sheds along the edge of the living quarters (1930s).
Digital copies of glass plate negatives preserved in the Archives for Cinema, Photography, and Sound Recording, Mongolia [1910s–1950s]. EAP264/1/9/2/71.

hours to vacate his Forbidden City "maṇḍala" by the warlord Feng Yuxiang nine months earlier. No longer did Han, Korean, Uyghur, Tibetan, or Mongol communities count the years according to the reign of Manchu rulers, as they had since the seventeenth century. Republican China was already a decade old. An autonomous Mongolian nation-state had separated from the flailing Qing in 1911. Urga had been transformed into its capital city—Neislel Küriye—eight years prior. A Tibetan incarnate lama had been enthroned as "holy king" of an autonomous Mongolian nation-state, its fraught existence measured in the years of his reign title, "Elevated by Many" (Mong. *Olana ergügdegsen*). In 1921, the urban environs where the "spiritual friend who pleases Mañjughoṣa" would give his tribute to the living Qing formation three years later had been the staging ground for the founding of the socialist Mongolian People's Republic (Bugude Nairamdakhu Mongγol Arad Ulus). The throne upon which "the spiritual friend" sat while teaching was no longer in the heart of Urga or even Neislel Küriye, but in the renamed Ulaγanbaγatur, or "Red Hero." On May 20, 1924, the "holy king" who had been "elevated by many" died. Laws were passed to prohibit identifying his, or any other, incarnation. Days and weeks soon proceeded with Gregorian names, no longer setting into time the body natural or body politic of the enlightened.

In the warm air of late summer 1924, Dashichoijurling thus lay in the heart of the world's second socialist nation, in an intellectual and political climate officially defined against imperial-era suppression by the Qing administration and its feudalist collaborators, the vast Tibeto-Mongolian-Siberian networks of Buddhist monasteries. Who would deliver such a message, so out of step with political reality? What monk (or god) would come to hear it?

This book is an attempt to answer such questions. My aim is to access the content of the social imagination of Buddhist scholars grappling with Qing religiosity and history beyond the regime's political end and beyond the totalizing, teleological discourses of the modern and modernization. The content of that imagination—which had its day between the Qing collapse in 1911 and the mass purge of monastics and monasticism in 1937—has been largely destroyed, fragmented by party rhetoric, buried by state violence, excluded by revisionist Soviet-era historiography, repurposed in the mythologies of diaspora and refugee communities, and exiled in geographies of academic knowledge about "Buddhism," "Asia," and its modern "History."

My work to find the otherwise ways of being in a post-Qing world—limited to a microhistorical portrait patched together from fragmentary sources—affirms what Prasenjit Duara, Dipesh Chakrabarty, and others have identified as an enduring problem for historians of twentieth-century Asia: the unselfconscious mobilization of the national subject, of national time, space, community, moral narratives, agents, and sovereignties, described using markers such as race, religion, rationalization, and a static, unilineal, progressive historical time.[15] To repurpose some wording from Peter Marshall's revisionist history of anarchism, this book therefore recognizes at the outset that Buddhism in Asia's heartland—poised between and beyond empire, nation, socialism, state violence, and exile—has been and remains not a victim but a product of the tyranny of fixed meanings. What lies beyond what Thomas Paine called the "Bastille of the word"?[16] How and where might we find it?

Setting the fixities of "Tibet," "Mongolia," "the West," "Asia," and "Buddhism" aside as best I can (while recognizing that the social location of my writing stubbornly demands slipping into their usage for comparative purposes), I treat networks of Inner Asian scholastic institutions during the Qing-socialist transition as a dynamic example of what Engseng Ho calls "inter-Asia space." Such an approach—stimulated by reflections upon globalized exchange that "is kicking anthropologists out of villages and historians out of nation-states"—promises to better "shed light on the social shapes of societies that are mobile, spatially expansive, and interactive with one another."[17]

The post-Qing monastic sources this book considers are vibrant examples of such interaction. I treat them as what Lisa Stenmark, drawing upon insights of feminist epistemologies, calls a "public discourse": a relationship between the knower and that which is known—a "relational epistemology"—and between the knower and society—a "situated knower."[18] Who the knower is fundamentally affects what is known. Tibeto-Mongolian monastic elites who during the Qing were the writers of society, as Michel de Certeau would have it, "knew" the post-Qing world in particular, relational ways that have so far been neglected. The worlds some of them wrote, as explored in these pages, collapse clear distinctions not only between an imperial and a postimperial moment but also between the contents of their monastic works and the academic literature and disciplinary tools modern scholars are trained to use in analyzing them. Here I follow Michel de Certeau even further, into the vanishing point between analytic procedures, textual product, and written trace: "an uncanny sort of passage," he would say, from the theoretically interminable domain of research into the "servitude" of writing.[19] How, I ask in these pages, were Buddhism, community, agency, and history written by monks, gods, and men (and not Bolsheviks, citizens, or the sovereign individual writ large) in the wake of a newly absent Qing?

Grappling with this question requires immediately confronting new zones of inter-Asian contact and exchange between revolutionary-era monastic authors, party ideologues, and harbingers of the human sciences that represent what Homi Bhaba calls "alien territory," a third space of hybrid cultural inscription and articulation beyond the nation, the Qing, or unilineal history.[20] The objects of historical inquiry and the usual tools and social spaces used to know them begin to unwind. My secondary sources are in my primary sources. The scientific academy was in the monastery. Ethnology, history, and philology made new knowledge about enlightened buddhas taking human rebirths like strings of a pearl. The intellectual products of Europe's Enlightenment unlocked antiquarian prophecy and tantric exegesis. The musing of conservative monks of the Qing gave form to scientific modernity. The modern, modernity, and modernization became negligible details in erstwhile global histories. And my long-dead protagonist has been reborn and will read these pages.

Géluk scholastic institutions elaborately defined themselves as interlocking sites for the movement of texts and literacy, medicine, ritual practices, material and visual culture, monastic discipline, and techniques for self and community cultivation among Russia, British India, the Qing, Japan, and all that sprang later from their imperial shells. Despite great regional differences in linguistic, economic, and political organization and affiliation, Géluk scholastic institutions like Dashichoijurling on the Khalkha steppes mobilized shared knowledge and knowledge-making practices between them. And these interpretative practices, as much as the narratives, inherited from centuries of cosmopolitan sense making across the many Sino-Tibeto-Mongolian frontiers, produced for a few short years an otherwise history for the post-Qing world and for Buddhist life in it.

In light of the stunning state violence that ends this story, what follows is necessarily a granular picture of history and self and community making. The very limited surviving sources allow for little in the way of grand comparison or archaeologies of the *Weltanschauung* or *mentalité* of hundreds of

FIGURE I.4 Zava Damdin painting.
Photograph by author.

thousands of monks either weathering the uncertainty of the postimperial moment or marching ahead bravely into a revolutionary future. Instead, I tell a story from the first-person perspective of a singular, altogether exceptional monk working at the Tibetan-Mongolian frontiers of Russia and China, in the global crosscurrents of early twentieth-century Khalkha Mongolia. Zava Damdin Lubsangdamdin (Tib. *Blo bzang rta mgrin*, 1867–1937) was one of the most prominent and prolific Inner Asian Buddhist thinkers to have lived during the late-and post-Qing periods. A complicated historian, mystic, logician, pilgrim, and abbot who defies easy categorization, Zava Damdin would be memorialized by Soviet-era historians as Mongolia's first modern intellectual and its last feudalist ideologue. His massive oeuvre—unfinished and hidden for decades as the monastic world it describes was battered into grass and sand—is the only collection of scholarly writing of equal scope and purpose to have survived the state-inflicted terror of the late 1930s.

Until new sources are discovered, these 417 texts in some 9,000 folios (all written in Tibetan, as was customary among Mongolian scholars at this time) offer our only substantive sources on just what those men and gods understood in August 1924 as they gathered at the feet of the "the spiritual friend who pleases Mañjughoṣa"—an epithet, it turns out, reserved by devoted disciples for Zava Damdin.

Zava Damdin: Writing the Ruins of the Qing

In a curious coincidence, in 1964 two dedicated studies published on either side of the Iron Curtain simultaneously memorialized Zava Damdin almost three decades after his death. The first was a Russian language literary history written firmly within the Soviet academy by Shagdaryn Bira titled *On Sh. Damdin's "Golden Book"* (Rus. *O "Zolotoi knige" Sh. Damdina*).[21] Reading in the overexposing and predictable light of historical materialism, Bira applauds Zava Damdin as a scholar of the Qing uniquely worthy of serious academic inquiry. Though ultimately this Khalkha monk remained beholden to "feudalist Lamaist ideology and Qing-era superstition," Bira considered Zava Damdin to have distinguished himself from the saffron-robed masses "since he did not seek to distance himself or his worldview from science, but on the contrary, he welcomed it."[22] This was quite opposite to those other monastics who attacked science and culture, "which had begun to flourish in Mongolia during the people's revolution of 1921."[23] Most striking for Bira was Zava Damdin's "rational" approach to the writing of history, an alluring dance with empirical methodologies and a flirtation with nascent scholarship in the human and natural sciences.

Also in 1964, across the trenches of the Cold War, Lokesh Chandra reproduced Zava Damdin's historical magnum opus, the 1931 *Golden Book* (Tib. *Gser gyi deb ther*; Mong. *Altan debter*), as volume 34 of his monumental *Śata-Piṭaka Series in Indo-Asian Literatures*.[24] As it happened, the great Indologist and Tibetanist reproduced the Dashichoijurling (Tib. *Bkra shis chos 'byor gling*) xylograph, a set of woodcut printing blocks that had been one of the last pre-purge projects of the monastery where "the spiritual friend who pleases Mañjughoṣa" had addressed his human and divine audience in 1924. Chandra's efforts brought Zava Damdin's work to shelves in research libraries around the world.

In a Romantic Orientalist tone quite different from Bira's study, Chandra noted somberly that "[Zava Damdin] had traversed the immense corpus of original sutras and tantras which had been translated from Sanskrit originals, and this intellectual feat earned him the appellation of *rtsa-ba bla-ma* or 'the guru who knows all the originals' [*zava lam* in Khalkha pronunciation]."[25] Damdin's life, body of work, and magnificent scholastic world—of a kind, in Chandra's telling, with the apex of classical Indian Buddhism and its successor monasteries in Tibet—had all come to a bloody close during the terror of the People's Revolution that began in earnest when Damdin died, in 1937. "The golden age of Mongolian chronicles (*chos-ḥbyuṅ*) closes with the Golden Annals in the twenties of our twentieth century. The Mongol lamas may no more chronicle the spread of the Dharma in their Northern Lands."[26]

Such competing narratives have given Zava Damdin's work a long and global life beyond their authors' death (and reincarnation). But just what those works recorded, what they sought to know, has been memorialized in ambiguous and contradictory registers. Consider the decidedly Whiggish prose of a 1974 Mongolian national history: therein, as in these pages, Zava Damdin's intellectual boundary-crossing attracted attention but confounded categorization and identification:

Among the historians of the Mongolian monarchy period mention should be made of Sh. Damdin (1867–1937). He was a historian who had formerly been a lama,[27] and wrote in Tibetan. Between 1900 and 1920 he wrote the following works: *Chronological Treatise, Short History of Fa-syang*, and others. In 1919 he began to write a history of Mongolia under the title *The Golden Book*. Although Damdin introduced a number of innovations by making use of contemporary historical data, nevertheless he was unable to free himself from the trammels of the feudal and religious ideology which were typical of Mongolian historiography of that period.[28]

Among the monks and patrons of Zava Damdin's revived Gobi Desert monastic community today—such as those who donated to the Taiwanese Corporate Body of the Buddha Educational Foundation to publish and distribute for free his entire *Collected Works*—Zava Damdin is venerated in the same breath as "the Gavj scholar of Khüree" and "Khalkha's Red Scholar."[29] This slippage is ironic, given that his contemporary publishers promote a brand of reform, modernist Humanist Buddhism (Ch. *renjian fojiao* 人間佛教) that Zava Damdin disparaged unrelentingly in the early years of the Mongolian revolution.

While Damdin's works cover all major topics of Géluk scholasticism, monastic administration, ritualism, and meditative self-cultivation as it was known to frontier Géluk scholars by the end of the Qing, and presume to unravel a narrative about the total history of the world itself, Zava Damdin's postimperial labor came to a much finer point. He was driven to "clarify" (Tib. *gsal*) and "order" (Tib. *bkod*) his revolutionary times. Occasionally he sought only to appropriately name (Tib. *zer*) ruptured temporalities, territories, communities, sovereignties, and religiosities: components of a situation some remember as "Asia's first modern revolution," which he knew as an incoherent crisis of category and practice unfixed from old certainties.[30] For generations, Tibetan and Mongolian Géluk scholars had produced Buddhism of the Qing, vast visions of power, ethnogenesis, and self and community in time and place. In a world now ablaze, his unenviable task was to either extend or close that narrative.

Monastery and Sovereignty, from the Qing to the People's Party

Polyglot, multiethnic Géluk monks had for centuries acted as go-betweens for Qing and tsarist powers all along the Tibeto-Mongolian frontiers. In the late nineteenth century, such monks were drawn into a Great Game that also now included Japan and the British Raj. By the twentieth century, "yellow hat" Géluk monastic networks extended between Central Tibet, north China, Beijing, and much of Mongol and Siberian territory, all the way to Saint Petersburg. While Russian, Manchu, Chinese, and Mongolian remained the regional bureaucratic languages of the law, the economy, and the records of state, literary Tibetan became the lingua franca for vast circuits of Buddhist intellectual exchange across the many frontiers of late-imperial central Eurasia. Often in Tibetan translation and fixed in Tibetan literary genres, local Mongolian and Buryat vernacular traditions were widely circulated and remade by being synthesized with, for example, the story of Tibet's imperial period (seventh–ninth centuries CE), translations of Chinese pilgrimage tales along the Silk Road to India, or Jesuit astronomy and cartography.

After the seventeenth century, as the Qing Empire continued to incorporate Tibetan and Mongolian communities into its fold, often by force, the projection of imperial power and social imagination was amplified (and sometimes strongly resisted) in Géluk monastic networks. As is well known, Qing sovereignty was characterized by rolling projects to define and systematize a multilingual and multiethnic empire (1644–1912). At the center of these were models of Manchu authority transposed simultaneously into local registers, histories, and associations. At the core of this self-and-community narrative was what Johan Elverskog has called the unified Qing-Géluk formation: a vast representation of sovereignty, community, and religiosity subsumed into the so-called "Two Systems" (Tib. *lugs gnyis*; Mong. *khoyar yosu*).[31] Even as Qing power in Inner Asia declined during the nineteenth century as a result of internal revolt and external military aggression, the Two Systems discourse in monastic writing largely endured. Polyglot monastic scholars became the dominant writers of society, translating histories previously tied to local banners, monastic estates, and the domains of the Chinggisid nobility into transregional and transhistorical sagas of enlightened intervention and ethnogenesis.

Much of the ideological context for this seventeenth-century development originated in thirteenth-century Tibetan interpretations of a recurring theme in many Mahāyāna and Tantric scriptural sources: that enlightened beings were present and available in the landscape, in architecture, in dreams, in material objects, and in the bodies of certain notable men (and only very rarely women).[32] Historians of the Qing Empire have largely focused on the so-called "Two Systems" as a relational model of authority shared between religious and political spheres (Tib. *chos srid*; Mong. *törü shasini*) and as an increasingly dominant discourse of diplomacy in Yuan, Ming, and especially Qing Inner Asia.[33] The more fundamental version of the relationship coordinated functions between a lay ruler-benefactor (Tib. *yon bdag*) and a religious preceptor-officiant (Skt. *dakṣiṇīya*; Tib. *mchod gnas*; Mong. *takil-un orun*). Beginning in the seventeenth century, this developed into a more unified political model of "associated religious and political [government]" (Tib. *chos srid zung 'brel*) seen as governed by buddhas and bodhisattvas playing the parts of monks and emperors. Wrapped in silk and saffron robes, these incarnations pronounced and then guarded the legal frameworks (Tib. *khrims*; Mong. *jasaγ*) of both the Dharma (Tib. *chos khrims*; Mong. *nom-un jasaγ*) and the mundane rule of a king, *khaγan*, or emperor (Tib. *rgyal khrims*; Mong. *khad-un jasaγ*).

Despite the erudition of shared discourses of imperial pluralism such as these, it must be noted that Mongolian or Tibetan subject communities were never simply institutional constructions, imaginary representations, or passive recipients of Qing identity politics. Inner Asian communities, and especially monastic elites, were active co-producers, mediators, and sometimes resistors of Qing imperial frameworks. Neither were minority peoples static, consensual, or mutually intelligible across their multiple frames of interpretation. Instead, local perspectives on the Manchu ruling elite and local participation in Qing sovereignty were formed in "mosaics of languages, events, and ideas organized in a manner so dense that they came to conceal infinite variations, innovations, and characteristics of actual populations."[34] The Qing was ever in the multiple and in process. And as Zava Damdin's oeuvre demonstrates, thinking time, space, community, and sovereignty via "Our Great Qing" (Mong. *Manu Yeke Cing*) endured the political endings of empire in unexpected and quite consequential ways.

For this reason, although it is customary to examine the Two Systems from within the study of the multiethnic and multilingual Qing, the postimperial sources I examine in this book demand a wider frame of reference.[35] In December 1911, Khalkha Buddhist monks and nobility from a variety of Qing administrative "banners" (Mong. *khosiyu*) met in secret to declare autonomy from a Qing Empire collapsing in the face of the Xinhai Rebellion. That consortium strategically elected the Jebtsundamba Khutuγtu, the highest of their incarnate lamas, as "Holy Emperor" (Mong. *Boγda Khaγan*) of a new Buddhist theocratic nation-state under the reign name "Elevated by the Many"

(Mong. *Olana ergügdegsen*). So began a brash and self-consciously modernist experiment at the heart of Asia whose state-centric histories have been described extensively elsewhere.[36] In revolutionary circles, progressive monks and lay intelligentsia twinned European models of nationalism, parliamentarianism, and industrial development with administrative structures and socioreligious hierarchies left over from the Qing.[37]

Geopolitical intrigues threatened the new nation almost immediately. A delegation from the Thirteenth Dalai Lama's Ganden Potrang administration (Tib. *Dga' ldan pho brang*), headed by the Buryat monk Agvan Dorjiev, signed a treaty of friendship and alliance with the Boɤda Gegegen's government in early 1913. However, neither fledgling state found any lasting or meaningful international recognition.[38] In the 1915 Kyakhta Agreement, tsarist Russia and an emboldened Republican China recognized Mongolia's autonomy but insisted the polity remain "Outer Mongolia." Vulnerable and with few options, the Mongolian delegation reluctantly recognized China's suzerainty. In 1919 Urga was occupied by Chinese forces and, in 1921, "liberated" by a motley band of White Russians led by the notorious Baron von Ungern-Sternberg. Mongolian socialists backed by Soviet forces ousted the Whites that same year and established a revolutionary regime referred to as the People's State (*Arad-un Ulus*). On July 11, 1921, the Boɤda Khaɤan was made into a constitutional monarch. Power now lay with a fractious band of leftist elites, "especially energetic activists suffering crises of identity, who became authors of nationalistic conceptions and ideals for the Asian country's development."[39] After the Boɤda Khaɤan's death in 1924, party leaders sought with uneven momentum and purpose to transform this sparse population from a "feudal" Qing outpost into the world's second socialist state.

The challenges the revolutionary factions faced in their project were mammoth. Mongolia was a vast nation with a largely illiterate population. The people's lives were centered—ideologically and economically—around the old "black" society of secular nobility (Mong. *khar-a ulus*) and the "yellow" society of Buddhist monastic establishments (Mong. *sir-a ulus*). The over eight hundred temples and monasteries that dotted the sparely populated steppes and deserts were nearly the only sedentary buildings.[40] Monastic estates and their vast networks of affiliation enjoyed near exclusive control over education, literacy, printing, and medicine. Therefore, they were the wellspring of economic, cultural, and political life. Incarnate lamas, or "living buddhas" (Tib. *sprul sku, skyes mchog*; Mong. *khubilγan, khutuγtu*) such as the Jebtsundambas and the Dalai Lama in distant Lhasa occupied an almost unassailable position as enlightenment embodied on the human stage, though the excesses and all-too-human abuses of individual incarnations evoked popular resentment, critique, and eschatology.[41] One third of all adult men were monks with some kind of formal monastic affiliation, the highest per capita rate of monasticism in two and a half thousand years of Buddhist history across Asia.[42]

For revolutionary ideologues and their Comintern advisors, the Mongolian situation presented a fundamental challenge to a historical materialism forged in the ecology of the Enlightenment and aimed at diagnosing the causes and outcomes of capitalism in industrialized Europe. The embellishments of Lenin, Trotsky, and others to make Russia fit the mold were inapplicable to Mongol lands. Who would be the proletariat of the steppes? Herders? Women? Lower-tier monastics? Just where was this land of livestock herders and monks situated on the received evolutionary charts of historical materialism? Responding to such questions, Lenin (reputedly) cautioned a delegation of prominent Mongolian socialists in 1921 that "the revolutionaries will have to put in a good deal of work in developing state, economic, and cultural activities before the herdsman elements become a proletarian mass, which may eventually help to 'transform' the People's Revolutionary Party into a Communist Party. A mere change of signboards is harmful and dangerous."[43]

Christopher Kaplonski writes that against the enduring authority of the Buddhist religious establishment, Asia's first socialist state remained contingent from 1921 to the purges of 1937; it occupied a liminal position, able to take direct military action against Buddhist monasteries but without the authority to impose the rule of law.[44] For this reason, a fundamental "lama problem" (*lama nar-yin asaγudal*) significantly hindered efforts to produce a socialist state in Asia between 1921 and 1937.

While the "lama problem" preoccupied leftist elements in the party, many founding members were more centrist monks and devoted lay Buddhists. They imagined not only that a purified, reformed Buddhism was uniquely adaptable to a socialist modernity but also that the classical Buddhist tradition had presaged the insights of Marx and Lenin. Long ago, Emanuel Sarkisyanz observed the tenacity and pervasiveness of Buddhist attempts to forge common ground with communism and communist utopianism in

Inner Asia.[45] For example, millenarian movements mobilized prophecies related to the imminent arrival of forces from the legendary Buddhist kingdom of Śambhala (Tib. *bde 'byung*) to rid Inner Asia of non-Buddhist barbarism. The equally pervasive epic tradition of King Gesar (Tib. *Gling ge sar*; Mong. *Geser Khan*) was put to similar use. Many Tibetan and Mongolian lamas had identified the tsar and his Romanov court as the fabled rulers of Śambhala, ready to fight the enemies of Buddhism (such as the British, Japanese, and Manchus). Troops marching to the orders of the early Mongolian communist leader Sükhbaatar reportedly sang Buddhist millenarian cadences. In the early days of Bolshevism, charismatic Buddhist leaders and tsarists came to power in polities bounded by newly imagined ethnic and national lines, as occurred in the short-lived theocracy of the Buddhist monk Samdan Tsydenov east of Lake Baikal.[46]

Between 1921 and 1937, Zava Damdin composed most of the historical and autobiographical works examined in these pages. During that time, socialists sought control by means of economic policies, education, educational reform, taxation, and cultivating strategic demographic and statistical information. They aimed to adopt a governmentality program: to reduce monks and monasteries to biodata points in a governable population. Kaplonski shows that legal and economic control, rather than brute force, was for much of the 1920s the preferred method by which the socialist government displaced monastic authority from the Mongol steppes and deserts.[47]

After some sixteen years, it became clear that the socialist party's biopolitics of containment had definitively failed. Monks, "living buddhas," and their monasteries escaped totalized state knowledge, legal inscription, and economic suffocation. To the dismay of party leaders and their Soviet advisors, by the mid-1930s Mongolia's monastic population had actually increased during a decade of socialist party rule. The people were faithful and loyal to their lamas. Class consciousness remained dormant. The economic clout of monastic estates and the hegemony of their colleges over most domains of cultural, social, and political life remained firm. Certain monks still climbed on thrones to tell men and gods about Mañjuśrī's intentions for them.

Owen Lattimore, with some dramatic flair, observed of Mongolian Buddhism in the early revolutionary period: "institutionally this religion, like one of its many-headed, thousand-armed deities, had a head to dominate every human thought and a hand to control every human action."[48] While it may be true that "in the long history of Buddhism perhaps no country or people in the world were as affected by the faith as were the Mongols of Great Mongolia,"[49] it took just years for it to be criminalized, and just months for the terror of state violence—enacted predominantly by Mongols upon other Mongols—to erase its previous hegemony.

In 1937, weeks after Zava Damdin's death, the "lama problem" received its bloody answer under the leadership of General Choibalsan. In only eighteen months, some forty thousand "counter-revolutionary elements," over half of them monks, were interrogated, tried, and shot at Stalin's behest.[50] At least 5 percent of the total population were put through show trials, felled by executioner's bullets, and buried in secret pits still being unearthed today. Hundreds of thousands more were imprisoned and sent to do forced labor. Mongolia's approximately eight hundred monasteries and temples, which Zava Damdin had meticulously catalogued, safeguarded, and sought to expand decades after the Qing collapse, were reduced to rubble (save three turned into storage facilities and then party museums). Buddhism receded from public life entirely, though as Caroline Humphrey notes, a "Soviet-style command economy" was not actually established in Mongolia until closer to the mid-twentieth century and was accompanied by private, buried forms of Buddhist religiosity.[51] Publicly, all continuity of monasticism and public religious practice other than for state propaganda purposes ceased until the democracy movement of 1990 and the Buddhist revival that followed.

Or so goes the usual state-centric version of events. Using the language of statistics, policy, and law and taking the just-invented national subject as protagonist, most modern studies of postimperial Mongolia have used the organizing categories of area studies to repeat a well-worn story about the marginalization and then suppression of religious life in a post-Qing world. This story is rehashed as an early migration and efflorescence of the Dharma, followed by a fall, neatly periodized into an imperial collapse, two revolutions (nationalist and then socialist), a purge, a Soviet era of religious suppression, and then a triumphant return with the democratic movement after 1990.[52] Such narratives bridge Hayden White's metahistorical modes of emplotment between Tragedy and Romance. They obscure much more than they reveal about the scope and desperate innovation of intellectual life in monastic colleges newly bereft of imperial context.[53]

To be fair, this partial picture is due to the paucity of sources. Our current historical picture of Buddhist life along the Mongol crossroads in the post-Qing world is overwhelmingly dependent upon state records such as census data, interrogation proceedings, and trial records from the 1920s and 1930s. In the bureaucratization of erasure, criminalized monks are ever silent. When they may speak, it is only of their crimes. The situation is made worse by disciplinary fault lines in the professional study of social, political, and religious history along the Tibeto-Russian-Chinese-Mongolian interface, as scholars have increasingly recognized.[54] Tibetanists have rarely looked at materials produced in Mongol lands, Mongolists have rarely plumbed the vast Tibetan-language monastic archive, and historians of the Soviet Union and Republican China have seldom delved deeply into the rarified world of Buddhist scholasticism along the Inner Asian frontiers.[55]

Because state archives have so overwhelmingly driven the historiography, the story of modernization in Inner Asia is organized too neatly between the imperial period and its aftermath, between Mongolian and Tibetan sources and traditions, between the national subject and what it excludes, and between the arrival of the "modern"—progress, self-mastery, social emancipation, science, technology, socialism, academic institutions, democracy, Europe—and the retreat of the "traditional"—stasis, superstition, other-mastery, suppression, folk tradition, Buddhism and shamanism, scholasticism, monastic institutions, feudalism, Asia.

Such dualisms are not tenable. The social imagination and active lives of the majority of monastics who did not become party cadres cannot be emplotted in the self-descriptive language of a state. Erstwhile cosmologies guided monastic lives during the modern formation of Inner Asia, yet we still know so little about them. Enter the traces of Zava Damdin's life and career, which begin to illuminate inter-Asian spaces, experiences, and exchanges beyond the Qing and the nation. His labor was profoundly dialogical, in sustained conversation with actors as diverse as the Dalai Lama, revolutionary soldiers, ethnologists, radical intellectuals, tantric yogis, Russian literary theorists, adventurers, Soviet Comintern agents, and early Buddhologists. The thousands of pages he left form a curious topography. They inscribe a social and religious imagination quite apart from what we know from state archives, reducible to neither tradition nor the modern, religion, science, monasticism, feudalism, or revolutionary progress. Damdin's was

FIGURE I.5 A gilded Buddha figure in a temple (location unknown) (1930s).
Digital copies of glass plate negatives preserved in the Archives for Cinema, Photography, and Sound Recording, Mongolia [1910s–1950s]. EAP264/1/9/3/107.

an otherwise world, periodized by enlightened presence and retreat, relational and situated, but nevertheless open to all manner of encounters, experiences, and mobility.

The Post-Qing Situation: Ruins and Anxiety

In the course of the research for this book, I have come to understand Zava Damdin's labor as an example of what some historians call "imperial formations." In the 1990s, Anne McClintock and Ann Laura Stoler drew upon currents in critical race theory and feminist scholarship to radicalize the study of colonialism.[56] The result was not only to productively gender colonial and imperial regimes. It was also a call for detailed analysis of the interweaving of sex, gender, and the economic into the cultural processes of imperialism and colonialism, and later, for Stoler, to seek out the "ruins" of such formations in the bodies, lives, and environment of postcolonial and postimperial subjects.[57] Ever since, a consensus of sorts has formed around the notion that sexual practice, discourse, and representation lay at the cornerstone of what Benjamin Cowan calls the "colonial order of things."[58]

In language more appropriate to the late- and postimperial sources this book considers, which must be thought of quite apart from the colonialisms of South Asia, Zava Damdin's writings illuminate the enduring legacies of "a Qing order of things" beyond its political ending. Damdin sought desperately to reconstitute that lost order so as to continue reproducing the Buddha's religion (Mong. *Burkhan-u shasin*) in Mañjuśrī's abandoned maṇḍala. This was less about safeguarding a geopolitics amenable to the status quo of Géluk monasticism than about maintaining the proximity to enlightened beings (playing the part of monks and emperors) required to make Buddhist life in its various institutional and social forms. The play of genre, gender, and sovereignty in Zava Damdin's prodigious writing illuminates (if, by scale of sources, only in part) a fear- and desire-infused cosmos severed from enlightened buddhas taking the always masculine form of emperors and monks.

I am further guided in these explorations by scholars such as Bernard Cohn to examine Qing religious and political legacies as necessarily twinned with the dominant structures of authority against which they took shape. Cohn was one of the first and most articulate anthropologists to draw attention to a dialectic in the study of previously colonized peoples that acknowledged the mutually constitutive nature of colonies and colonizer.[59] For him and the generations of scholars his work has inspired, the metropolis and colony, the European and the Other, become one field of analysis rather than an artificial and reductive model of Euro-American influence on "primitive" social life.[60] To further articulate his field of inquiry, Cohn borrowed Balandier's term: "the colonial situation." This was not understood as the unilineal effects of contact with European power, arts, and sciences, often described as "impact," "cultural contact," or "modernization"; nor was it to be viewed through a methodology "that seeks to sort what is introduced from what is indigenous."[61] Instead, the colonial situation as an analytical field united both the colonialist and "the indigene." My research shows that Zava Damdin's post-Qing intellectual labor is testament to this kind of "making the center from the periphery." Despite his sharp critique of revolutionary developments, Zava Damdin's historiography was deeply implicated in the nationalist and socialist reorganization of Mongolian society, even if his narratives exceeded and excluded their histories, territories, moral narratives, forms of authority, and religiosities.

Cohn's insights helps tangle the local production of time, place, and people with translocal processes of empire, national formation, and dispersed state violence in the ruins of the Qing.[62] Indeed, Zava Damdin never actually uses the word "revolution" in his work, nor does he refer explicitly to socialism, nationalism, or secularism. So writing about a generalized, tangled, and ambiguous "post-Qing situation" seems especially appropriate here. I hope thereby to expose the multivocal and in-process qualities of power and knowledge, the possibilities and paradoxes of authority and subjugation, and the multiple regimes of historicity that were put into motion in this small corner of the imperial ruins.

And yet, what specifically motivated Zava Damdin to write some two thousand pages of history after the empire, his dominant intellectual project amid the open possibilities and closures of his revolutionary situation? Why not ritual programs? Moral tracts?

Here too, certain insights and approaches from postcolonial scholarship on South Asia are useful, with care, outside a colonial context. Sara Suleri Goodyear and Brian Keith Axel have explored to fascinating effect how "colonial anxiety" motivated colonialists to emphasize the use of history and ethnography.[63] The constitutive power of such anxiety required them to produce knowledge about colonized peoples, which led to the assembly of vast colonial archives and the deployment of ethnographers and ethnography (whose scholarly products themselves became part of the colonial archive). What is relevant for the study of the late- and post-Qing period is the analytical emphasis of Goodyear and others upon the production of disparate categories of people, time, space, power, and religiosity through the representational strategies of ever-changing (and always contested) political disciplines.

Organization of Chapters

I have organized this book into two sections representing Zava Damdin's sharp distinction between an enchanted world that culminated in the Qing and a disenchanted world unfolding in his time of writing. In that binary periodization, Zava Damdin wrote the history of the world and the history of his own life. Chapters 1 and 4 draw from Zava Damdin's over one thousand pages of autobiographical writing, as well as hundreds of authorial intrusions in other works, which together represent the last literary self-stylizations of a Mongolian monk before the purges. I show how he used received Tibetan genres of "outer" and "inner" autobiography as a muted critique of his revolutionary times. In chapter 1 I track his rich narratives of early monastic training in Urga and his many mystical experiences across the still enchanted topography of the late Qing. Chapter 4 comes to the imperial collapse, when Zava Damdin became a senior monastic figure in Urga: an urban setting that was ground zero for first nationalist and then socialist revolution in Inner Asia. I explore the ways Zava Damdin turned to mass public ritualism and the expansion of scholastic education and monastic institutions while socialist violence against monks escalated. I conclude with oral histories collected from his still-living disciples about his death and the sorry fate of his monastic world in the bloody events of 1937.

Chapter 2 introduces readers to Zava Damdin's vast historicization of a trans-Asian, ethno-tantric Buddhist community that exceeded both Qing-era representations and the national subject. Following the narrative and interpretative templates of frontier cosmopolitan predecessors from the eighteenth and nineteenth centuries like Sumpa Khenpo and Mindrol Nomonhan, Zava Damdin leveraged the full weight of his scholastic training to understand his post-Qing world using material as diverse as French historical fiction, Khotanese prophecy, Finnish archaeology, Buddhist sutras, Tibetan doxography, elementary science textbooks, and Chinese pilgrimage tales. Repurposing Mikhail Bakhtin's differention between "real" and "empty" time in the epic and in the novel, I collect Zava Damdin's vast vision of the "real" time of the Inner Asian past, including his remarkable arguments for Mongol complicity in the Buddhist conversion of Eurasia. I conclude by exploring his mapping of lay, monastic, scholastic, and tantric kin-based communities from the pre-time of Indic antiquity to his twentieth-century present.

Chapter 3 focuses on Zava Damdin's long-standing project to historicize the enchantment of Eurasia by tracking the intervention of enlightened buddhas to create Asian social hierarchies, lay-monastic relations, sovereignty, law, and forms of knowledge among Turkic, Mongol, Tibetan, Chinese, and Indian communities. This is his vision of the "empty" time of Eurasian history, which he gleaned from a similarly creative meshing of Qing-era scholasticism and European arts and sciences. The interstice of real and empty time, which I call enchantment, was articulated in the "Two Systems" model of a unified religious and political authority. The Two Systems was for him, as it had been for his monastic predecessors, perfected in the Qing-Géluk partnership according to a well-worn model in his late-imperial scholastic tradition. This chapter tracks Zava Damdin's broad history of the Two Systems and the Qing, concluding with his sober and minimal description of the British invasion of Tibet in 1904 and the Qing collapse.

Chapter 5 surveys Zava Damdin's countermodern, cynical, and increasingly despondent theorization of the causes and direction of the disenchantment of Eurasia, a process elsewhere being celebrated as the national liberation of the Mongolian, Buryat, and Tibetan people from the tyranny of foreign imperial conquest and feudalist false consciousness. Counterintuitively, the focus of his critique was not state actors but his own Buddhist communities, whose nineteenth-century mistakes in relation to the enlightened he obsessively reconstructs as the primary causes of the Qing collapse, the disenchantment of Eurasia, and the end of history itself. This was the untwining of real and empty time, the cessation of the Two Systems, and the ending of the necessary conditions to reproduce Buddhist life in this world.

Chapter 6 explores Damdin's characterization of that crisis-saturated world guided by "post-Qing anxiety." He and those in his milieu were not explicitly concerned with violence or the ideology of state socialism, but rather with other features we often associate with modernization: new routes of social mobility, the authority of scientific knowledge, new forms of sovereignty governed by the unenlightened, and Buddhist reform movements, such as those championed by leaders of the early socialist movement with whom Zava Damdin enjoyed sustained but always critical correspondence. The chapter includes previously unstudied sources on revolutionary figures such as Jamsrano, the poet of Inner Asian socialism; Agvan Dorjiev, a Buryat Buddhist modernist and confidant of the Dalai Lama and Tsar Nikolai, Ts. Shcherbatsky, a founder of Euro-Russian Buddhist studies; M. Tubyansky, a member of the Bakhtin Circle, and many other prominent religious and scholarly figures deeply implicated in the modernist formations of Inner Asia.

In the conclusion I survey the impact of Damdin's work on refugee and diaspora Tibetan and Mongolian Buddhist thinkers since his death. While Zava Damdin's life and work are little known in scholarly or popular publications outside Mongolia, his post-Qing vision of the Eurasian past—from the deep time of Mongolia's Turkic roots, to the effect of Chinese pilgrimage tales on Tibetan historical consciousness, to the troublesome schisms associated with the Dorjé Shukden debate—has been profoundly influential within Inner Asian Buddhist literature. I close with a call for scholars to better attend to other neglected but widespread "countermodern" Buddhist responses across late- and postimperial and colonial Asia. Such attention would provide an urgently needed corrective to the hegemony of "transnationalism" and contact with European tradition as the primary trope for understanding twentieth-century Asian religiosity in its global contexts today, as well as illuminate the cosmos of those made invisible by modernist historiography and the hegemony of national peoples, territories, and histories.

PART I

Enchantment

ONE

Wandering

While the tracks of fleeing insects may appear as letters,
the insect is not an author.
Likewise, an ordinary person's activity, however virtuous,
is never the story of a holy life.

—ZAVA DAMDIN, *THE SUMMARY*

The best ethnographic study will never make the reader a native. . . . All that
the historian or ethnographer can do, and all that we can expect of them, is
to enlarge a specific experience to the dimensions of a more general one,
which thereby becomes accessible *as experience* to men of another country
or another epoch.

—CLAUDE LÉVI-STRAUSS, *STRUCTURAL ANTHROPOLOGY*

UIJING GÜNG, 1869: A mother attending children in a Gobi Desert felt yurt catches sight of her youngest son. He is once again sitting motionless, ignoring the play of siblings around him. He stares, never speaking, at the sky through the open roof. Is he stupid? Mute? She worries about him terribly. An aged nun comforts her. "Because this boy gazes uninterruptedly at the sky and the like, he must surely possess great virtue."[1] A great-grandmother offers more soothing words. "Though I have many great-grandchildren," she says with scripture in hand, "I wish to bequeath to him this precious Dharma object of my ancestors."[2]

*   *   *

Eastern Tibet, 1917: The oracle, his body enlivened by an otherwise unseen Dharma Protector, sputters *"Hri!"* The life and lives of a middle-aged monk in distant Urga who has put a question to him are reflected clearly in his divine mirror. Taktsang Rinpoché, that faraway monk's teacher, sits at the oracle's side awaiting answers he can pass on to his disciple. The deity animating the oracle knows that many lifetimes ago that Urga disciple was born in the city of Potal in south India. At the feet of a great yogi, he took refuge in the Buddhadharma, generated the far-reaching *bodhicitta* attitude aiming for enlightenment in order to benefit all sentient beings, and extensively served the teachings.[3] Tracking the courses of karma to the present, the oracle discerns that the ancient Indian adept has now taken rebirth in Khalkha to serve the Yellow Religion. Yet still more reflections of scattered lives dance across his divine mirror.

> He will excellently accomplish vast activities for the teachings
> but will encounter a few demonic obstacles.
> He will be fine if he puts effort into activities
> such as reciting the *Perfection of Wisdom Sūtras*,
> [undertaking] a close retreat of the Life-Conferring Goddess,
> and repeatedly [reciting] a longevity *sādhana*.
> For some seventy to eighty years,
> he will set uncountable disciples
> on the path to ripening and liberation.[4]

Looking further into the future, the oracle perceives that the distant Urga disciple will take rebirth in the pure land of Tuṣita and will sit at the feet of Buddha Maitreya in the company of other enlightened beings.[5] Addressing Taktsang Rinpoché directly, he intones, "Without a doubt [the activity of your disciple] will spread across the entire earth!"[6]

*   *   *

Na Küriye, 1918: Another oracle, possessed by another Dharma Protector, wheezes prophecies about the boy who stared at the sky, the disciple who centuries ago lived at the feet of an Indian yogi, the monk who now serves the Buddha's teachings in yurt temples on steppe grasses. This time, the Urga monk is present to hear directly about his future selves. The deity contorts its host in a trance. The oracle tells the monk he will be most successful in his Dharma practice. Though he will live to be eighty-eight, he will face obstacles at seventy-eight (c. 1945). With an appropriate ritual arsenal, the oracle says reassuringly, those obstacles can be purified without difficulty. "If you take refuge in the Triple Gem, your fame will spread everywhere and many sentient beings will respect you. Keep this in mind!"[7]

*   *   *

Ulayanbayatur, 1936: Racked with illness, the now elderly monk—he who stared at the sky, sat at his guru's feet in ancient India, served the Buddha's teaching in Mongol lands, and was told he would become famous—pens the last lines of the last text of his 9,000-page opus: his life story.[8] Now only dying plays upon his mind. The closing lines of this final text incise only an aspiration for rebirth in a Pure Land, where the enlightened now exclusively reside. Unlike all the other substantive texts among the 416 he wrote, this life story does not close with prayers for the flourishing of the Buddhadharma in the world, for the long life of personal teachers, or for the longevity of monasteries in the Khalkha crossroads. Such futures lie already abandoned.

His monkish world had been pulled to pieces. Teachers, fellow abbots, and disciples languished in prison awaiting show trials. Others had already been led to complete their life's karma on the lip of killing pits.

> In this way, for seventy years
> I have engaged in many activities of body, speech, and mind.
> But I am unable to write everything down
> or else I have forgotten.
> I am uncertain if all my activity has been virtuous or not. . . .

> If in this long text you see [only] a very ridiculous story,
> keep it in your mind that I was lying
> and simply offer all of it to the fire god!

> I was born in the last five hundred-year period of Śākyamuni's teachings.
> Even though I was young,
> I came to hold the appearance of a monk and joined the monastery.
> I spent my whole life studying, teaching, and building holy statues,
> but that activity is common, so who cares?

> When my consciousness goes to the next life,
> may it separate from nonvirtue, illusion, and fear!
> May the messengers of Maitreya Buddha show me the path
> so that I may be born without obstacle in Tuṣita![9]

He is hidden away in the modest home of lay siblings, and illness soon affirms the Buddha's teachings on impermanence. Within weeks, tens of thousands follow him along those paths that come after dying. They line up before judges, then crumple before firing squads.

At the end of pens and guns, the Yellow Religion is extinguished in Mongol lands with chilling bureaucratic efficiency.

"Wandering" in the Late Qing

That monk who as a boy stared at the sky, who sought his future in the mirrors of gasping spirits, and who penned his life story in the fog of state violence and illness was Zava Damdin. His 1936 autobiography was the last of his major compositions, a lifetime of writing that covered late imperial scholastic concerns from matters philosophical to ritual procedure, monastic order, contemplative techniques, and writing the past. Written soon before his death, this was the last iteration of nearly four decades of autobiographical writing, the only corpus of its kind by a Mongol monk to have survived the purges. This comes to us in dedicated autobiographies, authorial intrusions into dozens of other works, notes scratched in margins and colophons, letters, and prophetic accounts.

Zava Damdin's writing on the vast terrain of scholastic fields of knowledge—from arts and crafts to veterinary medicine, geography, logic, and methods to nonconceptually realize the ultimate nature of mind at death—essentially concern the nature of the world, how we know it, how we may know it more perfectly, and the effects such knowing might have on one's saṃsāric plight. Reading Damdin's other, nominally nonautobiographic works is still an intimate encounter with an author. Whether writing about the Kālacakra Tantra, Madhyamaka, medicine, the names of mountain gods, grammar, ethics, the sons of Chinggis Khan, or the domes of Saint Petersburg, Zava Damdin always inserted himself into the flow of narrative. His texts burst with notes and signs pointing to other works, stitched together with half-done corrections, clarificatory marginalia, and almost always with tender, first-person reflection.

The first of Zava Damdin's dedicated autobiographies is an expansive, three-volume effort written in the shared Tibeto-Mongolian genre of "record of teachings received" (Tib. *thob yig, gsang yig*). Such works construct genealogical maps of every religious transmission an (auto)biographical subject ever received—from the alphabet and first vows to the heights of tantric esotericism and sundry other highly restricted, secret instructions. "Records of teachings received" is a relatively neglected genre of historical writing from the Tibetan cultural sphere, despite the fact that they constitute "veritable goldmines for anyone engaged in the study of Tibetan literature from literary, bibliographical, or historical perspectives."[10] While the value of these records has long been recognized, systematic and comparative study has so far been lacking, with only a few notable exceptions.[11] Vostrikov, working in Russia contemporaneously with Zava Damdin, noted that genealogical records are "a quite distinctive class of Tibetan works" that serve to supplement but "go far beyond the framework of autobiographies" as "historico-literary works or records of oral and written traditions."[12]

Zava Damdin's work added to a series of prominent Mongol adaptions of this Tibetan genre, including most famously Zaya Paṇḍita Lubsangperinlei's (Tib. Dza ya paṇḍita blo bzang 'phrin las, 1642–1715) *Clear Mirror of Teachings Received* (Tib. *Thob yig gsal ba'i me long*).[13] The first "record of teachings received" ever written by a Khalkha monk, Zaya Paṇḍita's seventeenth-century map of transmission opens the Buddhist dispensation into Khalkha while Zava Damdin's work records its closure (until the postsocialist Buddhist revival occurring today).

The full title of Zava Damdin's effort is *The Record of Teachings Received That Tastes Some of the Ambrosial Nectar of the Virtuous, Holy Dharma in the Beginning, End, and Middle: A Catalogue of Precious Treasures of Profound, Vast, and Secret Advice* (hereafter, *The Catalogue*; Tib. *Thog mtha' bar du dge ba dam chos bdud rtsi'i zil mngar cung zhig myang ba'i thob yig zab rgyas gsang ba'i gdams pa rin chen gter gyi kha byang*).[14] It also has a secondary title: *The Manner by Which I, Lozang Tayang, Entered the Doorway of the Dharma by Progressively Listening, Receiving Vows, Transmissions, Commentaries, Initiations, and Subsequent Attainment* (Tib. *Blo bzang rta dbyangs rang nyid chos sgor zhugs te thos pa byed tshul gyi rim pa la sdom pa nod pa dang lung khrid dbang rjes thob tshul*). In all versions I have been able to find, *The Catalogue* is divided into three volumes. It is handwritten in uneven style, and gives the appearance of an imperfectly edited collection of short notes on clusters of lineage transmission from different years, hastily assembled as a draft for a later finished work. It is undated and without a colophon.

The earlier sections, which seem most finished, are interspersed with prose, so that the vast charting of Dharmic transmission from India to Tibet to Mongol lands and then to the autobiographical subject is enlivened in many places by personal reflection and expressions of tearful gratitude. In all, *The Catalogue* is a treasure trove of information about religious and social self-perception in the twilight of the Dharma in the Mongol ruins of the Qing. As we read in its opening lines,

> Through chance, I acquired just once a precious human life in the north of the north of the world in the land of Khalkha, on an auspicious day of the month in the Fire Rabbit year (1867) at the start of the fifteenth *rapjung*. I was named Lubsangagwang, the "Lazy Person in Yellow Robes." Because of my previous karmic latencies and the blessed causes and conditions of my Spiritual Friends, since the earliest stage of my life I gradually entered the gateway of the Dharma by first listening [to the teachings]; second, taking vows; third, [receiving] transmissions and instructions; fourth, [taking] initiations; and fifth, properly undertaking the "'subsequent attainment" [postmeditation practice].[15]

Jan-Ulrich Sobisch has observed that the seventeenth-century records of teachings received by the Great Fifth Dalai Lama and Zaya Paṇḍita were not only genre-changing due to their length. These works include narratives concerning the historical conditions of a particular lineage, thus shifting the genre from genealogy to prose history.[16] Zava Damdin, who inherited most of the Great Fifth and Zaya Paṇḍita's lineages and ways of writing about them, also bent this nominally genealogical genre to narrating the past more broadly. However, it was precisely what had been inscribed in maps of transmission associated with Zaya Paṇḍita—new subjectivities and collectivities founded on reproductive contact with masculine centers such as monks, monasteries, and "living buddhas"—that Zava Damdin increasingly believed had abandoned the post-Qing situation. Unlike previous authors of "records of teachings received" or life writing more generally, Damdin asked: What would count as a holy life story and as Dharmic transmission in the absence of the enlightened?

Answers are not forthcoming in the sprawling *Catalogue,* but we gain a much clearer picture in Zava Damdin's 1936 autobiography, the aforementioned *Summary of This Life's Activities* (hereafter: *The Summary*; Tib. *Rang Gi Byed Spyod Rags Bsdoms 'Di Snang Za Zi'i Rjes Gco*). This is a much shorter verse autobiography in thirty-three folios. Zava Damdin organized the story of his life into six *yeng-pa* or "wanderings" (Tib. *g.yengs pa*): 1) "Wandering

Without Thought During Childhood";[17] 2) "Wandering by Means of Study During Youth";[18] 3) "Wandering by Means of Textual Instruction During Youth";[19] 4) "Wandering by Means of Religious Teaching During Middle Age";[20] 5) "Wandering by Means of Protecting the Monastery During Old Age";[21] and 6) "Wandering with Uncertainty at the End of Life."[22]

Yeng-pa is a Tibetan word that usually refers to mental wandering, distraction, or agitation. In Zava Damdin's usage, *yeng-pa* had other meanings besides. It evoked an expected level of humility for a Buddhist monk who presumed to write about himself. As only *yeng-pa*, his entire life had been wasted through mundane distraction, mental wandering, and emotional agitation rather than virtuous self-cultivation through disciplined study and practice of the Buddhadharma. Zava Damdin also used *yeng-pa* to set his inter-Asian sojourns and exchanges in time as he "wandered" from youth to old age, as well as in space, as he "wandered" across vast stretches of the Qing Empire and then through the monastic circuits of revolutionary-era Khalkha. Through Géluk networks connecting Lhasa, Beijing, Urga, Irkutsk, and Saint Petersburg, Zava Damdin also "wandered" into the intimate presence of lineage-holding monks and incarnate lamas, by which he was formed first as a laymen, then as a novice and fully ordained monk, a scholar, a tantric disciple, and a tantric master.

Zava Damdin also used *yeng-pa* to describe his intellectual itinerancy between Europe and Inner Asia that is the subject of much of this book. Yet such pursuits always had a "place" in Michel de Certeau's double sense of the word: a social site and an associated set of knowledge practices or "operations." These amount to an interstice of institutional affiliations, technical procedures, permissions, and prohibitions at whose juncture historians, whether Gobi Desert monks or professionals today, write society.[23] A very direct way of delving into Zava Damdin's oeuvre and the post-Qing world it illuminates is to ask at the outset: What was "the place" from where Zava Damdin "wandered"? Where did he construct his texts? What were the places and associated techniques with which he fitted a post-Qing, revolutionary world with a past (and by that, a desired future)?

From when he first learned to read as a toddler to his death, Zava Damdin's life unfolded in the social site of the monastic college (Tib. *grwa tshang*; Mong. *datsang*). Places like Dashichoijurling, his college where he climbed upon a throne to address men and gods about the continuities of the Qing, had for centuries been the centers of intellectual activity across the late-imperial

Tibeto-Mongolian-Siberian frontiers. As Thuken Chökyi Nyima wrote in his widely circulated 1802 *Crystal Mirror: An Excellent Exposition That Shows the Sources and Assertions of All Tenet Systems*, a major influence upon Zava Damdin, under Qing patronage Mongol lands teemed with temples, monasteries, and monks, but ultimately "it is due to the philosophical monastic colleges (Tib. *mtshan nyid grwa tshang*) that the precious teachings have continually spread and increased."[24] In the time of Zava Damdin's writing, party agitators and revolutionary ideologues lamented the backwardness of the monastic colleges, as did Soviet-era historians long after the purges.

> In Mongolia a situation arose similar to that in medieval Europe where, as Engels put it, "the clergy retained a monopoly of [sic] intellectual education . . . and education itself had acquired a predominantly theological character. . . ." In such circumstances the feudal-religious elements in Mongol culture were sharply intensified as counter-weight to popular tradition. The Buddhist religion sought to control all the intellectual activities of the Mongols. . . . Tibet, as the home of Lamaism, became for the Mongols a unique centre not only of religious but also of any other kind of culture. . . . Under the Manchus Lamaism, which had become a reactionary force in the history of the Mongol people, constituted a great obstacle to Mongol cultural development . . . Lamaism was, in the hands of Manchu aggressors, a willing tool in the process of ideologically stupefying the nation.[25]

As if for posterity, sensing the destruction that would soon come, Zava Damdin concluded his 1931 history of Buddhism in Mongol lands with an extended catalogue of major monasteries across Inner and Outer Mongolia and Buryatia, with special attention to the type and number of monastic colleges and the Central Tibetan manuals they each followed (Tib. *yig cha*).[26]

Though always wandering from within the intellectual and institutional place of the monastic college, in the autonomous period and in the early years of the socialist revolution Zava Damdin became loosely affiliated with the newly established sites of the human sciences in Urga. These were connected with Russian institutions and directed by academically trained Buryat revolutionaries. Beginning in 1921, Zava Damdin became an affiliated member at the founding of the precursor to the Mongolian Academy of Science, the Mongolian Philological Institute (Mongol Bichig-un Sudur Küriyeleng). There and elsewhere in revolutionary Urga, he worked alongside and in conversation with historians, archaeologists, educators, physicians, ethnologists, and linguists from across Europe, Russia, and Siberia. As we shall see in the chapters that follow, despite his willing association, Damdin often adopted a hypercritical relationship with such characters and their scientific projects, articulated through sustained critical engagement with their ideas and knowledge practices. Despite the selective memories of Bira and other Soviet historians, as well as many in the Mongolian nationalist and Buddhist revival today, Zava Damdin's foray into science was only ever to diagnose the causes of the Qing collapse and, more generally, to bolster monastic positions against anticlerical and antireligious trends. To his unusual grave, Damdin, driven by Qing anxiety, sought doggedly to "wander" bravely across but also to police the boundaries of monastic college and scientific institute. In this decades-long effort, he voraciously attacked empiricism, which he considered a wayward and degenerate technique for knowing about the world. The "place" of Damdin's life, and thus of his ground-level interpretation of the bloody modernization of Asia's heartland, remained the monastic college to the bitter end.

Genre and Gender: Writing Inner and Outer Lives

From the place of the embattled monastic college, Zava Damdin's *yeng-pa* also occasionally folded time into space. Such literary contortions—rooted in the play of genre and gender inherited from Qing-era Buddhist literature—bear directly upon his dark story of Buddhism in a post-Qing world. Zava Damdin wrote with great tenderness about artifacts and spiritual treasures pulled from deep beneath the earth and from temple crevices at Mount Wutai and Beijing (those enchanted topographies emanated by Mañjuśrī that he publicly lauded when speaking as "the spiritual friend who pleases Mañjughoṣa"). Suddenly and unexpectedly, covered in dirt and dust, such holy lives and purifying objects became present in the very twilight of the empire as relics, words in stone, and magical trees. They became material examples of an enchanted topography of the Qing period he once knew, but which by the time of his 1936 life writing was only memory. From his late vantage, the salvific affordances of the absent Qing were inaccessible. Perhaps for this reason they appeared to memory with the greatest clarity.

The usual term for biography in Tibetan is *namtar* (Tib. *rnam thar*; Mong. *namtar*), meaning literally "a completely liberated [life]."[27] Tibetan *namtar* drew from Indic templates, especially those developed and systematized around the turn of the Common Era in the Central Asian Buddhist kingdoms of what we now call the Silk Road.[28] Most influential in this regard were standardized biographies of the historical Buddha Śākyamuni, which eventually were organized in the now familiar template of "The Twelve Deeds" (Skt. *Dvādaśabuddhakārya*; Tib. *Mdzad pa bcu gnyis*; Mong. *Arban khoyarüiles*). These widely circulated narratives and their visual representations portray the life of Prince Gautama from his privileged early days of luxury through his renunciation, asceticism, enlightenment, long teaching career, and passing, or *parinirvāṇa*. Other important south and central Eurasian influences included popular stories about the Buddha's previous lives known as *jātaka* (Tib. *skyes rabs*) and *avadāna* (Tib. *rtogs rjod*), a moralistic genre whose karmic framing linked the good and bad turns in a protagonist's life to the quality of their behavior in lives past.

Life writing began to be pursued with vigor in Tibetan cultural regions beginning in the twelfth century. Ever since, literati who were mostly monastics and almost exclusively men have written what became, along with historiographies (which were mostly collections of biographies), one of the most fertile and distinctive literary preoccupations of Inner Asia.[29] Although there are comparable examples from influential neighbors, (auto)biography in the hands of Tibetan authors reached heights unparalleled in the great literary cultures of either premodern India or China. It is thus no surprise that in the latter half of the seventeenth century, when Mongolians began participating en masse in Tibetan intellectual and religious traditions, life writing also became for Mongolian men of letters (and apparently never women), an enduring fixation (as it did also for some notable lay officials in the Tibetan government of the Qing period, as illuminated to fascinating effect by the late Elliot Sperling).[30] While Mongolian authors took up writing about their own and others' lives in the Tibetan language and on the Tibetan example in the seventeenth century, many Mongolian-language biographies also exist, such as those of the first Öndör Gegegen Zanabazar (1635–1723) and of his disciple Zaya Paṇḍita, the Chakhar Gevsh Lubsantsültim's prolific early nineteenth-century biography of the Géluk founder Tsongkhapa, and biographies of many prominent incarnate lamas from along the Tibeto-Mongol frontiers of the Qing, such as the Jangji-a (Tib. Lcang skya) and Thuken lines down to Zava Damdin's own friend and teacher, the Darva Paṇḍita Agwangchoijurdondubbalsang (d. 1924).[31]

Kurtis Schaeffer and Janet Gyatso have shown that in Tibet an efflorescence in life writing beginning in the seventeenth century not only drastically expanded the length and subject matter of (auto)biography but also
spawned a meta-tradition that debated the appropriate style and intended
purposes of such writing.[32] It is so far unmentioned in the quickly growing
scholarship on Tibetan life writing that polyglot Mongolian monks writing
along the Sino-Manchu-Tibetan-Mongolian frontiers of the Qing largely
drove the drastic expansion of the genre after the seventeenth century.
Examples include Jangji-a Khutuɣtu Rölpé Dorjé, Thuken Chökyi Nyima,
Sümbe Khambo Ishibaljur, Tongkhor Jamyang Tendzin Gyatso, Gombojab, the
Chakhar Gevsh, and Mindröl Nomon Han.[33] Also largely unexplored is that
this same group of frontier scholars wrote many synthetic histories, geographies, astrological works, and medical treatises of a kind that have also
recently been explored (individually, not yet comparatively) as alluring evidence for an early modernity in Tibet.[34]

Of great importance for this study of monastic interpretations of the Qing
collapse and the advent of a revolutionary modernity in Inner Asia, in the
received Géluk textual corpus that Zava Damdin inherited, life writing was
organized into subgenres describing increasing degrees of interiority.[35] In
nam-thar and an intimately related genre of autobiography known most
commonly as rang-nam (Tib. rang rnam; Mong. bej-e yin namtar), an "outer biography" (Tib. phyi rnam) would usually unfold on the template of a received
biography of the historical Buddha Śākyamuni, or else the life stories of other
eminent Indian and Tibetan monks and tantric yogis like Sakya Paṇḍita,
Ghaṇṭāpa, Milarepa, or the Bengali master and reformer Atiśa Dīpaṃkara
Śrijñāna.[36] The outer biography "typically begins with an early renunciation
of worldly life . . ., followed by the protagonist's meeting with teachers, taking
vows, entering retreat, acquiring students, teaching, and, finally, assuming
institutional positions."[37] It is a straightforward accounting of events, observ-
able to those outside the more proximate, intimate circle of close disciples.

The more rarified life story directed toward a guru's inner circle is called,
predictably, an "inner biography" (Tib. nang rnam). Such narratives describe
a more subjective, personal course of events related specifically to the successful application of Buddhist techniques of self-cultivation. The experience
of that accomplishment—such as radical shifts in perception and agency that
mark the transition from saṃsāra to enlightenment along so many "stages"
(Skt. bhūmi; Tib. sa; Mong. orun) and "paths" (Skt. mārga; Tib. lam; Mong.

mör)—is reserved for a subgenre known as "secret biography" (Tib. *gsang rnam*). Such narratives follow the intimate details of religious life that a protagonist would have shared only with a highly restricted circle of personal disciples. Secret biographies describe dreams, visions, direct encounters with enlightened beings, the revelation of spiritual treasures from sites such as the sky or the earth, and miraculous abilities like healing, manipulating the natural elements, or using tantric techniques to suppress threats to Buddhist institutions and polities.[38] Secret biography thus describes the very central, most interior aspects of a protagonist's life, offering a rarified and restricted view of the self quite distinct (though in practice never disconnected) from outward spheres of activity and the outer (auto)biographies that describe them.[39]

In his 1936 *Summary,* Zava Damdin was the last author to employ all three types of (auto)biographical writing in pre-purge Mongolia. As we shall see, the play of genre and gender, of interiority and exteriority, of an inner and outer life, is one of the ways that he set the post-Qing ruins into time. All Zava Damdin's descriptions of his mystical experiences and encounters, and of his religious formation through personal contact with enlightened beings and holy sites more generally, are written as "inner" and even "secret" biographical narratives of events that took place before the 1911 collapse of the Qing, at sites associated with imperial sovereignty and the Qing-Géluk formation specifically. By contrast, all personal events between 1911 and 1937 are narrated crisply in the style of "outer" biography. The literary effect is an alarming distancing from sacred, masculine centers, essences, and interiorities—a disenchantment that surged even as Zava Damdin matured into the most prominent and prolific religious leader in Mongolia, struggling to reproduce Buddhist life in a post-Qing world. His understated pivoting between "outer" and "inner" biographical genres reproduced a first-person polarity between an enchanted Qing and a dystopian post-Qing situation that is elaborated in his writing of global history explored later in this book.

Youthful Wandering from Home to Monastery

The boy who would be renowned as Zava Damdin was first named Lubsangagwang (Tib. Blo bzang ngag dbang), born close to the lunar new year in the midwinter of 1867 "at the lower white rock that is at the base of the mountain with prayer flags."[40] His was an aristocratic herding family of Khalkha ethnicity who lived in a small Gobi Desert administrative unit known then as Uijing Güng (Tib. Gho bi us dzing kung), some two hundred and fifty kilometers south of Urga, in Daichin Beij Banner of Tüshiyetü Khan Ayimaγ, one of four *ayima*γ making up Outer Mongolia during the Qing.[41] In today's Mongolia, this is near Delgertsogt, a small village in Central Gobi province (Dundgowi Aimag) near the revived Chöying Ösel Ling (Zava Damdin's home monastery at the end of life, today known as Delgeruun Choira and headed by his reincarnation).[42] Lubsangagwang was the fourth of ten siblings born to "ethical and intelligent parents" from a well-positioned family who may have been a part of the local nobility. Their family lineage was, according to *The Summary*, "well-behaved, long-lived, wealthy, and devoted to the Dharma."[43] Our author recalled that his childhood home was a happy one, "free from the two extremes" of excessive wealth or abject poverty.

Zava Damdin writes in *The Summary* that when he was born, a lama wearing a *paṇḍit*'s hat, clothed in religious robes, and carrying many Buddhist texts appeared to his mother in a dream. She requested blessings, and the

FIGURE 1.1 A nomad camp, Central Mongolia (1930s).
Digital copies of glass plate negatives preserved in the Archives for Cinema, Photography, and Sound Recording, Mongolia [1910s–1950s]. EAP264/1/8/6/100.

lama touched the texts to the crown of her head. Many other unusual signs accompanied Lubsangagwang's entry into the world, drawing the attention of locals. Before the customary protective rituals had been done three days after his birth, "non-Buddhist and Buddhist scholars" unanimously agreed that "this boy will certainly become a devotee of the Dharma!"[44] According to oral histories recently recorded by Zsuza Majer and Krisztina Teleki, though unmentioned by Zava Damdin in his autobiographical writing, upon his birth the local Noyan (noble) Tserendorji, who commanded Uijin Güng, took notice of the infant Lubsangagwang because unusual yellow flowers grew for three years at his birth site. The Noyan decided that later in life Lubsangagwang should become abbot of Tsaikhiurtiin khiid, the local banner monastery.[45]

Another noteworthy episode happened when the infant Lubsangagwang fell sick with a cold. His worried uncle Lubsangjinba, a monk in a nearby monastery who would become an important mentor, took him to be diagnosed by means of divination at the feet of a local Buddhist master. This was most likely Lubsangagwang's future root guru, Ācārya Sangjai, who would become a regular subject of Damdin's devotional biographical writing.[46] Stunned by the remarkable results of his divination, the master exclaimed, "This boy is extraordinary!" As both a therapeutic and symbolic act, Sangjai wrapped a monk's shawl around the boy's neck. We read in both *The Summary* and *The Catalogue* that Lubsangagwang, once fully recovered from illness, formally "entered the door of the teachings" at three years old by receiving the five *upāsaka* precepts of a lay male practitioner.[47]

The early sections of *The Summary,* written in 1936 by an ill monk facing dark times, fondly recall a childhood moving with gravitational force toward renunciant life. On family visits to the local monastery, Lubsangagwang would clamber onto the abbot's throne, just as he would a half century later on a summer's day in 1924 at Dashichoijurling to praise the absent Qing. Seated upon Gobi sands as a toddler, Lubsangagwang would ring discarded bells and drums, imitating ritual performances he would later spend half a century archiving, systematizing, and transmitting. He would also bring scarves to offer to people in the manner of a high lama blessing devotees, just as he would himself be blessed when in the presence of the major Inner Asian religious figures of his day.

Another notable (and characteristically gendered) sign of an early penchant for the ascetic life comes from an account in *The Summary* describing the birth of his younger sister. The toddler Lubsangagwang witnessed the birth in his family's *ger* (yurt) and was so repulsed that he cried out, "This is wicked!" He ran straightaway from the impure, saṃsāric company of the women in his lay home to stay for days in the purifying, masculine company of his uncle in the local monastery.[48] That disgusted movement across lay and monastic spaces became widely known in his community and received high praise.

When he was four years old, Lubsangagwang witnessed a student reciting a text, presumably a young monk practicing memorization. This was also a life-turning event propelling him toward monastic and then scholastic life. He begged his lama uncle to teach him to write, and learned both the "headed" (Tib. *dbu can*) and "headless" (Tib. *dbu med*) Tibetan scripts from his "master teacher" Sangjai in just three days. He also memorized core liturgies by listening to his uncle, who was the monastery's cantor (Tib. *dbu mdzad*; Mong. *umdzad*), recite them aloud. He could soon read on his own and began to work through not only the core ritual texts of the local banner monastery but also the liturgies of Guhyasamāja and Cakrasaṃvara used in the great monastic city of Urga to the north. The young savant also displayed a thorough and unexplainable base of knowledge about astrology, translation, and the vast pantheon of enlightened beings whose representations in wood, mud, and bronze populated monastic halls and family altars. Of that knowledge of statuary and painting, which seemed drawn from beyond his young life, the *Summary* records that "everyone thought it amazing." Knowing about representations of the enlightened, he later surmised, generated a storehouse of good karma responsible for saving his life from a childhood bout of smallpox (Tib. *'brum*).[49]

Despite such unusual knowledge and behavior, which in the narrative tropes of *namtar* would presage that a young child is the incarnation of either a buddha or a previous master, Lubsangagwang was to become famous not as a recognized "living buddha" but as a scholar. In the *Summary*, that momentous transition from lay to monastic life proceeded through a series of public declarations. The first followed "something terrible" that happened locally in his sixth year. To assuage its effects, monks did a ritual for which his mother offered a hat, new shoes, a sword, necklaces, and some cloth. Noticing the fabric being given away, the young Lubsangagwang cried out, "When I go to the prayer assembly I will need a shawl. Please, don't give away this cloth!"[50] Everyone became very happy and some even cried.

Around this time, Lubsangagwang saw two scholars with the elite *gabcu* (Tib. *dka' bcu*; Mong. *arban berketü*) degree in philosophical studies engaged in a dialectic contest, the bedrock of Géluk scholastic education and examination (Tib. *rtsod lan*; Mong. *nom khayaltsakh*). Zava Damdin recalls in *The Summary* that he was so enamored, he thereafter played at clapping his hands and stomping his feet in imitation of their formal debate gestures, the routinized performance of Géluk education then being repeated across Inner Asia, as well as in imperial centers like the Yunghe Temple in Beijing. One other important episode from his childhood "wanderings" came during a trip to the great monastic city of Urga with his father. During the days-long journey, "I said spontaneously, 'I will become a *géshé*!'"[51] "You will become a retreat lama," his father teased him, bragging to their companions, "If he joins the monastery, he may possibly become the *géshé* of (Yeke) Küriy-e [i.e., Urga]!"[52]

Lubsangagwang began that long road of memorization and dialectical competition to fulfill his father's playful dream at seven years old when he joined the banner monastery, most likely Tsakhiurtiin khiid[53] "the monastery of my homeland" (*skyes yul gyi dgon sde*) he identifies just once by name as Dorjé Tenpa (Tib. *Rdo rje bstan pa*; Mong. *Dorjidamba*). As a novice monk he was first charged with cleaning and helping to decorate the extravagant *balin* butter and tsampa offering cakes (Tib. *gtor ma*) that sit bulbous and fragrant at the center of most Mongolian and Tibetan Buddhist rituals. Following orders well, Lubsangagwang quickly solidified his position as a trusted acolyte to the master Sangjai and to his uncle. These connections provided the young monk protection from otherwise unexplained aggressions by "higher, middling, and lower people."

In the tender reminiscences of old age, enduring the calamity of revolutionary state violence, *The Summary* describes Lubsangagwang as a young boy intensely curious about the sacred topographies of the late Qing. He dreamed not only of the great monastic city of Urga to the north but also about the holy sites of Central Tibet such as the Jokhang Temple and the Dalai Lama's Potala Palace in Lhasa, as well as the "mother monasteries" of his Géluk tradition: Séra, Ganden, and that favored destination of Mongolian pupils, Drépung.[54] Like most burgeoning Buryat and Mongol scholastics of his day, he longed intensely to visit Lhasa, perhaps the most purifying and salvific site of the Qing-Géluk world. *The Summary* recalls that upon hearing of Lhasa from pilgrims and from senior monks who had spent decades there in study, the youthful Lubsangagwang was so astounded he would cry. For our elderly

FIGURE 1.2 A view of Gandan monastery in the background and east central part of Ulaanbaatar (early 1930s).
Digital copies of glass plate negatives preserved in the Archives for Cinema, Photography, and Sound Recording, Mongolia [1910s–1950s]. EAP264/1/12/1/37.

author this was a particularly difficult memory, since "due to the meager power of my previous life's karma, I never had a chance to see these [holy sites] as I grew older."[55]

To the Second Lhasa

Despite karmic deficits such as these, the young Lubsangagwang apparently had stores of merit enough to reach Urga, the "second Lhasa of the north."[56] A Russian observer, I. Maiskii, provides a lively description of Urga at the time:

Enormous Buddhist monasteries with temples and yurts shining with their bright whiteness, serving as chapels, thousands of yellow-and-red monks wearing pointed hats and carrying rosaries in their hands, a dusted and dirty trading square, very narrow and winding streets with nothing but palisades and wicket-gates in them, Mongol men on horses, Mongol women with [hair shaped like] horns and silver ornaments on their heads, long caravans of camels swaying slowly with packs on their humps, thousands of yellow-faced Chinese in their long caftans, Chinese and Mongolian signboards, and men and women squatting down to satisfy their physiological needs in the most crowded places.[57]

Having waited impatiently for more than two years to undertake the journey, he was finally excused by high monastic officials such as his abbot and a certain Toyin Gavj. Lubsangagwang excitedly departed sometime around 1883, when he was fifteen years old. This journey marks a major transition in his autobiographical writing. Most of the fifteen hundred folios of *The Catalogue,* his "record of teachings received," itemize hundreds of transmissions of canonical texts, oral teachings, and tantric initiations that he would receive, and then pass on anew, in Urga's temples over the course of his next fifty-five years.

Once in Urga, the young Gobi monk matriculated at the college of Gungachoiling (Tib. Kun dga' chos sbyor gling), "like a donkey joining the ranks of humans."[58] Gungachoiling was another, older name for Dashichoijurling, where forty years later Zava Damdin told about the absent emperor's prophecies to an audience of gods and men. The newest of three philosophical colleges in Urga, Gungachoiling had a curriculum based on the manuals of the Losel Ling College of Drépung monastery (Tib. 'Bras spungs blo gsal gling) near Lhasa. At Gungachoiling, Lubsangagwang began a lifelong course of study that he once characterized humbly as "like a dog fetching a stone," an unenthusiastic pursuit merely goaded along by others.[59] He first focused on *Collected Topics* (Tib. *bsdus grwa*), an introductory course in valid cognition (Skt. *pramāṇa*; Tib. *tshad ma*; Mong. *kemjiy-e*).[60] His first master in these scholastic pursuits was the "Lord of Exposition" Jigjid (Tib. Smra dbang Jigs byed), a prominent Urga scholar who, like his Gobi guru Sangjai, was known to have journeyed on pilgrimage to India. From statements in several of his autobiographical works that slip past their self-effacing tone, it appears Lubsangagwang quickly acquired a reputation in Urga for his abilities in memorization and debate. He moved quickly through his classes, passing the requisite exams with ease.

Of those early years studying with Jigjid, *The Summary* recalls,

FIGURE 1.3 Young lamas in Gandan monastery, Ulaanbaatar [1930s].
Digital copies of glass plate negatives preserved in the Archives for Cinema, Photography and Sound Recording, Mongolia [1910s–1950s]. EAP264/1/9/2/64.

When he first taught how to debate the colors,
   I was able to understand the syllogisms on my own and apply them to other
      subjects.
My lama became very happy
and he began teaching me the next class on *Summarized Topics.*
During the three sessions, I entered the third class.
At that time, I met the Supreme Refuge and Protector "Lord of Speech"
and I requested that we form a Dharma connection.
He said, "I will take you to Śambhala!"[61]

Zava Damdin recalls also being especially adept at memorizing canonical and exegetical texts, an essential ability that to this day functions as the foundation of Géluk dialectic education (the arsenal of raucous debate contests, where burgeoning scholars' names are made and broken, are hundreds or even thousands of pages of memorized texts):[62]

> When I was memorizing for my class,
> I could read a large folio about three times and would have it memorized.
> Though I was proud of myself,
> later I realized that my egoism had increased.
> I suppose I took up the actions of demons![63]

In only a few years, Lubsangagwang transitioned from a frustrated young monk in a provincial banner monastery to a gifted pupil in Mongolia's major scholastic center, and then to a teacher in his own right. For eight years, while studying and debating the different texts required for his advanced course of study leading to the elite *gabcu* degree, he began to simultaneously teach dialectics, logic, and epistemology to his juniors. Overextended by new pedagogical responsibilities, Zava Damdin recalls in *The Summary* that he had to limit his study of advanced topics like the *vinaya* monastic code and the *abhidharma* corpus to memorizing summary explanations from works like the *Four Divisions of the Vinaya Scripture* and its Indian commentaries.[64]

As a testament to his scholastic acumen, he continued to excel in his formal studies in the halls and debate courtyards of Gungachoiling despite his teaching load. "Whatever texts I could acquire, I studied."[65] Extracurricular interests included meditation manuals and pithy advice from the beloved Tibetan masters of the old Kadampa tradition (Tib. *Bka' gdams pa*) and the fundamental Géluk presentation of the "graduated stages of the path" to enlightenment (Tib. *lam rim*; Mong. *mör-ün jerge*). Other personal pursuits mentioned in *The Summary* include Nāgārjuna's *Fundamental Verses on the Middle Way*[66] and its "great commentary."[67] Zava Damdin recalls in *The Summary* that he was encouraged to tackle these classics of the Mahāyāna Buddhist tradition outside of other class requirements on the advice of an otherwise unmentioned teacher whom he identifies only with the Sanskrit name Sāmudra.[68]

Journey to Eastern Tibet

In the midst of a hectic schedule of teaching and voracious study, in 1899 "suddenly conditions arose so that I could go to Tibet."[69] By "Tibet" Zava

Damdin meant the major Géluk sites and teaching institutions in an area along the Sino-Tibetan-Mongolian frontiers known as Amdo (Tib. A mdo), largely contained today within the PRC's Qinghai province. It was the first of several formative trips across sacred topography in the twilight of the Qing. Zava Damdin's 1936 reminiscences are unaware, unconcerned, or unwilling to reflect upon the profound challenges the Qing was actually facing as he set off from Urga. Typical of all his writing in the revolutionary era, these narratives eschew political or ethnographic details and are saturated instead by visionary experiences, intense study, and prolonged devotional practice and meditation. At this juncture in the 1936 *Summary*, as the young monk finally makes contact with the holy land of Tibetan cultural regions, we see a marked transition in genre, from the "outer" biographical accounts of his early life to a mystic "inner" and even "secret" account of his wanderings across the enchanted late Qing.

That 1899 journey proceeded by way of Alashan monastery in Inner Mongolia.[70] There, Lubsangagwang met the "supreme incarnation of Jamyang Zhépa,"[71] one of the most important incarnations of the Sino-Tibetan-Mongolian frontiers, from whom he deeply drank "the nectar of Dharma."[72] Interestingly, this "worshipful encounter," or *jel* (Tib. *mjal*), occurred in a *yamen* (Ch. 衙門; Tib. *yā man*; Mong. *yamun*), either the Qing administrative office or perhaps the "Yamun süme" in nearby Bayankhota that had been founded in 1733.[73] Soon enough, he arrived at Kumbüm Jampa Ling monastery, founded at the reputed birthplace of the Géluk founder, Tsongkhapa (Mañjuśrī's other most important manifestation alongside the Manchu emperors who would patronize his lineage centuries later).[74]

At Kumbüm, Lubsangagwang engaged in devotional practices toward its many holy objects, especially the golden stupa that housed Tsongkhapa's relics until their destruction by Chinese forces in the 1950s (save a small portion of the mummified body housed inside, which a local man retrieved from the flames and ate, according to oral tradition). Lubsangagwang received teachings and transmissions from prominent local teachers on topics outside the core Géluk scholastic program, such as astrology, composition, and *kāvya* poetics. A few, rather elementary exercises in *kāvya* survive in Zava Damdin's *Collected Works*. A notable example is the *Brief Eulogy to Gadentegchenling* (Tib. *Dga' ldan theg chen gling gi bsngags pa mdo tsam brjod pa*), an exercise in thirty-two ornamental poetic modes expressing praise. Its colophon records that "the crazy Suddhi Wakāidha wrote this out by hand when he was thirty-three years old, on the auspicious day of the Female Pig year of the fifteenth *rabjung* [1899]."[75] A small selection will illustrate the scope and style of the poetic musings of a restless Mongol scholar thinking of distant Urga, who spilled much ink while "drunk like a bee" with new learning in Amdo.

FIRST: ORNAMENT OF THE OBJECT (*DPE'I RGYAN*)

All of the gorgeous land is like a sky.
The two monastic colleges appear as a sun and a moon.
The monastic residences and texts appear as stars.
Who is unsatisfied gazing upon this wondrous, magical display?[76]

SEVENTH: SUMMARY EXAMPLE (*BSDUS PA'I DPE*)

That hermitage, beautified by Gandhola.
Not only do its three supports
compare to Séra, Drépung, and Ganden,
so too do the pure behavior and view of its many thousands of monks.

ELEVENTH: EXAMPLE OF CONFUSION (*RMONGS PA'I DPE*)

There, whenever intelligent debaters
employ textual sources and logical reason
and make the sounds of debate,
the stupid imagine that a lion and tiger are fighting in the core of a mountain!
With their heart channel shaking, they flee!

THIRTEENTH: EXAMPLE OF DECISION (*GTAN PHEBS DPE*)

With a fearless confidence,
those monks can compete with even the Six Ornaments and the Two Superiors.
But their language, manner of dressing, and behavior appear different.
It is therefore sure they are not bearded Indians![77]

TWENTY-FIFTH: EXAMPLE OF THE IMPOSSIBLE (*SRID MIN DPE*)

The sun producing darkness,
the lotus flower emitting a wicked smell,
becoming less intelligent and acquiring a bad reputation from this monastery:
all are impossible![78]

Also at Kumbüm, the budding poet studied in the presence of Gyayak Trülku (Tib. Rgya yag sprul sku). This prominent incarnate lama provided a remarkable eyewitness account of a failed conversion of a local lama, the Māyang Paṇḍita, by the English missionary Cecil Polhill.[79]

Traveling to nearby Gönlung[80] and Chuzang monasteries,[81] Lubsangag-wang formally became a disciple of several lamas, including another of the main Géluk incarnations of the Inner Asian frontiers of the Qing: the Jangji-a Khutuɣtu.[82] He then returned to Kumbüm in order to take tantric initiation from Sertok Dorjé Chang.[83] There, his teacher Drotsang divined that Zava Damdin ought to cut his "Tibetan" odyssey short and return to Mongolia. Lubsangagwang dutifully left and faced the dangerous trip home in the company of a certain *ācārya*. "On the way," *The Summary* records, "whatever fearful situation occurred, whenever I made requests to the lama and the Triple Gem it immediately disappeared, which caused people to be amazed."[84]

Back in Urga and busy as ever with study, debate, and instruction, Lub-sangagwang took an opportunity to travel south to his Gobi homeland for what would be his last visit with his parents. While there he engaged in tantric rituals as an act of filial piety, performing purification ceremonies for a month on behalf of his elderly mother and father. Though grateful, his parents soon cut the visit short, saying:

You are our son, now return to Küriye [Urga]!
Because the compassion of the Triple Gem is unbiased
and because you reside there to study,
this [provides] more than enough virtue for us as well.[85]

With this memory, the elderly Zava Damdin intrudes into the temporal flow of the 1936 *Summary*. "Today, as I think about [my parents'] final testament, my heart is stirred and tears fall from my eyes."[86] After returning to his studies in Urga, he never saw them again: his mother died in late 1900, his father in the spring of 1901.

Just like his journey to Amdo, the loss of Lubsangagwang's parents marks a turning point in the trajectory of *The Summary*. The eager pupil and young pilgrim now began to occupy more senior administrative and pedagogical roles in the monastic scene of Urga and his Gobi homeland. This was when he, who since youth had had an irrepressible curiosity about history and antiquities, made a first tentative attempt to write about the past. He chose to write in the *ten-tsi* genre (Tib. *bstan rtsis*), a "chronology of the teachings" in Indian, Tibetan, and Mongol lands titled *Well-Explained Drop of Amṛta: A Brief Chronology of the Teachings in India, Tibet, and Mongolia* (Tib. *Rgya bod hor gsum gyi bstan rtsis rags bsdus legs bshad bdud rtsi'i thig pa*).[87] He would repeat the exercise in the Fire Rabbit year, 1927, when he wrote a *ten-tsi* about his hermitage and its webs of lineage affiliation.[88] *Drop of Amṛta*, like the fifteen hundred-folio "record of teachings received" he would write later, sought to position its author and his Qing-era monastic and lineage milieu in a direct temporal and spatial relationship with the Buddha and the dispensation of the teaching.

With the turn of the twentieth century (though the Gregorian calendar was unknown or unimportant to him; he would have marked this as drifting into the Iron Mouse year), Zava Damdin began to enjoy some renown as a popular teacher and an accomplished tantric practitioner sought after for the efficacy of his rituals. This is most evident in narratives spread across his autobiographical and historical works describing close personal contact, interaction, and gift giving with the many high incarnate lamas who arrived in Urga from across Tibet, Mongol lands, north China, and Buryatia, not least of which was the Thirteenth Dalai Lama. Of special note is Zava Damdin's relationship with the Darva Paṇḍita Agwangchoijurdondubbalsang, who in 1901 first invited Zava Damdin to reside and teach at his personal monastery, where the two became lifelong "Dharma friends." Exactly two decades later, Darva Paṇḍita would become one of the most active leaders in the early Mongolian socialist movement, writing populist tracts extolling the Buddhist virtue of Marxist-Leninism before his death in that fateful year of 1924.[89]

Despite a busy administrative and teaching schedule, Lubsangagwang— now of an appropriate maturity and stature to be called Zava Damdin in my account—was not yet finished with his studies. In the autumn of the Water Rabbit year, or 1903, one of his principal teachers in Urga offered him the opportunity to earn a shortcut degree, the so-called *parma géshé* course of study (Tib. *'phar ma dge shes*). With that qualification, Zava Damdin could more quickly embark on a series of scholarly examination tours (Tib. *grwa skor*) in and around the great monastic capital, a pursuit that would remain his primary public activity throughout the revolutionary period until 1936. He recalls that when he joined the advanced classes at the start of the Wood Snake year of 1905, "I couldn't compare to those (other) *géshés* who were studying the *vinaya* and *abhidharma*, and who had been studying for many years. I was a little embarrassed, and friends used shameful words."[90] Focusing more exclusively on his studies, he soon caught up with his peers to such an extent that "I was very happy and others were also amazed." Within months, Zava Damdin was appointed as teacher for his former critics.[91]

The Dalai Lama Comes to Town

At the turn of the twentieth century, escalations in the Great Game saw Britain preemptively responding to fears that the Russian Empire was exerting covert influence on the Tibetan frontiers of the British Raj, as it was then doing elsewhere in Central Asia. In 1904, the British viceroy ordered an invasion of Central Tibet under the leadership of Sir Francis Younghusband.[92] The penetration of Tibet, and especially of Lhasa, by British forces and the ensuing flight of the Dalai Lama was one of the most significant and jarring political events in late-imperial Buddhist Inner Asia. Under the advice of his Buryat tutor and confidant Agvan Dorjiev, the Thirteenth Dalai Lama, Tupten Gyatso, (Tib. Tā la'i bla ma Thub bstan rgya mtsho, 1876–1933) retreated nearly twenty-five hundred kilometers from Lhasa to Urga. There he sought asylum in the monastic city of the Eighth Jebtsundamba, who famously resented the competition for patronage and devotion that came with the Dalai Lama's residency. Despite the Jebtsundamba's misgivings, with great effort the Khalkha nobility and faithful funded the enormous and expensive Tibetan encampment for two years. In that time, the Dalai Lama taught widely and pursued a distressed diplomacy with envoys from Russia, America, and beyond before moving on to Mount Wutai and eastern Tibet.[93]

There is now a small body of scholarship on the Thirteenth Dalai Lama's time in Urga, a key moment in the geopolitics of the late Great Game, including about his divisive relationship with the Eighth Jebtsundampa Khutuɣtu, and his desperate political scramble to recruit help from Russia against both the British and the Qing.[94] In the later 1931 sections of his major historical work, *The Golden Book,* Zava Damdin provides a guarded account of the British invasion and the Dalai Lama's flight. Because of its historical interest as a previously unstudied firsthand account, I include a full translation here:

In the Wood Dragon year of the fifth *rapjung* [1904], an army of foreigners from Europe invaded Central Tibet. Because of that, the Lord of Refuge and Victor Precious One, along with some of his attendants, secretly escaped and passed along the northern route. They came to Chinese Sagyu through Upper Sok and then reached Khalkha Mongolia. Many individual bannermen lined the path to welcome him upon his arrival.

In the last month of winter, the party arrived at Gadentegchenling monastery at the center of Yeke Küriye [Urga]. That Spiritual Master with a Karap Jampa degree (Tib. *bka' rab 'byams pa*) and his students were divided, began teaching, and debated Buddhist texts. The Dalai Lama came to both colleges and they held Answerer's examinations, which he attended again and again. The Lord himself and his [Tibetan] disciples, incarnate lamas, and masters [in his entourage] all rose and debated.

High and low lamas and leaders of the center and borderlands of Mongolia, along with faithful laypeople and monastics, gathered every day like a raincloud. They visited him and asked for divinations, initiations, transmissions, and blessings. He fulfilled the wishes of all higher, lower, and middling beings. Like rivers gathering into the ocean, he received donations of material objects and animals from all directions.

At Gungachoiling, he gave the *bodhicitta* precepts principally to Tibetan and Mongolia lamas, reincarnated masters, and over three thousand monks. At his yellow encampment, he bestowed the great initiation of Avalokiteśvara three times, and widely spread the tradition of full monastic ordination. He gave five thousand silver coins to both monastic colleges in order to begin an allowance (Tib. *gsol phogs*) [system for the monks].

In the winter of the Wood Snake year [1905], he went to the encampment of the Chin Wang and received teachings from Jamyang Lama Tendar. During the summer of the Fire Horse year [1906], he went to the monastery of Zaya Paṇḍita. During the autumn, he went to the monastery of the Erdeni Jowo. He offered saffron water and then did a consecration. He also offered tens of thousands of butter lamps. Continuously day and night, he diligently made requests, prayers, auspicious recitations, and so forth. People recount that he said, "This Jowo statue is, in terms of blessings, no different than Lhasa's Jowo."

After that, he turned the reins of his horse toward the encampment of Sayin Noyan [Khan Ayimaγ]. From there, he departed for China's Gansu province by rail. He went to Mount Wutai and Beijing. He visited Emperor Guangxu [Ch. 光緒; Tib. Srid 'bar; 1871–1908]. Then he once more departed by rail to Kumbüm and beyond.

In the Earth Monkey year [1908], he returned to Tibet where he stayed, protecting and increasing the Buddhist teaching through the three wheels of activities.

One day in the Ox year [1924], the politicians of Central Tibet had an internal feud. Because of that, along with a few attendants, the Lord of Refuge [the Ninth Panchen Lama, Tupten Chökyi Nyima (Tib. *Thub bstan chos kyi nyi ma,* 1883–1937)] also secretly escaped via the northern route through Upper Sok and planned to come to Khalkha. However, when he arrived at Sagyu, the Yellow Chinese deceitfully directed him to Lanzhou. Because of that, he took the railway to Mount Wutai, Beijing, Mukden, and so on. These days, he resides in the land of the Forty-Nine Groups [i.e., Inner Mongolia] in order to benefit the teachings and sentient beings.

In this way, when a political or religious mishap (*jus nyer*) occurs in Tibet, both the Victor [the Dalai Lama] and his Son [the Panchen Lama] hasten to the Oirat and Khalkha regions. The reason for this is, as it says in Welmang (Bbal mang) Rinpoché's chronicle: "The Victorious Father and Son have expressed their respect. The seat of the Oirat is [the same as that of King] Songtsen [Gampo]. Khalkha is the seat of Chinggis [Khan]. These are places that attract the attentiveness of the Two Systems."

Though I need to explain much more on this topic, I am uninterested in being biased. People do not appreciate an honest statement, and so I will leave it all unsaid here.[95]

In the 1936 *Summary*, perhaps due to greater caution and self-censorship than he felt when undertaking the 1931 historical writing quoted above, Zava Damdin leaves out any further description of the political climate during the Dalai Lama's stay in Urga thirty years prior. He notes blandly that this was a happy time when "the most knowledgeable of Tibet, China, and Mongolia gathered here as if at a monastic assembly."[96]

FIGURE 1.4 The Thirteenth Dalai Lama in Mongolia (a photo copy) (1910s).
Digital copies of glass plate negatives preserved in the Archives for Cinema, Photography, and Sound Recording, Mongolia [1910s–1950s]. EAP264/1/8/2/2.

Regardless, the Dalai Lama's two-year stay in Urga was a critical time for Zava Damdin's development. New encounters shaped the interpretative tools he later used to make sense of the Qing ruins, as the visit facilitated intellectual exchanges with envoys of European and Russian arts and sciences. More notable in his autobiographical accounts are the regular personal interactions he enjoyed with the Dalai Lama. In 1905, Zava Damdin once even served as chief ritualist during a *sojong* (Tib. *gso sbyong*; Mong. *selbin*) monthly monastic confession and vow-purification ceremony presided over by the Dalai Lama.[97] Zava Damdin recalls that following that ritual performance, which included an oral recitation of both *Individual Liberation Sūtras*,[98] "[The Dalai Lama] showed his pleasure with me. He placed both of his hands on my head and said 'Wonderful' before giving me a very blessed statue of the Mañjughoṣa Lama [Tsongkhapa]."[99]

Many of the memories of Zava Damdin circulating in the Buddhist revitalization of contemporary Mongolia concern his scholastic performances in Urga while the Dalai Lama was in town. In those stories, Zava Damdin and a Mongolian team of luminary debaters (including the Darva Paṇḍita,

Borjgon Jamts, and Angi Shagdar) were pitted against the best Tibetan minds in the Dalai Lama's company, including the top scholars from the major Géluk institutions of Lhasa. Their battles were presided over by the Thirteenth Dalai Lama, as mentioned in passing in the account from the *Golden Book* translated above. According to several postsocialist oral traditions recorded by scholars such as Teleki, Majer, Khurelbaatar, and Luvsantseren, on several occasions the Dalai Lama sought to enter the most heated debates but was dissuaded by his Tibetan contingent lest he suffer the humiliation of losing in a test of scriptural knowledge and logic to Mongols. (In some versions of events, the Dalai Lama did lose to local Mongol monks and asked to become their disciple, a particularly politicized memory given the contested issue of Mongolia's dependence on Tibetan lamas to revive Buddhism in the postsocialist period).[100]

According to one remarkable memory circulating in today's revived Gandentegchenling monastery, Zava Damdin and his Mongol co-debaters defeated the Tibetans in a shocking, unbearable upset. Their victorious performance, which included contributions by Zava Damdin, was somehow recorded and pressed onto a record, brought back to Tibet, and played on a phonograph for top scholars in Lhasa. Having studied the virtuoso use of scripture and logic by the Mongols for years and prepared a counterattack, an elite team of Tibetan Lharampa *Géshés* (Tib. *dge shes lha rams pa*, the highest scholastic degree awarded in the Géluk school and only avaible from Lhasa institutions) were dispatched to Urga to defeat Zava Damdin and his compatriots and restore Tibetan supremacy in the multiethnic Qing-Géluk order.

Zava Damdin recorded none of this in his autobiographical writing. As in his narratives about mystic experiences on the slopes of Mount Wutai and on the streets of the Qing imperial capital some years later, what is noteworthy to him is the personal contact he enjoyed with the Dalai Lama and the transmissions, blessings, teachings, material boons, and respect he acquired as a consequence of that proximity. For example, while on a scholarly tour during the Great Prayer Festival at this time:

My knowledge and reputation grew greatly.
Nonbiased Realized Ones and others praised me as successful,
but this was just talk (*ca ca*)!
I understand that was all due to the power of karma, prayer, and the ripening
    of virtuous deeds.[101]

The Dalai Lama's visit also brought Zava Damdin into a more globalized series of intellectual connections that would last the remainder of his life. "In the spring [of 1905], it so happened that I had an audience with the Russian Shcherbatsky (Tib. Rgya ser Shra wā skhi) and [we] joyfully conversed about non-Buddhist and Buddhist doctrine."[102] After Sergey Fedorovich Oldenburg, Feodor Ippolitovich Shcherbatsky was one of the most prominent late imperial and early Soviet Buddhologists, whose works on logic and other philosophical topics remain widely available in many languages. (This warm but rather muted record of their meeting hardly matches Bira's 1964 description in his Soviet-era study of Damdin, which he described as "the grand event of [Zava Damdin's] life.")[103]

In all, 1906 was a year of both arrival and departure, of beginning and ending. Zava Damdin was awarded his *gabcu* degree, his dream since watching monks debate in the courtyard of his local Gobi monastery when wandering through youth decades earlier. This was the year the Dalai Lama left Khalkha (after months of delays and having thoroughly drained the collected resources of his hosts).[104] Unable to return to Central Tibet, he and his vast entourage headed to Eastern Tibet and China, stopping at Kumbüm monastery, Mount Wutai, and Beijing before returning to Lhasa in 1908.[105] Reflecting on his time spent with the Dalai Lama in *The Summary* in 1936, three years after the former's death, Zava Damdin writes in the characteristically muted and guarded tone of his late life, "I am very nostalgic."[106] This was also the year of Zava Damdin's departure from his monastic world into the enchanted topography of the waning Qing Empire.

His memorialization of that visionary, transformative wandering and quarter century of monastic leadership in the center of Inner Asian revolution is the topic of chapter 4. We must turn first to his revolutionary-era story of the enchantment of Eurasia. These histories of Qing time, space, communities, and religiosity, which he developed through a prodigious reading of the Eurasian literature newly available to him in revolutionary Khalkha, set the disenchantment, violence, and fractured temporalities of his revolutionary world into the sharpest relief.

TWO

Felt

World history is the record of the spirit's efforts to attain knowledge of
what it is in itself. The Orientals do not know that the spirit or man as such
are free in themselves. And because they do not know that, they are not
themselves free. They only know that One is free; but for this very reason,
such freedom is mere arbitrariness, savagery, and brutal passion, or a
milder and tamer version of this which is itself only an accident of nature,
and equally arbitrary.

—G.W.F. HEGEL, *LECTURES ON THE PHILOSOPHY OF WORLD HISTORY*

The sentient beings of Chinese, Mongol, and Tibetan lands have been enemies, friends, and strangers to one another for lifetimes without beginning. Even so, by emphasizing karmic connections between them we may
develop the minds of loving-kindness, compassion, and *bodhicitta*. Observing that hell has come to the human realm prior to or during our Degenerate Age, we must be encouraged in our practice of the Dharma.

—ZAVA DAMDIN, *THE MEMORANDA*

AGVAN DORJIEV WAS a master of discourses and disciplines forged elsewhere. Born in 1854 to the east of Lake Baikal on the Siberian frontier of tsarist Russia, Dorjiev (Tib. Ngag dbang blo bzang rdo rje) became philosophical
tutor (Tib. *mtshan zhabs*) to the Thirteenth Dalai Lama in Lhasa, a member
of the Russian Geographical Society in Saint Petersburg, an ambassador for
the Tibetan government in Beijing, a sought-after lecturer to Theosophists
in Paris, a wanted man in the British Raj, a confidant of Tsar Nikolai, a Soviet
Buddhist reformer, and, finally, a thought criminal who died on a gulag hos-
pital gurney after weeks of interrogation.[1]

In the Year of the Water Pig, 1923, Dorjiev wrote Zava Damdin a letter
about history and the historian's craft. They surely met already during the
Thirteenth Dalai Lama's stay in Urga, but Zava Damdin never recorded the

fact. Eight blunt questions driven by thinly veiled skepticism came in a missive with a deceptively pleasant note reading, in part, "I, the faithful beggar monk Vagindra [Dorjiev], held this letter to my crown and offer it to you accompanied by a silk scarf."[2] His "questions" were actually demands that Zava Damdin provide evidence, in the form of "reliable accounts" (Tib. *khungs ldan gtam*), for the often-radical claims the latter had made about the Eurasian Buddhist past in *The Dharma Conch*, a short historical work published in the 1910s.

The Dharma Conch, like the rest of the thousand pages of history Zava Damdin would write between 1900 and 1937, took the interpretative and narrative legacy of frontier, polyglot Géluk monks of the imperium and dramatically extended its purpose and scope of inquiry. He sought most of all to recognize signs concealed in the massive corpus of Eurasian literature available to him in Tibetan and Mongolian translation. These came bundled in texts already wrapped in silk and stored in dusty monastery libraries. The signs came also to scandalize literati circles in Khalkha on the pages of secular newspapers, in the halls of newly founded scientific academies, and in nationalist history projects. New sources and profoundly challenging new knowledge came also in personal exchanges with European, Russian, and Mongolian intellectuals, those networks of spies, diplomats, and academicians inventing "Asia," "Buddhism," "Mongolia," and "the modern" as objects of knowledge and reform.

Driven relentlessly by a Qing anxiety requiring that the postimperial situation be set into time, Zava Damdin sought to understand the deep history of his revolutionary present by bringing to bear on his Eurasianist sources the dexterities of a dialectician, an ethnologist, a tantric visionary, a philologist, a "wandering" pilgrim, and an archaeologist. Contrary to stories told by Soviet historians and Mongolian Buddhist revivalists today, he drew those "modernist" skills more from Qing-era scholastic practice than from the scientism prized by successive revolutionary parties. In Zava Damdin's hands, sources as diverse as French historical fiction, Mongolian oral tradition, Finnish archaeology, the Kālacakra Tantra, Khampa folk customs, and Chinese dynastic records spoke new stories about the Mongols, their claims upon the Dharma, the causes and consequences of the Qing collapse, and the possibilities of Buddhist life in a post-Qing world. Many of his monastic peers remained unconvinced, troubled even by his effort. Primary among them, it seems, was one of the most visible, powerful, and global Géluk scholars of the day: Agvan Dorjiev.

"As for those known as the Yeke Mongɣol," Dorjiev inquires in his 1923 letter, "where did their kin live long ago?" "Where have they ended up today and what are they named?" "Is 'the Land of Li' (which you identify as Khotan) not in fact a part of Nepal?" "According to the stone pillar inscriptions of King Aśoka, the birth year of the Buddha is calculated to more than 2500 years ago, but this contradicts our astrological system. In this case, are we to argue against [the dates of Aśoka's pillars] using logic and textual sources? Or do we just accept them?"[3]

In an undated letter Damdin wrote to the Buryat scholar Tseveen Jamsrano apologizing for losing money and misplacing a manuscript of a history of Erdene Zuu monastery the latter had commissioned, he remarks, "[Agvan Dorjiev] sent me several critiques of my *Root Verses of the History of the Dharma in Mongolia* [i.e., *The Dharma Conch*]. Although I can give answers to every one of his criticisms easily, I am busy right now with much to do and so cannot respond to him at this time."[4] When he did find time to respond, after the ornery Buryat had sent a second letter, Zava Damdin did indeed have ready answers, delivered brazenly and with force in the manner in which he had been challenged. He could handily supply evidence for the *longue durée* of Eurasian history, the form and structure of the physical universe, and the ancient peregrinations of Mongol peoples and their neighbors.

Damdin demurred only when asked, in Dorjiev's least condescending moment, how best to meet the steep challenges facing the Dharma in Soviet Russia and across postimperial Inner Asia. And that question confounded the Khalkha monk until his death. Over decades of historical research to find answers, his view of Eurasia's deep past appeared clearer than ever. The revolutionary present, however, remained unintelligible, and its future inscrutable.

*   *   *

When the Qing came undone in 1911, Zava Damdin focused his prodigious intellectual abilities on writing the past with intensity and purpose. He did so until he died in 1937, driven by relentless curiosity and a proclivity to archiving material culture, ritual traditions, historical narratives, and oral tradition going back to his youthful wanderings. As the Qing receded even further from view and a contingent socialist government sought to reform, then annex, and then abolish Buddhist monasticism, Damdin's writing of society became a desperate and then a hopeless project.

Childhood curiosities and Qing anxiety alone did not, however, compel him to press ink to a thousand folios of historiography. It was always others who demanded he order and inscribe the past. Holy kings, early scholars of Asia, the poets of revolution, living buddhas, a dazed Khalkha aristocracy, Lhasa abbots, and even a member of the Bakhtin Circle called upon Zava Damdin for clarity and reassurance, for stories, for a time and a place in the ruins of the Qing. They requested that he take up such writing with folded hands, money, and silk. And whenever he set down his pen or stopped dictating to his scribe, they insisted he begin again. Those appeals came from monastery and academy, from People's Congresses to Qing revivalist circles, in newly imagined places like "Asia" (Tib. A tsi ya) and "Europe" (Tib. Phe ring; Rgya ser). Such requests came when Zava Damdin was a young man awash in the certainties of the Qing, and when he was aged and certain that revolutionary events had exceeded history.

In exploring Zava Damdin's historical works in this chapter and in the remainder of this book, I have three rather modest aims. The first is to share with readers a cursory survey of their mostly unstudied content, a unique source on Buddhist thought during the collapse of the Qing Empire, the throes of "Asia's first modern revolution," and the early mechanization of state erasure in the Mongol crossroads. The second is to explore ways that a specific brand of frontier, polyglot, synthetic Géluk scholasticism forged during the Qing was put to use by Zava Damdin to engage and repurpose newly arriving Euro-Russian arts and sciences, especially as these concerned foreign concepts and practices such as "Asia," "Buddhism," empiricism, the national subject, and history. My final aim is to draw into relief a monastic representation of time, temporality, community, and sovereignty beyond both the Qing and the national subject. This hybridized third space responded to the unenviable demands on our author to interpret his postimperial world within a scholastic tradition gradually denied, in the most terrible fashion, its "place."

Historical Sources

As with his autobiographical writing and many of his over four hundred other works, Zava Damdin's synthetic histories close a centuries-long tradition of monastic historiography in Mongol lands. "The Mongol lamas may no more chronicle the spread of Dharma in their Northern Lands," as Lokesh Chandra put it somberly in 1964.[5] Damdin turned to matters historical soon after his 1899 wandering to the major monasteries and pilgrimage centers of Eastern Tibet. Flush with a pilgrim's fervor and literary skills learned at Kumbüm, he set brush to paper prodigiously, and almost without pause, for his remaining thirty-seven years. Almost in equal measure to the march of years—as a Qing realpolitik receded deeper into the fog of memory, as a People's Party and its antipathies crowded in—Zava Damdin turned increasingly to the authority of the past.

The result was a vast corpus of historical writing from 1900 to 1931, all in Tibetan. While a comprehensive overview is impossible here, these works can be loosely organized into four categories: major historical works completed between 1900 and 1931; middle-length historical works that deeply engaged European translations of Eurasian primary sources (especially Chinese and Mongolian ones) completed mainly between 1911 and 1927; minor historical studies embedded in dozens of nonhistorical works, such as an introduction to the ritual tradition of the protectoress Palden Lhamo, the making of medicinal pills, and monastic charters; and polemical letters on matters historical exchanged with progressive figures like Agvan Dorjiev and Jamsrano.

The first of Zava Damdin's major historical works was the aforementioned 1900 *Drop of Amṛta: A Well-Explained, Brief Chronology of the Teachings in India, Tibet, and Mongolia* (*Rgya bod hor gsum gyi bstan rtsis rags bsdus legs bshad bdud rtsi'i thig pa*).[6] Though this text is included in the index of various editions of Damdin's *Collected Works* to which I have access (always in volume *Kha*), it is never included in the contents as a separate work. Instead, it appears to have been inserted in part within the colophon of the 1931 *Golden Book* (also in volume *Kha*, just before its separate listing in the index).[7] Here the conquests of Chinggis Khan, the enlightenment of the Buddha Śākyamuni, the birth of Tsongkhapa, and the meeting of Altan Khan and the Third Dalai Lama are set in continuity with one another in a passage of years. So too is the authorial present—so that the ruins of the Qing have a time, if not a direction. Indexed works in colophons (if that is indeed where *The Drop of Amṛta* disappeared to) is representative of the mosaic quality of his later histories and (auto)biographies, which read as collections of short studies completed at different times, in different styles, with different spellings and conventions, often making different points and reading as if circumstances had precluded a final edit or revision.

Around a decade after *The Drop of Amṛta*, either soon before or just after the collapse of the Qing and the declaration of Mongol autonomy under the Eighth Jebtsundamba in 1911, Zava Damdin finished *The Sounding of the Auspicious Dharma Conch: The History of How the Precious, Holy Dharma Spread in the Land of Northerly Mongolia* (Tib. *Byang phyogs hor gyi yul du dam pa'i chos rin po che byung tshul gyi gtam rgyud*). Thirty-five folios long, this verse history in nine-syllable meter unfurled a historical vision Zava Damdin would continue to develop for the remainder of his life: the transmission of the Dharma into Mongol lands in three periods, guided in every case by enlightened intervention and culminating in the Qing-Géluk formation.

By the time of the Qing collapse, this was a well-worn story in both Mongolian language histories and the majority Tibetan language histories written in overlapping, intertextual genres like "Histories of the Dharma" (Tib. *chos 'byung*), general histories (Tib. *lo rgyus*), chronicles (Tib. *deb ther*), chronologies of the teachings (Tib. *bstan rtsis*), origin stories (Tib. *'byung khungs*), auto/biography (Tib. *rang rnam/rnam thar*), and royal and abbatial successions (Tib. *rgyal rabs/gdan rabs*).[8] The three dispensations story of the Dharma was ubiquitous in Géluk scholasticism by the twilight of the Qing, but Zava Damdin dramatically extended the scope of the earliest transmission using sources newly available in revolutionary Khalkha, even as he struggled to extend the story of the latter dispensation into the post-Qing situation.

Though Zava Damdin's histories were always written within the interpretative and narrative "site" of the Tibeto-Mongolian monastic college, by some accounts he was drafted unwillingly to contribute to the Boγda Khaγan's state history project toward the end of the Autonomous Period (1911–1919). In the early 1990s, at the start of the postsocialist opening of Mongolia, the scholar Khurelbaaar conducted oral history interviews with some of Zava Damdin's still-living disciples in his Gobi homeland. These include fascinating memories of Zava Damdin's love of hunting, the prayers most often recited by his herder father, and Damdin's apparent abilities in weapon repair ("It happened that the hunter's gun hadn't been shooting straight, and so the Lam took it apart, saw what was wrong, and fixed it. They said that after that, instead of killing one marmot, he could kill ten. This is a story about Zava Damdin"). Scattered in Khurelbaatar's study is the following anecdote about Zava Damdin's formation as a historian.

FELT

FIGURE 2.1 A lama sitting in front of his dwelling (location unknown) (1930s). Digital copies of glass plate negatives preserved in the Archives for Cinema, Photography, and Sound Recording, Mongolia [1910s–1950s]. EAP264/1/9/6/66.

Old Man Sereeter said the following: "Zava Lam did not really like the Eighth Boγda. The Boγda said, 'We shall produce a unified history of Khalkha.' He wanted Zava Damdin to write it and ordered a servant, 'Go visit him!' The lam [Zava Damdin] lived in a fenced-in, four-wall *ger* [yurt]. When the Boγda's messenger arrived and tried to enter the doorway, Zava Damdin yelled, 'Open the door quietly!' The servant came inside, took a seat, and passed along his message along with an offering scarf. Then the lam said, 'Though I do not want to, I am obliged to obey.' He took the offering scarf from the servant's hand and threw it down upon his pillow."[9]

Although I have been unable to reconstruct the extent of Zava Damdin's involvement, it appears that the "unified history of Khalkha" recalled by the elderly Sereeter became an eleven-volume state history commissioned by the

Boγda's government near the end of the Autonomous Period (c. 1918–19). The finished collaborative work appears to have been the *Commentary Upon the Right to Rule of the Mongolian State Based Upon Its National History* (Mong. *Ulus-un Teüke-yin Ner-e-yi Zarliγ-iyar Mongγol Ulus-un Shastir*). On the topic of the newly invented national subject, it was a massive study described by later Mongolian historians of the socialist period as advancing "the view that Mongolia has from time immemorial been an independent state which, after emerging from being a part of the Manchu Empire, was revived in the form of a Mongolian monarchy . . . it is still a noteworthy fact that the ideas of the national liberation movement did find expression to some extent in Mongolian historical writing at this time."[10]

Between the c. 1910 *Dharma Conch* and its major commentary, the 1931 *Golden Book*, Zava Damdin produced a series of mid-length histories that were intimately connected to new intellectual currents in post-Qing Mongolia and took him far from the received narratives of the *datsang* monastic colleges (but never from their interpretative traditions). In one sense, this period was avant-garde because of his synthetic and daring analyses, which have continued to supply Tibetan and Mongolian diaspora, refugee, and revivalist communities with an enduring historical frame to this day. In another sense quite apart from any of his arguments or insights, these works were radical simply for bringing many new Chinese and Mongolian primary sources into the Tibetan language and, thereby, to a geographically dispersed Tibetan reading public spanning the British Raj, Republican China, Russia, and after the purges of 1937, South Asia, the Pacific Rim, and the North Atlantic.

A standout example of his histories from this period, and of the global circulation of Euro-Russian scholarship that helped inspire them, is the *All-Illuminating Emanated Mirror That Reflects the Source of the Victor's Teachings: The Story of the Great Han-era Monk Faxian's Journey to the Land of Noble Ones* (hereafter: *The Mirror*; Tib. *Chen po hān gur gyi btsun pa phā hyin gyis 'phags pa'i yul du 'grims pa'i rnam thar rgyal bstan 'byung khungs kun gsal 'phrul kyi me long*). This was Zava Damdin's heavily annotated translation of the *Fuguoji*, or *Record of Buddhistic Kingdoms*, the famous fifth-century record of the Eastern Jin dynasty monk Faxian's (Ch. 法顯; Tib. Phā hyin, Phā shan; Mong. Fahiyen, c. 337–422) long pilgrimage from Chang'an to Buddhist India via the Silk Road. Xuanzang's 646 CE *Great Tang Records on the Western Regions* (大唐西域記 *Da tang xiyu ji*)—a later epic tale of a Chinese monk's pilgrimage to India via Buddhist Central Asia—had already been translated into Tibetan during the mid-seventeenth century by one of Zava Damdin's primary influences, the Beijing resident and Qing loyalist Güng Gombojab (c. 1692–1749). The older *Fuguoji*, however, had never been available to Tibetan or Mongolian readers.

In a 1970 Mongolian reproduction of Zava Damdin's translation of Faxian's *Fuguoji*, the academician B. Rinchen claims that Damdin completed this important work as an early member of the party scientific institute founded in 1921. Zava Damdin's colophon, however, records that it was translated in 1917, "during the virtuous waxing moon period in the tenth month of the female Fire Snake year." Its place of composition is listed as "the great temple of Glorious Da Küriy-e [Urga], a major teaching center foretold by the Victor."[11] Whatever its time and place of inscription, Faxian's text surely came into Zava Damdin's hands through new contacts with Euro-Russian scholars. As he explains in the early pages,

> There is a Chinese-language biography of one such *mahātman* who once journeyed to the Land of Noble Ones. Having discovered [that account], a foreigner European translated it into his native language. Its contents verified authentic research already undertaken about India. A Buryat lama-translator then translated that [European work] into Mongolian. The text that follows here is a translation of that [Mongolian translation] into Tibetan. Because [this text] has passed through many dialects, names and pronunciation for numerous places and communities have changed. I left whatever I encountered unchanged, just as I found them. We must recall that in the future it will be necessary to research other texts and reliable sources to [properly] identify these names and their pronunciation.[12]

As he readily admits, Zava Damdin's pioneering Tibetan translation was not made from the Chinese, but rather from a mid-eighteenth-century Mongolian translation of an 1836 French translation of the *Fuguoji* by Jean-Pierre Abél-Remussat, the first holder of a research chair in sinology in Europe. Abel-Rémussat's work, entitled *Foé Koué Ki; ou, Relations des royaumes bouddhiques: voyage dans la Tartarie, dans l'Afghanistan et dans l'Inde, exécuté, à la fin du IVe siècle, par Chy Fa Hian* brought the Buddha's life and ancient Buddhist India and Central Asia to European audiences for the first time. Within a few years, multiple English and German translations were in circulation. "For the European view of the life of the Buddha," writes Donald Lopez, "it was the first concerted attempt to identify the places in the Buddha's biography with actual locations in India. . . . Abel-Rémusat's work represents the most detailed life of the Buddha to appear in Europe up to that time."[13] It is little known that around the same time, Abel-Rémussat's work provided new resources for a Buryat Orientalist scholar and then our Khalkha monk to identify the places of a "Mongolian" Buddhist past "with actual locations in India" and Central Asia.

The first was Dorji Banzarov, whose Mongolian translation of Abel-Rémussat's *Foé Koué Ki* was titled *Journals of Travel to the Lands Where the Buddha's Scriptures Flourished* (Mong. *Burqan-u nom delgeregsen ulus-nuγud-tur jiγulčilγsan bičig*). Banzarov was a fascinating figure trained in ethnology and philology who read not only Tibetan but also several European languages. His translation is remarkably faithful to Abél-Remussat's French text. It is also a paradigmatic expression of late-tsarist projects to consolidate Asian borders through the production of geographical, botanical, and ethnological knowledge. Banzarov's work thus illustrates what Anya Bernstein describes as a new intellectual movement headed by certain Buryats to develop an "Asian Eurasianism" that evoked "Russia" to define itself against Asia;this inaugurated a long tradition of Buryat nationalism and Buddhist reform movements that were central to revolutionary developments in Mongolia.[14]

Christopher Atwood charges Banzarov's major scholarly contribution, *The Black Faith, Or Shamanism Among the Mongols,* with helping to cast a problematic mold in the study of Mongolian religions laden with "dubious first principles," such as that a foreign "Lamaism" rooted in Tibet could mask but never erase enduring shamanist sensibilities that were inherent in the Buryat and Mongol character.[15] In Zava Damdin's reading Banzarov's translation of the *Fuguoji* told the story of Buddhism in "Mongol" lands, and more specifically, of the earliest results of enlightened intervention into "Mongolian" communities. Zava Damdin would return to Faxian's *Fuguoji* in his 1931 *Golden Book* to "prove" his argument that "Mongols" not only had adopted Buddhism prior to the Chinese and the Tibetans but also had been the agents who brought Buddhism to ancient Tibetan and Chinese royal courts.

Zava Damdin's Tibetan translation of the *Fuguoji* comes to us in thirty-eight folios, organized into short chapters according to Abel-Rémussat's original and Banzarov's Mongolian version, but riven by intrusions, asides, and reflections. Damdin's text must therefore be treated as a stand-alone study as much as a translation. This is true also of his other translations of Chinese and Mongolian materials into Tibetan, which make up the bulk of his histo-riographic output in the 1920s. These were split compendiums with multiple authors, multiple narratives, and multiple conclusions alongside and within one another. Our author could not but jump into the narrative, to anxiously mine the ancient stories to make better sense of his post-Qing world.

In 1919, Zava Damdin began what would be his magnum opus, the 451-folio *Great, Amazing Golden Book: A Treatise Upon the History of the Northerly, Great Country of Mongolia* (hereafter: *The Golden Book*; Tib. *Byang phyogs chen po hor gyi rgyal khams kyi rtogs brjod kyi bstan bcos chen po ngo mtshar gser gyi deb ther*). This was ostensibly a commentary to the c. 1910 *The Dharma Conch*, but its narrative departs substantially from the root text even as it follows the same structure: first a discussion concerning the form and contents of the world, followed by the ways that political authority (Tib. *rgyal srid*) became con-nected to the Buddhadharma in Mongol lands in antiquity, during the Mongol and Yuan Empire, and then the reception of the Géluk school begin-ning with the Third Dalai Lama's conversion of Altan Khan of the Tümed in 1578 and extending across the Qing period and the socialist transition. Con-cluding discussions in both *The Golden Book* and *The Dharma Conch* include polemical attacks against the ancient Nyingma school of Tibet as an unsuit-able Dharma tradition for Mongol lands and "the uncommon, supreme qual-ities of the Géluk tradition." Unlike *The Dharma Conch*, *The Golden Book* includes some information about its composition in the colophon. In 1919, when autonomous Mongolia fell to Chinese and then White Russian occupa-tion, "the Da Lam Tseringdondub, he who possessed the vast eye of knowl-edge about religious and secular affairs, convened a conference discussion principally among the nobility of the government of Yeke-yin Küriy-e [Urga]. From this [discussion], many reasons were given why, by all means, it was absolutely necessary for me to write a great commentary upon a few stories concerning great Mongolia."[16]

> They constantly requested me until I could no longer decline and so I conceded. Therefore, that year I undertook this composition. When I had completed just two chapters, however, I again discarded this work on account of the frothing of fluctuating politics. Many virtuous friends from near and afar that possessed the eye of the Dharma sent me messages saying I must finish what remained. Upon receiving all that, I proceeded according to their wishes.[17]

In 1931, thinking presciently that "if texts were to become thoroughly scattered it will have been auspicious and excellent [for me to complete this work],"[18] Zava Damdin retreated to a small hermitage in his Gobi monastery and completed the remaining four chapters over the course of two months.

Other noteworthy examples of Zava Damdin's substantive histories, all of which we will encounter in the following pages, include a fifty-eight-folio, 1927 collection of Tibetan translations of Mongolian translations of Chinese and Manchu histories entitled *An Arrangement of Translations from Mongol Into Tibetan as an Appendix to the Memoranda Explanations of Great Mongolia's Ancient History* (hereafter: *The Memoranda*; Tib. *Chen po hor gyi yul gru'i sngon rabs kyi brjed byang shāstra'i zur rgyan du sog yig las bod skad du bsgyur te bkod pa*).[19] Related to this are two undated works that translate and analyze new sources on the history of the Sixteen Arhats, the eighteen-folio *Excellent Gift to Please Scholars: Old and New Prophecies of the Sixteen Arhats Together with Supplementary Explanations* (Tib. *Gnas brtan bcu drug gi lung bstan gsar rnyed 'phros dang bcas pa mkhas rnams mgu ba'i skyes bzang*)[20] and the fourteen-folio *Tibetan Translation of the Inscriptions for the Chinese Sixteen Arhats Together with a Supplementary Explanation* (Tib. *Rgya spar [sic] gnas brtan bcu drug gi zhal byang bod skad du bsgyur ba 'phros bshad dang bcas pa*).[21] In addition to these iconographical studies, Zava Damdin wrote fascinating histories of things. Stamps, statues, paintings, and the enchanted dirt and mortar of pilgrimage places, all enlivened by enlightened presence and tied inextricably to the Qing-Géluk formation, were regularly recorded on paper in the same way as people, as "liberated life [stories]" (Tib. *rnam thar*).[22]

Zava Damdin also wrote short histories on the origins of his monastic institutions in Urga and his desert homeland. A forty-four-folio local history of his Gobi monastic seat, Chöying Ösel Ling;[23] the nine-folio *Brief History of the Origins of Dashithoisamling* (Tib. *Bkra shis thos bsam gling gi 'byung khungs tho tsam*);[24] and the three-folio *Sweet Cooing of the Cuckoo: Praise to Dashiling* (Tib. *Bkra shis gling gi gnas bstod khu byug skad snyan*)[25] are a few of many examples.

In their modes of emplotment, genres of expression, scope of interest, and interpretative practice, Damdin's histories were written within the genres and interpretative expectations of his frontier Géluk scholastic world. This was a mold cast by polyglot intermediaries beginning in the seventeenth century, mostly monks and incarnate lamas who managed the political and intellectual interfaces among Beijing, Chinese cultural traditions, Jesuit science, developments in Russia, and their sundry Tibetan and Mongolian homelands. The results were genre-bending works on the past, biography, geography, doxography, astronomy, and medicine that have yet to attract any sustained comparative study, even though individually figures like Sumpa Khenpo Yéshé Peljor, Mindröl Nonom Han, Thuken Chökyi Nyima, Jangji-a Rolpé Dorjé, and the Longdröl Lama have been named as cosmopolitan scholars, in some cases as harbingers of "early modernity" beyond Europe.

This frontier scholastic corpus was Zava Damdin's primary resource, but his histories were not simply carbon copies of imperial narratives. They extended, and sometimes rejected, those narratives by adopting an extreme fidelity to synthetic interpretative practices. Just as the Üjümüchin West banner prince Gombojab (c. 1692–1749), working in the eighteenth century as headmaster of the Lifan Yuan's "Tangut" (i.e., Tibetan) school in Beijing, mined the Chinese record to introduce the history of Buddhism in China to Tibetan readers, Zava Damdin selectively mined European, Chinese, Manchu, and Indic sources to tell new stories about the Mongols, their histories, and their Buddhism. Such was his synthetic labor to render the Qing ruins sensible, to fit them with history and desired futures. Unlike the European-inflected professional history burgeoning amid party cadres and state-sponsored academies, a process Makoto Tachibana has explored as the separation of history from chronicle, Damdin's immense writing dramatically extended but never exceeded the Qing-Géluk narrative.[26]

And yet he became, for a time, a sought-after interlocutor for Mongolia's early scientific communities and their networks of European and Russian historians, Buddhologists, philologists, and ethnologists. In the early years of the socialist period (c. 1921–1927), between his work on the 1919 chapters and the 1931 chapters of the Golden Book, Zava Damdin remained a very active historian, despite "the frothing of fluctuating politics." He was made a founding member of the party's Mongolian Scientific Institute (Sinjileku Ukhaɣan-u Küriyeleng), then called the Institute of Scripts and Letters (Sudar Bichig-un Küriyeleng), a precursor to today's Mongolian Academy of Sciences (Kh. Mong. Mongol Ulsîn Shinjlekh Ukhaanî Akademi). There, unsurprisingly, he was tasked with researching the intersection of religion and politics in the Two Systems. L. Khurelbaatar and G. Luvsantseren, two contemporary scholars who have published in Mongolian on aspects of Zava Damdin's oeuvre, write, "in the early years of the People's Party, Zava

Damdin Gavj was a loosely affiliated member of the Mongolian Institute of Script and Letters. He took part in [examining] the unity (*khos*) of the tradition (*ulamjlal*) of religion and state, how this could be adopted in the new era of the state (*shine tsagiin töriin butshed*)."[27]

In Damdin's hands, cutting-edge Altaic linguistics from philology departments in Finland would bolster the foresights of ancient Khotanese prophecy. Paleography of Turkic stele would "clarify" cosmologies in the Abhidharma corpus. Photographs from Silk Road excavations would prove that "Mongols" had indeed brought Buddhism to the Tibetans in the seventh century. Dotted lines on round globes and German maps illuminated disjointed narratives in the Kālacakra Tantra, even as Zava Damdin elsewhere mocked the paucity of scientific claims for a round earth ("which they accept as if they actually could see it!").

The result was that Zava Damdin's late- and post-Qing histories found more "Mongols," by more names, in more places, who received more Dharmic transmissions, using more historical records, drawn from more Eurasian literary and scholarly traditions, than had any other monastic or professional historian before or since. Even those in Mongolia today who base their postsocialist revival upon his oeuvre cannot match its breadth of vision or the scope of its memorialization. Even so, its contents have until now remained unstudied in any depth or comparative light beyond a few summary studies of only a few works in the Mongolian and Russian academy.[28] The exception is their enduring legacy among Tibetan and Mongolian Géluk scholars in the global diaspora, explored in the conclusion of this book.

History Between the Real and the Empty

To avoid recapitulating the eccentricities and ethnocentricities of the West, as has occurred too often in the history of Buddhism and modernization in Asia, the individual and the event have everywhere to be treated as problematic. Just how are they formed, culturally and historically? In the case of Zava Damdin's post-Qing oeuvre, events, the individual, community, and space are constituted through the interplay of two distinct registers—the enlightened and the human—that, in Damdin's literary representation of the revolutionary era, had become worryingly disentangled.

Adapting Mikhail Bakhtin's differentiation between "empty" and "real" time helps illuminate the crisis of time, place, community, and self-fashioning that Zava Damdin and his milieu came to associate with the Qing ruins. Bakhtin—who similarly suffered under Soviet suppression after 1937 and whose colleague, the Orientalist scholar M. Tubyansky, was an interlocutor of Zava Damdin and a founding member in 1927 of the Soviet Institute of Buddhist Culture (*Institut Buddiyskoy Kul'tury*)—approached texts always as an "inscription lying on the boundary line between culture and a dead nature."[29] A text is a mute other that is evoked and enlivened in the space of particular readers arranged at a particular intersection of place and time. Drawing on biological metaphors, Bakhtin called such interstices a *chronotope*: "a unit for studying texts according to the ratio and nature of the temporal and spatial categories represented."[30] The chronotope is "the intrinsic connectedness of temporal and spatial relationships that are artistically expressed in literature. . . . In the literary artistic chronotope, spatial and temporal indications are fused into one carefully thought-out, concrete whole. Time, as it were, thickens, takes on flesh, becomes artistically visible, likewise, space becomes charged and responsive to the moments of time, plot, and history."[31] Bakhtin emphasized two such relationships. The first is "empty time," where characters are unaffected by narrative time or the unfolding of events, as in the Greek romance and epic.[32] The second is "real time," where characters are shaped by the events described, as in the novel.

The careful plotting of the human "real" and its intersections with the enlightened "empty" was Zava Damdin's primary historical objective, just as it had been for Tibetan monastic historians since the twelfth century and for Mongolians since the sixteenth. In Bakhtin's analysis of Greek romance and epic, literary time is empty when "events are not connected to each other in any causal relation; none of the events is linked in a sustained consequence."[33] Plots progress in such works, of course, but Bakhtin noticed that the characters involved are not shaped by the passage of time or formed by succeeding events. The same is true, I submit, of half of the subject matter of Inner Asian monastic histories: the enlightened beings who have intervened in, and thus enchanted, the Eurasian stage. Enlightened time, place, and subject are "empty" because they represent "an abstract pattern of rearrangeable events," in stasis relative to the ever-developing human histories of Eurasia.[34] The "enlightened" places, times, and subjects who occupy so much of Zava Damdin's historical attention are unaffected by the very chronology he inscribes. "These hours and days leave no trace, and therefore, one may have as many of them as one likes," as Bakhtin would have it.[35]

In the media ecosystems of Inner Asian scholasticism the enlightened bodhisattva Avalokiteśvara, for example, is no wiser, older, weaker, or stronger during his sixteenth-century intervention into Mongol space as the Third Dalai Lama, Sönam Gyatso, at the court of Altan Khan of the Tümed, than during his early twentieth-century arrival in Urga at the Thirteenth Dalai Lama, Tubten Gyatso. Nor is Mañjuśrī altered by his incarnation as Sakya Paṇḍita at the court of Göden Khan, as Jé Tsongkhapa on the debate courtyards of Central Tibet, or as the Qianlong emperor upon his throne at the Qing court. Vajrapāṇi, the embodiment of the skillful means of all the buddhas, does not learn a lesson or change his views between intervening in world affairs as Chinggis Khaan in the thirteenth century or as the Boγda Gegegen during the Autonomous Period in Khalkha.

As historical objects, these enlightened characters remained inscrutable for monastic historians such as Zava Damdin. The "events" of their intervention were discernible in the historical record among the ever changing, "real" histories of Eurasian peoples. Identifying and interpreting such intersections was the monastic historian's task. The "real" chronotope was for Bakhtin exploited mainly in the novel, a unique literary form that attracted so much of his analysis and reflection. The protagonists of such writing are not the static heroes of epic lore who wait patiently but unchanged as events roll by. The "real" are rather everyday people and places shaped by the temporal developments described in the text. Unlike the "empty" characters of Greek epic and romance, a "real" literary character accepts "some responsibility for the changes in his life."[36] The Mongols, the Xiongnu, the Khotanese, the Chinese, and the Tibetans as characters in monastic historiography had all changed fundamentally through their encounters with the enlightened. They were changing fundamentally again in Zava Damdin's dark times.

Like the authors of Greek epics and French novels, Inner Asian scholastic authors combined two literary times into their historiography. As the karmic causes (Skt. *hetu*; Tib. *rgyu*; Mong. *siltaγan*) of the Inner, South, and East Asian masses ripened in tandem with helping conditions (Skt. *pratyaya*; Tib. *rkyen*; Mong. *nöküchel*) in particular places and times, enlightened figures spontaneously intervened into the real time of the Eurasian stage. For Zava Damdin and his predecessors, the intellectual task was to delimit and narrate *both* the "real" human stage *and* the "empty" enlightened that periodically presented itself anew in, for example, the Yuan court of Khubilai Khaγan or the Mauryan Empire of Aśoka. It was Zava Damdin's anxiety-fueled challenge to interpret the revolutionary era using this scholastic model of intersecting time and causality, of the proximity of the real to the empty.

Felting Eurasia

As early as Gombojab's c. 1740 *History of Buddhism in China* (Tib. *Rgya nag chos 'byung*) and Rashipunsuγ's 1774–75 *Crystal Rosary* (Mong. *Bolor erike*), polyglot Mongolian historians deeply embedded in the Qing imperial project turned to Chinese language sources for a more expansive historical vision of the Mongolian people and their Buddhist dispensation. These mostly looked at Ming dynasty records like the *Yuan shi* (元史) and the *Gangjian huizang* (鋼鑑會纂), as well as select Buddhist literature like Xuanzang's pilgrimage tale. The result, long before Zava Damdin set ink to paper, was, as Johan Elverskog says, "a historiographical supposition that still resonates today in both nationalist discourse and academic inquiry: all the nomadic peoples north of the Great Wall are identified historically as Mongol; more important, since the Han dynasty they have been Buddhist."[37]

In the ruins of the Qing, Zava Damdin applied a creative philological technique to find even more Mongols and even more Mongol Buddhists than either Gombojab or Rashipunsuγ. This involved reading all references to *hor* and *sog* peoples in Tibetan language sources—ubiquitous but fluid ethnonyms applied in Tibetan translations of Indic and Central Asian sources as well as in indigenous writings to Turks, Persians, Indians, certain Muslims, and certain Tibetans (such as the rivals of the legendary King Gésar of Ling). For Zava Damdin, as for his cosmopolitan Qing predecessors, such references in received scripture and authoritative commentary were assuredly to "Mongols" of the Yeke Mongγol Ulus, in a direct continuity with his own Khalkha people and those other Mongols and Buryats he knew. By drastically extending the "real" history of the Mongols, in the post-Qing era Zava Damdin could thus "clarify" (Tib. *gsal*) and "order" (Tib. *bkod*) an even more expansive vision of the enchanting involvement of the "empty" enlightened upon the human stage. As he laments in the 1927 *Memoranda*: "In general, both

Buddhists and non-Buddhists claim that prior to Chinggis Khan the Mongols had neither a customary tradition (*tshul lugs*) nor a religious tradition (*chos lugs*). They also claim that [those pre-Chinggisid Mongols] amounted to only a few stupid people who dwelt in the company of monkeys and apes."[38] In correcting such mistaken views, Damdin produced an expansive vision of the Qing-Géluk formation as rooted in an especially deep pre-Chinggisid past.

Indeed, from Zava Damdin's vantage it appeared that the progeny of Chinggis had come to cover the globe, as just one example from a fascinating passage in the 1931 sections of *The Golden Book* illustrates:

In general, in ancient times there were the Forty Myriarchies (*khri skor*) in Mongol lands. From among those, when Boγda Chinggis Khan ruled most of the world he absorbed Chinese territory into these [myriarchies]. As a consequence, the populations of those regions mixed with one another. When Togen Temur Khaγan was dethroned, some Mongols remained behind and settled in China.

When Boγda Chinggis Khan appointed his sons and nephews, one by one, to be khans of individual dominions, they departed together with their subjects to those territories. In time, they were absorbed into those subject populations. That is why many Mongol peoples still reside in the area of easterly Japan (Rī wen gyi gling) and why Gushri Khan and his followers later settled in Tibet and became Dam-sok Mongols ('Dam sog). This is also why, later, a group of Khoshot Mongols called the Oirat Shomo (O'i lid kyi sho mo) retreated from a battle and escaped to an area in Upper Mongolia (Stod hor). This area is just to the west of Ngari's Ladakh. It exists even now and is called Khohugeröngöl Mongγol (Khwo hu ger mon gol). A few groups of Mongol peoples still live upon the slopes of a mountain in the east of the great city called Paṁbha (Paṁ bha) along the borders of northwest India. [When] the foreigner European Hong-sol stayed in that city, some of those local Mongols enjoined him, "We follow the tradition of Tsongkhapa. Many knowledgeable Mongol lamas travel along the railway (*lcags lam*). If you find a [candidate to be our] resident lama, please introduce him to us!"

Also, in time a few groups of Oirat Thorγuud Tib. Thor gwod) and Durvet (Dur bed) who abided over yonder in the direction of the setting sun became subjects of Russia. To the northwest of the land of Japan, there is a small area full of only Manchus called Sahalgön (Sa hal gon). There are also a few groups of Mongols living in America (A mrī ka'i gling), part of the northerly region.

From all this, it is clearly amazing that those of Mongol lineage who come and go, hither and thither, have become so dispersed between the oceans![39]

In the first place, Zava Damdin writes regularly that an absence of historical sources on the pre-Chinggisid Mongols was to be expected as a by-product of their ancient nomadic lifeway and oral culture strung across the grassy and sandy corridors of Eurasia. While some of those spectral Mongol figures may have written about their lives and communities, Zava Damdin surmises, their inscriptions must have been lost during endless cycles of conquest. As he puts it in *The Golden Book*,

> By comparing the words of the Victor [Buddha], non-Buddhist and Buddhist commentaries, and the earlier and more recent records of many great kingdoms, [we know that] this region of Greater Mongolia has existed for thousands of human years, comparable in age to the world itself. Nobody can deny this, whether wise or foolish or whether in our own or others' lands.
>
> Nevertheless, how the political order became connected to the arrival of the Victor's teaching is unclear in ancient Mongol writings, which are never explicit [on the subject]. Even nowadays, it remains very challenging to find [such sources] and so it is very difficult for anybody to provide a clear and detailed account.[40]

Zava Damdin frames his own historical pursuits as a remedy to all this. As he says in the concluding lines of the *Memoranda*, "In this way, I have described how the varieties of Mongolian peoples and successive ruling houses have had a continuous five-thousand-year history up until now. I have simply quoted selectively from the history books of the Chinese, the Mongols, and the Manchus that record a long history of hostilities."[41]

Specifically, Zava Damdin discussed the "real" history of the Mongols on the flat expanse of the southern continent of Jambudvīpa according to the classic divisions of the Abhidharma and Kālacakra Tantra corpus: as a "vessel"-like (Tib. *snod*) world inhabited by its "contents" (Tib. *bcud*), sentient beings including diverse human societies. By extending the scope and clarifying the details of the vessel and its contents as described previously by Qing-era scholars, Zava Damdin could also claim a radically new "empty" history of enlightened intervention, and more gravely, a very recent history of enlightened retreat.

The Vessel and Its Contents

In his introduction to a chapter entitled "Early Dispensation of Buddhism Into Mongolia" in *The Golden Book,* Zava Damdin sets out his historical vision of the vast, "real" Mongol stage. Synonymous at times with both Eurasia and Jambudvīpa, this was a site of collision of new discourses of nationalist territory, European racial topography, and the authoritative cosmologies of his Indian and Tibetan canonical sources.

> Like this, that which is called the "continent of Asia" (*A tsi ya'i gling*) is otherwise known as the "northeasterly country of Mongols." From where did the first settlers come to the lands of upper, lower, and middle Mongolia?[42] Concerning the ancestral proliferation and origins of the laity and farmers, the *Sayings* of the great Sakya patriarchs mention
>
> > In the north of the north of the world is [a land] called the "Kingdom of Great Mongolia" (Chen po hor gyi yul). [It possesses] three hundred and sixty different races (*mi rigs*) and seven hundred and twenty different languages.
> > [*Interlinear note:*] This country resembles a bird net. The hats of the inhabitants resemble a white hawk. Their boots resemble pig's snouts. They sustain themselves by means of tending the four types of livestock and by farming.
>
> Earlier and later prophecies say the same thing.[43]

Like in this grouping of modern European cartographic and ethnological terms with the prophetic pronouncements of twelfth-century Tibetan religious luminaries, Zava Damdin regularly attempts to extricate a singular Mongolian people (Tib. *hor sok mi rigs*) from his sources. One regular strategy was to identify a shared environment and social customs. "Indeed, most Mongol lands have fearsome sandy deserts with very little mountains, forests, or rivers. Because it is very cold, no one except those (who live) close to the border with places like China and Thokara can cultivate fields and so forth. There are few walled cities. Most people are nomads living in felt tents and sustaining themselves by means of horses, sheep, camels, and cattle."[44] A great expanse of unrecognized peoples—bound to one another by felt, livestock, ice, and sand in and out of the inner corridors of Eurasia—thus emerges in these works as part of the Mongol story.

Our author often describes his historical narratives as being told "from the perspective of the everyday Mongolian people" (*hor gyi mi byings kyi dbang du byas*). As he puts it characteristically in *The Golden Book*

Additionally, the biography of the great scholar of Lhotrak says:[45]

> Human genealogies have their source in the gods,
> just as waterways have their source in snow.

As this says, many earlier and more recent royal lineages of the Mongols descend from divine origins. Because the explanation of this is well known everywhere in our own and others' lands, in what follows I will describe the perspective of the common Mongolian people: those who possess the divinely originated paternal "bone" lineage (*rus*) and maternal lineage (*cho 'brang*).[46]

But what was the content of this shared, "everyday" experience of the "real" subjects populating these post-Qing histories and interacting in time and place with the "empty" enlightened?

In nearly all his historical writing between c. 1910 *The Dharma Conch* and the 1931 *Golden Book*, Zava Damdin used the resources at his disposal to create an all-embracing vision of the "Mongolian people" and their ancient history. The details encompass all Eurasian history as it was then known in the monastic colleges and new scientific institutes of the revolutionary period. The general contours of Zava Damdin's vision are laid out early in his writing, beginning with the opening lines of the "The Chapter That Reveals the Arrangement of Regions" (*Yul gru'i bkod pa bstan pa'i sarga*) from *The Dharma Conch*:

> As for how people settled here in this land of Mongolia:
> In olden times a goddess split from the heavenly realms
> and so was exiled to a golden mountain.
> Because of the gods' curse
> her body transformed into that of a demoness.
> She and five hundred other demons settled there.
> Because of that, the bodhisattva Opakchen,[47]
> in the company of five hundred merchants,
> came from India as a caravan leader

to the golden mountain
in order to request pure gold.
For that reason, their descendants came to possess the name "gold."
It says in *The Prophecy of Khotan Sūtra*[48]
that they were called "Hor people."
According to an ancient story,
a breakaway group of "Mutkals"[49] from the Land of Noble Ones [India]
departed from the right side of a snow mountain and settled in this region.
Over time, they spread and became upper, middle, and lower Hor.
The name [Mutkal] eventually became corrupted (*ming zur chag pa*)
And became widely known as "Mongγol."[50]

Looking for more hidden histories in corrupted names, in *The Memoranda, The Dharma Conch, The Emanated Mirror*, and *The Golden Book* Zava Damdin adopted a text-critical approach that excited later Soviet-era scholars such as Sh. Bira: here was a feudalist monk turning to scientific history, a rationalist awakening from the fog of religious superstition to the reign of fact. In reality, this was a well-worn interpretative operation from his frontier, imperial-era scholastic tradition. For example, in an early section from the opening chapter of *The Golden Book* entitled "Explanation of the Arrangement of the Vessel and Its Contents, Along with a History of its Origins" (*Snod bcud gyi bkod pa 'byung khungs lo rgyus dang bcas pa te bshad pa*):

Furthermore, there are five amazing, sacred places known in this world. Principal among these is Bodhgayā, in the center of India, where the buddhas of the three times reside. To the east is the land of the Lion of Speech, Mañjuśrī, which is Mount Wutai in China. To the south is Mount Potalaka, located on an island in the ocean, which is the abode of Avalokiteśvara and Tārā. In the west is the land of Vajrapāṇi called Oḍḍiyāna, the secret land of the *ḍākinī*s. In the north is Śambhala, the land of the seven Dharmarājas and the twenty-five Rikden kings.

Alternatively, according to Tibetan legends, at the top of this world is Tibet; in the "stem" (*yu ba*) are India, Kashmir, and Persia. In the "crane" (*krung krung*) are China and Jang Hor (*'Jang hor*). Surrounding all this are thirty-six barbarous lands wherein the holy Dharma never became established, including Lo, Do, Khatra, Kha-sok, Zha, Kha-sü, Mar, Tsa-pung, Mount Do-wo, Dram-tsa, Hu-tuk, Zha-ling, Trel-lak, Khyi-khyo, Dar-lok, Zhang-tsa-bya.[51]

From among all those, the abode of India is a jeweled land like the display of a silk canopy. Persia and the Li are lands fulfilling all desires in the shape of a chariot. Mongolia and China are amazing regions like a blossoming flower. Tibet is a snowy land shaped like a demon[ess] laid upon its back.

If I were to summarize what is said in the sūtras, tantras, śastras, and legends, this world is divided into five: the center, the east, the south, the west, and the north. From among those, Tibet, the Land of Li, Upper Hor, and so on are in the center. China and Great China, Mentsi[52] and the realm of the Manchus are lands in the east. The Land of Noble Ones [India], which may or may not include numerous islands, is the principal land of the south. In the west are many barbarous lands, such as the lands of Persia, the Torɣuud, many foreign lands including those of the Yi-wé,[53] Arabs, and the Tim-du. In the north are many Hor and Sok lands, such as the Yeke Mongɣol Ulus and many other regions populated by assorted barbarians, including the Hwasak,[54] Cossacks,[55] and Kyrgyz.[56] To the north of that is the supreme land of Śambhala, which includes the six great lands: the land of Tsampaka,[57] the Land of the Monkey, the land of Those Possessing Golden Eyes, Ruk-ma,[58] Buréma,[59] and the one called Gold.

In addition, the many abodes of the gods, demigods, *kiṃnaras*,[60] *gandharvas*,[61] *yakṣa*,[62] and *rākṣa* demons are regularly described. So too are many sublime abodes like deserts and the isolated wilderness, as well as bejeweled, snow-laden, and ice-covered expanses.[63]

Zava Damdin elaborates upon this vision of "real" place, time, and community in myriad ways. Reflecting upon a twelfth-century prophecy in the *Dharma Conch,* for example, he writes,

Sachen Kunga Nyingpo said that the land of the Mongols
is overall a place with three hundred and sixty different human races
and seven hundred and twenty different regional dialects.
It appears that this true.
For example, even in the Land of Noble Ones
previously there had been many Mongolian peoples
Who were called "Sukhapāna."[64]
Similarly, those of Mongol lineage
have long abided in barbarian lands including
Kashmir, Persia, and Turkestan.
Mongols of mixed lineage likewise live in Tibet, the Land of Li, and China.

Even in Russia, there are a great many
Cossock Tartars, Khalmyks, and Kyrgyz peoples, and so on.
In these ways, Mongolians span from the east to the west,
reaching the shores of the ocean.[65]

In these ways, on the basis of visions of Mongolian territory in the context of the "vessel-like world," Zava Damdin is able to describe its "contents," a vast Mongolian sphere of social and cultural affiliation.

In the *Dharma Conch*, Damdin broke down the Mongols into three ethnopolitical units, just as earlier frontier Géluk scholars of the Qing, such as the nineteenth-century cartographic historian Drakgön Zhapdrung Könchok Tenpa Rapgyé, had done for centuries.[66] Recovering their shared history in the Qing ruins was a point of regular consternation for our author, though he never doubts that such a shared identity had been an historical reality. As he puts it succinctly in *The Dharma Conch*:

It has been well known for a long time that Mongol lands
are divided into three: upper, lower, and middling.
When it comes time to actually identify these, however,
it becomes clear that these peoples have dispersed everywhere!
For this reason, earlier Tibetans would say that
Upper Hor and this region is called Yeke Mongγol.
Up until Hor-sok is called Upper Sok.
The four groups of Oirat, the seven groups of Khalkha,
the Bhata Hor, Urānghé, and so forth
are together counted as Middle Sok.
The Par-go, Buryat, and
forty-nine great divisions of the Solon Chakhar
are Lower Sok.
This identification is consistent with
non-Buddhist and Buddhist textual sources.[67]

In these ways, Zava Damdin recovered the "real" time, place, and communities of the Mongols through a critical analysis of stone inscriptions in Mongol grasses, various canonical histories and prophecies connected to the genesis of the "Rose-Apple Continent" of Jambudvīpa, oral traditions from Tibet and Mongolia, and nascent academic histories of "Asia," an always "foreign" (*phe ring*) category. But what unites a Mongolian historical subject of such capacious difference, beyond felt tents and cold winters?

After early sections of the *Dharma Conch*, the *Memoranda*, and the *Golden Book* focused on an ancient, shared "Mongol" past, Zava Damdin outlined a more familiar ethnic topography, such as of the Four Oirat and Seven Khalkha tribes. There is no space or need to endlessly summarize Zava Damdin's extensive but rather rote description here. A concise description from the closing lines of the first section of *The Dharma Conch* is representative:

> By comparing Chinese and Mongol writings,
> as well as the stone pillar inscriptions found across this land,
> it is clear that the Mongols are the peoples of the felt tent,
> those who subsist by tending the four types of livestock,
> hunting game, and so forth.
>
> We can still see the ruins of their towns and cities,
> like those of the so-called "White" and "Black" royal palaces,
> and also the remainders of fields that once were cultivated.
> Even today, traces of all this are evident in our central land.
>
> *Kye ma!*
>
> These days, we cannot find even the name
> of these ancient vessels and their contents!
> Having thought about this, those with wisdom eyes
> should find a path out of this situation![68]

Having himself trodden such a path, Zava Damdin elaborates his vast vision of a "real" Mongol past on the basis of shared religious and cultural traditions, often by pairing newly circulating Euro-Russian narratives with prophetic interpretation:

> As was mentioned before, in ancient times the Teachings of the Buddha spread in the Land of Li, and then similarly the Victor's Teachings spread into the connected territories of Mongolia and Greater Mongolia. Likewise, whenever the laws of religion and politics diminished in the Land of Li, the unified law of religion and politics would dwindle in Mongol lands as well.

Later, Mongol peoples became fragmented and a few groups scattered. The commitments of some to the Dharma remained unchanged, while others entered the backward Dharma of either the barbarians or the Hrisa Thosi (Tib. *hrī sa tho si*). Others came to possess neither a Dharma system nor even a customary tradition.

The majority of Mongol peoples continued to prostrate and make offerings to "Burkhan" (Tib. *pur han*), which may refer to either the Buddha or a war deity. Both [Buddhist] monks and Bön [shamanist] practitioners were called *baɣshi*. Their religious systems became indistinguishable and they were permitted to engage in practices such as reciting liturgies aloud.[69]

In these ways, Zava Damdin imagined a vast, shared Mongolian "real" drawn from his cosmopolitan sources. This was neither the Qing nor the nation, but a hybrid third time and space that set a vast stage for "empty" enlightened intervention and, in his time of writing, enlightened retreat.

Qing Ruins Between History and Chronicle

Like his Qing-era forebears working along the Sino-Tibetan-Mongolian interface, Zava Damdin developed his historical vision from a mosaic of Indic, Tibetan, Mongolian, Chinese, and sundry other Central Asian materials. He often allowed his sources to stand alongside one another, hazarding tentative interpretations but leaving any conclusions to future "unbiased scholars" who, he hoped, would extend his project into a post-Qing future. "Regarding the different regions of the Yeke Mongɣol Ulus, on the southern frontier are the Torɣuud, the Land of Noble Ones, the Land of Li, Tibet, China, and the Ka-li.[70] To the east is the great ocean. To the west is Lake Manasarovar and Turkey's Black Sea. To the north are some vast lands connected with Kailash, including Russia. Foreigners call all this 'the Continent of Asia.'"[71]

Reconciling the litany of spectral Mongolian peoples and histories that haunted so many texts, folk legends, and stones bearing half-discernible messages was Damdin's grand synthetic project. As he put it in the 1927 *Memoranda*:

Whatever the name, the meaning remains the same. Because of the effects of distance and time, it remains unclear whether some names were used to identify specific areas or peoples. In terms of their origins, we may divide the dialect of all Mongol peoples into three: Turkic, Mongol, and Manchu. Even so, in terms of origin, body color, beliefs, and behavior, there is no difference between any of them. In general, all nations have recognized this since long ago. All this is described in trustworthy non-Buddhist and Buddhist texts.[72]

These were visions of the Mongolian past unhinged from the rubrics of Qing ethnicity and ethnoreligious genesis. They looked beyond Chinggis Khan to a steppe history that led to neither India nor Tibet, but instead to Turkish civilizations, the Uyghurs, the ancient Xiongnu, and even "Asia" itself.

An early wellspring of such historical material specific to his post-Qing position was the *New Mirror* (Mong. *Shine Toli*), a secular newspaper published in Urga during the Boyda Khayanate period that, by all reports, caused an uproar among Buddhist monks. A tsarist representative in Urga named I. Y. Korostovets had started this paper in the early years of the twentieth century before it was taken over by the Buryat reformer and nationalist Tseveen Jamsrano, who had worked for the paper as a young progressive intellectual. The first edition under Jamsrano's watch in 1913 sold out immediately, consumed by a fascinated and outraged monastic audience. Its contents provided simple descriptive accounts of European knowledge about topics like "The Earth, the Continents," "Heat and Cold," "Wind and Atmosphere," "Thunder and Lightning," "The States of the World and Their Forms of Government," "The Development of Culture," "Race and Religion," and "The Life Expectancy of Man."

As new editions were printed, Mongolian readers encountered not only elementary science but also European literature and nascent scholarship on "Asia," "Buddhism," and the "Mongolian nation." These included excerpts from the works of Leo Tolstoy, Jules Verne, Robert Louis Stevenson, Jack London, and more.[73] Zava Damdin was an eager, though often suspicious, reader of *The New Mirror*. In his historiography he often turned to these works by "Euro-Russian scholars" (*rgya gser mkhas pa*) and "Westerners" (*phyogs nup pa*) to reinterpret and extend the Qing-era narrative. This is especially true in the 1931 *Golden Book*, but also in many of the middle-length translations and compendiums of primary sources he wrote during the 1920s.

Off all these new intellectual products circulating through revolutionary Khalkha, no two European sources were more influential in helping Damdin to extend the historical picture of the "real" Mongolian past than a research article by a Finnish linguist and the historical fiction of a Frenchman. The former was Gustaf John Ramstedt, who in 1912 at Jamsrano's request wrote an article for *The New Mirror* entirely in Mongolian, titled "A Short History of the Uyghurs" (Uiɣur ulus-un khuriyangɣui teüke).[74] Ramstedt recalled that this article was included "in a reader intended for school in Mongolia" as part of a Buryat-driven push for secular education during the Boɣda Khaɣan period.[75] Ramstedt's piece introduced the radical idea that Mongolians shared Turkic origins with other Central Asian peoples, not Buddhist kings in India or Tibet or even the minority sociopolitical identities that had been issuing from Qing centers for the last two and a half centuries.[76]

The effect of Ramstedt's work upon Zava Damdin was pronounced: he chose to translate it *in toto* into Tibetan with copious commentary and to include it in *The Golden Book*. Reading passages from his canonical sources anew in light of Ramstedt's study, Zava Damdin argued that the Xiongnu, an ancient Turkic tribe who lived north of China between the third century BCE and the first century CE, were in fact Mongols who had once practiced Manichaeism, as were the ancient Kitan, with whom the Mongols were bound through a shared language.[77] Zava Damdin encountered another formative extract of European histories of the Mongols in the pages of the *New Mirror*, David-Léon Cahun's 1877 *La Bannière bleue: Aventures d'un musulman, d'un chrétien et d'un païen à l'époque des croisades et de la conquête mongole* (*The Blue Banner: Adventures of a Muslim, a Christian, and a Pagan in the Age of the Crusades and the Mongol Conquest*), apparently unaware or uncaring that it was a work of fiction. Cahun's widely read book described a shared Turkic-Mongol past with much narrative embellishment, inspiring Turkish nationalist movements in the distant Ottoman Empire.[78] Like Ramstedt's study, Cahun's book had been translated into Mongolian by the nationalist Jamsrano (titled *Köke Mongɣol-un Köke Tuɣ*) with extracts published in *The New Mirror*. Zava Damdin translated both works into Tibetan, quoted them extensively in *The Golden Book*, and regularly referred to their contents in his own analysis and elaborations.

However, Zava Damdin's engagement with Euro-Russian arts and scientists was not limited to studies in translation. He was a sought-after interlocutor for several Russian academics, some of whom were pioneers in nascent academic fields such as Buddhology, ethnology, and Altaic studies. Mention of these encounters with Europeans and European documentation of "Mongol" history appear consistently in Zava Damdin's writing.

Some time ago, a Russian scholar showed me an image of some of the important people of [Kashmir and its Muslim neighbors], such as the king, ministers, and so forth, as well as the royal palace, some temples, and some stūpas. Of those, he said, "This is the motherland of you Mongol peoples, which is today part of India." He showed me [its location] by comparing the coordinates on both an atlas (*dra ris kyi kha byang*) and a globe (*sa'i go la'i kha byang*). If we reason based on the [presence of] temples and the stūpas, I think [those "Mongols" in the photographs] are still Buddhists.[79]

Just who this scholar may have been is unclear, but a small piece of evidence comes from a 1968 interview with Rabjamjamyan, a still-living personal disciple of Zava Damdin, who recalled, "When Zava Lam was in Küriy-e, he borrowed someone's horse to go somewhere. When the teacher was asked where he was going, he said 'There is a Russian at the consul who is very knowledgeable, and I am going to meet him.' This was Tubyanksy, whom the Mongols called Tuwasik or Tawansenge. He gave a few photographs to the *lam* [Zava Damdin], which had German descriptions on the back. Zava Damdin translated these into Mongolian."[80]

Indeed, it seems that Zava Damdin was in regular conversation with Mikhail Tubyansky, a student of Shcherbatsky and a prominent Russian Orientalist scholar in his own right. As Damdin notes in his 1936 autobiography,

In the spring of the Earth Dragon year (1928),
I gave the initiation and the transmission of *Yutok's Heart Essence*,[81]
and undertook the Nectar Accomplishing of Medicine [ritual].
Then I began a system of an ongoing academic tours (*grwa 'khor*)
for holders of the Menrampa medical degree (*Sman rams pa*).

That summer, I finished [overseeing the construction of]
principally the two "Stainless" stūpas and the other eight stūpas
as well as the assembly hall for the Lamrim Monastic College.
Then I returned to my monastic seat.

I was visited by the Russian Tubyansky (Tib. *thu wāe sig*),
who gave me Indian texts such as
[Dharmakīrti's] *Drops of Reasoning*[82] and so forth.
He then said that I must finish the remainder of my history of Mongolia.[83]

It was Tubyanksy who urged Zava Damdin to complete *The Golden Book*, which the latter had begun to write in 1919 at the behest of a China-centric consortium of nobility and monastic leaders but had set aside because of the difficult political situation. We can clearly understand this Russian Orientalist's anticipation of such a text. The purpose of Tubyansky's residence in Mongolia was in part to assess and document prerevolutionary Mongolian literature. This resulted in a 1935 article titled, tellingly, "Some Problems of Mongolian Literature in the Prerevolutionary Period" (Russ. *Nekotorye Problemy Mongol'skoi Literatury Dorevoly-Utsionnogo Perioda*).[84]

In a fascinating collision of my primary sources and my theoretical approach to their contents, Mikhail Tubyansky was an active member and resident Orientalist in the Bakhtin Circle. The fact was not lost on Soviet-era historians like Bira, whose short 1964 work on Zava Damdin has already been mentioned: "A few people such as the orientalists Shcherbatsky, Jamsrano, Tubyanski and others had an influential effect on Damdin's interest in modern science and culture, which were positively developing in Mongolia after the revolution."[85] Damdin regularly buttresses his interpretation of Indic prophecy, the Kālacakra Tantra, and Mongol oral tradition with documentary evidence gleaned from such scholars, often left unnamed, who for example were excavating ancient "Mongolian" writing on material culture being uncovered from Turkish, Kitanese, and Uyghur archaeological sites "after a thousand years of being buried."[86]

Finally, while Zava Damdin left no evidence that he ever read a nationalist or socialist history of Mongolia, the architects of an emergent Mongol ethnonational identity used Zava Damdin's works as data, as have Tibetan and Buryat monastic scholars crafting such narratives in the context of their global refugee and diaspora experience since the 1950s, and as have nationalist Buddhists in postsocialist Mongolia since 1990.[87] Anandin Amar, one of Mongolia's first nationalist historians and a colleague of Zava Damdin at the Institute of Scripts and Letters, at the end of his *Mongγol-un Tobci Teüke* (*A Brief History of Mongolia*) identifies Zava Damdin's works as his only source for Tibetan language historical materials on pre-Chinggisid Mongolia.[88]

All that said, we should not be surprised at such temporal and spatial pluralism in the ruins of the Qing. Myriam Revault d'Allonnes, like Reinhart Koselleck and Paul Ricoeur before her, writes in *La crise sans fin: essai sur l'expérience moderne du temps* that all sociopolitical transitions, especially revolutionary ones, are necessarily founded in "regimes of historicity" that are always in the plural. Each is made to mend, or in the case of modernists in Europe, to set into perpetuity the crisis of fractured time.[89] In such an interpretative and narrative light, Zava Damdin and his milieu set the post-Qing situation into a folded, binary time connecting the human "real" with the enlightened "empty." This was neither the time of the Qing nor the time of the nation. Mobilizing not just the narrative precedents but also the synthetic interpretative techniques of his scholastic forebears from the frontiers of the Qing, Zava Damdin mined his Eurasianist sources to fit more Mongols with more history than ever before. On that human stage, Zava Damdin could claim a vast history of enlightened intervention into "Mongol" communities: a deep history of proximity to enlightened agents playing the part of monks and kings required to produce and reproduce Buddhist life in its lay, monastic, scholastic, and tantric forms.

THREE

Milk

Indra's form is reflected
in the unblemished *baiḍūrya* ground.
So too are the bodies of the Lord of Subduers
mirrored in the purified groundlike mind of sentient beings.

—*THE SUBLIME CONTINUUM*, QUOTED IN
DARVA PAṆḌITA'S BIOGRAPHY

The Pure Land of Mañjuśrī will appear here on earth.
There [the one who] wears the savage color and who is the Lord of fortunate beings
and [the one who] makes the appearance of coming to earth as the second
Buddha
will unite together.
The abundances of politics and religion will then swell like a lake in
summer.

—PROPHECY BY TRÜLKU DRAKPA GYELTSEN (1619–1656)

During seven years of wrathful activity [Chinggis Khan] flooded the world
with blood from east to west. Because he did so, however, the milk of the
holy Dharma has flowed continuously until now.

—ZAVA DAMDIN, *THE GOLDEN BOOK*

IN AN ABSORBING study of affect and the modern experience, Svetlana
Boym writes that "political and cultural manifestations of longing" regularly accompany revolutionary transitions.[1] "Outbreaks of nostalgia" sur-
face neither evenly nor predictably. Such longing is never an artless crav-
ing for things as they were. The unrealized dreams of a prerevolutionary
time resurface to charm those cut from its histories. Old narratives pause,
unfinished, waiting where events left them to pursue a radical new course.
Biographies express aching and disorientation. Personal stories plod

forward but out of synch with collective truths, untethered from where they came from.

From the postrevolutionary vantage, writes Boym, prerevolutionary eras may become venerated and materialized, stagnant or golden, as in the aftermath of the October Revolution or *perestroika* and the end of the Soviet Union. The products of such exile may be pronounced and abundant. "In France it is not only the ancien regime that produced the revolution, but in some respect the revolution produced the ancien regime, giving it a shape, a sense of closure and a gilded aura."[2]

Like *perestroika* nostalgics, Zava Damdin mined the Eurasian textual record at his disposal and made the absent political Qing anew. In the process, however, he made a new story for the post-Qing world as well—a constellation of time, territory, community, sovereignty, and religious life beyond imperium, nation, and socialist project. Because of this, I am wary of drawing too much equivalence between Zava Damdin and the mainly European nostalgics Boym describes. Unlike Napoleonic poets and the rest, Zava Damdin kept the story of his life, his Buddhist institutions and communities, and the cosmos of the Khalkha crossroads in synch with collective stories from prerevolutionary times. He had known the imperium until middle age. Its story was the total order represented in the frontier Géluk histories, geographies, ritual collections, and prophecies he read. Though he knew the details of the Qing *political* ending, Zava Damdin continued to publicly sing the praises of a persistent Qing *formation* for years.

Zava Damdin used his historiography to populate the expansive "real" territories and communities of the Mongols, introduced in the previous chapter, with the "empty" deep history of enlightened beings intervening in human affairs as monks and emperors. This coming together of the real and the empty, of the human and the enlightened, is what I call enchantment. Such intersections were the primary event of history for him, as they had been for the Tibeto-Mongolian scholars of the Qing whom he read. The *splitting* of the real from the empty, which is how he came to know the form and direction of the imperial collapse and the post-Qing situation, I call disenchantment; it is my subject in the second half of this book.

Taking seriously discourses of presence and absence as a strategy to reclaim the marginalized histories of modernization has much in common with a turn to enchantment in revisionist histories and ethnographies of ground-level cultural production. Examples are as diverse as Dipesh

Chakrabarty's famous distinction between History 1 and 2, Robert Orsi's critique of ideologies of scholarship ("where the unseeing of god was a requirement of western modernity"), Michel de Certeau's explorations of contorted French nuns who spoke for the divinity and for devils when God became silent in the face of law and medicine, and Aisha Beliso-de Jesús's work on the "co-presences" of Santeria practitioners whose assemblages ever exceed the sovereignties of the individual and the nation.[3]

As we have seen, when Zava Damdin "recovered" the Mongol real from his dispersed Eurasian sources, he liberally supplemented his textual inheritance with the representations of a Euro-Russian academe and a popular literature in global circulation. His poaching, however, extended but never exceeded the grand events of the Qing-Géluk formation as they had been known. Drawing upon arts and the human sciences secured Zava Damdin a place in the Soviet-era historical record as a man of science, a pseudomodern, a lone rationalist afloat in a sea of feudalist abuse stained saffron. Although philology and archaeology helped him recover the lives of preliterate "Mongols" en masse, scientific discourses and practices did nothing to help illuminate the obscured histories of the enlightened and the contexts of their holy interventions upon the human stage. That analytical pursuit was Zava Damdin's major operation throughout the revolutionary era, a desperate intellectual pursuit that would determine whether the Buddhadharma could exceed the Qing.

The Enchantment of the Two Systems

In *The Dharma Conch, The Memoranda, The Golden Book, The Drop of Amṛta, The All-Illuminating Emanated Mirror,* and other of Zava Damdin's minor writings on the past, the history of the Dharma and of Eurasian civilization were always details in the total biography of the enlightened. The events and individuals of global history told a singular story.

> Although the Victors have equanimity toward sentient beings,
> [they are closest] to Mongolia, this northerly land of half-humans, half-demons.
> As objects of prostration and offerings for gods and sentient beings,
> through great effort and compassion

they have emanated here in this land
as sovereigns, ministers, *paṇḍita*s, *siddha*s, and translators.
Though it is critical that we explain the garlands of marvelous life stories
as an ornament for the ears of the learned,
detailed accounts are rarer than glimpsing a star during the day.
To that end, with whatever is my ability and understanding,
I have written this incomplete History of the Dharma
in China, Tibet, Mongolia, and the Land of Li
only to encourage scholars to write and speak further on the topic.
If in the future, O unbiased, great knowledgeable one with Dharma eyes,
you discover anything more on these subjects,
use this text as a basis and add more details.
Please enhance what I have done so that my efforts may be most fruitful![4]

Zava Damdin referred often to the events of enlightened presence upon the human stage not as "conversion" or some other universalized Judeo-Christian process that ought to be consigned only to the deceptions of World Religions textbooks. Contiguity with the enlightened provoked, in the metaphoric language he so loved, an alchemical upwelling of life-denying and life-giving bodily fluids that took each other's place over time. "An ocean of blood became an ocean of milk, and an isle of darkness became an isle of light" whenever and wherever the enlightened took on flesh in Eurasian history.[5] It was Zava Damdin's labor to claim as many of these events as possible for the Mongols.

For Zava Damdin and the previous generations of Géluk scholastic historians of the Qing—whose narratives he read voraciously and whose interpretive practices he applied liberally to the open questions of a post-Qing world—the deep history of Eurasia's enchantment was a braided one. Human history had been intermittently bound to masculinized sources of enlightened authority, to requisite scales of proximity for reproducing Buddhist subjects. From such associations had come the accouterments of civilization, like literature, medicine, law, state bureaucracy, taxation, architecture, visual and performing arts, and just war.

The culmination of the intersection of the unenlightened and the enlightened was the Two Systems of sociopolitical authority (Tib. *lugs gnyis*; Mong. *khoyar yosu*). During the seventeenth-century consolidation of Géluk

FIGURE 3.1 Young and old worship at a pagoda near Zuun monastery, Ulaanbaatar (1930s).
Digital copies of glass plate negatives preserved in the Archives for Cinema, Photography, and Sound Recording, Mongolia [1910s–1950s]. EAP264/1/9/6/13.

temporal and religious authority in Central Tibet under the Fifth Dalai Lama, the Regent Sanggyé Gyatso, and their Khoshud Mongol patron Güüshi Khan, ideologies of enlightened rulers, monks, and patrons benevolently working the gears of society gained new currency and application. This was especially centered on Avalokiteśvara, with whom the Dalai Lamas began to be recognized, and infused much of the political ideology and culture-making projects of the emergent Ganden Potrang (*Dga' ldan pho brang*), the seat of the Dalai Lama's government.

In time, the Two Systems became a dominant language of exchange between the ascendant Géluk seat of power and the emergent Qing Empire.[6] Of special note are aesthetic and narrative representations of the Dalai Lama as incarnation of Avalokiteśvara in concert with other incarnations such as the "Mañjuśrī Manchu Emperor." In state-sponsored visual and material culture, diplomatic exchanges, ritual traditions, and histories, the embodied enlightened presided over a total order heralded as "existence and peace replete" (Tib. *srid zhi'i phun tshogs*). Nancy Lin describes this new order with great insight as an "aesthetic of abundance [that] embraced and celebrated material wealth, variety, numerousness, and a vision of inclusiveness as the ethos of the court."[7] Fundamentally, this was the consolidation of a discourse of proximity, presence, and control, tied inextricably to a flourishing of peace, knowledge, influence, and self- and community transformation tied to Buddhist cultivation.

The Two Systems and its model of enlightened buddhas playing the part of religious and political leaders became a language of diplomacy among, for example, the Lhasa-based government of the Dalai Lamas, various Mongol rulers, and the Qing court for several centuries.[8] The Two Systems model also underpinned rolling projects by the Qing court to invent and project its authority in a variety of state-sponsored ritual programs, in artistic representations of the emperor as Mañjuśrī, and in the strategic patronage of a variety of key religious sites important to Tibetan and Mongolian Buddhists, like Mount Wutai, the "Five-Terraced Mountain," in Shanxi province (a site that Zava Damdin visited, following the route of the Thirteenth Dalai Lama).

Discourses such as these and the regimes of truth they sought to impose hardly represented the lived mentalities, political and social realities, or affiliations of even regional Géluk monastic communities in Central Tibet, never mind competing Buddhist traditions in Inner Asia or everyday people with little access to or opinion about the literary and diplomatic language of elite scholars and the aristocracy. Divisions and suspicions defined inter-Géluk relations in Tibet until the 1950s, including about the status and roles of the enlightened incarnate. The Mongols, and specifically cosmopolitan Mongolian Géluk scholars and incarnations who mediated the borderlands of the Qing, languished in their literary output within such aesthetics of abundance and all they entailed about place and time, the making and unmaking of selves and power.[9]

And indeed, the Two Systems had been central to Buddhist formation in Khalkha since the sixteenth century. Early on, polyglot Mongolian Buddhist scholars such as the seventeenth-century Zaya Paṇḍita and the unknown author of the *Erdeni-yin Tobci* consolidated an enduring vision of the connections between religion and state shared by Mongols, Manchus, and Tibetans.[10] An entire lexicon for this split authority developed in Inner Asian Buddhist historiography after the sixteenth century, such as the "Two Laws" or "Two Systems" (Tib. *chos srid lugs gnyis*; Mong. *khoyar yosu*) introduced above, as well as compound nouns that collapsed the two into one (Tib. *bstan srid, chos srid, bstan gzhung*; Mong. *törü shasin*). Split authority became complementary intervention in ubiquitous terms like the "unification of Dharma and politics" (Tib. *chos srid zung 'brel*). Early Manchu leaders, including even Hong Taiji (1592–1643), codified the translation of these terms into Manchu long before the Qing formation even bore that name; for example, *doro shajin*, clarifying that *doro* would hereafter mean only the Buddhadharma, not its previous general connotation of "ceremony."[11]

Such sources, and the theories of religiopolitical authority they coded, subsumed imperial law (Tib. *rgyal khrims*; Mong. *khad-un jasaγ*) into religious law (Tib. *chos khrims*; Mong. *nom-un jasaγ*). As the *Péma Katang* (one of the early Tibetan treatises to be translated into Mongolian by the Fifth Dalai Lama's disciples) puts it: "Then the king, being very delighted and performing many prostrations, established the religious law firmly like a silk knot, and brought together the imperial law, which is as heavy as Mount Yoke, one of the Seven Golden Mountains, and the religious law, which is smooth as a silk knot."[12]

In histories written in the century after Mongolians adopted the Yellow Religion in the sixteenth century, the concept of a unified dharmic and political authority became increasingly comMong. The early sixteenth-century *White History* (Mong. *Chagaan Teüke*) proclaimed its purpose as "a handbook to actualize these Two Laws rightly."[13] By the time of the Qing collapse in 1911/12, the Tibeto-Mongolian Géluk historical corpus took this concept for granted and had tracked its genesis into prehistory. By the time Zava Damdin was pressed to write his histories, Qing authority had long been situated as the natural political expression of the Buddhadharma since the time of Śākyamuni himself.[14]

Beyond a strategic language of political communication or the dominant subject of monastic histories, the Two Systems encapsulated inter-Asian, circulatory discourses about agency, time, place, and community. Enlightened intervention in the form of buddhas manifesting as emperors and monks to establish and unite religious and political law and Buddhist government in many ways became the story of the Buddhist dispensation itself, beginning with the early Buddhist kings of the Tibetan Yarlung dynasty, Chinggis Khan, the Yuan dynasty, the rise of the Géluk and the Dalai and Panchen lamas, the Jebtsubdambas in Urga, and that enlightened patron himself, the "Mañjuśrī Manchu Emperor." It is little noted in the scholarship on the Two Systems that, at its root, this was an ideology of contact and proximity to the enlightened. Such contact was required to make Buddhist selves, whether lay, monastic, scholastic, or tantric. The Two Systems represented a disciplinary field of masculinized practice of proximity that, Zava Damdin began to worry, was no longer possible in a post-Qing world.

Proximity and the Making of Buddhist Selves

Practices and associated ontologies of contiguity were, and remain, the principal means by which individuals in Inner Asia form as Buddhist subjects. Coming into proximity with enlightened presence is what allows them to fashion social, political, and religious selves.[15] Practitioners across the otherwise variable terrain of the Tibeto-Mongolian Buddhist world enter into beneficial relationships with purifying, generally masculinized and interiorized centers of enlightened agency, often referred to as *né* (Tib. *gnas*; Mong. *aγsan*), through routinized performances of "worshipful encounter," or *jé* (Tib. *mjal*; Mong. *jolγaγsan*). Toni Huber, Charlene Makley, Yael Bentor, Vesna Wallace, and Martin Mills have all separately argued that such orientations are operative among Tibetan and Mongolian Buddhists and that, other essential regional variations aside, the substantial and embodied nature of their relationships with powerful, purifying, enlightened presences are always emphasized.[16]

The efficacy of *né* is a function of an embodied moral purity (Tib. *dag pa*). Devoted contact with *né*—a holy place, a monastic compound, a shrine room, the words of an incarnate lama, hair or bones from the body, or, as from the current Dalai Lama, urine that is consumed in medicinal preparations by the ill—could cleanse (Tib. *sel ba*) the entire "psychophysical person" of its accumulated negative karma.[17] This karma, importantly, was indexed in the unclean state of the ordinary body and mind (Tib. *mi gtsang*). Purification through proximity clears obstacles to desired outcomes in this life and the next. As Charlene Makley argues in her ethnography of the spatial and gendered constructions of religious lives, authority, and Tibetan-Han communities of difference in contemporary Labrang monastery, "under Geluk mandalizaton both before and after the Chinese Communist Party intervention, everyday and ritual interactions among Tibetans in Labrang worked to reproduce a mandalic social geography, one characterized by the priority given to (purified) centrality over (impure) periphery."[18]

Martin Mills is at pains to point out in his work on authority and Géluk life in Lingshed monastery in Ladakh that the agents embedded in trans-Asian models of Buddhist subject formation are not "people" as such, "in the Rousseauian sense of collection of consciousness and subjective individuals," but instead "a matrix of chthonic forces and sources of symbolic power, within which 'people'—both lay and monastic—are both constituted and embedded."[19] In the middle of such maṇḍalic matrixes are incarnations of buddhas, clothed in saffron robes or royal gowns, holding court in monastic assemblies and imperial courts. Achieving proximity to sacred "centers" (Tib. bdus; gnas), "interiorities" (Tib. nang), and "essences" (Tib. bcud; snying) achieves distance from the usually mundane, usually feminized, usually lay, and always barbaric and polluting "border sites" (Tib. mtha') and "peripheries" (Tib. phyi).

To my knowledge, it has not been noted that such logics of contiguity are also wrapped up with the Two Systems as an object of monastic historical analysis and prose. The event of history for monk-historians in the Sino-Tibetan-Mongol frontiers of the Qing was the periodic incarnation of the "empty" enlightened to "subdue" (Tib. dul ba) the "real" Tibetan and Mongolian borderlands. An "outer" non-Buddhist (phyi pa) became an "inner" Buddhist (nang pa). A "frontier" (mtha' yul) became a "centerland" (dbus yul). An ocean of blood became an ocean of milk.

Consider the opening lines of Damdin's undated Some Studies on the Origins of Trashi Thösam Ling (Bkra Shis Thos Bsam Gling Gi 'byung Khungs Tho Tsam), a collection of legends and oral histories about the twenty-sixth monastic residence of Urga:[20]

In general, the holy Dharma was established in the time of the Heavenly Chinggis and Mañjunātha Sakya Paṇḍita. Specifically, the teachings of the Yellow Hat school were partly established by the kindness of the benefactor-recipient relationship (Tib. yon mchod) of Altan Dharmarāja and the Omniscient King of the Victorious Ones, Sönam Gyatso [the Third Dalai Lama]. At that time, to the

FIGURE 3.2 Young lamas and folks attending a religious ritual in Manzushir monastery, Central Mongolia (1930s).
Digital copies of glass plate negatives preserved in the Archives for Cinema, Photography, and Sound Recording, Mongolia [1910s–1950s]. EAP264/1/9/4/89.

extent of their individual capacities, [Mongols] pursued virtue by going for refuge, making offerings, taking the fundamental precepts, reciting the *maṇi* and *migtséma* [mantras], and so forth. Other than this, no monasteries based in pure ethics were founded that fostered such virtues as study and meditation. Therefore, the precious teachings of scripture and realization of sūtra and tantra neither spread nor flourished.

With the compassionate intention to set countless sentient beings of the borderlands during the Degenerate Age on the path to ripening and liberation, and having obtained the power of prayer to hold and protect the precious teachings of Jampel Nyingpo [i.e., Jé Tsongkhapa] that combine sūtra and tantra, the inner essence of the Buddha's teaching, by means of the supreme incarnation of the previous Refuge and Protector Jebtsundamba Lozang Tenpé Gyeltsen Pélzangpo's powerful prayer and intention, as well as by means of unthinkable manifestation of the three secret activities, all the lamas and lords of the four regions of

Khalkha entered into the enclosure of the political *vajra* fence of the Mañjuśrī [Manchu] Emperor. All this removed obstacles to the spread of the complete teachings of the Mañjuśrī Lama Tsongkhapa. Thereafter, all conducive conditions were gathered together for [receiving] all that they could wish for.[21]

For the Qing-era scholastics Zava Damdin read, contiguity with the enlightened was the primary event of history. Incarnations curated civilization and self-emancipation, both the sought-after objects of the historian's craft. Zava Damdin's labor in the ruins of the Qing interpreted his revolutionary times through this lens, not the national subject. His work produced two unique insights: that the history of the Mongols and their Buddhism was older than had ever previously been imagined, and that postimperial developments posed an irreconcilable crisis of exile from the enlightened that would end not only the reproduction of Buddhist life in the world but also the production of time and place as such.

The Early Spread

Like the synthetic Qing-era historians whom he read, such as Rashipunsuɣ and Mindröl Nomon Han, Zava Damdin organized his mosaic-like histories into "three waves" (Tib. *dar gsum*) of the Dharma's arrival upon Mongol shores. The first was an ancient spread of the Dharma into Mongol lands from India and Central Asian Buddhist city-states like Khotan. The middle dispensation came in the thirteenth and fourteenth centuries, flowing from Central Tibet into the court of Chinggis Khan during the Mongol Empire. Those first two dispensations, however, represented only an imperfect threading of the real with the empty. They were notable preludes to a more perfect and, Zava Damdin would later be forced to admit, final expression of the enchantment of the world, of the Dharma in Mongol lands. For Zava Damdin and his frontier interpretative community, that late and perfected spread was, unsurprisingly, inextricable from the Qing-Géluk formation.[22]

As we would expect, at the root of these waves of the Dharma was the "Land of the Noble Ones" (Tib. *'phags pa'i yul*). As elsewhere in Buddhist Asia, India, Indian religions, and Indian peoples had long occupied Tibetan and

Mongolian historians as the wellspring of not only the "inner field of knowledge" (Tib. *nang rig gnas*) of Buddhism but also of political ideologies and all other major and minor fields of cultural production, from medicine to astronomy, logic, poetics, and architecture. The pattern repeats across most all Tibetan sources used by Mongolian monk-historians over the course of the Qing, such as the Sakya historian Sonam Gyaltsen's (Bsod nams rgyal mtshan, 1312–1375) 1368 *Crystal Mirror of Royal Genealogies* (Tib. *Rgyal rabs gsal ba'i me long*), Tselpa Kunga Dorjé's (Tshal pa kun dga' rdo rje, 1309–1364) 1363 *Red Annals* (Tib. *Deb ther dmar po*), Butön's (Bu ston rin chen grub, 1290–1364) 1322 *Precious Treasury of Sayings* (*Bde bar gshegs pa'i gsal byed chos kyi 'byung gnas gsung rab rin po che'i mdzod*), Go Lotsawa Shönnu pél's ('Gos lo tsa ba gzhon nu dpal, 1392–1481) immensely influential c. 1478 *Blue Annals* (*Deb ther sngon po*), Pawo Tsuklak Trengwa's (Dpa' bo gtsug lag 'phreng ba, 1504–1566) influential 1564 *Scholar's Feast* (*Dam pa'i chos kyi 'khor los bsgyur ba rnams kyi byung ba gsal bar byed pa mkhas pa'i dga' ston ces bya ba'i legs par bshad pa*), Tāranātha's (Tā ra nā tha, 1575–1634) 1608 *History of Buddhism in India* (*Rgya gar chos 'byung*), and the Great Fifth Dalai Lama Ngakwang Lozang Gyatso's (Ta la'i bla ma Ngag dbang blo bzang rgya mtsho, 1617–1682) 1643 *Song of the Spring Queen* (*Bod kyi deb ther dpyid kyi rgyal mo'i glu dbyangs*).

Once Mongols began writing their own histories of the Dharma in the sixteenth century, contact with India was predictably emphasized via Tibetan lineages, continuous forms of emanated enlightened presence from antiquity to present, and thriving monastic and scholastic traditions on the model of Nālandā and Vikramaśīla. The sixteenth-century *White History of the Dharma with the Ten Virtues* (Mong. *Arban buyantu nom-un chaɣan teüke*), the 1662 *Precious Summary* (Mong. *Erdeni-yin Tobci*), the eighteenth-century *Golden Summary* (Mong. *Altan Tobci*), the c. 1774 *Crystal Rosary* (Mong. *Bolor Erike*), the c. 1748 *Auspicious Forest of Wish-fulfilling Trees* (Tib. *Dpag bsam ljon bzang*), and the *History of Buddhism in China* (Tib. *Rgya nag chos 'byung*) emphasized Mongolia's linear if distant relations to India via transmission, institutional continuity, and models of power and reproduction couched in the Two Systems.

In the twilight of that long historical tradition, Zava Damdin was full of innovation. Most notably, he argued that Mongols had enjoyed direct, enduring contact with India in ways that displaced and then reversed Tibet and Tibetans as intermediaries for the Dharma's passage to Mongol lands.

For example, from *The Golden Book*: "In general, most early and later Tibetan and Mongolian peoples have thought and declared that Indian arhats, paṇḍitas and so on never came to Mongolia to ensure the everlasting welfare [of the people here]. This is only because of the fault of not finding written records that describe the earliest spread of the Dharma in Mongol lands. It is clear that many Indian gurus did actually come here."[23]

With a skeptical, revolutionary-era audience in mind, Zava Damdin develops his argument by first mining the Chinese record (mostly from Gombojab's *History of Buddhism in China* and Faxian's *Journey to Buddhistic Kingdoms*). Since he had previously claimed vast swaths of central Eurasia as Mongol territory, his accounts of the journeys of Chinese masters to India and Indian gurus to China were full of descriptions of the "Mongol" Buddhist city-states they passed through along the Silk Road.

Since Zava Damdin had already claimed Uyghurs, Khotanese, Sogdians, Torγuud Mongols from Xinjiang, and other Central Asian peoples of the early Common Era like the Xiongun as "Mongols," historical arguments such as these were easy to defend, just as they been for his Qing predecessors. The idea that Mongolia had received an earlier Dharma transmission than China was already widely accepted in late-Qing Géluk historiography because of the works of Gombojab, Rashipunsuγ, Mindröl Nomon Han, Welmang Paṇḍita, Dharmatāla Damchö Gyatso, and many others. Zava Damdin not only agrees with them but pushes the logic of their argument into new territory concerning the complicity of Mongols in the Buddhist conversion of Tibet. "It is clear [in many sources] that Buddhism was established in Mongol lands long before it came to *either* Great China *or* Tibet."[24]

Concerning the familiar story of Mongolia's supposed reception of the Dharma prior to the Chinese, *The Dharma Conch, The Memoranda, The Golden Book*, and his other historical writings teem with evidence old and new.[25] We read, for example, about the military exploits of a certain "Lord of the [Southern] Chen [Dynasty]" whose sixth-century "Chinese army destroyed [Mongol] holy places, burning and obliterating the supports of enlightened body, speech, and mind [i.e., statues, texts, and stūpas]. They performed many cruel actions such as these." Elsewhere are more familiar stories. "During the reign of the Lord of the Han, the Chinese robbed some land from the Mongols. Even nowadays, some of those [old Mongolian] monasteries have become Chinese monasteries."[26] This later story was the centerpiece of this Qing-era historical position about Mongolian Buddhist history. According to Chinese sources read by Gombojab in the eighteenth century, the Han Dynasty (漢朝, 206 BCE–220 CE) emperor Wudi (武帝, 157–87 BCE) once sent military forces west into Xiongnu territory in central Eurasia looking for horses and conquest. His troops eventually returned with a statue of "a golden man" bundled up in their spoils, something Rashipunsuɣ and his frontier scholastic readers decided had been a statue of the Buddha Śākyamuni pilfered from the pious "Mongol" Xiongnu.[27]

Zava Damdin adds to the Qing-era record by Mongolizing not the Xiongnu but Khotan, a Silk Road city-state he identified as the oft-described "Land of Li" (Tib. *Li yul*) in Buddhist canonical sources. With that identification, the well-worn story of Buddhism's early arrival in imperial Tibet (c. sixth to ninth centuries) became a story of Mongol generosity.

> Based on the evidence, the Sixteen Arhats' enlightened activity gradually appeared in Khotan, Mongolia, China, and Tibet. Also the Chinese monk Faxian, who lived three hundred years before the Dharmarāja Songtsen [Gampo], and Xuanzang, who lived at the same time as Songtsen Gampo, both went to the Land of Noble Ones. Along the path, they observed that even at that time the Victor's teachings had become firmly established in Mongol lands.
>
> Also, when the great Sandalwood Jowo [statue] was brought to China from India, it passed through a Mongol region. Based on all this, there is no doubt that the sun of the Buddha's teaching came to Mongol lands long before China and Tibet. An intellectual could conclude that while it is possible that the teachings were established in *upper* Mongolia long ago, only the teachings of the black Bön [shamans] were practiced until the time of Chinggis Khan in Central and Lower Mongolia. If you believe this, it is true that there are those who worship the black Bön across upper, lower, and middle Mongolia even today. However, central and lower Mongolia were connected with the establishment of the Dharma in Khotan and so also possessed the Buddhadharma.[28]

Zava Damdin often bolstered such arguments by dwelling extensively on the story of pilgrims and students who traveled to the thriving Buddhist world of classical India. These were often from the Land of Li, which for Zava Damdin meant Khotan, which meant Mongol. "Those Indian scholars and paṇḍitas came to Mongolia and benefited the teachings and sentient beings. Furthermore, in the past Mongolian scholars went to India and studied the five fields of knowledge, became mahāpaṇḍitas, and then returned home and greatly served the Teachings in China, Tibet, and Mongolia. For example, among those who went to China was the Khotanese paṇḍita Shérap Pel and the Uyghur paṇḍita Dzayadāsa."[29]

Khotan was a Buddhist city-state that existed at the Indic-Persian cross-roads, a node in the Buddhist and Zoroastrian-dominated trading networks connecting China with central Eurasia and the Iranian and Indian worlds. The centrality of the Land of Li qua Khotan across the spectrum of Zava Damdin's revolutionary-era historiography cannot be overstated. It is the subject of, and evidence for, dozens of his arguments across all three dispensations, but especially the earliest. For instance, from *The Dharma Conch,*

> Reflection of the enlightened activity of all the Victors,
> manifested as a stainless goddess,
> O venerable, noble Tārā, by your compassion
> rain down auspicious, blossoming flowers!
> As for how the precious Victor's teachings
> arrived, spread, and increased here in this land of Mongolia,
> there was an earlier, later, and middling [spread].
> As for the first of those, it was prophesized in the *Ox Horn Sūtra*
> that by the power of the prayers and aspirations of the Buddha and his sons,
> once a hundred years have passed since the Teacher's *parinirvāṇa,*
> the teaching will spread into the land of Khotan,
> just as the holy Dharma spreads into upper Mongolia.

Zava Damdin's somewhat radical Mongol claim on Khotan was not without controversy and required persuasive evidence, which he presented characteristically using scholastic and European sources. Readers will recall Damdin's note in *The Golden Book,* quoted in the previous chapter, that describes a Russian scholar sharing photographs of contemporary Khotanese nobility and the ruins of Buddhist sites and stūpas that the Khalkha monk cross-referenced in an atlas (*'dra ris kyi kha byang*) and on a globe (*sa'i go la kha byang*). Emboldened by such synthetic analysis at the interstices of the monastic college and the scientific academy, of the chronicle and History, elsewhere Zava Damdin would turn away from European tools and knowledges to find ample evidence for the Mongol Khotan in his canonical sources. These primarily included the *Prophecy of the Land of Li Sūtra* and the *Oxhorn Prophecy Sūtra,* both filed in Kangyur collections of the Buddha's teachings translated into Tibetan and Mongolian (Tib. *Bka' gyur*; Mong. *Ganjuur*).[30] A plethora of other noncanonical works also buttressed his association of the Land of Li with Khotan, of Khotan with the Mongols, and of the Mongols with Indian Buddhism. The evidence was conclusive, as he states in one of dozens of examples from *The Golden Book*: "the great Mañjuśrī Emperor's Abhidharma commentary states 'all subsequent Hor and Sok [Mongol] peoples, including the Oirat and the Khalkha, are Khotanese peoples.' It is only ever described in this way!"[31]

In reality, it was not only ever described that way. In his post-Qing fervor to set a threatened Mongolian Buddhism into deep time, Zava Damdin waded into a long-standing historiographic battle that had raged in Tibet for centuries: just where in Jambudvīpa is "the Land of Li"? The details need not concern us, but the controversy was live in dispersed Géluk circles across Inner Asia in the early socialist period. Zava Damdin's certainty about the Mongolian Khotan attracted even Agvan Dorjiev's ire in 1923, when he challenged his Khalkha junior on the topic. Dorjiev wrote:

IV.

Concerning the identification of the Land of Li:
Nowadays in the kingdom of Nepal
there is a mountain called "Ox-Horn Prophecy"[32]
upon which is a throne for the unequaled Buddha.
Near the base of that mountain
is a place with a well-known
stūpa called "Sālagandha."
It seems that when the *śāstra*s of old
make mention of Li and Nepal,
they are referring to the same place,
or else to places near each other.
A great swath of wasteland obstructs
passage between Nepal, the Himalaya, and Tibet,
and that land [you describe] where Uyghurs, Indians,
and Mongol peoples once mingled together.
It takes months to traverse all the way [from Nepal]
to the north of the northeast of Nepal and Tibet.
Currently, within the borders of what

Europeans[33] call Turkestan,[34]
in a place known as Khong than
is a small city called Gyamili.[35]
This is misidentified as Li, which is actually in Nepal.
This area has many large and small monasteries,
meditation caves, and the three supports
that were completely destroyed
by the wicked, barbarian Muslims
before being abandoned.
At such a great distance from Nepal and Tibet,
it is problematic to recognize it as the Land of Li.[36]

Unfazed and assured in his interpretation, Zava Damdin responded brazenly on the correct identification, as well as the consequences of such an identification for an expanded history of the Dharma in Mongol lands. His response is too long to include here; he concludes by summarizing his rebuttal that Li could have been Nepal, away from "Mongol" Eurasia.

It is said that their colloquial language was different from India or China;
over time, Li's writing system became similar to Chinese;
their customary traditions were very similar to those of the Chinese;
their Dharma traditions and terminology were very similar to the Indians.
This is all mentioned in the histories of the Land of Li.
For all these reasons, Nepal and Li have dissimilar characteristics.
It is therefore undeniable that these two lands have no connection![37]

In such a view, not only had "Mongols" in and near Khotan received the Buddhist dispensation long before their influential neighbors, it was also abundantly apparent to Zava Damdin that "Mongol" Khotanese, Turks, and Sogdians first brought the Dharma to Tibet.

This position is elaborated upon in *The Golden Book* by reinterpreting very widely repeated legends about the so-called early Dharma Kings of the Tibetan Yarlung Empire who first received the Dharma. The first of these was Thothori Nyentsen (Tib. Tho tho ri gnyan btsan, c. fifth century CE). Zava Damdin rehearses the usual story that during Thothori's reign he received two foreign Buddhists from "Mongol" Khotan at court, the paṇḍita Losem Tso and the translator Litésé.[38] Realizing that their visit was in vain because the Tibetan court was illiterate and they could not understand each other's language, the monks returned to their homeland. They left some holy objects behind that were famously stored at court as object of a blind reverence.

But that was not the only time "Mongols" had helped usher in Tibet's reception of the Dharma, in Zava Damdin's telling. Another legendary story associated with Thothori Nyentsen's reign concerned Buddhist texts that miraculously fell upon the palace roof. *The Golden Book* "clarifies" that while hundreds of generations of Tibetan and Mongolian historians understood that these texts had fallen from the sky, this was a faulty attribution influenced by the practices of Tibetan Bönpo priests, who worship the sky.[39] In reality, Zava Damdin surmises, those Dharma texts arrived at the still non-Buddhist Tibetan court carried on a wind from the palace of the King of Za Hor, which refers to somewhere in Bengal but in Zava Damdin's telling is claimed assuredly as Mongol territory because the name contains the ethnonym *hor*.[40]

The same sort of assertion is repeated in relation to the early seventh-century King Songtsen Gampo, the next of the great Buddhist kings of the Tibetan Yarlung Empire. Songtsen Gampo, long considered an emanation of the enlightened buddha Avalokiteśvara, welcomed not only the Dharma but also literacy, architecture, medicine, and other civilizing accouterments to Tibet from neighboring regions. *The Golden Book* reminds us that "from Persia[41] and Mongolia (*sog yul*) in the west, [Songtsen Gampo] brought the treasure of wealth and bounty," and "from the northern lands of the Uyghur and Mongol peoples (*hor mi*), he adopted precedents of law and behavior." Also, "among the six inner ministers whom he commanded, one was a Mongol (*hor mi*)."[42]

Another revision concerns the story of two other monks from "Mongol" Khotan. A vision came to them that the bodhisattva Avalokiteśvara had manifested as a Dharma King in Tibet. Upon their arrival in the Land of Snows, they were shocked to see the corpses of executed criminals dangling from palace walls and other bloody evidence of a decidedly unenlightened sovereign. According to the usual story, which Zava Damdin repeats faithfully though with new connotations, the fearful misconceptions of the monks were cleared away upon meeting Songtsen Gampo, who awed them by revealing a seated Buddha Amitābha under his turban, convinced them that the corpses were all the play of enlightened manifestation, and then magically dispatched them back to Khotan (i.e., Mongolia) in an instant.[43]

A final illustration of Zava Damdin's argument concerns widely repeated stories about the last Dharma King of imperial Tibet, Trisong Detsen (Khri srong lde btsan, r. 755–797/804), considered to be an emanation of Mañjuśrī. Trisong Detsen was responsible for inviting the great Indian abbot Śāntarakṣita and the tantric master Padmasambhava to transmit the monastic code and tantric lineages into Tibet; together they built the first Tibetan monastery, Samyé;[44] and had the first group of Tibetans ordained as monks. In *The Dharma Conch* and *The Golden Book*, these standardized accounts require little alteration to tell Mongolian stories. For instance, in Damdin's telling of the famous story of Padmasambhava luring the Dharma Protector Péhar Gyalpo (Pe har rgyal po) from a monastery in distant "Bhata Hor" to become the protector of Samyé, Bhata Hor is a Mongol place of a kind with post-Qing Khalkha.[45] Zava Damdin also focuses on Sokpo Pelyangcan Zennya and Sokpo Taktri,key figures in the retinue of Padmasambhava and King Trisong Detsen.[46] Both had not only "Mongol" names, Zava Damdin claims, but also "Mongol bones" (Tib. *sog rus can*).

In these ways, Zava Damdin's subtle but radical narration of the early spread of the Dharma into Mongol lands centers Mongol munificence in the history of not just China but also Tibet. The abundance of Mongol actors in the early Buddhist scene of imperial Tibet, writes Zava Damdin, brought Mongolian religious terminologies into the Tibetan lexicon, though this was erased by the reforms of the last of the three great Dharma kings, Tri Rélpachen.[47]

THE MIDDLE SPREAD: VAJRAPĀṆI AND THE MONGOL EMPIRE

Seeing that the Victor's Teachings have flourished in China, Tibet, and Mongolia
in the last five hundred-year period
due to the three secret, magical emanations of the
Protectors of the Three Families of the Victor's Children,
I suppose it is due to my virtuous karma and aspirations that I was born in this
    country!

In the eyes of ordinary people, the wrathful and peaceful activities of
kings who are the emanations of bodhisattvas and demons appear the same.
However, when we clarify the white and black [nature] of their activities
everyone, including scholars and the stupid,

has the ability to examine the evidence based on the results of their actions.

[If you] put your head underneath the ass
of a barbarian engaged in nonvirtue,[48]
follow whatever they say as advice,
and then receive the fortunes of the murderous enemy,
what else will happen to you other than punishment by the Dharma Protector?

E MA!

Until I achieve the Stage of Patience on the Path of Preparation,[49]
may I never be reborn in an area where there are many holders of wrong view!
O Triple Gem, please bless me so that this request may come true![50]

So ends the second chapter of *The Golden Book*, entitled "An Explanation of How the Middle Spread of the Victor's Teachings Arrived from Tibet, Land of Snows, When Chinggis Khan, Turner of the Wheel of Power, Controlled Most of the World" (*Stobs kyi 'khor bsgyur zing gir rgyal pos 'dzam gling phal cher la dbang bsgyur zhin bod gangs can nas rgyal bstan bar dar byung tshul bshad pa*). These verses summarize and conclude what is a rather more conventional historical narrative about Mongolian Buddhism than Zava Damdin's innovative deep history about "Mongol" Khotan, Xiongnu, and the rest. As he rehashes stories about Chinggis Khan, the incarnation of Vajrapāṇi, establishing the disciplinary practices of contiguity with the enlightened known as the Two Systems in Mongol lands, a long interpretation about the causes and direction of the Qing collapse and a post-Qing Buddhism begins to take shape.

Damdin's version of events in the Middle Spread does not depart in any significant way from the story told by his imperial predecessors. We get a sense of his totalizing vision in a short summary section from *The Golden Book*:

In its first five hundred years, the teaching of the Buddha Śākyamuni flourished in the center and borderlands of the Land of Noble Ones [i.e., India]. During its final five hundred years, the domain of influence of the most exalted Lords of the Three Families flourished in Tibet, China, and Mongolia. From among those, it was the buddha activity of Mañjuśrī and Avalokiteśvara that caused the Dharma to gradually spread in China and Tibet. Later, when the time came for the Dharma to extend into Mongol lands, Vajrapāṇi emanated as Chinggis Khan and accomplished the buddha activity of causing the Victor's Teaching to flourish here. Earlier, Mongol lineages had been fragmented and scattered. He united them all into a single empire. In order to raise a great army, he gathered [the Mongols] together as his subjects through all manner of appropriate peaceful and wrathful activities.

Concerning the actual causes of the Dharma's flourishing in this land, there are both "establishing the favorable conditions" and "removing adverse conditions." In the former, both the support of the Royal Law (*rgyal khrims*) and the support of the Dharma Law (*chos khrims*) are required. In order to accomplish the first, [Chinggis Khan] adopted the way of wrathful activities on the basis of the Royal Law of China. In order to adopt the second, he subjugated [the people] principally by way of peaceful activities based upon the Dharmic Law of Tibet. At that time Buddhism was decreasing in India, which is why he never went there.[51]

In the context of this story, *The Dharma Conch* and *The Golden Book* each stage the history of the Dharma arriving into imperial Mongolia from Tibet in four acts. First is an early dispensation via the Tanguts (*Mi nyag*) prior to their obliteration by the "enlightened" Chinggis Khan. Second is an influential transmission to the Mongol court via hierarchs of the Tibetan Sakya school (*Sa skya pa*). Third is a less influential but still noteworthy diffusion by the head of the Tibetan Kagyu school (*Bka' brgyud pa*). The last act involves the consolidation of these transmissions in the founding of various temples and retreat centers in Mongolian lands associated with the ruling Chinggisid elite.[52]

Zava Damdin writes in *The Golden Annals*, for instance, that a certain Dungkurpa of Tsang in Central Tibet (Tib. *Gtsang pa Dung khur pa*) once traveled with seven disciples to do a retreat in Mongolia.[53] There he garnered the favor of locals (one shepherd in particular) and eventually, despite a language barrier, was called into the presence of "the holy Chinggis Khan." At first, Chinggis showed only a small amount of faith in this Tibetan. It took Dungkurpa's expert exorcism of a Mongol minister afflicted by a *teng* spirit (Tib. *steng gdon*) to incite the great Khan's favor and devotion. Chinggis presented Dungkurpa with a "certificate" (Tib. *lung bzang po*) recognizing his enlightened qualities. "People say that this was the first meeting between a

Mongolian khan and a Tibetan monk," notes Zava Damdin with gravitas.[54]
From this fortuitous encounter (later ruined, we read, by the jealous intervention of shamans),

> in the Fire Rabbit year of the fourth *rapjung*, two thousand and forty one years
> after the *parinirvāṇa* of the Buddha according to the system of Büton, the Boγda
> Khan [Chinggis Khaan] went to Central Tibet and entered into a patron-
> patronized (*mchod yon*) relationship with the Sakya hierarchs. From Ü and Tsang
> [Central Tibet] he requested the "three supports" [texts, stūpas, statuary]. All
> Mongol peoples developed unshakable faith. They made offerings, and took vows
> such as the *upāsaka* precepts. As such, the Middle Spread of the Dharma into Mon-
> gol lands proceeded like finding one's head. Concerning all this, it is said,
>
> > Because of the coupling of the Sun and Moon of Dharma and politics,
> > The festival of happiness and welfare swells like a summer lake![55]

In passages like these developed in numerous works, but especially in *The
Golden Book*, the messy affair of conquest and Mongol expansionism is glossed
by emphasizing their function: collateral damage quite necessary to unite
religious and political authority across Eurasia in a Two Systems model that
would culminate in the Qing formation. Enacted by the enlightened ruler
on horseback and conquering much of the known world, the goal was only
to more fully establish the circumstances for reproducing Buddhist life on
steppe grasses and Gobi sands. The blood of hundreds of thousands had
flowed during the Mongol Empire (and the Yuan dynasty) only to make room
for an ocean of milk. Enlightened buddhas began thereafter to emanate onto
the Mongol human stage. A complete Buddhist dispensation into Mongol
lands that came after, the "later spread," was thus inaugurated by the reproductive possibilities of contact with enlightened presence begun with
Chinggis Khan.

Zava Damdin emphasizes Chinggis's supposed final testament (Tib. *zhal
chems*) to his son and successor Ögedei, urging him to invite Lama Gungtangpa from Tibet as an object of veneration (*mchod gnas*) for the latter's
mother, Börte Üjin. Gungtangpa's arrival at Ögedei's court and his install-
ment as Head Lama (*bla mchod*) acts as a narrative pivot in this telling about
the "empty" enlightened intervening in stages in the Mongol "real." "People

say this was the first time a Mongol king received a tantric initiation."⁵⁶ It also "inaugurated a system whereby Uyghur and Mongol monks would chant the Dharma [in the Mongol court]."⁵⁷ The simultaneous production of Ögedei as Supreme Khaγan of a Mongol Empire and as an initiated tantric practitioner of illustrious lineage helps Zava Damdin justify the undeniable violence associated with his reign. The only actual victims of the Mongol Empire, we read, were "enemies of the Two Systems" such as the barbarous "red-faced Kyrgyz."

The Middle Spread thus proceeds by retelling widely told tales from frontier Géluk historiography of the Qing period. While the narratives change little in Zava Damdin's telling, sometimes the prodigious evidence is quite novel and noteworthy. After Ögedei's sons Güyük and Köten and their devoted Buddhist mother became disciples of Gungtangpa, Köten settled in the city of Liangzhou in the Tibetan hinterlands of Amdo. While campaigning against the Song dynasty in China, Köten ordered the scholar-saint Sakya Paṇḍita to his court from Sakya monastery in Central Tibet. Contrary to the histories of even Zava Damdin's most immediate Qing-era predecessors, neither *The Dharma Conch* nor *The Golden Book* contains descriptions of the violence enacted against Tibetan Buddhist monasteries such as Reting (Rwa sgreng dgon) by the forces of Köten's emissary Doorta. What is included, however, is a rare reproduction of the edict sent by Köten to Sakya Paṇḍita ordering him to the Mongol court at Liangzhou. Because an actual transcription of the contents of this letter is extremely rare in Tibeto-Mongolian historiography, the inclusion of a purported version in the *Golden Annals* has attracted the attention of scholars such as Dieter Schuh, who has remarked upon the rather aggressive tone of this rare transcription of the "invitation."⁵⁸

Since to my knowledge there has not yet been an English translation of this little-known (but no doubt apocryphal) letter, I include Zava Damdin's version from *The Golden Book* in full.

Khubilai's younger brothers named Darkhan Taiji and Doorda, in the company of their attendants, were officials who were commissioned to go to Tsang in the Wood Dragon year as messengers. The edict that they presented to the Gentle Protector Sakya Paṇḍita read as follows:

In dependence upon the glory of the merit of Tséring Namgyi Shémong (Tshe ring gnam gyi she mong), this is my royal order to you:

[112]

Sakya Paṇḍita Kunga Gyeltsen Pélzangpo, understand my speech! I need a lama who can show me what to adopt and what to discard in order to repay the kindness of my parents, heaven (*gnam*), and earth. Upon investigating, this person is you! Because of this, you must come here without thinking about the difficulty of the journey. If you say "I am old!," how many times in his previous lives did the Buddha give his body for the benefit of sentient beings? Wouldn't this contradict the commitments [associated with] your Dharma understanding? In light of all this, if you still do not come, I will order my army to harm many beings. Are you still not afraid (*skrag pa e yin*)? With these reasons in mind, you should think about how to benefit the Buddha's Teachings and many sentient beings. Then come here as quickly as possible! You will come to know monks from the easterly direction of the rising sun. I will give you five *dré* (*bre*) of silver; a silk, impearled Dharma robe with six thousand two hundred individual pearls; a *gölutang* (*gos lu tang*) lama shawl with shoes; two bundles of *khati khatsangma* (*kha to kha tshangs ma*) cloth; two pieces of *thönti khatsangma* (*thon ti kha tshangs ma*) cloth; and five types of silk in twenty long pieces. This message is sent with Dorsi Gön (*Rdor sri mgon*) and Doorta, and was written on the day of the auspicious new moon in the eight month of the Dragon year.[59]

The remainder of Zava Damdin's many descriptions of the "Middle Spread" in both *The Dharma Conch* and *The Golden Book* simply repeat what had become standard accounts in the Tibeto-Mongolian historical tradition. This involved the arrival of Sakya Paṇḍita's nephews and hierarchs of the Sakya school, Phakpa and Chakna Dorjé, at the Yuan court of Khubilai; their favor with the Khaγan; and the many cultural productions they performed beyond transmitting the Dharma to Chinggisid elites (such as inventing the Mongolian script). I will leave those widely known details aside and come finally to Zava Damdin's historicization of the Qing-Géluk formation, that central object of his historical inquiry and the primary instantiation of the enlightened "empty" upon the human stage.

The Latter Spread: Mañjuśrī's Maṇḍala Takes Form

In 1640, the Great Fifth Dalai Lama and the Panchen Lama wrote to Abahai (1592–1643), retroactively regarded as the founder of the Qing. They were responding to the Manchu leader's invitation for the Dalai Lama to visit Mukden, the capital of the quickly rising Jin state that would become the Qing. In their response, these two Géluk hierarchs addressed Abahai as "Mañjuśrī Great Emperor." Patricia Berger argues that this was a strategic evocation of an earlier prophecy by the Third Dalai Lama, Sönam Gyatso, who had made contact with the Tümed Mongols in the sixteenth century. Sönam Gyatso predicted that Mañjuśrī would one day manifest as a great ruler and unite with the Géluk school to unite and rule Tibetan, Mongolian, and Chinese lands. The highest clerics in the Géluk world apparently hoped that prophecy was finally coming true.

Such an association suited the Manchu ruling elite very well once they transitioned from their Jin state to the Qing Empire in 1644. As we have seen already, by the eighteenth and nineteenth centuries a tripartite tantric model of enlightened experience of the Géluk school was being applied to the political territory of the Qing: Mañjuśrī, the embodiment of the wisdom

FIGURE 3.3 A big Buddha statue in a temple, Ulaanbaatar (1930s).
Digital copies of glass plate negatives preserved in the Archives for Cinema, Photography, and Sound Recording, Mongolia [1910s–1950s]. EAP264/1/9/3/4.

of all buddhas, emanated as successive Manchu emperors; Avalokiteśvara, the embodiment of the compassion of all buddhas, manifested as successive Dalai Lamas in Tibet: and Vajrapāṇi, the embodiment of the skillful means and power of all buddhas, manifested as successive Jebtsundamba Khutᵧtus in Khalkha Mongolia. (The list was not so short, of course: the tsars and tsarinas were often recognized as White Tārā, as was the Russian President Medvedev more recently; the Panchen Lamas were recognized as Amitābha, and so on into the hundreds of *trülku* lineages across Inner Asia)

One of hundreds of examples from Zava Damdin's memorialization of the Qing is his glowing description of the Yongzheng emperor's (雍正, r. 1723–1736) "enlightened" life and works:

Later, Emperor [Yongzheng], who was Mañjuśrī appearing as a human being, . . . invited the previous Refuge and Protector Jebtsundamba, the object of his father's veneration, and many other great lamas . . . who were installed as Dharma Masters. They respected the Triple Gem upon their crown and worked to increase the Yellow Hat system. . . . Specifically, that Lord [Yongzheng] trained in the profound Madhyamaka view and developed great compassion toward all sentient beings, whom he happily protected by means of political and Dharmic law. . . . For these reasons, everywhere was pervaded by virtue and goodness!

Previous supreme beings have said, "That Emperor is the incarnation of Panchen Sonam Drakpa." Their reason is that when he was young at Singön, Gontrül [Panchen Sonam Drakpa] became very sad. Panchen Lozang Chögyen came to him in a vision, saying: "To the east is a city, Mañjuśrī's Pure Land, which you will one day protect. After that, you must bring light to the 'Dark Barbarian Country.' In conclusion, with a pure mind of loving-kindness and compassion, you must greatly benefit sentient beings!" [Sonam Drakpa then said]: "This is a sign that at the end of this life I will take rebirth in China. In the future, I will take rebirth just once in northerly Mongolia."

Elsewhere from the prophecies of that Lord [Panchen Sonam Drakpa]:

Although there are difficulties associated with our times, in order to help fortunate sentient beings who were born in the Pure Land of Mañjuśrī to the east, I will provide opportunities to practice virtue and goodness. For this reason I am very happy!

This completely makes sense.[60]

But it was not only Mañjuśrī upon the imperial throne who had intervened to bring the fullest expression of the Dharma, the Two Systems, to a world ordered by the Qing imperium. It was also a very important manifestation of Vajrapāṇi, the Jebtsundamba Khutγtus. Their story encapsulates the final dispensation into Mongol lands in Zava Damdin's and all other late imperial Géluk monastic histories. For Zava Damdin alone, their story also encapsulates the Qing collapse and the bloody tides of the revolutionary period, as we shall see in a later chapter.

In frontier Mongolian scholastic histories, the embodiment of the first Jebtsundamba Khutuγtu Zanabazar, born Ishidorji (Tib. Rje bstun dam pa ye shes rdo rje, 1635–1723), wedded the real with the empty. On November 4, 1635, he was born to the Tüshiyetü Khan Gömbödorji in the Borjigid lineage of the Mongol aristocracy descended from Chinggis Khan. Those noble blood and bones were further enlivened by the enlightened minds of two Tibetan masters, Tāranātha and Jamyang Chöjé, as recognized by the Fifth Dalai Lama and other Géluk authorities in Lhasa. The story of that enchanted, noble young man with Chinggisid flesh and an enlightened mind further braided together the real and empty histories of Eurasia when he submitted Khalkha to the Qing in 1691 in the face of Khoshud Mongol aggression. At a time when this capitulation was being derided by nationalist and socialist historians as inaugurating Mongolia's long feudalist repression, in Zava Damdin's view this act completed a deep history of Mongol flirtations with the enlightened architects of history.[61]

By the time Zanabazar was born, the ascent of the Géluk sect to political predominance and its spread into Eastern Tibet and Mongol lands were already well under way. With the help of the Khoshud Mongol Güüshi Khan's forces, the Dalai Lama and his Géluk school had defeated rival Buddhist sects and their Mongol military patrons. Under the Fifth Dalai Lama, Ngakwang Lozang Gyatso; his regent, Sanggyé Gyatso; and the Panchen Lama, Lozang Chökyi Gyeltsen, the Géluk sect entered into close relations with a relatively new Qing empire. Over the course of its rule, especially in the nineteenth century, major Géluk monasteries regularly opposed the policies of the Qing and were critical of the Dalai Lamas, the Jebtsundambas, and the Manchu emperors. From the literary perspectives of historiography made along the Tibeto-Mongol-Sino frontiers, if not always in the hearts and minds of Géluk monks on the ground, the

Qing-Géluk formation was definitively established in the blood and mind of the first Jebtsundamba Khutuγtu.

Indeed, despite many previous centuries of Mongolian Buddhist history in Zava Damdin's accounts, Zanabazar is the *ür*-Buddhist subject, the wellspring of the fullest instantiation of the Two Systems in Mongol history, an enlightened curator of the Qing-Géluk formation. As Damdin writes in *The Golden Book*,

> Even when the Refuge and Protector Jebtsundamba Lozang Tenpé Gyeltsen was young, he clearly bore the marks of a buddha. Because of that, he tamed all the arrogant beings of the center and borderlands and brought them to serve the Dharma. At that time, even though this land appeared as a country of demons, he overpowered them with his loving-kindness and compassion. Then he built the Riwo Gégyé (Ri bo dge rgyas) [i.e., Gandentegchenling monastery], established a monastic community, built the three supports, and also established a study system. The monks thereafter continually engaged in activities such as studying, contemplating, and meditating. He further established the Mahāyāna and Vajrayāna traditions. In this way, in this dark borderland he lit the fire of the holy Dharma. The heap of his kindness is impossible to repay! . . . Because of that, this frontier country was made yellow. He was immeasurably kind.[62]

The Dharma Conch offers a concise summary of all that followed from the first Jebtsundamba's life, extensively narrated in *The Golden Book*:

> According to the Dalai Lama's prophecy,
> the Jebtsundamba built a moveable monastery,
> which had a great main temple that was made like a tent out of white cloth.
> Not long after, tens of thousands of *saṅgha* members assembled.
> A Golden Age began for the study and practice of
> the sutra and tantra teachings of the Gaden [i.e., Géluk] tradition.
> That monastery was called Yeke Küriy-e [Great Encampment].

> Until today, Yeke Küriy-e monastery has been
> the great source for establishing and increasing
> the teachings of the Victorious Buddha in the north of the world.

Older generations have said that this is the reason why
a temple made of wood, stone, and earth was never built.

At that time, prodigious spiritual sons like the Great Learned Zaya Paṇḍita
and the great scholar Nomon Han
appeared, because long ago they had made
similar prayers and aspirations as the Supreme Refuge and Protector.

By the kindness of those holy beings,
thousands of monasteries endowed with good ethics
who each protected and spread the Yellow Hat tradition
were established in the four kingdoms of Khalkha
and in the individual lands of the eighty Jasags.

Infinite representations of the body, speech, and mind [of the buddhas]
were housed in those monasteries.
Some were brought from places such as India, China, Nepal, Tibet, and Khotan.
Other [holy objects] were personally built
by that Refuge and Protector and his spiritual sons.

In the range of the Royal Mountain Hanggas Henthi (hang kas hen thi
     rgyal ri)
is the retreat center of Elva Dorjé Trag.
At that place, images, seed syllables, *maṇi* syllables, the Kālacakra Mantra
and more have spontaneously appeared on rocks,
as have the hand- and footprints of the Supreme Lord of Refuge and others.

Furthermore, there are many amazing abodes of *arhat*s, bodhisattvas,
*paṇḍita*s, *mahāsiddha*s, Heruka Cakrasaṃvara Mother and Father,
As well as *ḍākini*s and Dharma Protectors.

In this way, because of the outer, inner, and secret
buddha activities of the successive incarnations
of the Highest Refuge and Protectors, Fathers and Sons,
who were nonbiased scholars and *siddha*s
who all gathered here in the remote region of Central Mongolia,
the taste of the marvelous festival of the

perfect qualities of the four abundances
has arisen at this time and in this place![63]

Such abundances were tied inextricably to the most fully manifest and perfected intersection of the real and the empty, the fruit of a requisite scale of
intimate proximity with the enlightened, and inaugurated at the Khalkha
crossroads by the early Jebtsundamba Khutuɣtus.

Centuries later, after the Qing collapse, when such discourse no longer
had any comprehensive religious or political reference, Zava Damdin turned
to a sustained excavation and examination of a global circuit of historical
sources to diagnose the causes and possible futures of his dismal moment.
What would be the disciplines of proximity required to make Buddhist lives
in a post-Qing world, when history seemed to have exceeded the event of
enlightened intersection with the human stage? Great masters then became
criminals. Monastic compounds came under economic and ideological siege.
Imperial centers were toppled. Empty, enlightened agents had vacated the
human real.

PART II
Disenchantment

FOUR

Wandering in a Post-Qing World

In the past, while the Buddha was alive and during times of peace, if someone worked hard to preserve the Buddhadharma the teachings would last for
millennia. In these savage times in our borderland, a person will accrue even
greater merit if they work to preserve the Buddhadharma for just a day.

—*THE GOLDEN BOOK*, 1931

IN *THE SUMMARY,* Zava Damdin's 1936 autobiography, our author organized the narrative of his life as so many "wanderings" or *yeng-pa*. The
story of his early wanderings between 1867 and the collapse of the Qing in
1911 is heavy with mystical experiences appropriate to "inner" and "secret"
biographical writing. Such restricted and inward-facing life writing com-
municated the personal experiences of a master for a select group of
reader-disciples, but also described transformative proximity to the purifying, generally masculinized interiorities represented by the guru, buddhas, bodhisattvas, and siddhas whose bodies, words, touch, and teachings
reproduced lay, monastic, scholastic, and tantric life in Asia's heartland.
Such inner life stories told of tantric transmission, pilgrimage, visionary
debates with long-dead Indian paṇḍits, dream voyages to hell or pure lands,
prophetic discernments in lake waves or foggy mirrors, miraculous movement through mountains and into bodies, and healing alchemy that made
medicine from poison and Buddhist disciples from spirits possessing hap-
less kings.

Zava Damdin continued to use such scales of proximity to memorialize
and invent the Qing as the culmination of three waves of Buddhist dispensation. This was also the language and logic he used to talk about his own
life as he approached middle age and seniority in Urga's monasteries, the
Dalai Lama left town in 1906, and the Qing gave way to the nation and to
socialist revolution.

[123]

Mystic Travels in the Late Qing: Mount Wutai and Beijing

Following the departure of the Thirteenth Dalai Lama, the preeminent "living Buddha" in Inner Asia, from Urga, *The Summary* describes a rush of stories about Zava Damdin's transformative contact with other sources of enlightened presence while on pilgrimage during the last years of the Qing Empire. Zava Damdin writes tersely that as the Dalai Lama and his entourage left, "I sold my yurt and other possessions and left my homeland for Mañjuśrī's Pure Land, Mount Wutai."[1]

Mount Wutai (Ch. 五臺山 Wutai shan; Tib. Ri bo rtse lnga; Mong. Ulai uula), which sits in contemporary Shanxi province of the People's Republic of China, long occupied a central place in the Mongolian religious imagination. As it did for Zava Damdin, pilgrimage to Wutai became a popular substitute for pilgrimages to Tibet or India among the Mongol faithful. In addition to its potency as a purifying site of enlightened presence (Mount Wutai is considered the abode on earth of Mañjuśrī), a field for creating merit and cleansing negative karma and other obstructions, the "Five-Peaked Mountain" became a cosmopolitan locus where goods and ideas were exchanged from across Inner and East Asia.[2] Johan Elverskog and Isabelle Charleux, among others, have shown that pilgrimage to Mañjuśrī's abode provided rare opportunities for Mongols of different administrative banners to interact with one another and with other communities, such as Tibetans and Han Chinese, from across the multiethnic Qing.[3] Such mixing in hostels and on the circumambulatory pathways seems to have helped generate Mongolian communal narratives as part of, and later against, the Qing formation.[4]

To my knowledge, Zava Damdin's tale of pilgrimage to Mount Wutai and then to the steps of the emperor's palace in Beijing is one of the very last record of such "wanderings" by a Mongolian monk prior to the purges. This was a journey to the very heart of the Qing-Géluk formation in its twilight, set to paper a quarter century into the post-Qing situation. In its narratives we see a profound switch in register from the sober accounting of an autobiography as teachings received and the "outer" details of scholastic training to an "interiorized" life saturated with transformative contact with the enlightened. Such contact was written about decades later, in 1936, with tears wetting cheeks and sighs of deep longing when such contact was impossible.

Zava Damdin left Urga for Wutai sometime in the spring of 1906. He arrived on the eve of the important festival of Ganden Ngachö (Tib. *dga' ldan lnga mchod*), a celebration of the life of the Géluk founder, Tsongkhapa Lozang Drakpa. As butter lamps blazed on the rooftops of temples across Wutai's terraces, our author "saw the face of Mañjuśrī" directly in a vision.[5] This contact with the enlightened architect of the Géluk school, he wrote, "changed my perspective, produced tears and [caused me] to recite the 'Three Praises' [to Mañjuśrī] aloud."[6]

That visionary scene appears elsewhere in Zava Damdin's historical writing with more details. In *The Golden Book*, our author characteristically ruptures the temporal flow of his description of Sakya Paṇḍita's thirteenth-century visit to Mount Wutai with his own story:

> After that, on his way the Dharma Lord [Sakya Paṇḍita] went to China's Mount Wutai on pilgrimage. One night he stopped and prayed to the Venerable One. He saw Mañjuśrī Lion of Speech along with four retinue deities. Among them was an Indian *sadhu* and a Mongol sky-goer (Skt. *ḍāka*; Tib. *mkha' gro*; Mong. *Oγtarγui ber yabuγci*). Sapaṇ wrote a *sadhana* about them and also gave the transmission of their practice.
>
> When I went to Mount Wutai, I [also] had a vision of Mañjuśrī Tsam Goma with four retinue deities. I asked an elderly Chinese monk, "Who were these retinue deities [in my vision]?" He replied, "I've heard that monks of bygone times would say that the *sadhu* holding the lion's nose is the Indian master Padampa [Sanggyé]. The sky-goer holding the sword near [Mañjuśrī] is Mongolia's Chinggis Khan." Other than this, I have never heard anything about who they are. Everyone knows that Padampa came to Mount Wutai. But Chinggis Khan as a retinue deity? I am shocked![7]

Here, the real and the empty intersect in the first person, a folding of time and space appropriate to life stories recounted in "inner" and "secret" autobiographical writing. In the black letters he pressed to the page as an old man, Zava Damdin could relive Qing time, Qing space, and Qing possibility. And what seems to have mattered most in his 1936 recollections was that exceptional contact with the enlightened was so publicly embraced and lauded upon Wutai's slopes.

Zava Damdin provides just one line in *The Summary* about his actual pilgrimage through the holy throughways and temples of Wutai ("I also gradually visited nearby holy sites"). Such "outer" details seem beside the point in this "inner" narrative, and he soon returns to more visionary contact with

FIGURE 4.1 Detail of Wutai shan sheng jing quan tu (1846).
Library of Congress Geography and Map Division, Washington, D.C. G7822.W8A3 1846 .G4.

the enlightened.[8] This comes first in stories about supramundane archaeological explorations Damdin and his companions undertook, never providing reasons or motivations for their labor. They set out first to find a buried
stūpa that supposedly housed a lock of Mañjuśrī's hair. Their search successful, Zava Damdin recalls, the joyful group "announced [our discovery] to
devoted monks and laypeople."[9] Soon thereafter, Zava Damdin and company
unearthed "two amazing stūpas, made by magic, from a place that had been
destroyed by some circumstance," inside a cavity in the Perfection of Wisdom Temple.[10] Pulling such sacred objects from the earth itself, we read,
brought devotion and financial donations from pilgrims and the residents
of Wutai. "In one month we received about ten thousand ounces of silver."[11]

Not all pious excavations were so successful. Damdin and companions
once set out on a hunt for the funerary stūpa of a fifteenth-century paṇḍita
named Śrī Aśraka.[12] The site seems to have been Yuanzhao Temple (Ch. 圓照寺;

Tib. Kun tu khyab pa'i lha khang), a major complex that Gray Tuttle writes had been associated with the spread of the Géluk school in China since the fifteenth century (when Jé Tsongkhapa sent his disciple Chöjé Śākya Yéshé in his stead to accept an imperial invitation to visit the Ming court).[13] Chöjé Śākya Yéshé and many later Géluk masters of the Qing had spent prolonged periods in the Yuanzhao Temple by the time Zava Damdin came digging. It is curious that the Khalkha pilgrim, flush with recent discovery, was so pre-occupied with locating the "lost" stūpa of this paṇḍita, since already in the eighteenth century Jangji-a Rolpé Dorjé identified the Yuanzhao Temple as having Paṇḍit Śri Aśraka's stūpa installed in its central courtyard.[14] (This may explain why Zava Damdin was unsuccessful in his dig, or perhaps the stūpa had gone missing since.) *The Summary* records that while turning earth around the temple grounds, Damdin accidentally unearthed a quadralingual white stone tablet from under a mud wall. Without elaborating or record-ing its inscription, he notes that fellow Mongolian, Tibetan, and Chinese pil-grims once again were appropriately awed by his findings, offering praise and money.[15]

Flush with these sublime visions and subterranean extractions, Zava Dam-din writes, he turned his attention from digging in the "thick earth" of Wutai to more traditional pilgrimage pursuits like circumambulation, prayer, man-tra recitation, and meditative retreat. These were all guided by a local lama he identifies only as the "Baɣshi with the Dorampa degree."[16] His attention tuned to devotional and meditative practice, he saw marvelous signs con-tinue to arise while he sat on the rock and mud of Mañjuśrī's maṇḍala. Solar and lunar eclipses and unusual lights danced in the sky. All the Tibetans and Mongols around him "were amazed."[17] Sometime later, as part of New Year celebrations at Pusading monastery (Ch. 菩薩頂), Zava Damdin partici-pated in a debate-examination on the Perfection of Wisdom corpus (Skt. *Prajñāpāramitā*; Tib. *Shes rab kyi pha rol tu phyin pa*; Mong. *Bilig-ün chinadu kijaɣar-a kürügsen*).[18] In the haughty tone of these autobiographical sections, he boasts, "[I] debated best [using] logic and scriptural sources."[19]

Without mentioning his reasons or the exact time, Zava Damdin left Mount Wutai and journeyed to the royal court of Beijing. He did so on a "fire-chariot" (Tib. *me'i shing rta*), perhaps the newly constructed Tianji-Lugouqiao railway line.[20] *The Summary* recalls in tender detail the awe this Gobi monk felt upon arriving at the true center of Mañjuśrī's maṇḍala, an imperial cap-ital enlivened by the enlightened, as he would tell the monks and gods

FIGURE 4.2 Peking Street (c. 1900).
Library of Congress Prints & Photographs Division, Washington, D.C., United States, LC-B2- 2153-10.

assembled at Dashichoijurling some fifteen years later. Zava Damdin headed straight to the Yonghe gong Temple (Ch. 雍和宮; Tib. Dga' ldan byin chags gling; Mong. Nairaldu nairaldakhu süm-e), the principal Tibeto-Mongolian monastery of the Qing capital.[21] Apparently basing himself at Yonghe gong while in Beijing (later in the autobiography we read that he conducted his monthly monastic confessions there with the assembly), he quickly wandered into the city and "saw the amazing design of the Outer and Inner Palace."[22] He then set out to visit the Miaoying Temple (Ch. 妙應寺), which houses to this day a large white stūpa constructed by his ancestors when they ruled China during the Yuan dynasty.

Despite being hundreds of miles of rail away from Mount Wutai, the enchanted would not be confined there. While looking for Miaoying in the busy streets of Beijing, Zava Damdin suddenly "arrived at a very old temple called Kong-je-ji, in the center of the city."[23] Upon arriving, "a very pure monk with seven or eight of his disciples welcomed me and let me see their old holy objects."[24] He was informed that the Sixteen Arhats had each visited the site in ancient times. One of these guardians of the Buddhist dispensation had planted a shoot from the Bodhi tree in India. Zava Damdin took all this in while shaded by its branches, like those that had shaded the Buddha Śākyamuni as he subdued Māra and his mind two thousand five hundred years before, in distant Bodhgayā.

The Chinese monks offered the astonished Khalkha pilgrim seven holy leaves fallen from the Bodhi tree before sending him on his way. As earlier in the *Summary*, Damdin couples narratives of visionary contact with the enlightened in Beijing with stories about the public recognition and wealth heaped on him as a consequence. "[Those of my party] who stayed on in Beijing during the summer and fall tried to investigate this tree. Many of them said they could not find it! Somebody said that maybe this was a magically emanated temple."[25] The suggestion is left unanswered, but the implication seems to have been that Zava Damdin unwittingly wandered beyond the normative time and place of Beijing into an encounter with enlightened presence, another topography, just as he had on Wutai's peaks and below its dirt. During the Qing, one bumped into the enlightened around every corner.

(However, just as when he was digging for Śrī Aśraka's "lost" stūpa, here too it seems that he and his companions took a lack of information for the miraculous. On a map of Beijing, even today, on the route between the Forbidden City [the "Inner and Outer" palace] and the Miaoying Temple, there is an ancient and famous Chinese Buddhist temple with the name Guangji [Zava Damdin had called his miraculous temple "Kong ji ji"]. This monastery dates to the Jin and has, to this day, a very prominent association with the Sixteen Arhats.)

Zava Damdin writes that he soon left Beijing to return to Mount Wutai, where he planned to stay another year. Because of an unexplained "circumstance," however, he hurried through some devotions on the holy mountain and started back to Khalkha sometime in late 1906 or early 1907. Within a few years, the Qing Empire came undone in the face of the Xinhai Rebellion. The Khalkha nobility and their monastic collaborators declared an autonomous nation-state, and the Géluk international order was cleaved from its imperial patrons. When Zava Damdin returned to Urga, he took up the responsibilities of a more accomplished scholar and a meditative master of some renown. His transition to senior positions in the monastic world came just as that "holy encampment" was set alight in Asia's first modern revolution. Reconciling those realities with his experiences in the centers of the holy Qing, from within the increasingly embattled monastic colleges, became his labor for the next thirty years.

Wandering Out of the Qing

Zava Damdin never provides explicit commentary on post-Qing political events in any of his over two thousand pages of revolutionary-era autobiography and historiography. Nor does he acknowledge his silence. At times he makes the faintest references to his pious strategy, as in *The Memorandum*:

> Due to my karma, I was born in a borderland country at the end of the Degenerate Age, but because of good conditions I was able to enter into the Buddha's teachings. A person like me should not fight with speech and mind. It is better to spend day and night putting effort into prayer. May whatever merit I and others of the three times have accumulated become the cause for the Victor's Teachings, which are the cause of all sentient beings' happiness, to endure long in this land. May we be blessed by the buddhas of the ten directions![26]

His capacious post-Qing writing never explicitly addresses a single People's Congress resolution, any policy of containment aimed at monasteries, the name of any revolutionary government or its leaders, or the show trials and executions that began to fell his friends and teachers before his own death. "Socialism" and "communism" are words that he seems never to have set to paper, even as he wrote prodigiously about his times at the very epicenter of Asia's first experiment with such state-building projects and in sustained conversation with revolutionary intellectuals. Similarly, the earlier autonomous Boγda Gegegen Khaγanate (1911–1919) goes unmentioned. Those perilous years for the Mongolian nation-state are glossed in *The Summary* simply as a time of "wandering through studies in middle age." Having returned from Wutai and Beijing to a nationalist revolution, Zava Damdin writes only, "I began to study, teach, and listen."[27]

Though he had already been awarded a *gabcu* monastic degree while the Dalai Lama was in Urga back in 1906, the immediate years after the Qing collapse were for Zava Damdin a time of extensive study, transmission (Tib. *lung*), tantric initiation (Tib. *dbang*), and little else. In Zava Damdin's telling, nothing of note happened in the sociopolitical landscape in December 1911, when a consortium of nobility joined with the Jebtsundamba Khutuγtu to declare an autonomous Buddhist theocratic state, abandoning a Qing empire already coming undone. Sando, the last Manchu *amban* to Urga, was given twenty-four hours to vacate the city. Yeke-yin Küriye or "the Great Encampment" (Urga)

FIGURE 4.3 Last Manchu governor in Mongolia, Sando (first on right in first row) (a photo copy) (1910s).
Digital copies of glass plate negatives preserved in the Archives for Cinema, Photography, and Sound Recording, Mongolia [1910s–1950s]. EAP264/1/8/13/54.

was renamed Neislel Küriye, the "National Encampment." The Jebtsundamba was elevated from the highest incarnate lama in Mongol lands to the position of Boγda Gegegen Khaγan, a religious and secular monarch ruling over an imperiled Mongolian nation-state. Zava Damdin seems not to have been bothered to record the fact. Perhaps in those dark days of 1936, when he wrote of his life in *The Summary,* he hesitated to entangle himself in any dangerous associations with those who used to be called the enlightened.

Writing Time and Society After the Qing

Zava Damdin's life and his monastic scene begins to slip out of official time in the years after his return from Wutai and Beijing. An emergent nationalist historiography began to fit the ruins of the Qing Empire with a new chronotope. In the words of a nearly contemporaneous state history:

> In 1911, European style, the third year of Hsüan T'ung of the Manchu or Ta Ch'ing Dynasty, the first day of the middle month of winter in the female white pig year of the fifteenth cycle, Mongol style, they initiated the independent state of Mongolia and established a separate country, raised the Holy Jebtsundamba Lama, the master of all, to be king of the country, and placed him on the great precious throne, putting all religious and secular power concurrently in his control, and they called the country Mongolia, and the reign period Exalted by All, and made Urga the capital of the country, and established the fine ministries.... It was agreed that in all matters and principles of state the old laws and regulations of the Manchu Dynasty should for the time being be followed as before.[28]

The new government of the Boγda Gegegen Khaγan declared, "Our Mongolia has been an independent state since the very beginning of its existence, and therefore according to the ancient law, Mongolia declares itself to be an independent state with a new government.... From now on, we Mongols will not submit to the Manchu and Chinese officials, whose power is being completely abolished."[29] When the Khalkha elites declared independence in 1911, "Mongol Urga was a natural choice for the capital against the smaller Manchu Uliyasutai, while the Khutuγtu, whose residence it was, was himself the only possible choice as king."[30]

In contrast to the emerging nationalist state rhetoric, Zava Damdin's entire autobiographical entry in *The Summary* for 1911 reads as follows (in the sober mode of outer biography, quite at odds with the "inner" visionary details and literary style that come just before at Wutai and Beijing during the late Qing):

In the spring of the Iron Pig year,
having gone to the monastery of the lama of Drak-ri
and having an audience with the lord Arhat,
I received experiential instructions on many
"Stages of the Path" and "Mind Training" [texts].

Also, from the heart disciple named Minjür
I received many teachings for nearly a month,
including principally an explanation of the
Perfection of Wisdom in Eight Thousand Lines.

During summer, I commissioned a silver statue
of the Gentle Protector Lama [Tsongkhapa]
for the local monastery in my homeland.
I offered the *gzung* ritual to it and then did the consecration.

From there I came back to my monastic seat [in Urga].
That winter, the [Darva] Paṇḍita came to Küriy-e
and gave profound teachings on the
"Three Terrifying Instructions" (Tib. *'jigs mdzad man ngag gsum*).[31]

And so goes Zava Damdin's literary self-representation over the entire Boγda Gegegen Khaγanate, until events in 1919 and 1920 intrude

Throughout, *The Summary* records only short travels to and from monasteries, initiations and teachings taken or given, meditation retreats undertaken, and a series of writing projects completed, such as a series of Madhyamaka commentaries in 1916 at the behest of the Ngak Ramjé. Such works built upon a widely read and quite original Madhyamaka commentary by Zava Damdin from 1899, entitled *Essence of the Ocean of Profound Meaning: A Discussion of the Concise Presentation of the Grounds and Paths of the Three Vehicles According to the System of the Perfection Vehicle* (hereafter: *The Essence*, Tib. *Phar Phyin Theg Pa'i Lugs Kyi Theg Pa Gsum Gyi Sa Dang Lam Gyi Rnam Par Bzhag Pa Mdo Tsam Du Brjod Pa*). *The Essence*, famed even today in the global Géluk scholastic scene as a late and radical departure from standardized scriptural positions, eschews the traditional interpretation of the grounds and paths of sutra from the Yogic Middle Way Autonomy School (Skt. Yogācārasvātantrika-mādhyamika; Tib. Rnal 'byor spyod pa). Instead, Damdin developed a unique analysis from the position of the Middle Way Consequentialist School (Skt. Prāsaṅgika-mādhyamika; Tib. Dbu ma thal 'gyur pa), considered by his Géluk tradition to encapsulate the Buddha's final and definitive statement on the nature of reality.[32]

Zava Damdin concludes this section of his autobiography, characteristically, at a seemingly random moment in time, out of step with the usual periodizations of revolutionary Inner Asia. Unmentioned by name in his works are the upheavals that came with the end of the Boγda Khaγanate, such as the Chinese occupation in 1919, their arrest of the Boγda on October 26, the violent "liberation" by the White Russian forces of Baron von Ungern-Sternberg on February 1, 1920, and then the victory of Mongolian revolutionary forces and their Soviet backers in July of that year.

> In the beginning of winter [of 1918–1919],
> when I was planning to travel to Upper Right Khalkha,
> the Noyan came to [visit] and said,
> "The abbot abandoned the monastic college, so you must go!"
>
> I had no choice and so made requests to the lama.
> [He told me] "For the benefit of the monastic college, you must go!"
> I decided this was due to the power of my karma.
> I arrived having had to cross an extremely frigid, snowy [landscape].
>
> The many years I spent doing this difficult job,
> such as building up the monastic college,
> Is a story I will tell separately.
>
> In the spring of the Earth Sheep year [1919],
> I went back to the monastic college and

I received the initiation of Mitra Gyatsa (*Mi dra brgya rtsa*)
from the Lord Ngakram (*Sngags rams rje*).

After that, I again returned and
we did the rainy season retreat in the monastic college.
The three holy objects and the offering materials
in the main temple's assembly hall and the shrine house
looked very nice and drew out the people's devotion.

During the fall, I went to the Thabin Estate (*Tha bin spyi so*)
And taught the *Great Stages of the Path to Enlightenment* (*Lam rim chen mo*).
Immediately after, I was invited to Küriy-e [Urga].
I went and they commanded that
I write the history of Mongol lands [i.e., *The Golden Book*].

At that time the Lord Ngakram passed away.
The honorable Lhatsün journeyed to China.
During the winter, I came back to the monastic college
and gave teachings to the students and engaged in other activities.

In the meantime, I wrote the *Praise to Shastri*
And *The Root Text of the Collected Topics*.[33]

[. . .]

In the spring [of 1920], at the abode of Chikti Kangyur (Chig thi'i
    bka' 'gyur),
I taught *The Great Stages of the Path to Enlightenment*,
And then again I returned to my monastic seat.
Though I wished to stay until winter,
I suspected a battle would soon break out between China and Mongolia.
I took whatever holy things I had in my quarters and left.

On the special occasion of *düzhi* (*dus gzhi*),
I dispatched the Dzédang *gabcu* to offer a *katag* scarf to Baγatur Wang
and begged him to spare the lives of two wicked ones

and three thousand Chinese.
Because of that, no one was killed.

During winter and spring,
by relying on the compassion of the Triple Gem,
the monastic and lay communities could abide without any misfortune.[34]

As the Mongolian People's Party adopted the unilinear, progressive time of the nation and the moral narratives of modernity (in their historical materialist versions), Zava Damdin turned with increased purpose to his otherwise histories of the Qing ruins.

We glean from the colophon to *The Golden Book* some ways that his profile as a monastic leader and intellectual drew him into political events during the dissolution of the autonomous government. He was asked to write *The Golden Book* at a time when nobility and monastic elites who were also opposed to the Boyda Gegegen Khayan invited Republican Chinese forces to reoccupy Khalkha. Though the details are sparse, it may be that the 1919 meeting of nobility and lamas convened by the last Tüshiyetü Khan, Dorjsuren Khoroljav (r. 1912–1922), who insisted Zava Damdin write *The Golden Book,* as described in its 1931 colophon, was connected to the "Revocation of Autonomy" movement formed against the Boyda's government that year. The nobles were more worried about instability associated with World War I, the Russian revolution, and violent White Russian pan-Mongolist movements looming to the north in the Transbaikal region, than reinstating some version of Qing sovereignty, but sought to submit to the Republican Chinese in a motion that was approved in the Chinese parliament, against the Boyda's protests, on October 19, 1919.[35]

As mentioned above, Damdin never references nationalism or socialism explicitly in any of his works. Yet in the 1927 *Memoranda,* he comes as close as ever to referencing (and actually bolstering) something like a pan-Mongolian national subject.

Oṃ Svasti!

Concerning the great land of Mongolia in the north of the world, which is renowned as a land tamed by the Venerable Vajrapāṇi: Although it has endured as a single community in Jambudvīpa for ten thousand human years, most of its peoples are nomads who [live] in felt tents and who herd domesticated animals.

It is their custom to move from one place to another. Because of that, in general since long ago there has only been an imperfect tradition of keeping records about lands, forts, human genealogy, and so on. Although some [records] do exist, I think that with each change in state these have been burned or else dispersed in the wind and destroyed.[36]

Lest Mongol nationalists and revivalists today became too excited, only a folio later in *The Memoranda* Damdin switches registers entirely and argues that Mongolia originated "in the land of China, the field of Mañjuśrī's dominion."[37] The colophon to that work gives a sense of his hybrid temporalization of the Mongols and their Buddhism, never of the Qing or the nation, echoed elsewhere in his histories explored above.

Here I have described the continuous, five-thousand-year history of the varieties of Mongol peoples and the succession of their rulers. [I used] histories of the Chinese, Mongols, and Manchus that record a long history of conflict. I principally focused on kings, ministers, military, and bandits. I tried to avoid other topics in order not to [fall into] foolish chatter (Tib. *ngag 'khyal*). Although when I wrote this commentary I put in only a little effort, I heard from a few laypeople, monks, and intellectuals (*rtog ldan*) that it would be useful to help understand this topic.

In general both Buddhist and non-Buddhist peoples claim that before Chinggis Khan appeared the Mongols had neither a customary tradition (Tib. *tshul lugs*) nor a Dharma system (Tib. *chos lugs*). They have also claimed that [in Mongolia] there were just a few stupid people who lived with monkeys and apes. Many people have felt this way. In order to remove their wrong views, in general in *saṃsāra*, especially in the land where we have been born, the wheel of anger, attachment, and ignorance turns continuously. Because of that, since long ago we have not escaped from and are still drowning in *saṃsāra*. If you are able to contemplate this, then you will understand that a precious human life and the Triple Gem are very difficult to find.[38] Then we will understand that the world of the six types of beings—whether higher or lower, happy or suffering—is impermanent and without essence. Then we will cultivate the mind of renunciation [that desires] to escape from *saṃsāra*.[39]

Similar motives emerge in Zava Damdin's other statements about the challenges and opportunities he faced when writing about society with any certainty.

In this *śāstra* you have read stories about many wicked kings, ministers, and bandits. These are unsuitable topics for a monk to explain! However, their stories were told in histories written by generations of previous scholars, and so there must be some special meaning to them. Therefore, here I have explained [them again].

I have traveled to many different regions, been to their libraries, and read many erudite texts. All of these I have understood. However, I know that there are many texts, each with multiple meanings and perspectives. It is therefore difficult to settle upon a single interpretation. For that reason and because of the nature of my own understanding, it is quite possible that I have made many mistakes. Please, forgive me![40]

In some cases, Zava Damdin describes his motivation for writing history in profoundly local terms: in order to inscribe and preserve oral traditions, for example, or else to clarify genealogical descent and differentiate communities of Mongols from their neighbors. In a short historical work about a favorite retreat in his Gobi monastery entitled *An Account of Bringing Together Mother and Son: A History of the Merging of the Old and New Hermitages*, he writes:

Since long ago, those in the region of Khalkha's Uijing Güng have been nomads. There has never been a library in either the monasteries or the settlements. As a consequence, [locals] don't know anything about their bone lineages, previous generations, lama lineage, and so on.

The ancient Tibetans would say:

If you don't know your ancestry,
you are like a forest monkey.
If you don't know your relations,
you are the same as a deceitful turquoise dragon.
If you don't know your ancestors' history,
you are like an orphan. . . .

For those reasons, even if the history I record is already known to the oral tradition, my hope is that it becomes beneficial over the short and long term.[41]

Elsewhere, Zava Damdin similarly declares that it would be "very beneficial over the short and long term" to recover an immense Eurasian history for the Mongols.

FIGURE 4.4 A religious ritual begins, Ulaanbaatar (1930s).
Digital copies of glass plate negatives preserved in the Archives for Cinema, Photography, and Sound Recording, Mongolia [1910s–1950s]. EAP264/1/9/6/111.

Defending the Dharma in Socialist Mongolia, 1921–1937

Muted though they are about contemporary politics, Zava Damdin's reminiscences about the tumultuous transition from the Boɣda Gegegen Khaɣanate to the socialist period are those of a scholar, pilgrim, meditator, and historian settling uncomfortably into monastic leadership at the heart of the world's second socialist state. Consider the *yeng-pa* wanderings he used to title the late chapters of *The Summary:* "Wandering by Means of Protecting the Monastery During Old Age"[42] and "Wandering by Means of Uncertainty at the End of Life."[43] Despite such solemn characterizations from his position in 1936, Zava Damdin was an extremely active builder of scholastic, monastic, and public Buddhist practice throughout the 1920s. Not only did he fund the building and expansion of several scholastic colleges in Urga and in his Gobi homeland, he also paid for new statuary, text collections, and other supports necessary for the ritual life of the many monasteries under his care. Publicly Zava Damdin began to lead large-scale teachings and tantric initiations, such as *maṇi* recitations and pill blessings, Maitreya processions, and Kālacakra empowerments. This clearly speaks to his rising prominence as a respected senior teacher among monastics and the laity. It was in this period, in 1924, that he publicly taught on the enduring Qing formation as "the spiritual friend who pleases Mañjughoṣa."

Despite the rigors of his schedule and the pace of his writing, as the 1920s progressed Zava Damdin more regularly retired from Urga, now renamed Ulaγanbaγatur (Red Hero), south to his Gobi homeland to perform religious functions for his kinsmen and the old aristocracy. According to the *Summary*, Zava Damdin founded more than half of the temples and scholastic colleges of his Gobi monastery, Chöying Ösel Ling, between 1918 and at least 1926. "We gathered objects, donated wealth and many animals from nearby and afar into the treasury of our monastery's administrator."[44] In the Wood Ox year, 1925, due to another set of unmentioned though seemingly nefarious circumstances, Zava Damdin's position at Chöying Ösel Ling was suddenly elevated so that he would "take over responsibilities as abbot."[45]

In that role, which was becoming an exposed and perilous one as party policies swung rightward, then leftward at the end of the 1920s, Damdin dramatically expanded the scholastic curricula and colleges. He built a tantric monastic college (*rgyud grwa*) in 1922; a philosophical college (*mtshan nyig grwa tshang*) in 1926, based on the manuals (*yig cha*) of Drépung Gomang college in Central Tibet; and in 1935, he founded another philosophical college that used the manuals of Losél Ling, Drépung's other famous college.[46] Just months before his death and the brutal destruction of all his monasteries, Zava Damdin had brought the great scholastic traditions of Lhasa, that holy city he tearfully regretted never seeing, to his rural Gobi homeland. The frontier became the center, if for only a moment.

Indeed, as the 1920 entries blur into those of the 1930s in *The Summary*, nearly every account is of Zava Damdin's activities to found, fund, build, and consecrate all manner of monastic infrastructure in his Gobi monastery. In addition to replicas of the great philosophical colleges of Drépung in Lhasa, Zava Damdin conceived of, paid for, consecrated, and organized the curricula for new medical and astrological institutes, primary assembly halls, monastic residences, and hermitages.

In addition to abbatial duties and building monastic colleges on Gobi sands, a fascinating and very regular preoccupation of Zava Damdin during the socialist period was to standardize the examination systems in medicine, astrology, and tantric studies. Connected to this work, he sought to routinize a set of "scholar tours" (Tib. *grwa 'khor*). These required advanced students to travel between regional colleges, debate their areas of specialization, and be subjected to intense scrutiny and evaluation before earning their degrees.

> In the spring of the Earth Dragon year (1928),
> I gave the initiation and the transmission of *Yutok's Heart Essence*,[47]
> and the Nectar Accomplishing of Medicine [ritual].
> Then I began a system of an ongoingscholar tour
> for those holding a Menrampa degree (Tib. *Sman rams pa*, i.e., medical degree).[48]

In such narratives we get a sense of the enduring exchange of bodies and knowledge that continued largely unabated during the 1920s and 1930s across the monastic networks of Tibet, Mongolia, and Siberia. At least in one small corner of the Gobi, Buddhism in Mongol lands grew substantially during the early socialist period, not only in terms of monastic population or reformist accommodation but as a feverish push to establish and renovate a complete Géluk scholastic program in the ruins of the Qing.

Many large-scale public events that the *Summary* describes in these later sections were connected to the Kālacakra tantric cycle. And this should hardly surprise us, since Zava Damdin's expertise in the Kālacakra system and his commentaries on its interpretation and practice have been widely consulted by Tibetan and Mongolian monastic scholars and tantric practitioners to this day. This includes the present Fourteenth Dalai Lama, who until the mid-1990s relied upon Zava Damdin's commentary in his public teachings on the Kālacakra around the world.[49]

There is little explicit evidence in the *Summary* that Zava Damdin's turn to the Kālacakra so late in the revolutionary period was related to its longstanding connection to millenarian traditions in Inner Asia. However, the increasingly intense pressure of the nascent socialist movement at home and tremendous danger on Mongolia's border to the north in Russia and the south in China was being met elsewhere by evoking the Kālacakra *imaginaire*. For example, in the face of revolution in Russia, Agvan Dorjiev and other Buryat

FIGURE 4.5 People attending a religious ritual ceremony, Ulaanbaatar (1930s). Digital copies of glass plate negatives preserved in the Archives for Cinema, Photography, and Sound Recording, Mongolia [1910s–1950s]. EAP264/1/9/6/21.

Buddhist leaders cast the tsar into Śambhalist narratives of Buddhist political ascendency using Kālacakra imagery. The Thirteenth Dalai Lama had performed a mass Kālacakra initiation in China while in exile after the British invasion in 1904, and the exiled Ninth Panchen Lama would perform the initiation in Beijing for one hundred thousand devotees in 1932 and on many other occasions as well. Inner Asian Buddhist mediation of postimperial political developments, from the October 17 revolution to the "liberation" of Tibet by the PRC in the 1950s and in the hands of the current Dalai Lama, the many decades of refugee Tibetan experience, was filtered through the Kālacakra, and specifically, the Śambhala legends.[50]

Zava Damdin was, among all his other abilities, a recognized master of this complex tantric system. He remarks in several places that the Kālacakra system became increasingly central to his own effort to "protect" the monasteries under his charge as the Qing receded further from view. He was giving large-scale public initiations as late as 1935, building specially dedicated temples, undertaking long retreats focused on this deity, elaborating courses of scholastic study in this system for his disciples, initiating "Kālacakra Scholar's Tours" (*Dus 'khor gyi grwa 'khor*) in 1931 and 1933, and self-publishing his commentaries on the stages and paths of Kālacakra practice as late as 1934.[51] As the revolutionary period progressed, he also undertook many archival projects related to this tradition, collecting and ordering endangered ritual systems and composing commentaries for them. The corpus of his writing on the Kālacakra continues to circulate widely in today's globalized Géluk scholastic circles, being the most recognizable portion of his over four hundred works alongside *The Golden Book*, his unusual Madhyamaka commentaries, and, more controversially, his Dorjé Shukden ritual collections.

Wandering Into Death

The increasingly muted style of the closing sections of *The Summary* stand in the sharpest contrast with the extravagant stories of contact with the enlightened that organize Zava Damdin's life story during the twilight of the Qing. The Dalai Lama no longer came to Urga. Relics no longer shook free from the thick earth of Wutai. Mañjuśrī no longer appeared in the sky with Chinggis Khan at his side. The branches of the Bodhi tree no longer offered relief from the sun. Mañjuśrī, Avalokiteśvara, and Vajrapāṇi no longer held court in monastery or palace. Reduced to a nearly annalistic bareness, the last "wandering" of Zava Damdin's life covers the four years leading up to and including 1936, the year before his death and the purges. These terse accounts, organized by the seasons, tell of a few scholastic tours, ill health, and in one instance, an intervention into the immoral behavior of two unnamed politicians. He titled this last section of his last work "Wandering with Uncertainty at the End of Life."

Knowing how difficult the situation was becoming for Mongolia's Buddhist institutions and monastics, contemporary readers of the *Summary* are left wondering whether Zava Damdin was restricted, perhaps actively persecuted, at any point before 1937. Even without many details, his death and the end of the Dharma in Mongolia hang ominously just beyond the text. This is most evident in the final "scene" of the autobiography, an entry where Zava Damdin writes of being a year into a solitary retreat in his yurt, apparently without monastic affiliation, duty, or identity.

The yurt itself, as opposed to the monastery that had been his home since his youth, is a poignant sign of a disoriented return. The cries of a newborn sister ringing in his ears, he had run from the "wicked" and polluted, feminized, exterior felted dome of family life as a youth to the monastery, where he had lived for over six decades. Now he languished once more in the smell of camel hair felt, separated from the monastic places he yearned for. An interlinear note inserted by an unknown hand states that this seclusion was part of Zava Damdin's final testament (*bka' chems*) to undertake a six-year retreat.[52] Perhaps this was a "retreat" in both the religious and the more normative sense? There was very real danger for him at this time. Many of his teachers, colleagues, and students had passed out of life already at the sound of a judge's gavel and then the crack of a rifle.

In the colophon to the *Summary*, likely some of the last lines he ever wrote, Zava Damdin situates his life explicitly in Buddhist institutional and doctrinal space, into history one last time. He was "born in the last five hundred years of Śākyamuni's teachings"; he had come to "hold the signs of a monk and joined a monastery"; and he had spent his time "studying, teaching, [and] building holy statues," even if, in his own words, such piety was simply "a common activity, so who cares?"[53] Of the hundreds of colophons Zava Damdin penned to his substantive works, the *Summary*'s is the only one that does not dedicate the merit of composition to the flourishing of the Dharma in Mongol lands. Here are the last lines to the last life story:

> In that way, I did many activities of body, speech, and mind,
> until my seventieth year [1937],
> but I am unable to write everything down
> and also I have forgotten.
> I am uncertain if it has all been virtuous action or not.
> For instance, while the tracks of fleeing insects may appear as letters,
> the insect is not an author.
> Likewise, an ordinary person's activity, however virtuous,
> is never the story of a holy life.
> If some of my actions become the cause of enlightenment
> because of the power of [making contact with] holy objects,

then that would be a wonderful outcome.
If in this long text you see only a very ridiculous story,
keep in mind that I was lying
and offer it all to the fire god![54]

Our author ends with an uncharacteristically personal focus:

When my consciousness goes to the next life,
may it separate from nonvirtue, illusion, and fear.
May messengers of Maitreya Buddha show me the path,
and may I be born without difficulty in Tuṣita Pure Land![55]

Perhaps his prayers worked. Zava Damdin died just before socialist forces descended upon the monastic establishments whose history he had written and which he had headed and defended for decades. Within months these were reduced to rubble and the vast monastic population killed, imprisoned, or disrobed.

Beyond the horizon of his autobiographical writing, we glean some more specific details of Zava Damdin's death, his funerary rituals, and the sad fate of his monastic institutions in another set of first-person narratives collected by Mongolian scholars and journalists after the collapse of the socialist system. The most revealing come in a series of oral history interviews that J. Choidorj and G. Akim undertook with some of Zava Damdin's still-living disciples in the early 1990s. Many of these informants had been very young monks in Zava Damdin's circle when the master died and oceans of blood rose higher. Since the 1990 Democratic Revolution, they had rejoined newly opened Buddhist monasteries.[56] Choidorj interviewed a monk named Sharav who had been present at Chöying Ösel Ling during Zava Damdin's funeral and the aftermath, and in 1997 Akim interviewed Myatav Lam, an eighty-year-old monk who had reentered monastic life after the end of the socialist period in 1990. Myatav had been a direct disciple of Zava Damdin and had been tasked by the elderly lama to lead his funeral according to a special tradition.

According to Sharav, at the end of his life in 1937 Zava Damdin was no longer living in a monastery. At the time of his death by natural causes, he resided in an Ulaγanbaγatur home under the care of a brother named Puntsag and a younger sister named Gündinjal. With the help of many devotees,

Zava Damdin's corpse was loaded onto a carriage drawn by a white horse.[57] The funerary procession then began the long journey from Ulaɣanbaɣatur to Uijing Güng in the Gobi and to Zava Damdin's home monastery, Chöying Ösel Ling. At the monastery, Myatav set Zava Damdin's corpse alight according to a very particular tradition that he and his lama had clarified before the latter's passing (Myatav describes it in his interview as involving a special tripod). Unusually, Zava Damdin's ashes were collected into an urn and buried, per the deceased's instructions. According to Myatav, Zava Damdin was only the second lama from this area whose ashes were interred according to this exceptional custom.[58]

Either in his old age or after his passing, Zava Damdin had been succeeded in the abbotship of Chöying Ösel Ling. Sharav said that soon after Zava Damdin's death, this Khambo Lam also died (naturally or by execution is left unclear) and a monk named Minjüür took his place. Very soon after, in the autumn of 1937, Minjüür and Sharav, along with forty-five others, were arrested and imprisoned. According to Myatav, the rest of the remaining monks, perhaps still numbering in the hundreds, were executed (according to oral traditions at the site today, there were over seven hundred monks resident just before the purges, most of whom were killed). Chöying Ösel Ling, newly built, was destroyed. Only the foundations of the monastic colleges remained. During the communalization initiatives, closer to mid-century, some of the monks' residences (Mong. *ayimaɣ*) were converted into storage sheds. You can still see them there today, shells drying in the sun, as a revived monastery has risen in the last two decades.

FIVE

Vacant Thrones

None of the previous seven [Jebtsundamba] khutukhtas [*sic*] was allowed to live too long. It is a sign of decadence that [. . .] the eighth khutukhta [*sic*], who was born in 1871, has succeeded in asserting his right to live so long as this. But his life has been a worthless one. He has a great predilection for strong liquors, he is very fond of cards, he likes the yellow, glittering metal more than anything else in the world, and, so far from passing his time in pious devotion, he rides in a motor car, plays the piano, listens to the phonograph, and has surrounded himself with a little harem.

—*THE WASHINGTON POST,* 1914

JUST AS I hesitate to brand Zava Damdin a nostalgic of a kind with eighteenth-century French intellectuals or *perestroika* poets, I resist reducing his post-Qing works to either an embrace or a rejection of the revolutionary modern taking hold of Inner Asia. The global circuit of the human sciences provided Zava Damdin with new knowledge about "Asia," "Mongolia," and "Buddhism." He used that learning to extend, and sometime to exceed, the Qing-era historical template of his frontier monastic predecessors. In conversations across desks in the Institute of Scripts and Letters, in the pages of *The New Mirror,* in letters demanding or defending historical interpretation, or in poring over photographs in embassy sitting rooms, Zava Damdin leveraged the synthetic impulses of his polyglot, frontier tradition to try to fit imperial ruins with a time and place. Knowledge gleaned from the globally circulating human sciences allowed him to use canonical sources in speaking back to changing times. Altaic linguistics enlivened prophecies delivered by the Buddha upon dusty Silk Road hilltops. Paleography clarified a "Mongolian history" of the Dharma that moved in panniers carried by Turkic horsemen through Eurasia's grassy corridors. Philology and the history of religions provided knowledge and social contexts in which Indian treatises on logic and Chinese pilgrimage tales changed hands and found new life in new languages.

While Zava Damdin enthusiastically extended the scope of the everyday "real" story of the Mongols and their neighbors on the basis of Euro-Russian sources, his histories of "empty" enlightened intervention into that human stage remained dependent upon synthetic sources and scholastic knowledge practices inherited from the late imperium. Prophetic interpretation, creative reconstructions of "corrupted names," critical readings of texts, and documenting oral tradition were all centuries-old techniques employed in the polyglot ecologies of the frontier monastic college. He poached professional historiography and the fruits of other foreign disciplines focused on Asia to tell an otherwise history, one that never simply repeated European or Qing discourses. He mined a few products of paleography and archaeology, but never adopted their methods or pursued their goals. He noted the idea of "Asia" but only described Jambudvīpa.

In this sense, despite the claims of Soviet historians and of revivalists in Mongolia today, Zava Damdin stubbornly remained a Géluk scholars of the Qing long past its political endings. He did not simply synthesize religious experience and rationality or reason, but claimed "reason and systematicity . . . [as] the very prerequisites for spiritual realization and action."[1] José Cabezón describes four fundamental orientations to knowledge and liberation in Géluk scholasticism that are exemplified in Zava Damdin's engagements with the intellectual diversity of revolutionary Khalkha. First, the universe is understood to be accessible, intelligible, and knowable, or, "at the very least everything that is of soteric importance is understandable through rational inquiry."[2] Second, scholastic movements are tradition oriented, meaning they display a strong historical consciousness and foreground the maintenance and preservation of tradition and lineage. Importantly, "preserving tradition" means "to preserve its intellectual underpinnings, [which consist primarily of] rational inquiry into doctrine."[3] Third, rational inquiry not only is essential for maintaining internal continuity and orthodoxy within a scholastic tradition but also is "considered essential to *distinguishing* that tradition from others, and to *demonstrating* its relative superiority to others."[4] Finally, by means of a particular tradition of rational inquiry, scholars must often confront and systematize a vast, disjointed, and contradictory scriptural corpus.

To his death, Zava Damdin remained oriented to knowledge, knowledge practices, and knowledge pluralism in the terms Cabezón describes. While he was a sought-after interlocutor for Russian Buddhologists and Buryat Mongolists, his narrative and interpretative authorities remained those seventeenth- to nineteenth-century border-crossing, polyglot scholars from the Sino-Mongolian-Tibetan frontiers, such as Sumpa Khenpo Yéshé Peljor, Gombojab, Thuken Chökyi Nyima, Jangji-a Rolpé Dorjé, Mindrol Nomön Han, and Panchen Lama Lozang Chökyi Gyeltsen. As a result of his labor in the ruins of the Qing, the "Mongols" were invested with more history and more Buddhism than had ever been written before. This drew on new Eurasianist knowledge in the inter-Asian zones of contact and exchange opened in revolutionary times, but only ever told about the "three dispensations" and the events of enlightened manifestation.

As a result, the deep time of "real" Mongolian history, actors, and territories never appeared more clearly. Nor did the history of "empty" enlightened intervention into Mongol lands, with all the possibilities for contact and transformation this entailed. But what about the present? The future? What about the practice and social spaces of scholasticism as the revolution grew older, allies in the party were silenced, and modernist reformers of Buddhism became emboldened? Clarity in regard to all this was hardly forthcoming. Still, Zava Damdin turned resolutely to the authority of the past to know the revolutionary present and to try to direct the post-Qing future. If the universe is understood to be accessible, intelligible, and knowable, as his Géluk tradition insisted, he ought to have been able to render revolutionary events sensible, at least to determine what was of soteric importance in an ocean of blood.

Writing the Political End of the Qing Empire

For Zava Damdin and his milieu, Qing time, territories, communities, and forms of sovereignty endured and exceeded the newly invented national subject and its attended histories, forms of power, and spheres of affiliation. Still, he was aware that the Qing had ended politically. His brief description of the fact in *The Golden Book* would be the last reference to any specific regime, political actor, policy, or government in his histories or letters. As a framing device, Zava Damdin characteristically mines the prophetic record. Writing in 1931, he describes the 1911 collapse of the Qing as a future event foretold by none other than Mañjuśrī and the seventeenth-century Géluk master Drakpa Gyeltsen (Tib. *Grags pa rgyal mtshan*, 1619–1656):

> [As it says in *The Root Tantra of Mañjuśrī*]: "While [the Manchu emperor] lives, the strong political system of the previous Manchu emperors and the pure teachings of the Jamgön Lama [Tsongkhapa] will remain united. Sentient beings from the center and borderlands will enjoy a festival of religion and politics."
>
> How do we know this? From Trülku Drakpa Gyeltsen's prophecy:

> To the east, in a land where everything is done according to the Dharma, a ruler who is the manifestation of Mañjuśrī will appear. By legalizing the ten virtuous actions, all sentient beings will become happy and peaceful. This ruler will respect the reddish-yellow Wish-fulfilling Jewel [i.e., the monastic community] upon his crown.

> As it says in *The Root Tantra of Mañjuśrī*:

> Due to the nature of [our degenerate] times, sixty years after Emperor Daoguang (Srid gsal, r. 1821–1851) the "house of political and religious law" will become looser and looser in both central and border lands. In time, loyalty (*grya*) to the union of the teachings and political authority will be severed in China, Tibet, and Mongolia. Then, [the Two Systems] will transform into fragrant food for the barbarians of the ends of the earth. In time, the [two] systems will be destroyed. Those foreigners will then make [their own] supplications.[5]

In case his readers had not drawn the obvious conclusion, Zava Damdin laments: "It is certain that all this has now come to fruition!"

Searching for What Is Holy

But how exactly had this sorry state of affairs come to be? While Zava Damdin's earlier histories offer descriptions of the post-Qing crisis (the topic of the next chapter), it seems that only after twenty years of inquiry did he come up with a historical interpretation. His identification of the causes of the oceans of blood awash in Mongol lands does not implicate communists, but the behavior of everyday monks, lamas, and even the "living buddhas" who had long been at the center of Buddhist life in Inner Asia. Just as the events of history had always been the intersections of the enlightened empty with the human real, so too would the end of history take place at their junctures.

Like most of his presentist narratives, Zava Damdin's critiques of Buddhist institutionalism and his diagnosis of what was elsewhere being called modernization in Asia's heartland are dispersed across the 1931 sections of *The Golden Book*, in small asides or laments that tumble into other narratives. We have already seen some examples, drawn from classical Buddhist sources on monastic decline associated with the dissolution of the teachings. Specifically, these are associated with the "five degenerations"[6] that are commonly understood to be signs of the gradual decline of the Buddha's teachings during the "age of degeneration,"[7] when no buddha will appear in the world.[8] As the age rots from the inside, such expectations about the wearing of time upon the Buddhadharma usually manifest in monastic degeneracy, social reversals, and disrespect for the sanctity of Buddhist teachings, persons, and places.[9]

While the above quote from *Root Tantra of Mañjuśrī* suggests that the Qing-Géluk formation would endure based on the "loyalty" (Tib. *rgya*) of its subjects, in a much later section of *The Golden Book* Zava Damdin comes to his own conclusion:

> [As Nāgārjuna] writes in *The Precious Garland: Advice to the King*: "Always be broad-minded and undertake very broad deeds. From broad actions come broad results...."
>
> If you look at the biographies of various Mongol rulers, they completely acted as Nāgārjuna advised.... However, eventually both the patronized and patrons adopted extremist behavior and went well beyond political and Dharmic law. That's why the precious Sandalwood Jowo statue, no different than the actual living Buddha, flew off into the sky. After that, just as the wind disappears, so too did the emperor.[10]

Here is a fascinating proposition about the causes and conditions of the Qing collapse, with much consequence for monastic leaders such as Zava Damdin: the gilded era of the Dharma had putrefied from the inside due to excessive and degenerate behavior. This was hardly a unique position.

Regional Mongolian unrest against aristocratic and monastic abuses was a regular occurrence in the nineteenth and early twentieth centuries. Often given context by prophecy, such protest movements carefully distinguished the sanctity of an incarnate lama's title from the sorry behavior of its all-too-human, temporary occupant (such as lamas whipping poor herders to death for unpaid loans).[11]

This split allegiance and critique was one of the steepest challenges the Mongolian People's Revolutionary Party faced when trying to activate class consciousness among a newly imagined proletarian population of nomadic pastoralists and "lower-class monks." The downtrodden could readily admit abuses but could not forsake loyalty to the monastery, the idea of enlightened manifestation, and the personal and community cultivation that could come from disciplines of proximity.

Just how Zava Damdin sided with such popular movements in his own life remains unverified in the extant written sources. But how could the degeneracy Zava Damdin identifies after the mid-nineteenth century reign of Daoguang be reconciled with the vast story of the enlightened intervening in human affairs from a time before time was recorded? What, in other words, were the temporal, territorial, religious, and political implications of such excess on the monastic and imperial thrones, the "centers" supposedly binding together the social, political, and religious worlds of Eurasia? It seems, most basically, that part of the disorientation Zava Damdin and others in his milieu experienced in the post-Qing situation was a confusion of social categories, for example between monk and layperson, between nobility and commoner, between scholastic and scientist, and most egregiously, between the holy and the mundane.

And this confusion also drove forward successive socialist party policies against the Buddhist establishment from 1921 to the events of 1937. As Christopher Kaplonski has noted, the fledgling socialist state remained contingent against the enduring authority of the Buddhist religious establishment; it occupied a liminal position between enacting direct military action against Buddhist monasteries and having the authority to impose the rule of law. This was fundamentally an issue of competing definitions of authority. A confusion of terms thus beleaguered the first historical effort to produce socialism in Asia and hobbled efforts by conservative monastic leaders like Zava Damdin to circulate a persuasive counternarrative.

FIGURE 5.1 A State Khural (grand meeting) in session, Ulaanbaatar (1920s).
Digital copies of glass plate negatives preserved in the Archives for Cinema, Photography, and Sound Recording, Mongolia [1910s–1950s]. EAP264/1/8/7/23.

Interestingly, Kaplonski's work asks not only why state violence is enacted and how, but also why and when widespread state violence is avoided. Why did the new government take so long to kill the lamas? How exactly were they (especially the "living buddhas") made killable? Answering these critical questions, Kaplonski draws upon two key theoretical traditions in the (historical) anthropology of political violence. The first, explaining why it took so long, emerges from the work of Italian philosopher Giorgio Agamben on the "state of exception." The second, explaining how they were made killable, is a line of revisionist anthropology that has approached statehood and sovereignty as dynamic, contingent, and contested rather than stable, consensual, and legitimate. This characterization of revolutionary Mongolia is only bolstered when we turn to monastic sources like Zava Damdin's.

Agamben's notion of the state of exception pivots on a curious Roman legal concept of *homo sacer*. A *homo sacer* (a sacred person) was someone legally stripped of citizenship who could be killed but not sacrificed.[12] In Agamben's view, *homo sacer* began a long Euro-American tradition he calls the state of exception: political power founded in legal exclusions enacted during "states of emergency." The result is a legal construct of sovereignty that functions "at once excluding bare life from and capturing it within the political order, the state of exception actually constituted, in its very separateness, the hidden foundation on which the entire political system rested."[13]

Kaplonski shows that to immediately identify and exclude *homo sacer* in the Mongolian case—as the Nazis had done to Jews during the Holocaust and as the Americans have done to "enemy combatants" in Guantanamo and to Central American children brought illegally to the southern border—was untenable. Setting state power opposite bare life presumes a position of power that the Mongolian socialists did not possess. Walter Benjamin's opinion that the state of emergency in which we live is no longer the exception but the rule was true of revolutionary Mongolia in the 1920s and 1930s. However, the government was at pains to make it appear not to be the case: an actual state of emergency (Mong. *onts bayidal*) was declared only during an armed rebellion in 1932. Producing bare life as an exercise of established power eluded the socialist party. And this was precisely the problem.

Buddhist monastics and especially the living buddhas were too heavy with social meaning: they resisted being reduced to a killable subject position. Covert assassinations, death squads, and the like would have delegitimized any claims to sovereignty the socialists hoped to make. Weber's classic observation that a state is an entity with "a monopoly of the legitimate use of physical force" is inverted in Kaplonski's analysis: the Mongolian socialist state needed to gain legitimacy in order to use physical force at all.

Acquiring the authority and legitimacy to render monks killable thus became fundamental. Kaplonski focuses on a series of strategies used by socialist leaders to contain and exclude the sovereignty of the Buddhist establishment. Foucault's insights on governmentality are important here, but his notion of the population can hardly account for the exceptional social meaning of "living buddhas" in Mongolia, who remained unkillable in Agamben's sense and unknowable in a Foucauldian biopolitical sense. The crisis of classification, felt by both socialist leaders and monastic leaders like Zava Damdin, found partial and deadly resolution in the turn to law.

Knowing, legality, and economic deployment, rather than brute force, unexpectedly emerged as the backdrop for the killing of 5 percent of Mongolia's population in just eighteen months.

Beginning unevenly in the late 1920s and reaching fever pitch in 1937, economic and ideological routes legally available to monastics were gradually tightened. Counter-revolutionaries were tried, convicted, and punished with prison sentences or death. Guilt or innocence was decided in a court, in other words. "The exception needs to be contained, to be made unexceptional. To do otherwise, to highlight the exception, could be read as highlighting the contingent nature of the state." Abiding by norms and regulations helped mediate the delicate sovereignty of the socialist government and it was hoped, would help invent a strong socialist polity in Mongolia. "The system had to be seen as functioning to be seen to be normal."[14]

However, this normally functioning, cautious legal strategy to contain the Buddhist establishment ultimately failed. By the mid-1930s, after a decade

FIGURE 5.5 Persons imprisoned under the "antination group" label during the Great Purge of the 1930s (a photo poster) (1930s).
Digital copies of glass plate negatives preserved in the Archives for Cinema, Photography, and Sound Recording, Mongolia [1910s–1950s]. EAP264/1/8/14/152.

FIGURE 5.3 Historical books and documents temporarily stored in an abandoned temple, Ulaanbaatar (1940s).
Digital copies of glass plate negatives preserved in the Archives for Cinema, Photography, and Sound Recording, Mongolia [1910s–1950s]. EAP264/1/10/1/15.

of socialist party rule, the monastic population had actually increased. The faith and loyalty of the people were hardly opposed to their lamas. Class consciousness remained dormant. Only when it became clear that these had definitively failed was the final technology of exception—a desperate, mass exercise of state violence—implemented.

Working in another register entirely, Zava Damdin sought to order the crises of the revolutionary period by asking not who could be killed but who could still be "called a holy being" (Tib. *skyes bu dam pa zhes pa*) in the post-Qing situation? Specifically, who still embodied enlightened presence in the imperial ruins?

To begin his discussion, Zava Damdin once again turns to a Qing-era authority from his interpretative community, the Jangji-a Khutuɣtu Rolpé Dorjé.

FIGURE 5.4 An abandoned temple, Ulaanbaatar (1930s).
Digital copies of glass plate negatives preserved in the Archives for Cinema, Photography, and Sound Recording, Mongolia [1910s–1950s]. EAP264/1/9/6/83.

The All-Knowing Jangji-a wrote:

It is taught that [noble beings]
do not destroy their practice by means of knowledge,
nor do they destroy their uprightness by means of practice.[15]

But what of incarnate lamas, those "living buddhas" who were the very embodiment of enlightened presence in Inner Asian Buddhist institutions, the manifestation of the empty enlightened authority that brought to Mongol lands, previously in darkness and awash with blood, the sovereignty of the Two Systems? On this topic Zava Damdin has much to say.

For example, after a long section in *The Golden Book* describing the biographies of Mongolian lamas responsible for the Buddhist dispensation into Mongolia after the original Mongolian Buddhist subject, the seventeenth-century Jebtsundamba Khutuɣtu Zanabazar, Zava Damdin makes Jangji-a's terse definition of a "holy being" more nuanced. This comes from a citation attributed to yet another Qing-era cosmopolitan Géluk monk from the Sino-Tibetan-Mongolian borderlands, Gungtang Könchok Tenpé Drönmé (Tib. Gung thang dkon mchog bstan pa'i sgron me, 1762–1823), the third incarnation of the influential Gungthang incarnate lineage.

> An incarnation [of a buddha] arises in this world to benefit the teachings. Their activity must "make a handprint" [i.e., impact] through teaching and medita-tion. [Otherwise] they can become a support for the effects of cyclic existence. If in *saṃsāra* we find a rich family's son [i.e., a falsely identified incarnation], we could just ask them [for wealth]!
>
> Anyone from the history of scholars, noble and respectable beings who pro-tect and increase the Buddhist teachings, and also those who guide all sentient beings to higher realms and to enlightenment: those are noble beings.[16]

Zava Damdin makes his intention clear: "Nowadays, those with the name of 'lama,' 'incarnate,' or 'noble one' just turn the wheel of attachment, anger, and ignorance and destroy the Victor's teaching. In this way, all sentient beings are escorted to the lower realms. Those are definitely not noble beings. Forget it! We must understand this!"

And for Zava Damdin, understanding his post-Qing world required a his-torical understanding of just when the enlightened had left the human stage, when true incarnate lamas and emperors last walked upon Eurasian soil, and when charlatans donned their robes and sat in phony maṇḍalas.

The Fifth Jebtsundamba and the Prehistory of the Qing Ruins

To answer such questions, we must set the above discussion into its full con-text in the 1931 sections of *The Golden Book*. There it comes after a glowing, devoted rehearsal of the life story of the First to the Fifth Jebtsundamba Khutuɣtus, or Zanabazar to Tsültimjigmidambajaltsan (Tib. Tshul khrims 'jig med bstan pa'i rgyal mtshan,1815–1841) and then a damning, dismissive summary of the degenerate, duplicitous lives of the Sixth to the Eighth Jebt-sundambas (the Eighth was enthroned as the Boɣda Gegegen Khaɣan in 1911 and sought out Zava Damdin to write the history of his imperiled state).

As we have seen, the first Jebtsundambas were central to all post-seventeenth century religiopolitical histories of Mongolia in Zava Damdin's histories as well as in those of his Qing predecessors. Uniting bodies animated by Chinggisid blood with the enlightened minds of deceased Tibetan masters, the early Jebtsundambas had inaugurated the Géluk dispensation to Mongol lands, had appropriately submitted the Khalkha to the Mañjuśrī Manchu Emperor, and had acted as enlightened architects of the founding of mass monasticism and scholasticism in Khalkha lands—all in dialogue with those other enlightened incarnations managing Inner Asia: the Dalai and Panchen Lamas in Tibet, the Qing emperor, and various other incarnations across the Sino-Tibetan-Mongolian frontier.

Zava Damdin evokes that long history in *The Golden Book* as context for what had happened to produce the turmoil, violence, frustrated routes to proximity, and convoluted social categories in the postimperium.

Furthermore, in earlier times when Atiśa came to Tibet, he saw two wild yaks on the mountainside of Sakya, and he prophesied that "In the future, two Mahākālas will perform buddha activity here. These will be 'Gur' and 'Zhel' [i.e., *mgon po gur* and *mgon po zhal*]." He then pointed to the white earth and said, "There, seven *Dhi* syllables, one *Śrī* syllable, and one *Hūṃ* syllable will appear in succession. There will be seven emanations of Mañjuśrī, one emanation of Avalokiteśvara, and a single emanation of Vajrapāṇi who will benefit sentient beings." Among those who appeared at Glorious Sakya [monastery], the emanation of Mañjuśrī was Sapaṇ, the emanation of Avalokiteshvara was Pakpa, and the emanation of Vajrapāṇi was "Chinese Chakna (*rgya nag phyag na*, i.e., Chakna Dorjé)."

Because of those three, Chinese, Tibetans, and Mongols developed a singular loyalty to [the unified] teachings and political authority. Our lama forefathers also prophesied that "When China, Tibet, and Mongolia become separated and cut off from political authority, the virtuous teachings will deteriorate in all three lands." Upon consideration, it is beginning to seem as if the time described in that prophecy has now arrived. Therefore, the knowledgeable should rely upon conscientiousness and devote themselves to the virtuous Dharma![17]

The founding of the Qing-Géluk formation, the twinning of the enlightened and the human, the very possibility of proximity was a story that began fully in Mongol lands with the First Jebtsundamba Khutuɣtu.

According to Zava Damdin's decades-long investigation, the story of its ending began not with the Qing collapse in 1911 or with socialist policies of exception in the 1920s and 1930s, but with the death of the Fifth Jebtsundamba in 1841.

This historical argument, to my knowledge quite unique to Zava Damdin's oeuvre, comes in 1931 sections of *The Golden Book* after an extended description of the life of the Fifth Jebtsundamba. Though he lived only a short time, he built on the legacy of his prolific predecessor, the Fourth Jebtsundamba Lubsangtübdanwangchug (Tib. Blo bzang thub bstan dbang phyug, 1775–1813), who had profoundly shaped the institutional, ritual, and social structure of Khalkha Buddhist life.[18] In Zava Damdin's telling, the Fourth had notably established the two principal philosophical colleges of Urga and had transmitted both the Kālacakra and the Dorjé Shukden lineage to Mongol

FIGURE 5.2 Drawing by Jügder, completed in 1912, depicting Khuree (Ulaanbaatar), National Central Museum, Ulaanbaatar (1930s). See Uranchimeg Tsultemin, "Cartographic Anxieties in Mongolia: The Bogd Khan's Picture-Map." *Cross-Currents: East Asian History and Cultural Review* 21 (2016): 66–87.
Digital copies of glass plate negatives preserved in the Archives for Cinema, Photography, and Sound Recording, Mongolia [1910s–1950s]. EAP264/1/8/15/38.

lands. The Fifth, according to Zava Damdin, not only had reestablished Gadentegchenling monastery but also had provided detailed public instructions to the Mongolian monastic and lay population about constructing stūpas, statuary, *thangka* paintings, and pilgrimage routes through the sacred urban interior of Urga. The Fifth had acted, Zava Damdin is careful to tell his readers, in close consultation with those other major embodiments of the enlightened: the Ninth Dalai Lama, the Seventh Panchen Lama, and the Daoguang emperor.[19]

Like the Fifth Dalai Lama, Ngakwang Lozang Gyatso (1617–1682), the Fifth Jebtsundamba Khutuytu sought to materialize the Yellow Tradition in the Khalkha crossroads of the Qing anew. Unlike the Dalai Lama and his famous regent, Sanggyé Gyatso, the Fifth Jebtsundamba did not just aim to project a synthetic vision of authority that could subsume political and religious rivals or to standardize the scholastic program of the dispersed Géluk monastic colleges.[20] The Jebtsundampa's task was profoundly spatial: to settle a previously itinerant Urga, to establish a material base for the Khalkha devoted, to facilitate pilgrimage, and to routinize lay contact with the massive monastic community. It was, in other words, to set up a context wherein "users" of Urga, to adopt language from Michel de Certeau, would be fashioned into devoted and virtuous subjects of the Qing-Géluk formation by moving along circumambulatory routes and coming into purifying proximity with Urga's monks, relics, statuary, stūpas, and buddhas in human bodies.[21]

As in much of his careful diagnosis of the causes of the Qing collapse and the disenchantment of Eurasia, Zava Damdin turned to a careful reading of prophecy and oral tradition as he centered the Fifth Jebtsundamba in his story of the Qing collapse and revolutionary crisis. In the late sections of *The Golden Book*, Zava Damdin finds most of his evidence in statements that were attributed to the Fifth Jebtsundamba while Urga was being rematerialized as a sedentary monastic seat on the River Tüül. With hindsight, Zava Damdin interprets the Fifth's prophecies to the Urga faithful as prescient warnings. He repeatedly laments that headless monks and foolhardy laity in the mid-nineteenth century had misinterpreted "auspicious signs" and ignored the Jebtsundamba Khutuytu's orders.

A few examples illuminate the character of each prophecy and its interpretation in Zava Damdin's two extended biographical sketches of the Fifth Jebtsundamba. Each entry describes an episode from the Fifth Jebtsundamba's life, a prophecy given or received, and then Zava Damdin's interpretation of their meaning from his vantage in the post-Qing situation.

> At that time, [the Fifth Jebtsundamba's] uncle-abbot went to Tibet. He had written a prophecy in the Ox Tiger year [1829] and this was offered to the Panchen Rinpoché. When his uncle returned, the Panchen Rinpoché sent a letter with him that said, "In this situation, whatever you think will come to be." The Panchen also praised him. The meaning of all this is that in relation to prophecies, if you do not mistakenly interpret the auspicious signs, when the time comes everything will happen as foretold.
>
> Nowadays, out of delusion people create and declare all manner of prophecies. That is because Dharmic and political law is not strict enough. It is all the drama of crazy people! If you investigate the prophecy of the Lord of Refuge [Fifth Jebtsundamba] with great care, he is saying that in the future the Victor's teaching will be destroyed. That is now happening.[22]

A little further on in *The Golden Book* is another of the Fifth Jebtsundamba's prophetic evaluations of the near future in Khalkha. Here, however, the subject is degenerate monasticism, the target of many of the Buddhist reform movements in play in the post-Qing and post-tsarist periods that, ironically, Zava Damdin so vehemently attacked (as we will see in the next chapter).

> [The Fifth Jebtsundamba said:] If you do not protect your *samaya* commitments and your vows, do not correctly follow the lama and spiritual master, do not have faith in the Triple Gem from the bottom of your heart, go against the Vinaya by destroying the full or novice ordination vows using the profound Vajrayāna teaching as an excuse while still wearing Dharma robes, then you deceive the good followers of the Buddha Śākyamuni.
>
> If we engage in these many wicked actions, this will become a cause to harm the lives of the upholders of the Buddha's teachings. In this land, it is undeniable that situations like famine, contagious diseases (*nad rim*), and quarrels among people from other lands [are occurring]. This unwanted [prophesied] situation has now appeared.[23]

A final series of prophecies delivered by the Fifth Jebtsundamba, followed by Zava Damdin's interpretation in light of the revolutionary calamity, concerned the mobility of Urga, a monastic city of felt and wood that until the time of the Fourth Jebtsundamba had been relocated dozens of times.

> The merit of disciples has decreased and demonic activities have increased. [Monks] no longer reside continuously in Yeke Küriy-e [Urga] or at Gaden-tegchenling monastery according to the instructions of the Great Refuge and Protector [Jebtsundamba]. Though he prudently left a testament, because of wrong prayer and fiendish influence, [the city's residents] ignored [his orders] even though they knew about it. Yeke Küriy-e, Kalapa, and both tantric colleges were then moved back to the old ruins [i.e., their previous location, before the Fourth's resettlement].
>
> This was all prophesied by the Lord: "I established [Ganden]tegchenling in order to teach the Dharma. Monks have joined in order to practice the profound teaching of the Mahāyāna and the Vajrayāna. [It will be] intentionally destroyed by the yellow wind. I have no confidence that the Buddhadharma will remain established here."
>
> Alas! The Lord said, "If Yeke Küriy-e is continually resettled in the wrong location, eventually it will become a city of female slaves (*bron mo*)!" He would say this again and again. Nowadays, old people are repeating this. If I think about it, since current events are simply the ripening of karma, what can I do?[24]

Again, in these late pages in *The Golden Book*, Zava Damdin finds occasion to insert his times into stories about one of the Fifth's particularly opaque forewarnings:

> While slapping his fingers on the throne and displaying sadness, he said:
>
> *A re!* All of you have not thought carefully enough! In the future, all bad circumstances will appear from [receiving gifts from the Qing emperor]!
>
> Until now, even scholars could not elucidate the meaning of that prophecy. Today, even an old shepherd could explain it![25]

While there are many more examples than these in Zava Damdin's late histories, their general meaning is summarized in a concluding note about the Fifth Jebtsundamba.

The Lord said:

> All of you [listen]! The understanding of higher persons will become lower,
>   and the understanding of lower persons will become higher.
> Higher beings will become scared of lower beings.
> If it turns out not to happen like this, this will be better.
> We can only hope, as we have no other options!

> Since ancient times, [Mongol, Tibetan, and Chinese peoples] acted in accor-
> dance with the Two Systems of religion and politics. In the future, if we change
> this behavior at the main monastic seat of Yeke Küriy-e, then higher and lower
> beings will come to misunderstand each other. That sort of degeneration all
> started after the Lord of Refuge [the Fifth Jebtsundamba] passed away.[26]

The Fifth Jebtsundamba's death was thus, according to *The Golden Book*, the
beginning of the end of the enlightened organization of human society. The
real and the empty began to unbraid due to the heedlessness of Urga's lay
and monastic residents. The contexts for proximity and self- and community cultivation inaugurated by Zanabazar and routinized by the Fourth and
Fifth Jebtsundambas had become tearful memory.

In a rare message of hope to readers of *The Golden Book*, suggesting that at
the very least there was something pious to do in light of this terrible situation, Zava Damdin implores: "Nowadays, all of us who follow [the Fifth Jebtsundamba's] advice must practice and protect the Dharma.... We should
not live by means of wrong livelihood, should make effort [in virtuous prac-
tice], and increase the Mahāyāna and Vajrayāna teachings of the Jamgön
Lama [Tsongkhapa]. In this way, we can repay the kindness of the Revered
Father."[27] Still, the picture remained grim. As he says remorsefully, "[today]
our religion has become killing."

But what of the Sixth to Eighth Jebtsundambas, those humans who only
wore the robes and adopted the name of the enlightened? If they could not
be categorized as "holy beings," what were they?

In Zava Damdin's view, their fraudulence—and the Qing imperial collapse
generally—was a product more than a cause of the disenchantment of Eurasia. They represented the occupation of the empty enlightened by the
human real alone. Thus, any of the purificatory possibilities associated with
proximity and interiority that had organized frontier Géluk practice for
centuries (and Buddhist life in general among "Mongol" communities

FIGURE 5.6 Young Bogd Khan (painting), religious leader of all Mongolia, National Central Museum, Ulaanbaatar (1930s).
Digital copies of glass plate negatives preserved in the Archives for Cinema, Photography, and Sound Recording, Mongolia [1910s–1950s]. EAP264/1/9/3/9.

spread between India, Khotan, and the Pacific for millennia before) were negated. Zava Damdin writes that in the ninety years since the enlightened Fifth passed away, his throne had been occupied only by scoundrels and imposters, responsible for "pulling the Buddhadharma down by its feet." In a requisite scholastic move, his interpretation is bolstered by authoritative scripture and logic. He cites from a variety of Tibetan authors similarly critical of the excesses and abuses of the incarnate *trülku,* a tradition that gave

Inner Asia so many "living buddhas" and enlightened khans and emperors. Zava Damdin is at pains to note that incarnation of the enlightened, and even their occasional enthronement in monastery and palace, occurred in the past as a spontaneous outcome of enlightened experience. He does not doubt that buddhas exist or that they express their enlightenment by taking embodiment among sentient beings. His critique of events and figures after the Fifth Jebtsundamba, told by citing authoritative Tibetan authors, is about how corrupt the institution of incarnation had become.

His sources in *The Golden Book* include a number of Géluk figures who lived on the Sino-Mongol-Tibetan frontiers of Amdo and Kham between the seventeenth and nineteenth centuries. For example, from Réla Trülku's autobiography (Rwa bla sprul sku):

> After a lama passes away people stop making donations. For some of his student-attendants, who think only about this life, the thought naturally arises:
>
>> Since this lama passed away
>> we will no longer receive donations.
>> So if we identify an incarnation of the previous lama
>> we will receive many donations
>> and we will therefore not have to rely on others for food and clothing.[28]

Réla Trülku continues by lamenting that these worldly attendants simply choose a nice-looking and intelligent young boy and call him the incarnation, a particularly debased act since this inspires the laity to offer whatever little money, clothing, and wealth they have to the boy as if he were an actual Refuge and Protector. Reflecting on his own identification as a *trülku*, which Réla Trülku considered invalid and politically expedient, he writes that any parents and attendants who subject a young boy to becoming a recognized incarnation must be "either demons or nonvirtuous friends."[29]

Another representative example quoted in *The Golden Book* is the scathing assessment of *trülku*s by Gungtang Tenpé Dronmé (Gung thang bstan pa'i sgron me, 1762–1823). In *The Golden Book,* Zava Damdin uses Tenpé Dronmé's tongue-in-cheek praise to "living buddhas" writ large as a very directed attack against the Sixth to the Eighth Jebtsundambas, and thereby against all those who claim enlightened names and privilege in a disenchanted world.

To the great lama who sits at the front of the monastic assembly,
to the incarnation who is like a fake flower,
and to those who are like a simple dancer
wearing the mask of scholars and practitioners:
before guiding others, you must guide yourself!

In these ways, Zava Damdin's decades-long investigation of the Eurasian historical record led him to this prognostication of the post-Qing situation: this was a crisis provoked by the unwinding of secular and religious authority, the enlightened had retreated from the human stage, and the necessary scales of proximity to purifying masculine centers required to reproduce Buddhist life had collapsed. The long enchantment of Eurasia, a story extending back to the Buddha and heavily featuring "Mongols," had now ceased, most likely irreversibly.

At stake in all these scattered laments, just as it had been for party leaders hoping to render living buddhas killable, was the status and definition of "those who are called a holy person" in the postimperial period. Those bodies of monks and emperors who previously had been enlivened by enlightened presence now moved only according to the *saṃsāric* time of the human real. Such were the causal mechanics of disenchantment of Eurasia. An ocean of blood had swept away an ocean of milk. The prospects for the religious life in the ruins of the Qing were dismal indeed, incoherent in light of insufferable forms of social mobility, violence, lay-monastic mixing, and especially, perverted scientific knowing.

SIX

Blood

Regarding this project [*The Golden Book*], you must not give up on completing the remainder. Since it now appears that in the future others will not be able to finish it, by all means finish the writing yourself!

—PALDEN LOZANG OF TRASHI KHYIL MONASTERY
TO ZAVA DAMDIN

Playing on the still strong religious feelings of the *arat*, the lamas strove to arouse in the people a distrust and enmity toward the new system, to make them fight for their interests. But life dethroned the old idols, conquered superstition and dispersed the religious narcotic, displaying that behind the slogans of the Buddhist monks for a crusading campaign there was nothing except weak anger and hatred toward the democratic system. Gradually, the people stopped treating the lamas as a God-chosen order beyond the judgment of the common people.

—LUDMILLA K. GERASIMOVICH

The young crystal child of the east will thrice milk a painted cow.
On the first try, the "three whites" [milk, curd, and butter]
will flow and be put to use.
On the middling and last attempt, instead of milk and the rest,
blood will flow.

—PROPHECY BY DRAKPA GYELTSEN (1619–1656),
QUOTED IN *THE GOLDEN BOOK*

UNLIKE THE USUAL, embattled markers of the modern and modernization, Zava Damdin's oeuvre unwinds a story of postimperial Eurasia from elsewhere, beyond the national subject and its histories, territories, communities, and agencies. His unique interpretation of when, how, and why the enlightened had left the human stage was his periodization of the Qing-socialist transition. This final chapter explores the ways that Zava

Damdin wrote post-Qing Inner Asia society in the bloody wake of that departure.

Like so much of his *Collected Works*, Zava Damdin's writings on new currents in revolutionary Mongolia, on religious and social life in a newly disenchanted world, are the only surviving descriptions of equal scope and purpose by a monastic of that era. They are partial and idiosyncratic but still invaluable, offering an unparalleled view of modernist development from within the embattled interpretative and social places of the *datsang* monastic colleges. Unlike in archives of interrogation records and trial proceedings, where monks could speak only about their crimes, in his letters, polemics, and histories Zava Damdin could speak on his own terms and deploy other discourse, if always guardedly. In such traces we also see how indebted the better-known authors of revolution in Mongolia were to conservative monastic leaders such as Damdin who remained outside the party and never adopted the master moral narratives of nation, history, progress, the individual, religion, race, proletariat emancipation, and the like. Nor did he adopt the knowledge practices that claimed to know those social categories using methods like ethnology or philology. Empiricism and the hard sciences represented an especially unbearable affront. Of greatest consequence for illuminating a fuller picture of Buddhist and social thought at the underside of modernization in Asia, Zava Damdin did not periodize his times using contact with European tradition as an epochal break. Such contact, couched in words like "revolution" and "progress" that he never used, was for him only the debris of an otherwise, grander story of disenchantment and departure that began with the last breaths of the Fifth Jebtsundamba.

Like the rest of his writing examined in these pages, Zava Damdin's interpretations of the revolutionary present came not in dedicated works or chapters but in short asides, tangents, and notes made in passing spread over dozens of texts and some two thousand folios. Faint laments and shallow sighs break suddenly into narratives about the legendary exploits of the Sixteen Arhats, the qualities of special stamps, and the movement of felt temples for the Mongolian *saṃgha*. Gathering them together in the following pages illuminates a rough and often incoherent response to the post-Qing world. Here is one man making sense of quickly moving times, using resources from his past and from his present, rarely advancing a consistent critique. He wrote anxiously in different contexts and periods on what he thought was wrong with the post-Qing situation, before he was made to speak for others in Soviet histories, Buddhist revivalist movements, and splintered transnational Géluk politics hashed out in cyberspace or Dharma center board meetings in Switzerland, Beijing, or Vancouver. Here is what he wrote long before he was reborn to speak for himself anew.

The Post-Qing Situation

Just as he did when diagnosing the deep and near causes of the Qing collapse, to understand revolutionary events Zava Damdin regularly turns to a small corpus of prophetic sources, supplemented in places by visionary pronouncements attributed to important Géluk lamas of his frontier, imperial-era predecessors. The works of Trülku Drakpa Gyeltsen, today infamous for his associations with the Dorjé Shukden schism, are central, as are "elegant sayings" (Tib. *legs bshad*) literature on matters political by figures like Nāgārjuna and Sakya Paṇḍita. The Kālacakra tantric corpus, the *Root Tantra of Mañjuśrī*, and the Vinaya and Abhidharma canonical collections also provided Zava Damdin with a critical arsenal. So too did many unattributed statements by the Buddha and "ancient lamas," as well as oral tradition and local legend.

Zava Damdin never identifies a revolutionary-era political event, figure, government, or policy by name (other than the reviled Eighth Boɣda Gegegen Jebtsundamba). I have suggested that this was in part self-censorship. Zava Damdin wrote some of his most extensive historical and autobiographical works at a time when his close teachers and peers, such as the Manjushir Khutuɣtu, faced party tribunals and then executioners. Beyond self-censorship and often leaving his late works incomplete (they often read as drafts and unpolished collections of smaller studies), our author was himself struggling to make sense of the world in real time, as a historian and rather global intellectual but also as a monastic leader, a custodian of scholarly tradition, as public ritualist, and as a tantric master. In other words, the crisis of the post-Qing was not only an object of intellectual inquiry for him. It was a radically disorienting set of circumstances that challenged Zava Damdin and others in his milieu to reassert a cohesive and persuasive narrative frame in the absence of the Qing and the Two Systems. And in this, by their own admission, they failed.

Convinced that the enlightened had left the human stage, that disciplines
of proximity could no longer organize Buddhist life, that the "low now controlled the high," Zava Damdin sought to diagnose the bloody, profane state
of his tradition. His characterization of post-Qing degeneracy identifies an
external and internal set of circumstances. The former include foreign military aggression, the influence of "Westerner" science, and unenlightened
state control. The latter include laxity and corruption within the monastic
order, the aggression of non-Buddhist Muslims and other barbaric peoples
(Tib. *kla klo*) within the Mongol fold, Buddhist reform initiatives, and new,
polluting routes for social mobility among the everyday population.[1]

Zava Damdin concludes chapter 2 of the *Golden Book*, a 1919 composition
entitled "The Manner by Which the Teachings [Came to Mongolia] from India
During the Earlier Spread," with a characteristic warning about ethical
laxity and its consequences lifted from an unidentified sūtra or Vinaya
scripture.

As for how someone enters the monkhood once the Degenerate Age has arrived
and after the results and accomplishments of the Buddha's teachings are complete, it is as follows. As is said in the fragments of former prophecies [by the
Buddha],

At that time, the Subduer's teaching
will completely disappear.
Monks, novices, and
nuns will become miserly and
will forever engage in
wrongdoing and deception.
That will be a thoroughly impure time.
My teachings will no longer remain.
[Monastics] will seek out a house and a wife.
At that time, the laity will scrutinize other's wives
and have affairs.
At that time, only the signs and names [of practitioners] will persist.
All of their resentments will come from habit.
They will harm one another, and
heretics will suppress most [of them].
All the gods will also cause harm.

As this says, the fourfold *saṃgha*[2] will break their respective ethical discipline and disagree with one another, which will in turn become the cause for heretical barbarians to overpower them and for the gods and Dharma Protectors to punish them. . . . After I depart for nirvāṇa, many sentient beings will arise and most ordinary beings, by their nature, will follow teachers [who preach] harming others as the Dharma. In that way, they will cut the root of their virtue. The Noble system [i.e., the Buddhadharma] will disappear.

This all describes our present situation.[3]

In the *Golden Book*, such prophetic diagnosis is often connected to the vitality and authority of the absent Two Systems, that central scaffolding of the absent Qing-Géluk formation.

Another representative example comes in *The Golden Book* during a long summary of the biographies of Tibetan Buddhists from the Sakya school, credited with converting the court of the Mongol Empire in the thirteenth century during "The Middling Spread of the Dharma": "Those three [Sakya Paṇḍita, Pakpa Lama, and Chakna Dorjé] all acted with similar loyalty to the Two Systems. Ancient lamas prophesied, 'When political authority (Tib. *rgyal srid*) is lost in China, Tibet, and Mongolia, all three lands will also lose the Buddhadharma.' If you consider this, [it is clear that] the time [anticipated in] this prophecy is now approaching. The knowledgeable should be careful and make effort in virtuous activity!"[4]

Another illustrative example comes from the *Golden Book*'s final sections, a 1931 chapter entitled "The Manner in Which the Yellow Hat Teaching Arrived [in Mongol Lands]:"

Trülku Drakpa Gyeltsen prophesied:

Later, during the Degenerate Age, there will arise a deceptive, nonvirtuous spectacle. The simple-minded will be confused. How worthy of compassion are those [confused beings] who will not realize their situation? At that time, they will be truly crippled on the plane of cyclic existence. They will be unable to find a protector, and they will fall into the abyss of the lower realms. Even though they will walk, they will do so with a stagger.

May I show the path to those miserable ones! Red-faced demons will arise as kings in the borderlands and will destroy Dharmic law, and the miserable will wander everywhere. At that time, may I emanate as a Dharma Minister and influence the king's power!

This has all come exactly true, just as it was said.

For this reason, what should we do now that the Reviving Hell has transferred into the land of humans here and now? It is as Welmang Paṇḍita has said:[5]

E MA HO!

The Triple World is impermanent like an autumn cloud.
Beings are born and die as if they were attending a dance.
The life of sentient beings is like lightning in the sky,
and moves swiftly like a waterfall on a steep mountain face.
Whatever is gathered is dispersed and whatever is collected is lost.
In the end, whatever is superior becomes very weak.
Whoever is born will eventually die.

At that time, Dharma is the only protector, so be careful, accept and reject the white and black activities [respectively]!

We should think carefully about the excellent meaning of this advice, and we must be careful with karma and its result.[6]

Elsewhere, the possibility of manipulating karmic causality to survive, or perhaps even reverse, the crisis of the post-Qing situation seems more remote. From another 1931 chapter entitled "The Manner by Which the Two Systems Came to Abide in the Center of Hor [i.e., Khalkha]" in *The Golden Book*, we read:

According to Glorious Nāgārjuna:

If one correctly practices the system of human law (*mi chos*) it is not a long way to travel to the god realm. If you climb the ladder from the human realm to the god realm, liberation is not far off!

That being said, nowadays all high and low beings, monastics and laity alike, in general practice the Ten Nonvirtuous Actions, and especially those actions that reverse the yoke of Dharma and politics. We can see directly with our own eyes the suffering that is uninterruptedly experienced because of the turning of the wheel of disease, weapons, and famine. This is like experiencing the sufferings of the Three Lower Realms.[7]

As for all this, it is a reality that the distinguishing feature of the karma of the world's inhabitants is that the results of actions are infallible and that the three true meanings of the Buddha's instructions and prophecies really come true!

Of this, it is also said in the *Transmission of the Vinaya*:[8]

> As for what was previously not custom or Dharma, today it has become famous as [our] customs and [our] Dharma.

This is said again and again [in the scriptures]. As it says in the *Sūtra on the Application of Mindfulness*:[9]

> Because of actions that function as a condition to split the customary and Dharma traditions—[such as when] the living beings of the world do not respect rulers or chieftains, do not respect father or mother, do not respect virtuous protectors or Brahmins, do not respect gods or lamas, and so forth— the demons of the black side of the world and the power of humans and non- humans in demonic abodes spread while the gods of the white side of the world and the power of humans and nonhumans in the godly abodes decline.

This is said again and again.[10]

The Problematic Visibility of "a People"

Zava Damdin regularly identifies the increased social mobility of the Mongolian *arad* masses as a defining, lamentable quality of the postimpe- rium. In People's Party Congresses occurring elsewhere in Urga, the pro- letariat were being lionized in the moral narratives of class emacipation. Zava Damdin saw only a disordering of the requisite scales of proximity between laity and monastics, commoner and nobility, enlightened and *saṃsāric* that had been so fully manifest in the Qing-Géluk formation. He had lived that reality in the early part of his life, while seeing Mañjuśrī in the sky and sitting in the shade of the Bodhi tree in emanated Chinese temples while the awed faithful poured praise and riches upon him. In the *The Golden Book*, after a section describing the hereditary rulers of Zava Damdin's *ayimaɣ*, he writes, "The sovereign Mañjuśrī Emperor praised the successive Tüshiyetü Khans as the rulers of Khalkha."[11] As the noble blood of Chinggis flowed into the revolutionary present, however, its course had become dangerously redirected.

Nowadays, as it is said in Lhatsün Jangchup Ö's *Letter That Reverses Mantra:*[12]

> Increasing copulation creates disorder in human lineages;
> increase liberation, and by this, stop sleeping [with] goats and sheep!

It is now the case that nearly everyone, from lamas and rulers to everyday monks and laypeople, are adulterers (*byi bo byed mkhan*). Consequently human lineages have become confused in both the center and the borderlands. Of this, it is said, "The father's sons are only a very few, [while] the mother's sons are everyone!" Because such faulty deeds have now descended upon us, we should all feel very shameful!

The rulers of ancient India, China, Mongolia, and Tibet made extremly strict laws [on this matter]. The purpose was not just to murder children, but to stop [the people from] entering the doorway of copulation that counts as sexual misconduct. As it says here, [to do this] is to sever the tradition of the [Sixteen] Pure Human Laws.[13] Because of this, do not disparage the laws of such kings as being the base actions of misbehaving humans. . . .

In earlier times, rulers together with their ministers and subjects generally abided by the Ten Virtuous Actions, and in particular by the Sixteen Pure Human Laws. Thus [they upheld] the glorious Two Systems. This was the means by which, from the point of view of what seemed merely like a diversion, they traveled in stages along the right path to truly high and definite [i.e., better rebirth and liberation].[14]

Elsewhere in his late historical writing, Zava Damdin had been preoccupied with defining "holy beings" in the post-Qing situation. His prodigious efforts turned up nothing but charlatans with the robes, thrones, and names of the enlightened. Similarly, in many passages such as the above, he was intent on investigating, perhaps even influencing and managing, a problematic ambiguity between nobility and commoners and between monastics and the laity. A quite related set of intolerably confused categories was more specific to his revolutionary era and to his own intellectual itinerancy: the polluted mixing of monastery and scientific academy, of monk and scientist, and of worlds known by scholastic interpretation and empiricism.

Like Feeding Milk to Snakes: The Perils of Buddhist Reform

The object of Zava Damdin's critique in this regard was a series of Buddhist reform movements that developed in revolutionary Buryatia and Mongolia over the course of the Boγda Khaγanate and the early years of the socialist period. For a few years, cultural elites both in the monastery and in party offices (or, as was often the case, progressive monastics and lay Buddhists working for the party) debated the nature, structure, and potential of Buddhism to contribute to a rationalized, equitable, nationalized, and progress-oriented future in Inner Asia. Progressive Buryat literati played a central role in the Buddhist scene of post-Qing Mongolia. Their clique managed the interface not only of globally circulating human and natural sciences with Buddhism but also of a nascent Buddhology and Orientalist scholarship with scholastic knowledge and knowledge practice.

These drivers of monastic reform in Buryat and Mongol communities in the nationalist and socialist revolutionary period were a group of Siberian intellectuals known as the "Buryat Intelligentsia," a name coined in 1956 by Robert Rupen, who first introduced this group to scholarly audiences outside of the Soviet sphere. Members were usually educated in the Russian academy. Though the monumental fact remains as yet little studied, some were among the earliest native ethnographers and indigenous Asianist scholars trained in the human sciences and then deployed to study their homelands. This group had its origins in the pioneering careers of two late nineteenth-century Buryat scholars: Dorji Banzarov (1822–1855) and Galsan Gomboev (1822–1863). It was Banzarov who produce the Mongolian translation of Faxian's pilgrimage tale that Zava Damdin later brought into Tibetan to such interesting effect. The more widely known of the Buryat Intelligentsia were Batudalai Ochirov (1875–1934), Mikhai Bogdanov (1878–1919); Agvan Dorjiev (1854–1938), Elbekdorji Rinchino (1885–1937), Gombojab Tsybikov (1873–1930), Badzar Baradin (1878–1937), and Tseveen Jamsrano (1880–1942).[15]

Their deeply politicized intellectual projects were far ranging, sometimes contradictory, and unevenly affiliated with shifting sources of power and patronage in Russia and Mongolia. For these reasons, members of this fraternity have been memorialized individually and together as nationalists, pan-Mongolists, Buddhist reformers, Russian (tsarist and Soviet) agents, and less nefariously, as scholars and educators of high accomplishment who eventually became victims of revolutionary events.[16] Involved in Buryat nationalist movements in the early twentieth century and then in autonomous Mongolia under the Jebtsundamba Khutuγtu after 1911, many of these scholars retreated to Buryatia when Chinese and White Russian forces occupied Urga between 1919 and 1921. Responding to the Russian revolution of November 1917, some of this loosely affiliated group formed the Buryat National Committee (Rus. Burnatskom) in support of the provisional government and in order to once again advance the cause of Buryat and pan-Mongolian autonomy.[17]

Dismissed as "bourgeois nationalists" by the Soviets after they swept into Siberia, this group disbanded and refocused their efforts on forming the socialist Mongolian People's Party (renamed the Mongolian People's Revolutionary Party in 1924) in cooperation with subversive Khalkha cells already organizing in Urga. In the retrospective words of one of them, "[We] constituted the cultural *avant-garde* among Mongolian tribes, introducing and leading the revolutionary ideas of our time."[18] The fermentation of those ideas began in response to a politics of land and territory that pushed back against forced Slavic migration and the advances of the Orthodox Church. In time their dissident projects inspired progressive debates across Inner Asia and integrated Inner Asia into such debates in Russia and, at mid-century, the People's Republic of China. Recurring topics of inquiry for the Buryat Intelligentsia included the nature of nomadic existence, clan and tribal organization, the issue of russification, political autonomy, the judicial system, military service, education, language, epic and literature, religion, socialism, universal suffrage, and even women's rights.[19]

As the Buryat National Committee was dismissed by the Soviets and the platform of the Mongolian People's Party was drafted, many members continued to think about what the place of Buddhism would be in a new, post-imperial Inner Asia. Tseveen Jamsrano, for example, was the author of the Mongolian socialist platform and a great systematizer, interpreter, and reformer of Buryat-Mongolian tradition. He became a key member of the Mongolian delegation that negotiated the Kyakhta Treaty in 1915 among Mongolia, Russia, and China. "Given that the talks were being attended by these people, with Russian and European educational background, it was possible to conduct negotiations with a full legal understanding of alien terms such as sovereignty, suzerainty, and autonomy."[20] Closer to home, Jamsrano contributed to the Buryatatskii Nacional'nyi Komitet (Buryat

FIGURE 6.1 One of the founders of the Mongolian Academy of Sciences, Jamsran Tseveen (a photo copy) (1940s).
Digital copies of glass plate negatives preserved in the Archives for Cinema, Photography, and Sound Recording, Mongolia [1910s–1950s]. EAP264/1/10/1/144.

National Committee), a short-lived autonomous government created in Buryatia after the October Revolution in 1917.

Jamsrano also made Buddhism inseparable from the Mongolian national subject. Not only was the Dharma and Buddhist social infrastructure implicit in the unity of a broad Mongol national family, he regularly declared, these were its very precondition, the "shelter of the national spirit." After 1921, Jamsrano was also among the most vocal advocates for keeping Buddhism centered in socialist reforms planned for the Soviet

Union and the Mongolian People's Republic. "Seeing that the basic aims of our Party and of Buddhism are both the welfare of the people," he once wrote, "there is no conflict between the two of them. . . . . Our Party wants to see the Buddhist Faith flourishing in a pure form, and approves of lamas who stay in their lamaseries, reciting the scriptures and faithfully observing their vows."[21]

FIGURE 6.2 Agvan Dorjiev at the Second Global Buddhist Assembly, December 22, 1925. Archive of A. I. Breslavce, Moscow, Russia.

Another reformist figure of similar stature and goals was the abbot, diplomat, and scholar Agvan Dorjiev, whose letter challenging Zava Damdin's histories we have encountered already. In a 1905 correspondence with the Buryat National Culture Society, Dorjiev wrote of the need for Buddhist scholasticism to accommodate the fruits of European modernity, especially the sciences:

> Without appropriating the global human culture which takes more and more prominence today, our lamas are definitely unable to follow the Buddhist religion properly. Without knowledge of the general cultural norms and ideas they won't be able to spread their religion both within their nation and among other peoples as well. They lack the knowledge to do it. That is the reason why our lamas need to study European sciences. They need to learn mathematics, natural sciences, cosmology, and so forth.[22]

Jamsrano and Dorjiev worked for years in the Soviet Union and the Mongolian People's Republic to modernize Buddhist monasticism, and scholastic education specifically, to meet modernist challenges and possibilities.

To the reformers among the Buryat Intelligentsia and their collaborators in Mongolia, a revitalization of Buddhism's institutions and practices was sorely needed. Anya Bernstein summarizes the aims of what became known simply as the "reform movement" (Rus. *obnovlencheskoye dvizhenie*) as remaking the administrative system of Buddhism, eliminating excess wealth from monasteries, emphasizing monks' adherence to the rules of the Vinaya, opening secular schools at monasteries, and using contemporary European literature on Buddhism.[23]

While the general scope of the reform movement may have been shared, the reforms that actually took place were always local and motivated by charismatic individuals, small clusters of monasteries, and regional political desires often working at cross-purposes with Bolshevism. Rupen claimed that the "Buryat attachment to collective land ownership resulted in a built-in sympathy for 'socialism,'" but elsewhere in Buryatia the revolution was received without such sympathy.[24] Amid a trend of forming local Buryat nationalist movements and polities,[25] antisocialist regional political groups also articulated and legitimated their agendas by drawing upon new discourses of "original Buddhism" and nationalism. A particularly fascinating example comes from east of Lake Baikal, in Khori Aimag. There, in reaction to the events of 1917, a consortium of nobles and clergy elevated the monk Samdan Tsydenov to the position of "Dharmarāja of the Three Worlds and a Holder of the Religious and Civil Spheres of Authority." Nikolay Tsyrempilov has shown how Tsydenov's anti-Bolshevik theocratic polity, soon crushed by Soviet authorities, initiated its own Buddhist reform initiatives that elaborately fetishized the tsarist Russian state and its deposed political leaders.[26]

Of the many goals of the Buddhist reform movement in Mongolia during the early socialist period, the issue of harmonizing European secular education with "traditional Mongol culture" (in ways expressed by Dorjiev in his letter to the Buryat National Culture Committee above) was paramount. Baradin, for example, wanted to introduce European science into the traditional monastic curriculum in order to oppose "the 'vulgar and superstitious Lamaism' to the 'pure' Indian Buddhism and insisting on viewing Buddhism not as a religion but as an ethical philosophy with Buddha not as a god but as an ingenious thinker and philosopher."[27]

Whatever their differences, this earlier generation of Buryat visionaries remained committed to creating policies through which Buddhist monastic education could be reformed in harmony with the techno-rationalist and egalitarian ideology of state socialism. Medicine, literacy, printing, and the structures of economic and political hegemony would be pulled from the grip of monastic estates and the private holdings of living buddhas and moved into a rationalized public sphere directed by the people's party. Such reforms would begin by standardizing and recentering literary Mongolian (instead of Tibetan) and introducing nonmonastics and non-Buddhist subject matter into the monastic curriculum. Plans to hybridize monastic colleges by involving the laity and secular European education inspired Jamsrano to look for direction in a letter to the most prominent and accomplished scholar of his time, Zava Damdin.

The details of Zava Damdin's personal relationship with the layman Jamsrano remain unclear; they knew each other and shared a long history of intellectual exchange. In 1912 Jamsrano was headmaster of Urga's few nonmonastic schools and in 1913 he directed *The New Mirror*, Mongolia's first secular newspaper. In the pages of *The New Mirror*, Zava Damdin read Ramstedt's article on the Turkic origins of the Mongols and Cahun's *La bannière bleue*, which he translated into Tibetan and included as evidence for the deep history of the Mongol real in *The Golden Book*. Jamsrano was also responsible for forming scientific associations in Urga, such as the Institute for Scripts and Letters, of which Zava Damdin was an early member. That Zava Damdin spoke personally and on multiple occasions to Shcherbatsky, Tubyansky, and other European Orientalist scholars probably also included Jamsrano in some way, since the Buryat was an accomplished field researcher and textualual scholar who often acted as go-between for foreign scholars wanting to work in Mongolia.[28]

I have been able to locate only one undated version of Jamsrano's letter exchange with Zava Damdin on the matter of restructuring monastic education, that central issue for Buddhist reformers in post-Qing and post-tsarist Inner Asia, as well as in late-colonial Sri Lanka and Burma, imperial Japan, and Republican China. Jamsrano's fascinating letter to Damdin on reviving monastic education was translated from Mongolian into Tibetan for posterity and preserved in volume 1 (*ga*) of the latter's seventeen-volume *Collected Works*.[29] The eight-folio text contains both Jamsrano's inquiry and Zava Damdin's reply and is titled *The Amber Rosary: A Reply to the Knowledgeable Translator Tséwang's Consultation* (hereafter: *The Amber Rosary: Mkhyen ldan lo tsā ba tshe dbang gi gros lan spos shel phreng ba*).

Jamsrano's project, described in verse to Zava Damdin, was to use the riches of homegrown Buddhist monastic education to counter the loss of Buryats and Mongolians who were leaving Mongolia and Buryatia for advanced studies in foreign academic institutions. Having left, Jamsrano laments, they "end up forgetting the detailed meaning of our holy Dharma system. They no longer study or contemplate [the Dharma] in even a cursory way." Most egregiously, "this becomes the reason certain people adopt wrong views."[30]

Jamsrano reveals to Zava Damdin that he feels obligated to build a local school "in order to stop" the revolutionary-era brain drain.[31] Jamsrano had in mind a hybrid monastic college whose cohorts of "Buddhist and non-Buddhist monks and laity" would study not in Tibetan but in Mongolian. Upon graduation, alumni would be able to "greatly benefit both politics and religion . . . and provide both direct and indirect service to non-Buddhist and Buddhist countries."[32] For a conservative figure like Zava Damdin, Jamsrano's school was profoundly disruptive not just because of the hybrid curriculum. The mixed student body was intolerable. Both monks and laymen, and therefore neither from our abbot's perspective, Jamsrano's students were an ideal type being imagined across Buddhist reform initiatives as a "black [i.e., lay] lama" (Mong. *khara lam*).[33]

To extend the curricula and traditional social boundaries of the Buddhist monastery to meet such radical expectations and goals, Jamsrano guilelessly proposes to Zava Damdin that teams of translators chosen by the latter hasten to translate logical texts from the Tibetan-language Géluk scholastic program into Mongolian so that they could be studied in his new school. "You are a paṇḍita who is knowledgeable in the five major fields of knowledge, and also you have many scholar-students. Please, could you share the names who would be suitable, [especially those] with the ability to translate monastic manuals on logic. Could you write to us who would be most suitable to translate which text?"[34] A note is inserted by an unknown hand at the end of Jamsrano's letter explaining that it had been sent to Zava Damdin to discuss his newly established school for Mongolian, Russian, and other foreign laypeople and monks to study logic and epistemology in the Mongolian language.[35]

Also written in verse and included in *The Amber Rosary*, Zava Damdin's response opens with a familiar reverence for Jamsrano. Then come the critiques.

It is amazing that here in our great land, which is now the center of Mongolia,
[where] the political system has become as stable as a vajra rock,
there is now a general school [that teaches] Buddhist and non-Buddhist texts
[and] opens its doors to [people from] the four directions.
Nowadays, the desire to benefit Buddhadharma and sentient beings
is difficult to find even among the highest-ranking monks.
From among all nonbiased scholars, who would not admire
this motivation that you, a layperson, [possess]?[36]

At first amiable, Zava Damdin's response soon assaults Jamsrano's proposal to blur the boundaries between the curricula of monastic colleges and "everyday (lay) schools" (*slob grwa*). To reaffirm proper scales of proximity and distance, predictably, Zava Damdin turns to the authority of received Indian and Tibetan tradition:

If you examine traditions of countries with the unity of Dharma and politics,
such as India, the source of knowledge, and so on,
only the first four of the five major fields of knowledge
are ever taught to the laity, and the laity continually study [only] those subjects.

Even a paṇḍita who knew all five of the major sciences
[at first would] study the [four] general fields of knowledge while a householder.
After becoming a monk, it is against the rules of religion and politics
to intentionally study those first four [fields of knowledge].
That is the reason earlier Indian, Tibetan, and Mongolian
Dharma adepts, kings, and ministers, all those with great wisdom,
never established a tradition of having grammar schools (*yi ge'i grwa*)
teach topics like monastic manuals about logic
or having novice and fully ordained monks join [such mundane schools].
If monks and lay students mix, it is like [mixing] milk and water;
they will be no shame or modesty between them.
They will look down on, condemn, criticize, scorn, and slander [each other],
    and so forth.
Many objectionable circumstances, which can harm both religion and politics,
    will arise.
Political leaders who control the Dharma and Dharma leaders who control
    politics
are both very inauspicious signs.

All this is clarified in the *History of Buddhism in China*, and so forth.[37]

In addition to the "shame" of mixing lay with monastic students, Jams-rano's proposed reforms would disrupt the entire course of monastic study and limit the possibility of salvation itself:

In India, there were never Buddhist or non-Buddhist monks who studied in
    [lay] schools.
When the Buddha did study in an everyday school, he was not turning the
    Wheel of the Dharma;
we also have to consider the reason for this.
Specifically, the reason for gradually practicing the Threefold Training
in the supreme Teacher's system is to study the Tripiṭaka in stages.
First you must receive vows, then you can study.
The Buddha never gave a layperson permission to join a [monastic] class
about the Vinaya, even if they were a holy being.
As for barbarians and non-Buddhists, there is no question [that they cannot
    join such a school]![38]

In addition to compromising monastic purity contra received tradition, Jamsrano's proposal contains a more fundamental defect, in Zava Damdin's view: it ignores karmic causality, the fundamental mechanics of monastic and lay life.

> Although the laity do occasionally stay in this monastery, that is only because an administrator did not follow the rules properly.
> If you look at any monastery's constitution (bca' yig),
> there has clearly never been a tradition of nonmonastics staying permanently in a monastery.
> What's more, [when a] student studies the life story of a Buddhist or non-Buddhist teacher,
> if their karmic potentialities (bag chags) awaken, they are powerless to not become a follower of the Buddha.
> If they do not have such potentialities, even if we teach them the vast and profound Dharma,
> like giving milk to a snake, it is possible to destroy our own and other's enlightenment.
> Therefore, in this situation both scholars and the stupid must be careful![39]

The effect of all this, in Zava Damdin's damning rejection, is to kill the very liberatory potential of Buddhist monastic education in a fool's rush to accommodate the values and forms of (foreign) socialist reform.

> In conclusion, if in a lay school we teach logical texts, how to rely on a spiritual teacher, and so forth,
>
> We must do so according to the Vinaya.
> In this case, the student body must be monks, as I mentioned earlier.
> We already have a monastery, so we do not need a new, separate school.
> If we do not care about how to rely on a spiritual teacher, and so forth,
> is it enough to just teach [students] the black letters?
> If we do so, we destroy the root of knowledge and
> incur the fault of burning the Buddhist teaching in a great fire.

. . . .

In previous times, because of the nature of their activities,
some people who served the Buddhadharma created more harm than benefit,
or else created temporary benefit but long-term harm.
That is why it is better to have self-control![40]

In these ways, Zava Damdin leverages the weight of received tradition to reject Jamsrano's innovative project. For Damdin, social personae, the mechanics of self- and community cultivation, and the authority of monks and monastery needed clarification, not erosion, in the post-Qing period.

A final example of monastic reform being deployed by interlocutors of Zava Damdin comes from Agvan Dorjiev. By the time of the October Revolution he had spent many years as a vocal advocate for Tibetan and Buryat interests in his capacity as close confidant and tutor to the Thirteenth Dalai Lama, Tupten Gyatso. On the Dalai Lama's behalf, Dorjiev traveled extensively, from the courts of the Qing emperor and the tsar to England, Germany, India, Urga, and France. A reformist in Bolshevist times, Dorjiev developed a new alphabet for the Buryat people that he hoped would promote ethnic unity and oppose russification.[41] He also wrote prefaces to books intended for Buryat youth on the virtues of literacy, diligence, and right conduct.

Like other Buryats and Mongols involved in early socialist-inspired Buddhist reforms and nationalist projects, Dorjiev would soon succumb to hardline factions and endure a series of arrests and, eventually, death in a Soviet prison. Dorjiev wrote his autobiography (one of the few of his works currently available) sometime after the 1917 revolution.[42] It offers a rare glimpse of Buddhist ecclesiastical accomodations amid the ever-changing expectations of Bolshevism. Socialism promised a political and social modernity that Dorviev approved of, even if he lamented the fall of the tsar (which he explains in his autobiography as being the result of, variously, Rasputin, Christian ["long beard"] interference, or simply the general corruption of noble classes). As for the Bolsheviks themselves, Dorjiev wrote with cautious (perhaps guarded, given the political climate) optimism, while still being willing to acknowledge and deride the violence that had followed upon the revolution:

Out of pity for the worn out, impoverished people, the officials, chiefs, rich people and merchants, the great exploiters who oppressed the poor people,

were destroyed without a trace. Lenin (Tib. *le nyin*), the head of the Bolsheviks (Tib. *sbol zhe sbeg*) who intended to take better care of the poor, along
with the many followers, controlled the government. . . . While communism
[Tib. *khom mon*] is a good system, those who gave power to it acted badly, tyr-
annizing everyone at the time when various bad and immoral people entered
the party. Because of those people, communism has acquired a bad name.
Since there were few who practiced communism correctly, they have become
disliked.[43]

Later in his autobiography, Dorjiev describes his efforts to improve the
quality of monastic education and purge corruption in the monastic ranks
of Buryatia (and, by extension, Mongolia and Tibet) in response to the rise
of socialism. At this point, he pauses to muse about just what sort of excesses
had reduced the Buddhist tradition (and monasticism specifically) to such
lows, causing the laity to lose faith, the clergy to mix Buddhism with "shamanism," and the Bolsheviks to condemn their exploitation of the faithful.[44]
Such were the reflections, newly possible in the post-1917 period and eventually leading to firing squads, that occupied ecclesiastical figures and lay
devotees like Dorjiev and Jamsrano.

We Buddhist monks have few desires and are content, even when we need assistance. But, especially in later times in Mongolia, as the groups of monks keeping the monastic discipline grew larger and larger, small numbers did as they
pleased and became extremely attached to wealth and leisure. Some accumulated homes, furnishings and clothing with an even greater sense of attachment
than ordinary people. Some monks, acting shamelessly and without conscience,
did not consider, even in the corner of their thoughts, the rules set down by the
Buddha. When outsiders saw them, they found it easy to confuse their actions
with the Buddha's teachings. The patrons were especially misled by the teachings of lamas who mixed shamanism [with the Buddhadharma]. Many criticized
the monks saying, "All they think about is how happy they will be when the donations for their liturgies are collected."[45]

These sorts of critical reassessments of monastics and their institutions in
light of new and increasingly felt pressures from Soviet centers of power
prompted Buryat Buddhist leaders such as Dorjiev to remake Buddhist
monasticism (or at least, to think about what remaking it would entail). Their

rationale was both anachronistic and defensive. Buddhism needed to return to its puritan, ascetic roots in order to survive. A fundamentalist Dharma and *saṃgha*, not the corrupted superstitions and self-interest of living tradition, would automatically be compatible with new socialist visions of modernity.

It is no coincidence that at this time many lamas in Siberia and Mongolia went to work writing tracts arguing that, among other things, the Buddha had been a materialist, the original anticapitalist, and the forerunner to Lenin.[46]

Empiricism and the Knowledge of Fools

In Agvan Dorjiev's 1923 letter to Zava Damdin on matters of history and the historian's craft, seven of the eight questions leveled pointed challenges to the Khalkha scholar on specific issues of historical interpretation. The Land of Li was Nepal, not Khotan. Mindröl Nonom Han's geographies were a farce. The Mongols had not been Turks.

Dorjiev's final question, the least condescending and sincere of his "queries," turns from past to present, from history to strategy.

VIII.

Especially nowadays in this area,
many people reject the existence of past and future lives.
They accept as valid knowledge[47]
only direct perception (Skt. *pratyakṣa*; Tib. *mngon sum*; Mong. *ile bodatu*)
but not inference (Skt *anumāna*; Tib. *rjes dpag*).[48]
If we can overcome perverted views such as these,
held by those who do not accept [rebirth],
it is possible they might once again become Buddhists.
Since none other than you possess one thousand [wisdom] eyes,
who else could [wield] hundreds of sharp logical reasons
powerful enough to completely obliterate such a wrong view?[49]

Zava Damdin declines to answer Dorjiev's questions directly, but his humble response reveals a shared concern about the threat of exclusively

valuing "direct cognition," by which they mean empiricism, and not inference, by which Buddhist logical texts claim one can validly know about
unseen phenomena like karma, rebirth, and the Buddha's three bodies.
Zava Damdin responds:

VIII.

In ancient times, the King of Subduers, his heirs,
and all Indian paṇḍitas and siddhas used their powers
to defeat barbarian *tīrthika* heretics
using magical displays and the force of their mind.
Whereas the unfortunate, perverted teachings
of the barbarian *tīrthikas* have grown and spread,
nowadays, small-minded people like me
cannot tame even our own minds.
Wishing to tame the minds of others is therefore
an object of ridicule for all gods, demons, and humans.
In the same way, if you do not develop your own insight,
this is just another example of the above.
By taking hold of knowledge and
refuting the false views of opponents,
the intelligent may claim the pride of brave warriors.
But, if most Tibetan and Mongolian practitioners,
successors to the heirs of Śākyamuni,
are haughty, then they harm the Dharma with their speech.
Present-day Europeans,
those who have been forever born in places without the Dharma,
appear as either faithful or stupid.
They read the scriptures and their commentaries strangely.
However, such wrong views
are connected to the Buddha's activities.
An exceedingly wise Mahātman such as yourself
should pray to be reborn in a Pure Land.
I, an uninfluential person,
pursue purification, prayer, and so forth
so that in this life and the next,
I do not come to hold the wrong views of the barbarians.[50]

Their shared concern was not with the contents of non-Buddhist knowledge: both Dorjiev and Zava Damdin made generous, strategic use of European arts and sciences. What was at stake were the *practices* of knowledge they tied to "Europo-Russia" (Tib. *rgya ser*) and "the West" (Tib. *phyogs nu pa*). Empiricism, or valid knowledge gleaned from direct, sense-based cognition, in their scholastic terms, was only a partial accounting of the world. And now it was being enshrined in constitutions, people's platforms, party schools, and the monastic college.

While Zava Damdin demurred in 1923 to employ "the sharp sword of logical reason" against the new legitimacy of empiricism, he was emboldened to make such an attack in various 1919 and 1931 sections of *The Golden Book*. For example, late in the text Zava Damdin pauses to mock the paucity and degeneracy of "European" scientific empiricism with an assuredness that Agvan Dorjiev would have appreciated eight years earlier.

> Today, barbarian non-Buddhists write about typologies of insects and how many fish there are in the four different types of ocean in this world, and so forth. They write about such meaningless and mistaken topics and conceitedly claim they are writing [authentic] commentary [*śāstra*, i.e., that they are producing worthwhile knowledge].
>
> Even if we are just pretending to debate or compose texts, whatever we do, we must focus on the benefits to sentient beings in light of liberation. The Lord of Logic [Dharmakīrti] said in *Commentary on Valid Cognition*:[51]
>
>> They don't know, but teach others.
>> The deluded listen carefully to whatever is said.
>> [Instead], you must find some scholar or Knowledgeable One.
>
> That is why in whatever [non-Buddhist scholars] say, we must investigate whether it can become the cause of enlightenment or not. Whether they know the count of insects or not, this is useless for me. I believe "valid people" (*skyes bu tshad ma*) are people who know which things to accept and which things not to accept, and what is the cause of enlightenment.[52]

In Zava Damdin's effort to define what remains valid, holy, and worthwhile in a post-Qing world, he predictably evokes the authority of the Indian logician Dharmakīrti. The *Commentary on Valid Cognition* was and remains the very bedrock of Géluk scholastic education, providing the contours and modes of logical analysis used to clarify the definitive and interpretative meaning of the Buddhist doctrine (and all other knowledge besides). If all the world is knowable and all knowledge is to be evaluated and ordered, as Cabezón says of Géluk scholastic orientations, then it is *prāmaṇa* logic as interpretative technique that knows such worlds and orders all knowledge.[53] For revolutionary-era scholars like Dorjiev and Zava Damdin, scientific knowledge and the worlds such knowledge described could not be ignored.

In both *The Golden Book* and *The Dharma Conch*, an elementary problem Zava Damdin faced was to reconcile contradictory claims in Buddhist canonical sources regarding the physical layout of the universe and its "contents" (*bcu*, i.e., sentient beings). We have seen already how he described the topography of Eurasia and the vast Mongol communities who had long resided there. In addition, Zava Damdin was deeply concerned to evaluate and synthesize competing cosmological claims in his canonical sources regarding the shape of the world. This was quite unlike the structure of monastic histories he read and other models from the late Qing. Dharmatāla's 1889 *Rosary of White Lotuses*, for instance, begins with a "General Account of the Emergence and Spread of Buddhism in the World."[54] Gushri Tsépel's 1819 *History of Buddhism in Mongolia* begins with the early "enlightened" kings of Tibet, their connection to the *ür*-ruler Mahāsammata, and their work to bring Buddhism there during the Yarlung empire. It quickly becomes apparent that Zava Damdin's attention was aimed at relativizing, if not refuting, the troubling cosmological propositions of European science concerning the objectionable idea that the earth is round.

Zava Damdin delves into this topic in the opening, 1919 folios of the *Golden Book* with a quote from the *Flower Garland Sūtra*[55] on the nature and form of the waters bounding Eurasia whose stories he will soon tell.[56]

In the lands of all directions oceans have appeared;
several are round and several are triangular.
In several directions are [oceans in the shape of a] square.
Moreover, [in the end] it is the ocean of karma
That "writes" the form [of these waters].[57]

This last point is most important for Damdin. It provides a scriptural authority for what I call his "karmic relativity" defense against a threatening empiricism and scientific descriptions of the world.

There are a variety of ways of explaining the number, size, measure, and so forth of the underlying maṇḍala base, the mountains, the oceans, the continents, and so forth in the sūtras and tantras, such as in the "higher" and "lower" Abhidharma,[58] the Kālacakra Tantra, and so on. However, these are never mutually contradictory. Those [topographies] are not established from their own side, but rather they are established from the karma of sentient beings. In our own world, many different oceans, mountains, and islands have all appeared at once. These might appear to the vision of one sentient being, but not another . . . because of this, we cannot object if one sentient being remains blind to what another sees.[59]

This point, which pre-emptively provides an explanation for the contradictions found in the Abhidharma and Kālacakra presentations of the "arrangement of the world and its beings" he is about to describe, is further supplemented by a classic example found in Buddhist sources. He writes that if a god, a human being, and a hungry ghost were to gather in front of one cup of water, "at that time, because of their different karma, for one it would appear as nectar, for one it would appear as water, and for one it would appear as pus. While this is true, we would not say that there is more than one cup of water."[60]

The point of all this is that Buddhist canonical sources describe the world in which we live differently because we experience it differently through karmic veils, the illusory perception as though through so many tinted glasses and hairs in eyes. Therefore, opposing Buddhist scriptures are not invalid, partial, or limited on the topic. Competing accounts are simply tailored to the dispositions of beings. The contradictions are ultimately noncontradictory. They also, it seems, prove their "enlightened" providence, since the assumption is that different presentations depend on an omniscient reading of the karmic potential of any given textual audience. Scientists, whose elementary descriptions of the world and its beings Zava Damdin had read in the pages of *The New Mirror*, possessed no enlightened insight. Most pitifully, they believed that what appeared through the microscope could be accounted for validly.

So, [when] non-Buddhist barbarians use their many different instruments to investigate all over the world, it is not necessary that they see by means of their direct cognition in the same way as is described in the sūtras and tantras. This is so since most of them are obscured by karma and [so the canonical] presentation remains hidden to them. [Additionally, in relation to] some of these [topographical descriptions], their names and objects have changed over time: today they are identified differently, and have different shapes, etc.

This is what leads the superficial intellectuals (*rtog ge pa*) of Europe (*yi wa ro pa*) to use their technologies to describe this world as being shaped like an egg [i.e., round] and continually rotating. They actually believe they perceive this!

[This is all akin to] the "Story of the Eighteen Blind People Describing the Elephant" depicted in the *Compendium of the Great Vehicle*.[61]

According to Zava Damdin, these foreign scientists claim that their tools allow them to produce knowledge about the world only by means of direct cognition (*mngon sum*). He, like Agvan Dorjiev and many Géluk scholars since, characterized empiricism and scientific bodies of knowledge in these terms. But in Géluk scholasticism, direct perception was considered only the most basic kind of knowing. Absent in the scientism so lauded by revolutionary governments was a complementary but critical sort of knowledge based in inference, which could know truths that would ever remain hidden to the obscured senses of *saṃsāric* beings.

Unique to the monastic college, inference had been prized in ages past. The hidden objects it could know included much of the Buddhist tradition that was being abandoned and attacked amid the rationalist advances of Buddhist reformers and socialist agitators: that enlightened beings played the role of men, that lives extend beyond a single body, that medicine enlivened by mantra can cure, that merit and virtue sticks to a mental continuum after it comes into proximity with a monk or monastery, and that social distinctions between laity and monastics, between academy and monastery, between the holy and the mundane, matter.

Conclusion

There is no more important or more difficult work in the world than the work that you, the intellectuals of Mongolia, have so courageously begun. . . . Translate just those European books which give the clearest expression to the principle of activity, of mental exertion, striving for active freedom, not for the freedom of inaction.

—LETTER FROM MAXIM GORKY TO E. BATUKHAN, MAY 19, 1925

AS I TYPE these words in the early summer heat of Southern California, in his revived Gobi Desert monastery Zava Damdin's current incarnation prepares to celebrate the one hundred and fiftieth anniversary of the birth of his previous incarnation, the protagonist of this book. Not just the memory but the person of Zava Damdin remains active today in defining and categorizing the holy in Inner Asia. In the transnational networks that have guided the postsocialist Buddhist revival in Mongolia, and in the folding of empty and real time that once again allows the enlightened to manifest in Inner Asian bodies, Zava Damdin has reappeared. Between his death in the midst of the chaos of the purges and directing an international conference to be held in his predecessor's name today, the "stubborn logician of the north" has continued to give form and history to generations of refugee and diaspora Mongolians, Tibetans, and convert followers from across China, Russia, and the North Atlantic.

Just as Zava Damdin drew on the synthetic scholasticism of Qing-era monks to make sense of his post-Qing world, so too have generations of refugee and revivalist monks used Zava Damdin's synthetic writing to make sense of their transplanted lives, dispersed centers, and memories of violent erasure and suppression. Zava Damdin's hybrid construction of Inner Asian Buddhist narratives, neither of the Qing nor of the socialist nation, has been well suited to fit transplanted people into time. Though his works are often without any attribution to their author, or else with attributions to him

FIGURE C.1 The revived Delgeriin Choira monastery.
Photograph by author.

under different names that isolate them from one another, Zava Damdin's intellectual legacy has been profoundly influential.

Several years ago, already well into this research, I once again made the long journey south from Ulaanbaatar city to the revived Gobi desert monastery of Zava Damdin.[1] This is known today as Delgeriin Choira but was called Chöying Osel Ling (Tib. *Chos dbyings 'od gsal gling*) in the revolutionary period. Over the years I had come to know the small monastic community, many of the local townspeople and herders, and the current incarnation of Zava Damdin, known as Zava Damdin Renbüchi Luwsandarjaa (1976–). On this occasion, Zava Renbüchi sat upon his throne in front of the monastic assembly and a large audience of lay devotees, having just finished several days of prosperity rituals. I was welcomed with tea by the young monks and with kisses from Renbüchi's mother and sister, who lived on site with other lay members of his extended family.

The memory of the previous Zava Damdin, the protagonist of this book, was (and remains) everywhere in that monastery and around the nearby town of Delgertsogt. Zava Damdin's enlightened mind is thought to animate the body of Zava Renbüchi, who regularly wears the tattered robes of his predecessor, as well as a small mustache reminiscent of the many portraits of Zava Damdin that decorate the monastic grounds, local museums, and a public statue in town. A fifteen-foot statue of Damdin dominates the altar space of the main yurt temple wherein we gathered that evening. Everyday items associated with Zava Damdin are treated as contact relics, from the small yurt he once used while on pilgrimage (perhaps to Mount Wutai?) to cooking utensils and a kettle. These are displayed alongside the usual images of buddhas, bodhisattvas, and tantric deities as sacred "supports" for the merit accrual and purification of devotees. Through revived disciplines of proximity in relation to them and to Zava Damdin's incarnation upon the nearby throne, Buddhist selves are once again reproducing in this small stretch of the Gobi.

The material effects of Zava Damdin, like so much of the material culture of Mongolia's postsocialist Buddhist revival (1990 to present), had been recovered from boxes buried in the sand by monks anticipating the purges of the late 1930s or else collected from elderly disciples who kept them in secret during the long socialist period. Some of them, including a very elderly nun attending the ritual events that day, had been present in 1937 as a young girl when monks took the trunks to bury in the desert just before military trucks arrived to take the monks. The legitimacy, contours, and content of this particular postsocialist Buddhist revival are founded in the materiality of Zava Damdin. His prominent display is working to mediate new memories, forms of social relation, and religious sensibilities at Delgeriin Choira Monastery, in affiliated monasteries and organizations across Mongolia, and in transnational hubs of patrons and Dharma centers spread around the world, such as in China, Switzerland, South India, Canada, Korea, and America.[2] For years now, Zava Renbüchi has brought his messaging to mass media, including regular long-form television interviews and a YouTube channel.[3]

My own research interest in the previous Zava Damdin and his historiography had always been warmly received in his revived monastic community, but, I sensed, treated with some misgiving. This was understandable, given the labor of these monks to repair a local tradition erased so ruthlessly within living memory. I was apprehensive upon arriving at the Gobi monastery that particular evening, as I have been many times since, because Zava Renbüchi knew that I had been working on translating and studying his predecessor's historical works. These are valuable cultural commodities that he himself had been translating from Tibetan into modern Cyrillic Mongolian. He and his monks regularly cite their contents as they give shape to their revivalist project, from explaining architectural choices in newly rebuilt temples to ritual programs and the curriculum of Buddhist summer camps for urban youth.

As he warmly inquired about my study that evening, still atop the throne and in front of his large community, the politics and complicated reception of the present research once again became clear. "It is wonderful that you are studying the work of Zava Damdin, but not just anyone can understand the contents of those histories," he reminded me. "Their meaning is profound, and not easily understood by common people." Most pointedly, Zava Renbüchi publicly mused that "Zava Damdin's histories are like a golden key to all history, and must be protected." The comfortable distance that a historian often enjoys between the dead and the place of writing vanished very quickly into the quiet, cool Gobi night. So too did the presumptions of exploring the histories of those affected by state violence in a distant university, quite removed from its traumas, ruins, and buried kettles. Nothing felt natural or comfortable as Renbüchi's words hung in the air in the crowded temple. There I sat, face to face with someone whom all those herders, young monks mumbling prayers, old women prostrating, and city men taking snuff and sipping fermented horse milk (*airag*) considered to be the very subject of my research.

It was a great experience to be so troubled and exposed, then and many times since. In memory of Zava Renbüchi's cautious but ever-warm support over the years (and in humble acknowledgment that the present study will not meet his expectations), I think again of his image of "the golden key to all history" as I finish my writing.The scope of the content of Zava Damdin's writing of society and history, the lost intellectual and religious life they represent, and the dizzying mosaic of sources, lines of inquiry, and historico-philosophic arguments they contain has made developing a cohesive (never mind a comprehensive) analysis difficult, to put it mildly.

In completing this book I have returned often to something Carlo Ginzburg said of the religious imagination of his famous protagonist, the sixteenth-century miller Menocchio: after years of exploring traces of his life and writing, Zava Damdin remains for me "a dispersed fragment, reaching us by chance, of an obscure shadowy world that can be reconnected to our own history only by an arbitrary act. To respect its residue of unintelligibility that resists any attempt at analysis does not mean succumbing to a foolish fascination for the exotic and incomprehensible. It is simply taking note of a historical mutilation of which, in a certain sense, we ourselves are the victims."[4] I feel compelled to acknowledge this victimhood, my mutilation of these sources, to those readers who have been personally affected by and implicated in the desolation of the Qing-socialist transition.

In light of Zava Renbüchi's comments, I take comfort from Zava Damdin's own reflections on the disorienting project of writing the past in a post-Qing world. I feel compelled to echo his self-deprecating apology to readers: "I have traveled to many different countries, been to their libraries, and read many scholarly texts, and all of those I understand. But I know that there are many different texts with many different meanings and many different perspectives, so it is difficult to draw only a single point. As such and because of [the limits of] my understanding, it is possible that I made many mistakes, so please forgive me!"[5]

I also ask forgiveness from those in Mongolia today who have helped with the research for this book but whose challenges, personal histories of violence and struggle, strategic conceptions of a presocialist past, and belief in an enduring national subject are not represented here. Their expectation was that I would write about a little recognized, golden era of the Dharma in Mongolia. Instead, my reading of Zava Damdin's work and my research into its context led to a book about the intersection of local knowledge practices with processes of a world historical order, about anxious creativity in the face of state violence, and about the periodization and interpretation of modernization in Asia beyond the national subject and its histories, territories, and communities. While I have tried to include as much of Zava Damdin's own words in these pages as space and genre would allow, this book is not the compendium of annotated translations my Mongolian friends and hosts expected, but more of what Brian Keith Axel once called "the politics of living the ongoing connections or disjunctures of futures and pasts in heterogenous presents."[6] I apologize sincerely to them for the mixed categories.

Zava Damdin in Global Circulation

The afterlife of Zava Damdin and his ideas are not limited to an ideological form of the Buddhist revival in Mongolia today, nor to the body of a present-day man enchanted by his mental continuum. Zava Damdin's vision of the Dharma, the social site of the monastery, of history, and of Inner Asian community in the Qing ruins—deterritorialized and depoliticized by revolutionary events—has had an enormous impact on narratives produced by Tibetan and Mongolian Géluk scholars writing on religious life in the global diaspora and refugee community over the last eighty years. His works and interpretation, though often not by name and rarely considered together, also continue to influence Euro-American academic representations of Inner Asian Buddhist life as well as the transnational community of converts to the Géluk school.

From the perspective of many in the now globalized Tibeto-Mongolian Buddhist tradition, Zava Damdin was a prolific and prominent figure at the height of Mongolian Buddhism during the late Qing, a firsthand witness of its decline and erasure in the revolutionary period, and a major actor in the reenchantment of Mongolia's troubled postsocialist society. Although Zava Damdin eventually decided that revolutionary events had exceeded history, that reproducing Buddhist life was no longer possible, those who came later were not so burdened. To my knowledge, there are two comprehensive histories of the Dharma in Mongol lands written by Géluk scholars since the purges and the global exodus of Tibetan and Mongolian people. The first is the 1965 *History of the Dharma, a Lamp on Scripture and Reasoning* (Tib. *Chos 'byung lung rigs sgron me*) by the famous Buryat scholar and abbot of the revived Drépung Gomang monastery in South India, Ngakwang Nyima (Tib. Ngag dbang nyi ma, 1907–1990).[7] The other is the 1991 *Transparent Mirror* (Tib. *Dwangs gsal me long*) by Jampel Shérap (Tib. 'Jam dpal shes rab, dates unknown).[8] Both were written by Buryat-Mongol Géluk scholars living in the refugee monastic settlements of the Tibetan community in India, and both use Zava Damdin's histories as authoritative in nearly every regard.

Specifically, this "lamp" and this "mirror" make extensive use of Zava Damdin's works on what I have been calling the deep time of the "real" history of the Mongols, and on that basis, the earliest spread of the Dharma into "Mongol" communities. It seems that the innovative positions Zava Damdin took on the deep history of "Mongol" history using scholastic and newly arriving European sources, which for figures like Agvan Dorjiev were intolerable departures from received tradition, have become a standard reference since the violence of the late 1930s in Mongolia and in the 1950s and 1960s in Tibet. Extensively quoting his revolutionary-era works, Ngakwang Nyima and Jampel Shérap each introduce their story about "Mongol" contact with the enlightened wellsprings of tradition in India and Khotan. They string together quotes by Damdin about the *longue durée* of the enchantment of Eurasia, and "Mongol" agency in the Buddhicization of not just China but also Tibet.[9]

Damdin's claims on the deep time of Mongols and Mongol Buddhism have thus entered into global circulation. Not repeated in these diaspora histories at all are Zava Damdin's extensive theorization about the Qing-Géluk formation as the perfection of the Two Systems, the culmination of history itself. Nor do we see Tibetan or Mongolian scholastics adopt or even reference Damdin's somber argument about the end of enlightened presence on earth. While the Qianlong and Shunzhi emperors may still keep their "Mañjuśrī Emperor" monikers in these diaspora texts, the ambiguity of the imperial ruins that so confounded Zava Damdin goes unmentioned. The crisis he diagnosed in the post-Qing situation—a ruptured contiguity to the masculinized, enlightened centers required to reproduce Buddhist life—seems to have already been repaired for these later authors, who lived and worked in reestablished monastic networks in South India with all requisite proximities intact.

But Zava Damdin's legacy is not confined to revived monastic communities or to his revolutionary-era histories. While he has not attracted any sustained scholarly attention until now, fragments and traces of his oeuvre have long been known to Euro-American Buddhist studies scholars, though often under disconnected authorial names scattered in footnotes in reference to his unusual and prolific work on matters epistemic, logical, and philosophical. For example, his philosophical and tantric commentaries are still prominent in the intellectual culture of Tibetan Géluk philosophical colleges in exile and for that reason have received some scholarly notice. His Madhyamaka commentary, *The Essence*, not only continues to be debated in monastic courtyards but also has been prominently featured in an earlier era of philosophy-heavy American scholarship on Tibetan Buddhism.[10] Tibetologists have also noted Zava Damdin's works on epistemology[11] and some of his conclusions related to Tibetan historical development (for instance, Köden Khan's supposed letter to Sakya Paṇḍita and the biography of the Third Dalai Lama).[12]

At the behest of the current Dalai Lama—who until 1996 used Zava Damdin's commentaries around the world in his many large-scale Kālacakra initiations—José Cabezón translated Zava Damdin's one hundred-and-eight-verse *Praise to Great Compassion* for distribution to Western devotees (the only complete translation of a work by Zava Damdin into a Western language of which I am aware).[13] In that parochial vein, Zava Damdin's commentaries on "mind training" (Tib. *blo sbyong*) have also been referenced in popular works on contemplative practice by contemporary Tibetan Buddhist lamas teaching in Europe and America.[14]

While it deserves a major study of its own, unburdened by the biases of contemporary politics and schisms, a major part of Zava Damdin's enduring influence on the global Tibeto-Mongolian Buddhist tradition has to do with the profile of his writings and ritual collections among followers of the deeply divisive protector deity Dorjé Shukden (Tib. Rdo rje shugs ldan; Mon. Dorjishugdan). Zava Damdin received and transmitted the practice of Shukden in Khalkha on several occasions and also wrote the basis of what has become the standard ritual collection, or bé-bum (Tib. be'u 'bum). In an entry from the Summary for 1920, for example, Zava Damdin recalls that he set out to compile this in response to Lord Ngakram's final testament:[15]

> In the spring of the Steel Monkey year [1920]
> I went to the monastic college and the Lord Lhatsün returned from China.
> He gave me a copy of the 8,000-Verse Prajñāpāramitā Sūtra.
> I gave him the explanation and transmission of the Great Stages of the Path
> and the ritual of generating bodhicitta.
>
> At that time, amazing signs emerged,
> and I realized that this was due to the blessing
> of the super being himself
> and of the Dharma.
>
> According to the final testament of the Lord Ngakram,
> in order to arrange the bé bum
> I received from Nyönné Trülku (Smyong gnas sprul sku)
> the sadhana collection (grub khor) of Gyelchen Dorje Shugden.[16]

Later, in the entry for 1922, we read: "At that time, the Lhasa trülku sent the thangka painting of 'Gyalchen Dorjé Shukden with a Head Wrap' from Sarthaulai."

Zava Damdin's works on Dorjé Shukden have thus situated him posthumously as a node in this inter-Asian and transnational rift (which includes three murders) that currently divides Géluk communities from Malibu to Lhasa, Delhi to Ulaanbaatar. The current incarnation of Zava Damdin and his root lama, Guru Deva Rinpoché (who compiled and published Zava

FIGURE C.2 "Зава Дамдин Гэгээнтэний Шүгдэн сахиусны тухай айлдсан айлдал
[Zava Lam Discusses the Blessed Protector Shugden]".
YouTube Video, 1:29:50, April 29, 2014, https://www.youtube.com/watch?v=K1il-7AtQs4.

Damdin's *Collected Works* in 1975–76), have become key figureheads in the global Shukden movement, adding a retroactive partisanship to the memory of Zava Damdin.

Beyond contemporary schisms in the global Géluk community, Zava Damdin's records of active transmission of Shukden practice in Mongolia and between Mongolia and Tibet complicate the historical position of several prominent Tibetanists and Buddhist studies scholars on Shukden, which generally take the position of the current Dalai Lama and the Tibetan government in exile. For example, writing soon after the ban, Georges Dreyfus reduces the history of this controversial practice to sectarian movements in Lhasa in the early twentieth century, and more immediately to the person and disciples of Phabongkha Dechen Nyingpo (which includes the present Dalai Lama's two principal tutors and most other Géluk lamas who brought their Dharma to Europe, North America, and South and Southeast Asia between 1959 and 1996).[17] The implications of Zava Damdin's complicity in spreading the Shukden tradition on the Khalkha frontier of the Tibetan cultural world, far away from Phabongka's so-called Géluk fundamentalism movement in Central Tibet, requires its own sustained study and cannot be pursued here. The point is that among Shukden devotees the world over (who, because of their persecution, often refer to themselves as the "Jews of Tibetan Buddhism"), Zava Damdin and his oeuvre have become central in an alternative historicization of the Géluk tradition and, more broadly, of religion and politics in Inner Asia since the mid-seventeenth century.

In recent years, these split sympathies and histories have continued to cleave the global Géluk, with major monasteries in exile like Ganden now split into two and every Géluk community required to side with either the Dalai Lama and his government or the alternative order of Shukden practitioners (*Shugs ldan pa*), including such immanent figures as an emeritus "Throne Holder of the Ganden Tradition" (*Dga' ldan khri pa*), the elected head of the Géluk school.

The competing times, places, authorities, and communities of Géluk formation—and of the person of Zava Damdin specifically—have thus exceeded imperial decline, revolutionary violence, the displacement of diaspora, democratic and capitalist revival and circulation, and a global embrace of Tibetan Buddhism.

Countermodern Buddhism and Its Global Circulations

Zava Damdin's historical works rejected the modern and its associated knowledge practices *tout court*. Still, they drew some of their evidence from intellectual and cultural products of a nascent Euro-Russian academe and popular Western works interested in classical Asia and the "primitive," "original," "pure" Buddhism of Gautama and his first disciples. As Zava Damdin worked through his scholastic education, English, Russian, German, and Japanese translations of Pāli, Sanskrit, Gāndhārī, Kharoṣṭhī, Uyghur, Old Tibetan, and other textual materials began circulating into Inner Asian monastic communities such as those of Urga. Unearthed from desert ruins, sealed caves, forgotten libraries, and other graves, these works were rendered into academic texts and popular literature, both of which he avidly read in Mongolian translation, rendered into Tibetan, and used to set the post-Qing world into time.

Unlike the widely studied "Buddhist Modernists" in Japan, Myanmar, Sri Lanka, and Tibet, who reimagined a Buddhism already legible to the national subject and to the Romantic Orientalist, Protestant, and scientist tastes of Western audiences and progressive circles in Asia, Zava Damdin was deeply engaged with such sources and the knowledge practices that produced them for decidedly other purposes. The products of his reception of new sources on the Buddhist past, mediated largely through the Euro-Russian academy and popular presses, was a hybrid, countermodern Buddhism.

This was a routinized poaching of nonscholastic knowledge, a familiar exercise in Géluk scholasticism from the Mongol frontiers of the Qing. As we have seen, Zava Damdin set his post-Qing world into time beyond the Qing and the national subject, its unilinear histories, bounded communities, moral narratives, expected forms of agency, and "rationalizing" ambitions for emancipation, development, and material progress. Countermodern Buddhisms such as Zava Damdin's are to be found across postcolonial and imperial Asia but have received hardly any sustained scholarly attention, compared to our many histories of modernist Buddhisms that ironically reproduce, by monopoly of ink and paper if not intention, that which they seek to set into history: that contact with the European tradition has been synonymous with epochal breaks in Asian cultural history.

The role of Buddhism in the modern formation of Asia, and of the modernist varieties of Buddhism that developed as a result, continues to fascinate both scholars and a popular global readership of converts and revivalists. A robust subfield has developed under the heading of Buddhist modernism, or Protestant Buddhism.[18] Of particular interest have been late- and postcolonial and imperial figures, movements, and works that invented various national Buddhisms (such as in China, Sri Lanka, Japan, and Burma), reflecting a cluster of influences tied to European traditions. Scientific rationalism, monotheism, Romantic Orientalism, democracy, and capitalism are just some of the more popular examples.

The sources for this research have been a vocal minority of late nineteenth- and early twentieth-century Buddhist intellectuals trained in local monastic fields of knowledge as well as European arts, sciences, and political theory. There are widely read and widely taught recent monographs on individual reformists like Gendün Chöpel, D. T. Suzuki, Ledi Sayadaw, Tarui Tōkichi, and Anagarika Dharmapala. The fruits of their

CONCLUSION

mediation, as the authors of many of these works have so clearly shown, remain the most recognizable and popular form of Buddhism embraced by Euro-American converts today. In those pages we discover the startlingly recent remaking of popular, supposedly antique practices like Theravādan insight meditation or the more familiar features of Zen thought, which somehow arrived on American shores already packaged as a legible Eastern Philosophy.

In Zava Damdin's struggles to make sense of a post-Qing world and to lead Buddhist institutions in the absence of enlightened presence on the imperial throne or in the monastery lie previously unexamined traces of the diverse economies of an emerging globalization. Many of the organizing categories familiar to our current historiography of twentieth-century Inner Asia are simply absent, such as the shifting between the imperial epoch and the postimperial moment, exiting from servitude to national autonomy, the experience of moral and material deregulation, new forms of social mobility, industrialization, and the promises of nationalist and socialist "development."

Damdin's modes of engaging new secular categories of national self-representation and governance—which are Talal Asad's way of situating science, religion, and ethnicity—are couched in other terms, a third register beyond the Qing and the national subject.[19] Social and religious legacies exceed political endings. Topographies of the social imagination inhabited fleetingly by victims of postimperial events reaggregate. And most important, contact with Euro-American traditions no longer demarcate the arrival of modernity, or any other epochal break. Such contact is only a detail in the total biography of Mañjuśrī, in the debris of a vast history of law, security, and reproductive possibility.

I take Zava Damdin's written traces as a challenge to scholars of cultural history in modernizing Inner Asia to better attend to such neglected but widespread "countermodern" Buddhist formations across late- and postimperial and colonial Asia. Such a comparative effort would provide an urgent corrective to the hegemony of "transnationalism" and contact with European tradition as the primary trope for understanding twentieth-century Asian religiosity in its global contexts of circulation, and would better illuminate the otherwise histories of those made invisible in the rationalist creation of national peoples, territories, histories, and religions (which, it seems to me, is really what we mean by Buddhist modernism).

For example, David McMahan, whose ongoing work on Buddhist modernism remains a milestone in the study of twentieth- and twenty-first-century Buddhist formation, has aimed

> to illuminate not only how Buddhism's encounter with modernity has changed it but also how the conditions of modernity have created implicit parameters for what interpretations of Buddhism become possible and impossible. . . . How and why have certain elements of the Buddhist traditions been selected as serving the needs of the modern world, while others have been ignored or suppressed? How has Buddhism fit into the metanarratives of American and European culture, and into those of an increasingly globalized modernity?[20]

Zava Damdin's work (and that of similar thinkers across postimperial and postcolonial Asia) allows us to reverse these questions and ask instead: what elements of monastic and scholarly traditions were passed over as serving the needs of the modern world? How have certain monastic and scholastic formations and associated knowledge practices remained incommensurable with the metanarratives of a globalized modernity? How do the parameters of Enlightenment-derived modernities exile certain formulations of the subject, time, territory, community, and religiosity but not others?

The illegibility of such sources to modernist discourses and moral narratives requires attention to what Saba Mahmood calls "those conditions of discursive formation that require and produce the kind of subjects who may speak in its name."[21] Those conditions also offer the possibility of bringing the study of Buddhist formation in revolutionary Inner Asia into better conversation with the fractured social representation of time in the "age of revolution" (1750–1850) in Europe, whose memory Asian revolutionaries so often invoked but whose terms are unknown in these monastic sources.[22] Hybrid, countermodern Buddhisms like Zava Damdin's do not occupy the territory of religion or the political, the private or the public, the imperial/colonial or its aftermath, the renounced monk or the national citizen. All is crisis and open, disorienting possibility.

By this we might productively set into the plural the personal and global stories that have made up the diversity of Buddhist life between empire and nation, at the crossing tides of milk and blood.

Notes

Introduction

1. "Grand Abbot of Mongolia, One of Three Living Buddhas, May Soon Lose Throne Through the Diplomacy of Russia," *The Washington Post*, April 5, 1914, E2.

2. Since Urga (modern-day Ulaanbaatar) was renamed on at least two or three occasions in the period examined in these pages, for the sake of clarity I will keep "Urga" throughout but will note in passing when such changes occurred. I justify this decision based also on the variety of names and spellings in the sources examined. For example, Urga is itself a Russian corruption of *Örgüge* (Kh. Mon. *Örgöö*), meaning palace, a reference to the roaming monastic encampment of the first Jebtsundamba Khutuɣtu, Zanabazar (1635–1723). By Zava Damdin's time, Urga was known in Mongolian as *Boɣda-yin Küriy-e*, *Yeke Küriy-e*, and *Da Küriy-e*. In Khalkha pronunciation, and in the Cyrillic spelling reforms that came in the socialist period after Zava Damdin's death in 1937, these were *Bogdiin Khüree*, *Ikh Khüree*, and *Da Khüree* respectively. An added layer is that in the Tibetan-language monastic sources examined in this book, Urga is commonly referred to as *hu rel chen mo* or *dā hu re*.

3. Blo bzang rta mgrin, "Dam Pa Gong Ma'i Gsang Ba'i Lung Bstan 'ga' Zhig Gi Don Mchan Bus Gsal Bar Byas Pa," in *Rje Btsun Blo Bzang Rta Dbyangs Kyi Gsung 'Bum*, vol. 14 (New Delhi: Mongolian Lama Guru Deva, 1975), 360.

4. Mañjughoṣa (Tib. *'Jam dbyangs*) is an epithet for the bodhisattva Mañjuśrī (Tib. *'Jam dpal dbyangs*).

5. The colophon to this text indicates that the prophecy and the commentary offered by the "spiritual friend who pleases Mañjughoṣa" at Dashichoijurling were printed using differently colored text. However, in the black-and-white version preserved in Zava Damdin's collected works, the only way to distinguish the original and its annotation are by different font sizes. These are so intermingled that it would be nonsensical to distinguish between them in my English translation. For example:

"'on te blon po [blang dor la rmongs pa'i] ma rig [pa] can / mi dge'i [spyod pa'i] dbang du gyur [pa] dag [byung srid] kyang."

6. Blo bzang rta mgrin, "Dam Pa Gong Ma'i Gsang Ba'i Lung Bstan 'ga' Zhig Gi Don Mchan Bus Gsal Bar Byas Pa," 360.

7. Blo bzang rta mgrin, "Dam Pa Gong Ma'i Gsang Ba'i Lung Bstan 'ga' Zhig Gi Don Mchan Bus Gsal Bar Byas Pa," 361.

8. Blo bzang rta mgrin, "Dam Pa Gong Ma'i Gsang Ba'i Lung Bstan 'ga' Zhig Gi Don Mchan Bus Gsal Bar Byas Pa," 360.

9. Blo bzang rta mgrin, "Dam Pa Gong Ma'i Gsang Ba'i Lung Bstan 'ga' Zhig Gi Don Mchan Bus Gsal Bar Byas Pa," 361.

10. Blo bzang rta mgrin, "Dam Pa Gong Ma'i Gsang Ba'i Lung Bstan 'ga' Zhig Gi Don Mchan Bus Gsal Bar Byas Pa," 363.

11. Blo bzang rta mgrin, "Dam Pa Gong Ma'i Gsang Ba'i Lung Bstan 'ga' Zhig Gi Don Mchan Bus Gsal Bar Byas Pa," 361.

12. On the long history of Tibetan-Han Buddhist exchange, see Matthew Kapstein, ed., *Buddhism Between Tibet and China* (Boston: Wisdom, 2009). On the prominent role of Tibetan Buddhist lamas and traditions in Republican-era China, see Gray Tuttle, *Tibetan Buddhists in the Making of Modern China* (New York: Columbia University Press, 2007).

13. Blo bzang rta mgrin, "Dam Pa Gong Ma'i Gsang Ba'i Lung Bstan 'ga' Zhig Gi Don Mchan Bus Gsal Bar Byas Pa," 363.

14. Blo bzang rta mgrin, "Dam Pa Gong Ma'i Gsang Ba'i Lung Bstan 'ga' Zhig Gi Don Mchan Bus Gsal Bar Byas Pa," 363.

15. Prasenjit Duara, *Rescuing History from the Nation: Questioning Narratives of Modern China* (Chicago: University of Chicago Press, 1996); Dipesh Chakrabarty, *Provincializing Europe: Postcolonial Thought and Historical Difference* (Princeton, N.J.: Princeton University Press, 2009).

16. Peter Marshall, *Demanding the Impossible: A History of Anarchism* (Oakland, Calif.: PM Press, 2010), x.

17. Engseng Ho, "Inter-Asian Concepts for Mobile Societies," *The Journal of Asian Studies* 76, no. 4 (2017): 907.

18. Lisa L. Stenmark, "Going Public: Feminist Epistemologies, Hannah Arendt, and the Science-and-Religion Discourse," in *The Oxford Handbook of Religion and Science*, ed. Philip Clayton (New York: Oxford University Press, 2008), 822.

19. Michel de Certeau, *The Writing of History*, trans. Tom Conley (New York: Columbia University Press, 1988), 86.

20. Homi K Bhabha, *The Location of Culture* (London; New York: Routledge Classics, 1994), 38.

21. Sh Bira, *O "Zolotoi knige" Sh. Damdina [On Sh. Damdin's "Golden Book"]* (Ulan-Bator: Izd-vo Akademii nauk MNR, 1964).

22. Bira, *O "Zolotoi knige" Sh. Damdina*, 20.

23. Bira, *O "Zolotoi knige" Sh. Damdina*, 20.

24. Blo-bzaṅ-rta-mgrin, *The Golden Annals of Lamaism Being the Original Tibetan Text of the Hor-Chos-Ḥbyuṅ of Blo-Bzaṅ-Rta-Mgrin Entitled 'Jam Gliṅ Byaṅ Phyogs Chen Po Hor Gyi Rgyal Khams Kyi Rtogs Pa Brjod Pa'i Bstan Bcos Chen Po Dpyod Ldan Mgu Byed Ṅo Mćhar*

Gser Gyi Deb Ther, ed. Lokesh Chandra, Śata-Piṭaka 34 (New Delhi: International Academy of Indian Culture, 1964).

25. Blo-bzaṅ-rta-mgrin, *The Golden Annals of Lamaism*, v.

26. Blo-bzaṅ-rta-mgrin, *The Golden Annals of Lamaism*, v.

27. I have yet to see any evidence, or even mention in any other source, that Zava Damdin ever disrobed or formally disaffiliated himself from his monastic duties.

28. William A. Brown, Urgunge Onon, and B. Shirendev, *History of the Mongolian People's Republic* (Cambridge, Mass.; London: East Asian Research Center, Harvard University, 1976), 264.

29. "Ryedaktoprîn Taniltsuulga," in *Rje Btsun Blo Bzang Rta Dbyangs Kyi Gsung 'Bum*, vol. 17 (New Delhi: Mongolian Lama Guru Deva, 1975), 569.

30. Urgunge Onon and Derrick Pritchatt, *Asia's First Modern Revolution: Mongolia Proclaims Its Independence in 1911* (Leiden; New York: E. J. Brill, 1989).

31. Johan Elverskog, "Mongol Time Enters a Qing World," in *Time, Temporality, and Imperial Transition : East Asia from Ming to Qing*, ed. Lynn A. Struve (Honolulu: Association for Asian Studies and University of Hawai'i Press, 2005); Johan Elverskog, *Our Great Qing : The Mongols, Buddhism, and the State in Late Imperial China* (Honolulu: University of Hawai'i Press, 2006); Pamela Kyle Crossley, *A Translucent Mirror : History and Identity in Qing Imperial Ideology* (Berkeley: University of California Press, 1999); Peter C. Perdue, *China Marches West : The Qing Conquest of Central Eurasia* (Cambridge, Mass.: Belknap Press of Harvard University Press, 2005); Patricia Ann Berger, *Empire of Emptiness : Buddhist Art and Political Authority in Qing China* (Honolulu: University of Hawaii Press, 2003); Isabelle Charleux, "Mongol Pilgrimages to Wutai Shan in the Late Qing Dynasty," *JIATS* 6 (December 2011): 275–326; Stacey Van Vleet, "Medicine, Monasteries and Empire: Rethinking Tibetan Buddhism in Qing China," (Ph.D. diss., Columbia University, 2015); Peter Schwieger, *The Dalai Lama and the Emperor of China: A Political History of the Tibetan Institution of Reincarnation* (New York: Columbia University Press, 2015); Xiangyun Wang, "Tibetan Buddhism at the Court of Qing: The Life and Work of LCang-Skya Rol-Pa'i-Rdo-Rje, 1717–86," unpublished ms., 1995; Johan Elverskog, "Wutai Shan, Qing Cosmopolitanism, and the Mongols," *Journal of the International Association of Tibetan Studies* 6 (2011): 243–74; David M. Farquhar, "Emperor as Bodhisattva in the Governance of Ch'ing Empire," *Harvard Journal of Asiatic Studies* 38, no. 1 (1978).

32. For important studies of the few autobiographies written by women in Tibet, see Holly Gayley, *Love Letters from Golok: A Tantric Couple in Modern Tibet* (New York: Columbia University Press, 2016); Sarah Jacoby, *Love and Liberation: Autobiographical Writings of the Tibetan Buddhist Visionary Sera Khandro* (New York: Columbia University Press, 2014); Kurtis R. Schaeffer, *Himalayan Hermitess: The Life of a Tibetan Buddhist Nun* (New York: Oxford University Press, 2004).

33. Elverskog, "Mongol Time Enters a Qing World"; Elverskog, *Our Great Qing*; Johan Elverskog, *The Jewel Translucent Sūtra : Altan Khan and the Mongols in the Sixteenth Century* (Leiden; Boston: Brill, 2003); Ġoncuġjab and Johan Elverskog, *The Pearl Rosary: Mongol Historiography in Early Nineteenth-Century Ordos* (Bloomington, Ind.: Mongolia Society, 2007); Schwieger, *The Dalai Lama and the Emperor of China*; Ishihama Yumiko, "The Notion of 'Buddhist Government' (chos srid) Shared by Tibet, Mongol, and

Manchu in the Early 17th Century," in *The Relationship Between Religion and State (chos srid zung 'brel) in Traditional Tibet: Proceedings of a Seminar held in Lumbini, Nepal, March 2000*, ed. Christoph Cüppers (Lumbini: Lumbini International Research Institute, 2004), 15–31; Crossley, *A Translucent Mirror*; Pamela Kyle Crossley, Helen F. Siu, and Donald S. Sutton, *Empire at the Margins : Culture, Ethnicity, and Frontier in Early Modern China* (Berkeley: University of California Press, 2006); Berger, *Empire of Emptiness*.

34. Pamela Crossley, "Pluralité Impériale et Identités Subjectives Dans La Chine Des Qing," *Annales, Histoires, Sciences Sociales* 63e Année, no. 3 (June 2008): 597.

35. Carl Johan Elverskog, "Buddhism, History and Power: The Jewel Translucent Sutra and the Formation of Mongol Identity" (Ph.D. diss., Indiana University, 2000), ProQuest Dissertations & Theses (PQDT) (MSTAR_304600342); Elverskog, "Mongol Time Enters a Qing World"; Elverskog, *Our Great Qing*; Ishihama Yumiko, "The Notion of 'Buddhist Government' (chos srid) Shared by Tibet, Mongol, and Manchu in the Early 17th Century"; Crossley, *A Translucent Mirror*; Mark C. Elliott, *The Manchu Way: The Eight Banners and Ethnic Identity in Late Imperial China* (Stanford, Calif.: Stanford University Press, 2001); Schwieger, *The Dalai Lama and the Emperor of China*.

36. Ivan Sablin, *Governing Post-Imperial Siberia and Mongolia, 1911-1924: Buddhism, Socialism, and Nationalism in State and Autonomy Building* (London; New York: Routledge, 2017); Dindub and John G. Hangin, *A Brief History of Mongolia in the Autonomous Period* (Bloomington, Ind.: Mongolia Society, 1977); Charles Roskelly Bawden, *A Contemporary Mongolian Account of the Period of Autonomy*, 1st ed., vol. 4 (Bloomington, Ind.: The Mongolia Society, 1970); Onon and Pritchatt, *Asia's First Modern Revolution*; Thomas E. Ewing, *Between the Hammer and the Anvil? : Chinese and Russian Policies in Outer Mongolia, 1911-1921* (Bloomington: Research Institute for Inner Asian Studies, Indiana University, 1980); Emget Ookhnoi Batsaikhan, *Bogd Jebtsundamba Khutuktu, The Last King of Mongolia* (Ulaanbaatar: Admon., 2009); B. Shirendyb, *By-Passing Capitalism* (Ulaanbaatar: Mongolian People's Republic State Press, 1968); Baabar, *History of Mongolia*, ed. Christopher Kaplonski (Ulaanbaatar: Monsudar Publishing, 2004); Brown, Urgunge Onon, and Shiréndév, *History of the Mongolian People's Republic*; Robert Arthur Rupen, *How Mongolia Is Really Ruled : A Political History of the Mongolian People's Republic, 1900-1978* (Stanford, Calif.: Hoover Institution Press, Stanford University, 1979); Sh. Natsagdorzh, Kh. Perlee, and Khureelen Tuukhiin, *Khalkhyn tuukh* (Ulaanbaatar: ["Bembi San" KhKhK], 2008); Stephen Kotkin and Bruce A. Elleman, *Mongolia in the Twentieth Century : Landlocked Cosmopolitan* (Armonk, N.Y.: M. E. Sharpe, 1999); I. M. Mayskiy, *Mongoliya Nakanune Revolyutsii (Mongolia on the Eve of Revolution)* (Mongolia: Oriental Literature Press, 1959); A. Amar et al., *Mongolyn tovč tüüh* (Ulaanbaatar: So·embo Printing, 2006); Uradyn Erden Bulag, *Nationalism and Hybridity in Mongolia* (Oxford; New York: Clarendon Press; Oxford University Press, 1998); Owen Lattimore, *Nationalism and Revolution in Mongolia: With a Translation from the Mongol of Sh. Nachukdorji's Life of Sukebatur* (New York: Oxford University Press, 1955); Christopher Kaplonski, *Truth, History and Politics in Mongolia : The Memory of Heroes* (London; New York: RoutledgeCurzon, 2004).

37. Dindub and Hangin, *A Brief History of Mongolia in the Autonomous Period*.

38. Lobsang Tenpa, "The 1913 Mongol-Tibet Treaty and the Dalai Lama's Proclamation of Independence," *The Tibet Journal* 37, no. 2 (2012): 3–29.

39. Sanders, *Mongolia*, 26.

40. Rinchen, *Mongol Ard Ulsyn Ugsaatny Sudlal, Khelnïi Shinzhleliïn Atlas = Atlas Ethnologique et Linguistique de La République Populaire de Mongolie* (Ulaanbaatar: BNMAU Shinzhlekh ukhaany akademi, 1979).

41. Rebecca Empson, *Time, Causality and Prophecy in the Mongolian Cultural Region: Visions of the Future* (Folkestone: Global Oriental, 2006).

42. Then, as today, monasticism in Mongol lands does not demand celibacy or abandoning familial duties in ways expected of Géluk monastics in Tibetan communities.

43. Vladimir Il'ich Lenin, *Collected Works* (Moscow: Progress Publishers, 1972), 42:360–61.

44. Christopher Kaplonski, *The Lama Question: Violence, Sovereignty, and Exception in Early Socialist Mongolia* (Honolulu: University of Hawai'i Press, 2014).

45. Emanuel Sarkisyanz, "Communism and Lamaist Utopianism in Central Asia," *The Review of Politics* 20, no. 4 (1958): 623–33.

46. Nikolay Tsyrempilov, "Samdan Tsydenov and His Buddhist Theocratic Project," in *Biographies of Eminent Mongol Buddhists*, ed. Johan Elverskog (Halle: IITBS, International Institute for Tibetan and Buddhist Studies, 2008), 117–38.

47. Kaplonski, *The Lama Question*.

48. Lattimore, *Nationalism and Revolution in Mongolia*, 81.

49. Larry William Moses, *The Political Role of Mongol Buddhism* (Bloomington: Indiana University Press, 1977), 5.

50. Sh. Sandag, Harry H. Kendall, and Frederic E. Wakeman, *Poisoned Arrows : The Stalin-Choibalsan Mongolian Massacres, 1921-1941* (Boulder, Colo.: Westview Press, 2000).

51. Caroline Humphrey, "Remembering an Enemy: The Bogd Khaan in Twentieth-Century Mongolia," in *Memory, History, and Opposition Under State Socialism*, ed. Rubie S. Watson (Sante Fe, N.M.: School of American Research Press, 1994), 21–44.

52. For example: Kaplonski, *Truth, History and Politics in Mongolia*; Kaplonski, *The Lama Question*; Baabar, *History of Mongolia*; Robert A. Rupen, *Mongols of the Twentieth Century* (Bloomington: Indiana University Press, 1964); Rupen, *How Mongolia Is Really Ruled*; Charles R. Bawden, *The Modern History of Mongolia* (New York: Praeger, 1968); Ivan Jakovlevitsch Korostovets and Erich Hauer, *Von Cinggis Khan zur Sowjetrepublik; eine kurze Geschichte der Mongolei unter besonderer Bercksichtigung der neuesten Zeit* (Berlin; Leipzig: W. de Gruyter & Co., 1926); B. Shirendyb, *V.I. Lenin I Mongolyskiy Narod (V.I. Lenin and the Mongolian People)*, n.p., n.d.; Alan J. K. Sanders, *The People's Republic of Mongolia: A General Reference Guide* (London; New York: Oxford University Press, 1968); Sneath, David and Christopher Kaplonski, *The History of Mongolia 3, The Qing Period Twentieth-Century Mongolia* (Folkestone, Ky.: Global Orient, 2010); George G. S. Murphy, *Soviet Mongolia: A Study of the Oldest Political Satellite* (Berkeley: University of California Press, 1966); I. Maiskii, *Sovremennaya Mongoliya* (Irkutsk, R.S.F.S.R.: Gosudarstvennoe Izdatel'stvo, Irkutskoe Otdeleniye, 1921); Irina Y. Morozova, *Socialist Revolutions in Asia : The Social History of Mongolia in the Twentieth Century* (Abingdon, Oxon; New York: Routledge, 2009); Thomas E. Ewing, "Russia, China, and the Origins of the Mongolian People's Republic, 1911–1921: A Reappraisal," *The Slavonic and East European Review* 58, no. 3 (1980): 399–421; Marie-Dominique Even, "Ritual Efficacy or Spiritual Quest? Buddhism and Modernity in Post-Communist Mongolia," in

Revisiting Rituals in a Changing Tibetan World, ed. Katia Buffetrille (Leiden: Brill, 2012), 241–72; Owen Lattimore et al., "Religion and Revolution in Mongolia," *Modern Asian Studies* 1, no. 1 (1967): 81–94; Sandag, Kendall, and Wakeman, *Poisoned Arrows*; Owen Lattimore, *Nomads and Commissars: Mongolia Revisited* (New York: Oxford University Press, 1962); Lattimore, *Nationalism and Revolution in Mongolia*; Sanders, *Mongolia* ; A. P. Okladnikov et al., *Istorija Mongolskoj Narodnoj Respubliki* (Moskva: Nauka, 1983); Larry William Moses, *Introduction to Mongolian History and Culture* (Bloomington: Research Institute for Inner Asian Studies, Indiana University, 1985); Kh. Ts. Raldin, "Great October and the Affirmation of the Socialist Mongolian Nation," *Studia Historica* 7, no. 3 (1968); Ookhnoĭn Batsaĭkhan, Zorigtyn Lonzhid, and Olon Uls Sudlalyn Khŭrėėlėn (Mongolyn Shinzhlėkh Ukhaany Akademi), *Bogdo Jebtsundamba Khutuktu, the Last King of Mongolia: Mongolia's National Revolution of 1911 : Research Work* (Ulaanbaatar: Admon, 2009); S. Purevzhav, *BNMAU-D sum khiid, lam naryn asuudlyg shiidverlesen ní : 1921-1940 on* (Ulaanbaatar: Ulsyn khevleliin khereg erkhlekh khoroo, 1965); Ewing, *Between the Hammer and the Anvil?*; Onon and Pritchatt, *Asia's First Modern Revolution1*. For important corrections and complications of that narrative, see Christopher Pratt Atwood, *Young Mongols and Vigilantes in Inner Mongolia's Interregnum Decades, 1911-1931* (Leiden: Brill, 2002); Bulag, *Nationalism and Hybridity in Mongolia*; Munkh-Erdene Lhamsuren, "The Mongolian Nationality Lexicon: From the Chinggisid Lineage to Mongolian Nationality (From the Seventeenth to the Early Twentieth Century)," *Inner Asia* 8, no. 1 (2006): 51–98; Elverskog, "Buddhism, History and Power."

53. Hayden V. White, *Metahistory : The Historical Imagination in Nineteenth-Century Europe* (Baltimore: Johns Hopkins University Press, 1973).

54. Johan Elverskog, "Tibetocentrism, Religious Conversion and the Study of Mongolian Buddhism," in *The Mongolia-Tibet Interface : Opening New Research Terrains in Inner Asia : PIATS 2003 : Tibetan Studies : Proceedings of the Tenth Seminar of the International Association for Tibetan Studies, Oxford, 2003*, ed. Uradyn E. Bulag and Hildegard G.M. Diemberger (Leiden; Boston: Brill, 2007); Christopher P. Atwood, "Buddhism and Popular Ritual in Mongolian Religion: A Reexamination of the Fire Cult," *History of Religions* 36, no. 2 (1996): 112–39; Hildegard Diemberger and Uradyn Bulag, "Towards Critical Studies of the Mongolian-Tibet Interface," in *The Mongolia-Tibet Interface : Opening New Research Terrains in Inner Asia : PIATS 2003 : Tibetan Studies : Proceedings of the Tenth Seminar of the International Association for Tibetan Studies, Oxford, 2003* (Leiden; Boston: Brill, 2007).

55. Though of course there are many exceptions to these trends. Notable examples are the pioneering work of Byambaa Ragchaa to create inventories of Tibetan language works by Mongolian authors and a growing body of revisionist studies that deeply considers the Tibet-Mongol interface by scholars such as Agata Bareja-Starzyńska, Nikolay Tsyrempilov, György Kara, Uradyn Bulag, Vesna Wallace, Christopher Atwood, Hildegard Diemberger, Yumiko Ishihama, Krisztina Teleki, Vladimir Uspensky, Erdenibayar, Isabelle Charleux, Brian Baumann, Uranchimeg Tsultem, Johan Elverskog, Stacey Van Vleet, Zsuzsa Majer, Kiril Alekseev, Karénina Kollmar-Paulenz, Sangseraima Ujeed, and ErdeneBaatar Erdene-Ochir.

56. Ann Laura Stoler and Carole McGranahan, "Refiguring Imperial Terrains," in *Imperial Formations*, ed. Ann Laura. Stoler, Carole McGranahan, and Peter C. Perdue (Santa Fe, N.M.: School for Advanced Research Press, 2007), 3–42.

57. Ann Laura Stoler, *Imperial Debris : On Ruins and Ruination* (Durham, N.C.: Duke University Press, 2013).

58. Benjamin A. Cowan, Nicole M. Guidotti-Hernández, and Jason Ruiz, "Sexing Empire: Editors' Introduction," *Radical History Review* 123 (2015): 2.

59. Bernard S. Cohn, "India as a Racial, Linguistic, and Cultural Area," in *Introducing India in Liberal Education*, ed. Milton Singer (Chicago: University of Chicago Press, 1957).

60. "In the historical situation of colonialism, both white rulers and indigenous peoples were constantly involved in representing to each other what they were doing. Whites everywhere came into other peoples' worlds with models and logics, means of representation, forms of knowledge and action, with which they adapted to the construction of new environments, peoples by new 'others.' By the same token, these 'others' had to restructure their worlds to encompass the fact of white domination and their powerlessness." Bernard S. Cohn, *An Anthropologist Among the Historians and Other Essays* (Delhi: Oxford University Press, 1987), 144.

61. Cohn, *An Anthropologist Among the Historians,* 44.

62. Bernard S. Cohn, *Colonialism and Its Forms of Knowledge: The British in India* (Princeton, N.J.: Princeton University Press, 1996).

63. Sara Suleri Goodyear, *The Rhetoric of English India* (Chicago: University of Chicago Press, 1992); Bernard S. Cohn, *Colonialism and Its Forms of Knowledge* (Princeton, NJ: Princeton University Press, 1996); Brian Keith Axel, *The Nation's Tortured Body: Violence, Representation, and the Formation of a Sikh "Diaspora"* (Durham, NC: Duke University Press, 2001).

1. Wandering

1. Blo bzang rta mgrin, "Rang Gi Byed Spyod Rags Bsdoms 'Di Snang Za Zi'i Rjes Gco," in *Rje Btsun Blo Bzang Rta Dbyangs Kyi Gsung 'Bum*, vol. 11 (New Delhi: Mongolian Lama Guru Deva, 1975), 172.

2. Blo bzang rta mgrin, "Rang Gi Byed Spyod Rags Bsdoms 'Di Snang Za Zi'i Rjes Gco," 172.

3. Blo bzang rta mgrin, "Sprul Pa'i Chos Skyong Chen Po'i Sger Gyi Lung Bstan Snga Phyir Phebs Pa Gnyis," in *Rje Btsun Blo Bzang Rta Dbyangs Kyi Gsung 'Bum*, vol. 14 (New Delhi: Mongolian Lama Guru Deva, 1975), 368.

4. Blo bzang rta mgrin, "Sprul Pa'i Chos Skyong Chen Po'i Sger Gyi Lung Bstan Snga Phyir Phebs Pa Gnyis," 369.

5. In Tuṣita Pure Land, Jé Tsongkhapa Lozang Drakpa (Tib. Rje tsong kha pa blo bzang grags pa, 1357–1419), the founder of the Géluk tradition, takes on the form of Jampel Nyingpo (Tib. 'Jam dpal snying po).

6. Blo bzang rta mgrin, "Sprul Pa'i Chos Skyong Chen Po'i Sger Gyi Lung Bstan Snga Phyir Phebs Pa Gnyis," 370.

7. Blo bzang rta mgrin, "Sprul Pa'i Chos Skyong Chen Po'i Sger Gyi Lung Bstan Snga Phyir Phebs Pa Gnyis," 374.

8. More specifically, his autobiography was the last of his *dated* works. A great many smaller texts, scraps, letters, and notes come to us undated, though in my reading none explicitly references events after 1936. Given Damdin's ill health during his final years and the terrible political climate, I am confident that the autobiography was his last major textual project.

9. Blo bzang rta mgrin, "Rang Gi Byed Spyod Rags Bsdoms 'Di Snang Za Zi'i Rjes Gco," 203.

10. Jan-Ulrich Sobisch, "The 'Records of Teachings Received' in the Collected Works of A Mes Zhabs: An Untapped Source for the Study of Sa Skya Pa Biographies," in *Tibet, Past and Present: Tibetan Studies I. PIATS 2000: Tibetan Studies: Proceedings of the Ninth Seminar of the International Association Fro Tibetan Studies, Leiden 2000* (Leiden; Boston; Köln: Brill, 2002), 1, 2:161.

11. For scholarship on *gsan yig/thob yig,* see V. P. Vassilijev, "Die Auf Den Buddhismus Bezüglichen Werke Der Universitätsbibliothek Zu Kasan," *Melanges Asiatiques 2* (1856): 347–86; Manfred Taube, "Die Bedeutung Eiheimischer Bibliographien Für Die Erforschung Der Tibetischen Literatur," *Studia Asiae, Festschrift Zum 70. Geburtstag von Johannes Schubert* (1968):277–99; A. I. Vostrikov, *Tibetan Historical Literature* (Richmond, Surrey: Curzon Press, 1994); Sobisch, "The 'Records of Teachings Received' in the Collected Works of A Mes Zhabs"; Leonard W.J. van der Kuijp, "On the Life and Political Career of T'ai Si Tu Byang Chub Rgyal Mtshan," in *Tibetan History and Language: Studies Dedicated to Uray Gèza on His Seventieth Birthday.* E. Steinkellner, eds.Wiener Studien Zur Tibetologie Und Buddhismuskunde 26 (Wien: Arbeitskreis für Tibetische und Buddhistische Studien); Günter Grönbold, "Materialen Zur Geschichte Des Ṣaḍaṅga-Yoga: III. Die Guru-Reihen Im Buddhistischen Ṣaḍaṅga-Yoga," *Zentralasiatische Studien* 16 (1982): 337–47; David Paul Jackson and Sa-skya Paṇḍi-ta Kun-dga'-rgyal-mtshan, *The Entrance Gate for the Wise (Section III): Sa-Skya Paṇḍita on Indian and Tibetan Traditions of Pramāṇa and Philosophical Debate* (Wien: Arbeitskreis für Tibetische und Buddhistische Studien, Universität Wien, 1987); David Paul Jackson, *A History of Tibetan Painting: The Great Tibetan Painters and Their Traditions* (Wien: Verlag der Österreichischen Akademie der Wissenschaften, 1996); David P. Jackson, "Enlightenment by a Single Means: Tibetan Contriversies on the 'Self-Sufficient White Remedy' (Dkar Po Chig Thub)," in *Beiträge Zur Kultur- Und Geistesgeschichte Asiens,* vol. 12 (Wien: Verlag der Österreichischen Akademie der Wissenschaften, n.d.); Dan Martin and Yael Bentor, *Tibetan Histories : A Bibliography of Tibetan-Language Historical Works* (London: Serindia, 1997); E. Gene Smith and Kurtis R. Schaeffer, *Among Tibetan Texts : History and Literature of the Himalayan Plateau* (Boston: Wisdom, 2001).

12. Vostrikov, *Tibetan Historical Literature,* 199.

13. bLo bzang 'phrin las, *ShAkya'i Btsun Pa Blo Bzang 'phrin Las Kyi Zab Pa Dang Rgya Che Ba'i Dam Pa'i Chos Kyi Thob Yig Gsal Ba'i Me Long,* 4 vols. (New Delhi: International Academy of Indian Culture, 1981). See Sangseraima Ujeed, "The Thob Yig Gsal Ba'i Me Long by Dza-Ya Paṇḍita Blo-Bzang 'phin-Las (1642–1715): An Enquiry into Biographies as Lineage History" (Ph.D. diss., University of Oxford, 2017).

14. Blo bzang rta mgrin, "Thog Mtha' Bar Du Dge Ba Dam Chos Bdud Rtsi'i Zil Mngar Cung Zhig Myang Ba'i Thob Yig Zab Rgyas Gsang Ba'i Gdams Pa Rin Chen Gter

Gyi Kha Byang," in *Rje Btsun Blo Bzang Rta Dbyangs Kyi Gsung 'Bum*, 17 vols. (New Delhi: Mongolian Lama Guru Deva, 1975), vols. 15–17: 7–502 (pod dang po), 7–508 (pod gnyis pa), 7–560 (pod gsum pa).

15. Blo bzang rta mgrin, "Rang Gi Byed Spyod Rags Bsdoms 'Di Snang Za Zi'i Rjes Gco," 5.

16. Sobisch, "The 'Records of Teachings Received,'" 163.

17. *Byis pa'i dus su bsam med du g.yengs pa'i byed.* Blo bzang rta mgrin, "Rang Gi Byed Spyod Rags Bsdoms 'Di Snang Za Zi'i Rjes Gco," 170–75.

18. *Gzhon nu'i dus su slob gnyer gyis g.yengs pa'i byed.* Blo bzang rta mgrin, "Rang Gi Byed Spyod Rags Bsdoms 'Di Snang Za Zi'i Rjes Gco," 175–78.

19. *Lang tsho'i dus su dpe khrid kyis g.yengs pa'i byed.* Blo bzang rta mgrin, "Rang Gi Byed Spyod Rags Bsdoms 'Di Snang Za Zi'i Rjes Gco," 178–82.

20. *Dar yol ba'i dus su bka' chos kyis g.yengs byed.* Blo bzang rta mgrin, "Rang Gi Byed Spyod Rags Bsdoms 'Di Snang Za Zi'i Rjes Gco," 182–91.

21. *Rga ba'i dus su dgon skyong gis g.yengs pa'i byed.* Blo bzang rta mgrin, "Rang Gi Byed Spyod Rags Bsdoms 'Di Snang Za Zi'i Rjes Gco," 191–99.

22. *Rga ba'i dus su dgon skyong kyis kyi [sic.] g.yengs pa'i byed.* Blo bzang rta mgrin, "Rang Gi Byed Spyod Rags Bsdoms 'Di Snang Za Zi'i Rjes Gco," 199–203.

23. Michel de Certeau, "The Historiographic Operation," in *The Writing of History* (New York: Columbia University Press, 1988), 58.

24. D. Choijamts and Sh. Choimaa, eds., *Mongolîn Burkhanî Shashanî Tüükhen Surwalj: Töwd Khelt Surwaljiin Orchuulga, Mailbar, Müükhiin On Tsagiin Khelkhees*, trans. D. Bürnee and D. Enkhtör (Ulaanbaatar: Enekhüü Toliig London Dakhi Tövdiin Sangiin Tuslamjtai Khevlev, 2004), 68.

25. William A. Brown, Urgunge Onon, and B. Shirendev, *History of the Mongolian People's Republic* (Cambridge, Mass.: East Asian Research Center, Harvard University, 1976), 221.

26. Krisztina Teleki published a Hungarian translation of the Outer Mongolian monasteries from this section of the Golden Book. Building on her work, I produced an English translation of that entire section, and in addition of Zava Damdin's descriptions of the Inner and Outer Mongolia and Buryatia sections. See Krisztina Teleki, "Mongólia Kolostorai Az Arany Krónika Jegyzéke Alapján," in *Bolor-un gerel: Kristályfény : Tanulmányok Kara György Professzor 70. Születésnapjának Tiszteletére*, ed. Ágnes Birtalan, 2 vols. (Budapest: Eötvös Lóránd Tudományegyetem, Belső-ázsiai Tanszék, 2005), 2:773–90; Matthew W. King, "A 1931 Survey of Mongolian Monastic Colleges from the Golden Book (Altan Devter)," in *Sources of Mongolian Buddhism*, ed. Vesna Wallace (New York: Oxford University Press, forthcoming).

27. Tibetan was the literary language of Zava Damdin and most other Mongolian Buddhist scholars of the Qing after the eighteenth century.

28. Relevant references on *namtar* include: Andrew Quintman, "Between History and Biography: Notes on Zhi Byed Ri Pa's 'Illuminating Lamp of Sun and Moon Beams,' a Fourteenth-Century Biographical State of the Field," *Revue d'Etudes Tibétaines*, no. 23 (Avril 2012): 5–41; Janet Gyatso, *Apparitions of the Self: The Secret Autobiographies of a Tibetan Visionary : A Translation and Study of Jigme Lingpa's Dancing Moon in the Water and Ḍākki's Grand Secret-Talk* (Princeton, N.J.: Princeton

University Press, 1998); Andrew Quintman, *The Yogin and the Madman: Reading the Biographical Corpus of Tibet's Great Saint Milarepa* (New York: Columbia University Press, 2013); International Association for Tibetan Studies, Seminar, and Johan Elverskog, *Biographies of Eminent Mongol Buddhists: PIATS 2006, Tibetan Studies, Proceedings of the Eleventh Seminar of the International Association for Tibetan Studies, Königswinter 2006* (Halle: IITBS, International Institute for Tibetan and Buddhist Studies, 2008).

29. For some important studies of the few Inner Asian autobiographies written by women, see Kurtis R Schaeffer, *Himalayan Hermitess: The Life of a Tibetan Buddhist Nun* (New York: Oxford University Press, 2004); Sarah Jacoby, *Love and Liberation: Autobiographical Writings of the Tibetan Buddhist Visionary Sera Khandro* (New York: Columbia University Press, 2014); Holly Gayley, *Love Letters from Golok: A Tantric Couple in Modern Tibet* (New York: Columbia University Press, 2016).

30. For a few examples, new and old, see: Johan Elverskog, ed., *Biographies of Eminent Mongol Buddhists* (Halle: IITBS, International Institute for Tibetan and Buddhist Studies, 2008); Agata Bareja-Starzyńska, "The Mongolian Incarnation of Jo Nang Pa Taranatha Kun Dga' Snying Po: Ondor Gegeen Zanabazar Blo Bzang Bstan Pa'i Rgyal Mtshan (1635–1723): A Case Study of the Tibeto-Mongolian Relationship," *The Tibet Journal* 34, no. 3–4 (2009): 243+; John Snelling, *Buddhism in Russia: The Story of Agvan Dorzhiev, Lhasa's Emissary to the Tzar* (Shaftesbury, Dorset; Rockport, Mass.: Element, 1993); Paul Hyer and Sechin Jagchid, *A Mongolian Living Buddha: Biography of the Kanjurwa Khutughtu* (Albany: State University of New York Press, 1983); Owen Lattimore, Fujiko Isono, and Diluv Khutagt, *The Diluv Khutagt: Memoirs and Autobiography of a Mongol Buddhist Reincarnation in Religion and Revolution* (Wiesbaden: O. Harrassowitz, 1982).

31. Agata Bareja-Starzyńska, *The Biography of the First Khalkha Jetsundampa Zanabazar by Zaya Pandita Luvsanprinlei: Studies, Annotated Translation, Transliteration, and Facsimile* (Warsaw: Dom Wydawniczy ELIPSA, 2015); Bareja-Starzynska, "The Mongolian Incarnation of Jo Nang Pa Taranatha Kun Dga' Snying Po"; Blo-bzaṅ-tshul-khrims and Rudolf Kaschewsky, *Das Leben Des Lamaistischen Heiligen Tsongkhapa Blo-Bzan-Grags-Pa (1357-1419): Dargestellt Und Erlautert Anhand Seiner Vita "Quellort Allen Gluckes"* (Wiesbaden: O. Harrassowitz, 1917); Ngag dbang chos 'byor don grub, *Khyab Bdag Rdo Rje'i 'chang 'Dar Pa Paṇḍita Nga Dbang Chos 'Byor Don Grub Dpal Bzang Po'i Skyes Rabs Rnam Thar Dang Gsung Thoral* (Ulaanbaatar, Mongolia: R. Byambaa, 2011).

32. Kurtis Schaeffer, "Tibetan Biography: Growth and Criticism," in *Editions, Éditions: L'Écrit Au Tibet, Évolution et Devenir* (München: Indus Verlag, 2010); Kurtis Schaeffer, "New Scholarship in Tibet, 1650–1700," in *Forms of Knowledge in Early Modern Asia: Explorations in the Intellectual History of India and Tibet, 1500-1800*, ed. Sheldon Pollock (Durham, N.C.: Duke University Press, 2011), 291–310; Gyatso, *Apparitions of the Self*; Janet Gyatso, "Experience, Empiricism, and the Fortunes of Authority: Tibetan Medicine and Buddhism on the Eve of Modernity," in *Forms of Knowledge in Early Modern Asia: Explorations in the Intellectual History of India and Tibet, 1500-1800*, ed. Sheldon Pollock (Durham, N.C.: Duke University Press, 2011), 311–35; Matthew W. King, "Fragments from Gesar's Iron Chain: Biography as Aesthetics of Empire in the Minor Works of the Chahar Gewsh Lubsansültim (1747–1810)," in *The Many Faces of Ling Gesar: Contributions in Honour of the Late R. A. Stein*, ed. Matthew Kapstein and Charles Ramble (Leiden: Brill, forthcoming).

33. Sum pa mkhan po ye shes dpal 'byor (1704–1788); Lcang skya (gsum pa) rol pa'i rdo rje (1717–1786); Thu'u bkwan (gsum pa) blo bzang chos kyi nyi ma (1737–1802); Stong khor (drug pa) 'jam dbyangs bstan 'dzin rgya mtsho (1753–1798); Cha har dge shes blo bzang tshul khrims (1747–1810); Smin grol no min han (bzhi pa) 'jam dpal chos kyi bstan 'dzin 'phrin las (1789–1839).

34. Schaeffer, "New Scholarship in Tibet, 1650–1700"; Matthew Kapstein, "Just Where on Jambudvīpa Are We? New Geographical Knowledge and Old Cosmological Schemes in Eighteenth-Century Tibet," in *Forms of Knowledge in Early Modern Asia : Explorations in the Intellectual History of India and Tibet, 1500-1800*, ed. S. Pollock (Durham, N.C.: Duke University Press, 2011), 336–64; bTsan-po Bla-ma and Turrell V. Wylie, *The Geography of Tibet According to the 'dZam-Gling-RGyas-BShad* (Roma: Istituto italiano per il Medio ed Estremo Oriente, 1962); Gray Tuttle, "Challenging Central Tibet's Dominance of History: The 'Oceanic Book,' a Nineteenth-Century Politico-Religious Geographic History," in *Mapping the Modern in Tibet*, ed. Gray Tuttle ([Andiast, Switzerland]: IITBS, International Institute for Tibetan and Buddhist Studies GmbH, 2011), 135–72; Gray Tuttle, *Mapping the Modern in Tibet, PIATS 2006: Tibetan Studies: Proceedings of the Eleventh Seminar of the International Association for Tibetan Studies* (Königswinter: International Institute for Tibetan and Buddhist Studies GmbH, 2011); Lobsang Yongdan, "Tibet Charts the World: The Btsan Po No Mon Han's Detailed Description of the World, an Early Major Scientific Work in Tibet," in *Mapping the Modern in Tibet*, ed. Gray Tuttle ([Andiast, Switzerland]: IITBS, International Institute for Tibetan and Buddhist Studies GmbH, 2011); Janet Gyatso, *Being Human in a Buddhist World: An Intellectual History of Medicine in Early Modern Tibet* (New York: Columbia University Press, 2015).

35. For more detailed descriptions of classificatory schemes used in Tibetan auto/biography see Gyatso, *Apparitions of the Self*, 102–6; Janet Gyatso, "Turning Personal: Recent Work on Autobiography in Tibetan Studies," *The Journal of Asian Studies* 75, no. 1 (2016): 229–35; Janet Gyatso, "From the Autobiography of a Visionary," in *Religions of Tibet in Practice*, ed. Donald S. Lopez (Princeton, N.J.: Princeton University Press, 1997), 369–75; Jacoby, *Love and Liberation*; Bstan-'dzin-nor-bu, Benjamin Bogin, and Bstan-'dzin-nor-bu, *The Illuminated Life of the Great Yolmowa* (Chicago: Serindia Contemporary, 2013); Elijah S. Ary, *Authorized Lives: Biography and the Early Formation of Geluk Identity* (Somerville, Mass.: Wisdom, 2015); Quintman, *The Yogin and the Madman*; Quintman, "Between History and Biography."

36. In a biographical tradition that took shape in the so-called "renaissance period" of postimperial Tibet (eleventh–twelfth century), Padmasambhava (Tib. Padma 'byung gnas), the "Lotus Born," was an Indian tantric master from the eighth century widely memorialized for having facilitated the transmission of Buddhist (especially tantric) traditions to imperial Tibet. For example, see Ye-śes-mtsho-rgyal, Tarthang Tulku, and gter-ston O-rgyan-glin-pa, *The Life and Liberation of Padmasambhava, Padma Bka' Thaṅ* (Berkeley, Calif.: Dharma Publications, 2007). Milarepa (Tib. Mi la ras pa, 1052–1135) was a Tibetan meditator and lineage master of the Bka' brgyud sect who continues to serve as the paradigmatic yogi in Inner Asian Buddhist traditions. Tsangnyön Heruka (Tib. Gtsang smyon he ru ka, 1452–1507) assembled his biographical corpus in the late fifteenth century; it continues to serve as a template for writing the lives of so-called "mad yogis" (see Quintman, *The Yogin and the Madman*).

37. Gyatso, *Apparitions of the Self*, 111. While such outlines became the convention for writing the general lives of Inner Asian masters, Janet Gyatso argues that these ought to still be considered auto/biography proper and not instances of self-effacing genres such as epic or genealogy. Tibetan (and, as we shall see, Mongolian) Buddhist authors, she notes, often juxtapose formulaic religious narratives ("I took these vows, and built this monastery, and did this meditation retreat") with a pronounced "interest in the ordinary vicissitudes of the self" (112).

38. Critically, the language of interiority and the "self" inscribed in such texts, especially in autobiography, does not simply correspond to the privatized or individualized subject of post-Enlightenent autobiography in Europe. For important and lucid differentiations, see Jacoby, *Love and Liberation*, 14–17; Gyatso, "Turning Personal"; Gayley, *Love Letters from Golok*.

39. It will be clear to anyone who has read even a small selection of *namtar* that in practice individual texts generally incorporate narrative elements from all three subgenres. Jan Willis has argued that in any individual text, each narrative level strategically draws forth a particular response in its readers. The outer biography tells the reader about the course of historical events (and might include key details about a particular polity, genealogy, or monastery). The inner biography inspires readers to emulate the exemplary life of the protagonist, and more broadly, to cultivate devotion to associated teaching lineages and institutions. The secret biography, Willis claims, serves as a road map for readers who are suitably advanced—initiated and learned, in other words—and who are prepared to emulate the protagonist along his or her road to self-cultivation (Janice Dean Willis, *Enlightened Beings: Life Stories from the Ganden Oral Tradition* [Boston: Wisdom, 1995], 5–6).

40. Blo bzang rta mgrin, "Rang Gi Byed Spyod Rags Bsdoms 'Di Snang Za Zi'i Rjes Gco," 170–71.

41. Tib. *Gho bi us dzing kung.*

42. For a fascinating history based on the memories of still living disciples and the current incarnation of Zava Damdin, see Zsuzsa Majer, "Delgeriin Choir, the Monastery of Zawa Lam Damdin in the Gobi," in *Zentralasiatische Studien Des Seminars Für Sprach- Und Kulturwissenschaft Zentralasiens Der Universität Bonn* (Andiast: International Institute for Tibetan and Buddhist Studies, 2013), 41:7–42.

43. Blo bzang rta mgrin, "Rang Gi Byed Spyod Rags Bsdoms 'Di Snang Za Zi'i Rjes Gco," 171.

44. Blo bzang rta mgrin, "Rang Gi Byed Spyod Rags Bsdoms 'Di Snang Za Zi'i Rjes Gco," 171.

45. Majer, "Delgeriin Choir, the Monastery of Zawa Lam Damdin in the Gobi," 19.

46. For a translation of Zava Damdin's primary biography of Sanjai (Kh. Mong. Sanjaa), see Matthew King, "Beautifying Ornament for the Mind of the Faithful: A Praise-Biography of My Root Lama Vajradhara, He Who Possesses the Three Types of Kindness, the Great Mahāpaṇḍita Endowed with Excellent Discipline and Learning Named 'Sanjaa,'" in *Sources of Mongolian Buddhism,* ed. Vesna Wallace (New York: Oxford University Press, forthcoming); Blo bzang rta mgrin, "Bka' Drin Gsum Ldan Rtsa Ba'i Bla Ma Rdo Rje 'chang Mkhan Chen Sangs Rgyas Mtshan Can Gyi Rnam Thar Gsol 'Debs Dad Ldan Yid Kyi Mdzas Rgyan," in *Rje Btsun Blo Bzang Rta Dbyangs Kyi Gsung 'Bum,* 17 vols. (New Delhi: Mongolian Lama Guru Deva, 1975), 1:7–19.

47. I.e., to not kill, steal, engage in sexual misconduct, lie, or consume intoxicants. Blo bzang rta mgrin, "Rang Gi Byed Spyod Rags Bsdoms 'Di Snang Za Zi'i Rjes Gco," 5.

48. Blo bzang rta mgrin, "Rang Gi Byed Spyod Rags Bsdoms 'Di Snang Za Zi'i Rjes Gco," 172.

49. Blo bzang rta mgrin, "Rang Gi Byed Spyod Rags Bsdoms 'Di Snang Za Zi'i Rjes Gco," 173.

50. Blo bzang rta mgrin, "Rang Gi Byed Spyod Rags Bsdoms 'Di Snang Za Zi'i Rjes Gco," 173.

51. Blo bzang rta mgrin, "Rang Gi Byed Spyod Rags Bsdoms 'Di Snang Za Zi'i Rjes Gco," 173.

52. Blo bzang rta mgrin, "Rang Gi Byed Spyod Rags Bsdoms 'Di Snang Za Zi'i Rjes Gco," 173.

53. Majer, "Delgeriin Choir, the Monastery of Zawa Lam Damdin in the Gobi," 9.

54. There are three great Géluk monasteries located in Central Tibet, all founded by Tsongkhapa himself or by his direct disciples. These were some of the largest monastic universities in the world until the Cultural Revolution of the 1960s, and at times housed a monastic population drawn from as far away as Rome, Siberia, Korea, and Japan. Sera monastery (Tib. *Se ra dgon pa*) is located some five kilometers north of Lhasa's central temple complex, and was founded in 1419 by one of Tsongkhapa's disciples. Ganden Namgyal Ling monastery (TIB. *Dga' ldan rnam rgyal gling dgon pa*) founded by Tsongkhapa himself in 1409, is located some thirty-five kilometers northeast of central Lhasa. To the west of Lhasa is Drépung (Tib. *'Bras spungs dgon pa*). Founded in 1416, it was the largest of the three with a maximum population of 10,000 monks in the 1930s. For this reason, it was often identified by European travelers as the largest monastery in the world (for example: Frederick Spencer Chapman, *Lhasa, the Holy City* [(London: Chatto and Windus, 1939], 195). Gomang college (Tib. *Sgo mang grwa tshang*) of Drépung seems to have been the preferred monastic home for Mongol, Buryat, and Tuvan pupils over the course of the Qing.

55. Blo bzang rta mgrin, "Rang Gi Byed Spyod Rags Bsdoms 'Di Snang Za Zi'i Rjes Gco," 174.

56. For fascinating studies of religious, political, and artistic life in Urga at this time, see the work of Uranchimeg Tsultem, including: Uranchimeg Tsultemin, "Ikh Khüree: A Nomadic Monastery and the Later Buddhist Art of Mongolia" (Ph.D. diss., University of California, Berkeley, 2009); Uranchimeg Tsultemin, "Cartographic Anxieties in Mongolia: The Bogd Khan's Picture-Map," *Cross-Currents: East Asian History and Cultural Review* 21 (2016): 66–87. An important, long-running project to document the lost monastic world of Urga (Ikh Khüree) comes from the scholarship of Teleki and Majer. In English, see Krisztina Teleki, *Monasteries and Temples of Bogdiin Khuree* (Ulaanbaatar: Institute of History, Mongolian Academy of Sciences, 2011). See also the digital version, much expanded under the direction of Sue Byrne and many other collaborators: Mongolîn Süm Khiidiin Tüükhen Towchoo/Documentation of Mongolian Monasteries (mongoliantemples.org). For a classic, eyewitness account of the monastic scene in late-imperial era Mongolia, see Alekseĭ Matveevich Pozdneev and John Richard Krueger, *Religion and Ritual in Society: Lamaist Buddhism in Late Nineteenth-Century Mongolia* (Bloomington, Ind.: The Mongolia Society, 1978).

57. I. Maiskii, *Sovremennaya Mongoliya* (Irkutsk, R.S.F.S.R.: Gosudarstvennoe Izdatel'stvo, Irkutskoe Otdeleniye, 1921). Quoted from Jerzy Tulisow et al., eds., *In the Heart of Mongolia: 100th Anniversary of W. Kotwicz's Expedition to Mongolia in 1912: Studies and Selected Source Materials* (Crakow: Polish Academy of Arts and Sciences, 2012), 31.

58. bLo bzang rta mgrin, "Thog Mtha' Bar Du Dge Ba Dam Chos Bdud Rtsi'i Zil Mngar Cung Zhig Myang Ba'i Thob Yig Zab Rgyas Gsang Ba'i Gdams Pa Rin Chen Gter Gyi Kha Byang," 6.

59. bLo bzang rta mgrin, "Thog Mtha' Bar Du Dge Ba Dam Chos Bdud Rtsi'i Zil Mngar Cung Zhig Myang Ba'i Thob Yig Zab Rgyas Gsang Ba'i Gdams Pa Rin Chen Gter Gyi Kha Byang," 6.

60. *Summarized Topics* is a preliminary subject in the logical formulation of arguments (Tib. *rtags rigs*), epistemology (*blo rigs*), and dialectics (*rtsod sgrub rig pa*). For overviews of Géluk scholasticism in a variety of places and periods, and examined from a variety of methodological perspectives, see: Daniel Perdue and Phur-bu-lcog Byams-pa-rgya-mtsho, *Debate in Tibetan Buddhism* (Ithaca, N.Y.: Snow Lion, 1992); Guy Newland, "Debate Manuals (Yig Cha) in DGe Lugs Monastic Colleges," in *Tibetan Literature: Studies in Genre*, ed. José Ignacio Cabezón and Roger R Jackson (Ithaca, N.Y.: Snow Lion, 1996), 202–16; Michael Lempert, *Discipline and Debate: The Language of Violence in a Tibetan Buddhist Monastery* (Berkeley: University of California Press, 2012); Tom J. F Tillemans, "Formal and Semantic Aspects of Tibetan Buddhist Debate Logic," *Journal of Indian Philosophy* 17 (1989); Bernard Carmona et al., "Formation transdisciplinaire, trajet anthropologique et tradition tibétaine: Recherche sur l'ingenium de la pratique du débat dans l'Ecole Gelugpa" (SCD de l'université de Tours, 2012); Daniel Perdue, *The Course in Buddhist Reasoning and Debate: An Asian Approach to Analytical Thinking Drawn from Indian and Tibetan Sources* (Boston: Snow Lion, 2013); Georges B. J. Dreyfus, *The Sound of Two Hands Clapping: The Education of a Tibetan Buddhist Monk* (Berkeley: University of California Press, 2003); Lempert, *Discipline and Debate*; José Ignacio Cabezón, *Buddhism and Language: A Study of Indo-Tibetan Scholasticism* (Albany, N.Y.: State University of New York Press, 1994); Elijah S. Ary, *Authorized Lives: Biography and the Early Formation of Geluk Identity* (Boston: Wisdom, 2015).

61. Blo bzang rta mgrin, "Rang Gi Byed Spyod Rags Bsdoms 'Di Snang Za Zi'i Rjes Gco," 175.

62. Memorization is also a central exercise in the monastic education of the other Tibetan Buddhist schools. On the rigors of memorization and its place in the Géluk curriculum, see Dreyfus, *The Sound of Two Hands Clapping*.

63. Blo bzang rta mgrin, "Rang Gi Byed Spyod Rags Bsdoms 'Di Snang Za Zi'i Rjes Gco," 175.

64. Tib. *'Dul ba lung sde bzhi*. The "four divisions" are commonly listed as: 1) 'Dul ba rnam 'byed, 2) 'Dul ba lung gzhi, 3) 'Dul ba phran tshegs, 4) 'Dul ba gzhung dam pa.

65. Blo bzang rta mgrin, "Rang Gi Byed Spyod Rags Bsdoms 'Di Snang Za Zi'i Rjes Gco," 177.

66. Skt. *Mūlamadhyamakakārikā*; Tib. *Dbu ma rtsa ba'i tshig le'u byas pa shes rab ches bya ba*.

67. This probably refers to Candrakīrti's classic seventh-cenutury verse-by-verse commentary *The Clear Words* (Skt. *Prasannapadā*; Tib. *dbu ma rtsa ba'i 'grel pa tshig gsal ba*), but could also be Tsongkhapa's *Rtsa she tik chen rigs pa'i rgya mtsho*.

68. Blo bzang rta mgrin, "Rang Gi Byed Spyod Rags Bsdoms 'Di Snang Za Zi'i Rjes Gco," 177.

69. Blo bzang rta mgrin, 179.

70. Tib. *A lag sha.* This major stopover for Mongols traveling to Eastern Tibet was found in the Alashan district (Ch. 阿拉善) near contemporary Yinchuan in Ningxia province. Alashan was home to several important Géluk monasteries and lines of incarnate lamas, foremost of which was Agwangdandar (Tib. Ngag dbang bstan dar, 1759–1831) whose works are widely referenced and commented upon by Zava Damdin.

71. This would have been the fourth 'Jam dbyangs bzhad pa, Bskal bzang thub bstan dbang phyug (1856–1916), a Géluk prelate enthroned at Bla brang bkra shis 'khyil monastery who met the Guangxu Emperor in Beijing in 1898.

72. Blo bzang rta mgrin (1975–1976). "Rang gi byed spyod rags bsdoms 'di snang za zi'i rjes gcod." In gsung 'bum/_blo bzang rta mgrin 11:169–203. New Delhi: Mongolian Lama Guru Deva, 1975), 178.

73. John Watt described the nineteenth-century Qing yamen as "one of the most conspicuous institutions in Ch'ing society, for it was the principal vehicle of political administration in a civilization that placed great emphasis on administration. . . . The county yamen served also as the main center for negotiation between bureaucratic government and informal local authority. . . . In short, the county-level yamen served both as the leading government instrument of public authority and as the primary arena of political exchange" (John R. Watt, "The Yamen and Urban Administration," in *The City in Late Imperial China*, ed. George William Skinner [Stanford, Calif.: Stanford University Press, 1977], 353). Isabelle Charleux lists Yamun süme in "Buddhist Monasteries in Southern Mongolia," in *The Buddhist Monastery: A Cross-Cultural Survey*, ed. Pierre Pichard and F Lagirarde (Paris: École française d'extrême-orient, 2003), 12.

74. Tib. *Sku 'bum byams pa gling.* Located near Xining city in the eastern Tibetan cultural region of Amdo (in what is today Qinghai province in the People's Republic of China), this monastery was founded by the Third Dalai Lama in 1583 at the putative birth site of the fourteenth-century founder of Zava Damdin's Géluk school, Rje Tsong kha pa blo bzang grags pa (1357–1419). By the end of the nineteenth century, it had long been a favored pilgrimage site for devotees from across Inner Asia north and east of the Tibetan cultural region, as well as for Han and Manchu devotees.

75. Blo bzang rta mgrin, "Dga' Ldan Theg Chen Gling Gi Bsngags Pa Mdo Tsam Brjod Pa," in *Rje Btsun Blo Bzang Rta Dbyangs Kyi Gsung 'Bum* (New Delhi: Mongolian Lama Guru Deva, 1975), 1:634.

76. Blo bzang rta mgrin, "Dga' Ldan Theg Chen Gling Gi Bsngags Pa Mdo Tsam Brjod Pa," 628.

77. Blo bzang rta mgrin, "Dga' Ldan Theg Chen Gling Gi Bsngags Pa Mdo Tsam Brjod Pa," 629.

78. Blo bzang rta mgrin, "Dga' Ldan Theg Chen Gling Gi Bsngags Pa Mdo Tsam Brjod Pa," 632.

79. Matthew W. King and Pamela E. Klassen, "Suppressing the Mad Elephant: Missionaries, Lamas, and the Mediation of Sacred Historiographies in the Tibetan Borderlands," *History and Anthropology* 26, no. 5 (October 20, 2015): 529–52.

80. *Dgon lung byams pa gling*, in contemporary Haidong district, Qinghai province.

81. *Chu bzang dgon dga' ldan mi 'gyur gling*, also in contemporary Haidong District, Qinghai province.

82. Tib. *Lcang skya*; Mong. *Jangji-a*; Ch. *Zhangjia*.

83. Tib. *Gser gtog rdo rje chang*.

84. Blo bzang rta mgrin, "Rang Gi Byed Spyod Rags Bsdoms 'Di Snang Za Zi'i Rjes Gco," 179.

85. Blo bzang rta mgrin, "Rang Gi Byed Spyod Rags Bsdoms 'Di Snang Za Zi'i Rjes Gco," 180.

86. Blo bzang rta mgrin, "Rang Gi Byed Spyod Rags Bsdoms 'Di Snang Za Zi'i Rjes Gco," 180.

87. Blo bzang rta mgrin, "Rgya Bod Hor Gsum Gyi Bstan Rtsis Rags Bsdus Legs Bshad Bdud Rtsi'i Thig Pa," in *Rje Btsun Blo Bzang Rta Dbyangs Gyi Gsung 'Bum*, 17 vols. (New Delhi: Mongolian Lama Guru Deva, 1975), vol. 1.

88. Blo bzang rta mgrin, "Rang Dgon Bstan Rtsis," in *Rje Btsun Blo Bzang Rta Dbyangs Kyi Gsung 'Bum*, 17 vols. (New Delhi: Mongolian Lama Guru Deva, 1975), 11:295–98.

89. Zava Damdin mentions Darva Paṇḍita in several colophons when dedicating works to him or citing him as inspiration for their composition. In some cases, Darva Paṇḍita and his monastic milieu were the primary topics of his writing, such as in "The Pleasant Voice of the Cuckoo: A Song in Praise of the Sacred Place of the Monastic Seat of Dashidarjailing from the Mouth of the Refuge of Northerly Beings and the Teachings, the Incarnate Lama, Precious One, Darva Paṇḍita" (Blo bzang rta mgrin, "Bkra Shis Gling Gi Gnas Bstod Khu Byug Skad Snyan," in *Rje Btsun Blo Bzang Rta Dbyangs Gyi Gsung 'Bum*, 17 vols. [New Delhi: Mongolian Lama Guru Deva, 1975], 1:637–40). Several texts were written by Zava Damdin according to Darva Paṇḍita's instruction or inspiration, such as one on monastic discipline, composed "In accordance with the desire . . . of the matchless friend of the teachings and beings, the Precious Emanation Body, Darva Paṇḍita." In addition to these is a brief biography of Darva Paṇḍita's previous lives (*'khrungs rabs*) entitled "Reverential Verses Producing Faith and Joy Enumerating the Previous Lives of the Friend of the Teachings and Beings in [this] Northerly Direction, the Supreme Incarnation, Precious One, Darva Paṇḍita" (Blo bzang rta mgrin, "Byang Phyogs Bstan 'gro'i Rtsa Lag Mchog Sprul Rin Po Che Dar Ba Paṇḍita'i 'Khrungs Rabs Gsol 'Debs Dad Ldan Dga' Bskyed," in *Rje Btsun Blo Bzang Rta Dbyangs Kyi Gsung 'Bum*, 17 vols. [New Delhi: Mongolian Lama Guru Deva, 1975], 6:259–64). For an introduction to the incarnation line of the Darva Paṇḍitas in India, Nepal, Tibet, and Mongolia, see L. Chaloupkova and D. Dashbadrakh, "About the Biography of Darpa Pandita Called The Beautiful Jewel Rosary of Victorious Teaching," *Archiv Orientalni* 71 (2003): 285–92.

90. Blo bzang rta mgrin, "Rang Gi Byed Spyod Rags Bsdoms 'Di Snang Za Zi'i Rjes Gco," 182.

91. Blo bzang rta mgrin, "Rang Gi Byed Spyod Rags Bsdoms 'Di Snang Za Zi'i Rjes Gco," 183.

92. See Melvyn C Goldstein, *A History of Modern Tibet, 1913-1951: The Demise of the Lamaist State* (Berkeley: University of California Press, 1989), 45–47.

93. Thub bstan rgya mtsho, 1876–1933.

94. For example: Boryn Zhambal et al., *Tales of an Old Lama* (Tring, UK: Institute of Buddhist Studies, 1997); Charles Alfred Bell, *Portrait of a Dalai Lama: The Life and Times of the Great Thirteenth* (London: Wisdom, 1987); Sampildondov Chuluun and Uradyn E. Bulag, *The Thirteenth Dalai Lama on the Run (1904–1906): Archival Documents from Mongolia* (Leiden: Brill, 2013).

95. Blo bzang rta mgrin, "Byang Phyogs Chen Po Hor Gyi Rgyal Khams Kyi Rtogs Brjod Kyi Bstan Bcos Chen Po Ngo Mtshar Gser Gyi Deb Ther," in *Rje Btsun Blo Bzang Rta Dbyangs Kyi Gsung 'Bum* (New Delhi: Mongolian Lama Guru Deva, 1975), 2:411–13. I would like to sincerely thank one of my anonymous reviewers who kindly pointed out a very careless error I had made in my translation of the section on the Panchen Lama in this citation. For more on the critical role of the Ninth Panchen Lama in the religious and political affairs of post-Qing Inner Asia, see Fabienne Jagou, *The Ninth Panchen Lama (1883–1937): A Life at the Crossroads of Sino-Tibetan Relations*, trans. Rebecca Bissett Buechel (Chiang Mai: Silkworm, 2011); Gray Tuttle, *Tibetan Buddhists in the Making of Modern China* (New York: Columbia University Press, 2005).

96. Blo bzang rta mgrin, "Rang Gi Byed Spyod Rags Bsdoms 'Di Snang Za Zi'i Rjes Gco," 182.

97. *gso sbyong.*

98. Skt. *Prātimokṣasūtra*; Tib. *So sor thar pa'i mdo.*

99. Blo bzang rta mgrin, "Rang Gi Byed Spyod Rags Bsdoms 'Di Snang Za Zi'i Rjes Gco," 183.

100. Krisztina Teleki, "Bogdiin Khüree: Monasteries and Temples of the Mongolian Capital (1651–1938)," *Études Mongoles, Sibériennes, Centralasiatiques et Tibétaines* 40 (2009); Majer, "Delgeriin Choir, the Monastery of Zawa Lam Damdin in the Gobi"; Lkhamsurengiin Khurelbaatar and G. Luvsantseren, *Ogtorguin tsagaan gardi*, vol. II (Ulaanbaatar: Mongol Uls, Shinzhlekh Ukhaany Akademiin Khel Zokhiolyn Khureelen, 1996).

101. Blo bzang rta mgrin, "Rang Gi Byed Spyod Rags Bsdoms 'Di Snang Za Zi'i Rjes Gco," 182.

102. Blo bzang rta mgrin, "Rang Gi Byed Spyod Rags Bsdoms 'Di Snang Za Zi'i Rjes Gco," 183.

103. Sh. Bira, *O "Zolotoi knige" Sh. Damdina [On Sh. Damdin's "Golden Book"]* (Ulan-Bator: Izd-vo Akademii nauk MNR, 1964), 6.

104. On the details of the economic and political toll of the Dalai Lama's stay, see Chuluun and Bulag, *The Thirteenth Dalai Lama on the Run (1904–1906).*

105. See Bell, *Portrait of a Dalai Lama*; Goldstein, *A History of Modern Tibet, 1913–1951.*

106. Blo bzang rta mgrin, "Rang Gi Byed Spyod Rags Bsdoms 'Di Snang Za Zi'i Rjes Gco," 183.

2. Felt

1. For an annotated translation of this complete letter and Zava Damdin's response, see Matthew W. King, "Agvan Dorjiev's Questions About the Past and

Future of Mongolian Buddhism," in *Sources of Mongolian Buddhism,* ed. Vesna Wallace (New York: Oxford University Press, forthcoming). On Agvan Dorjiev's life, see: Nikolay Tsyrempilov, "The Open and Secret Diplomacy of Tsarist and Soviet Russia in Tibet: The Role of Agvan Dorzhiev (1912–1925)," in *Asiatic Russia: Imperial Power in Religional and International Contexts,* ed. Tomochiko Uyama (London and New York: Routledge, 2012); John Snelling, *Buddhism in Russia: The Story of Agvan Dorzhiev, Lhasa's Emissary to the Tzar* (Rockport, Mass.: Element Books Limited, 1993); Agvan Dorjiev, Thubten Jigme Norbu, and Dan Martin, *Dorjiev: Memoirs of a Tibetan Diplomat* (Tokyo: Hokke bunka kenkyū, 1991); Yeshen-Khorlo and Robert Montgomery Dugarava-Montgomery, "The Buriat Alphabet of Agvan Dorzhiev," in *Mongolia in the Twentieth Century,* ed. Stephen and Bruce A. Elleman Kotkin (Armonk, N.Y.; London: M. E. Sharpe, 1999), 79–97; Nikolai Kuleshov, "Agvan Dorjiev, the Dalai Lama's Ambassador," *Asian Affairs* 23, no. 1 (1992): 20–33.

2. Blo bzang rta mgrin [Agvan Dorjiev], "Mtshan Zhabs Mkhan Chen Gyis Chos 'Byung Las Brtsams Te Bka' 'dri Gnang Ba'i Chab Shog," in *Rje Btsun Blo Bzang Rta Dbyangs Kyi Gsung 'Bum,* vol. 2 (New Delhi: Mongolian Lama Guru Deva, 1975), 554.

3. Blo bzang rta mgrin, "Mtshan Zhabs Mkhan Chen Gyi Dogs Lan Tshangs Pa'i Drang Thig," in *Rje Btsun Blo Bzang Rta Dbyangs Kyi Gsung 'Bum,* 17 vols. (New Delhi: Mongolian Lama Guru Deva, 1975), 2:561–72.

4. Lkhamsurengiin Khurelbaatar and G. Luvsantseren, *Ogtorguin tsagaan gardi* (Ulaanbaatar: Mongol Uls, Shinzhlekh Ukhaany Akademiin Khel Zokhiolyn Khureelen, 1996), II:237.

5. Blo-bzaṅ-rta-mgrin, *The Golden Annals of Lamaism Being the Original Tibetan Text of the Hor-Chos-Ḥbyuṅ of Blo-Bzaṅ-Rta-Mgrin Entitled 'Jam Gliṅ Byaṅ Phyogs Chen Po Hor Gyi Rgyal Khams Kyi Rtogs Pa Brjod Pa'i Bstan Bcos Chen Po Dpyod Ldan Mgu Byed Ṅo Mćhar Gser Gyi Deb Ther,* ed. Lokesh Chandra, Śata-Piṭaka 34 (New Delhi: International Academy of Indian Culture, 1964), v.

6. Blo bzang rta mgrin, "Rgya Bod Hor Gsum Gyi Bstan Rtsis Rags Bsdus Legs Bshad Bdud Rtsi'i Thig Pa," in *Rje Btsun Blo Bzang Rta Dbyangs Gyi Gsung 'Bum,* 17 vols. (New Delhi: Mongolian Lama Guru Deva, 1975), vol. 1.

7. Blo bzang rta mgrin, "Byang Phyogs Chen Po Hor Gyi Rgyal Khams Kyi Rtogs Brjod Kyi Bstan Bcos Chen Po Ngo Mtshar Gser Gyi Deb Ther," in *Rje Btsun Blo Bzang Rta Dbyangs Kyi Gsung 'Bum* (New Delhi: Mongolian Lama Guru Deva, 1975), 2:481–82.

8. I note these genres in passing to provide general readers with a sense of the breadth of historical writing available to Zava Damdin in the early twentieth century. Specialist readers will know already that in practice these "genres" usually shared subject matter, literary styles, and rhetoric.

9. Khurelbaatar and Luvsantseren, *Ogtorguin tsagaan gardi,* II:230.

10. William A. Brown, Urgunge Onon, and B. Shirendev, *History of the Mongolian People's Republic* ([Cambridge, Mass.: East Asian Research Center, Harvard University, 1976), 263.

11. Blo bzang rta mgrin, "Btsun Pa Phā Hyin Gyis 'phags Pa'i Yul Du 'Grims Pa'i Rnam Thar Rje Nyid Kyis Gsar 'Gyur Mchan Dang Bcas Pa," in *Rje Btsun Blo Bzang Rta Dbyangs Kyi Gsung 'Bum* (New Delhi: Mongolian Lama Guru Deva, 1975), 1:242.

12. Blo bzang rta mgrin, "Btsun Pa Phā Hyin Gyis 'phags Pa'i Yul Du 'Grims Pa'i Rnam Thar Rje Nyid Kyis Gsar 'Gyur Mchan Dang Bcas Pa," 242.

2. FELT

13. Donald S. Lopez, *Strange Tales of an Oriental Idol: An Anthology of Early European Portrayals of the Buddha* (Chicago: University of Chicago Press, 2016), 225.

14. Anya Bernstein, "Pilgrims, Fieldworkers, and Secret Agents: Buryat Buddhologists and the History of an Eurasian Imaginary," *Inner Asia* 11, no. 1 (2009): 23–45.

15. Christopher P. Atwood, "Buddhism and Popular Ritual in Mongolian Religion: A Reexamination of the Fire Cult," *History of Religions* 36, no. 2 (1996): 113.

16. Blo bzang rta mgrin, "Byang Phyogs Chen Po Hor Gyi Rgyal Khams Kyi Rtogs Brjod Kyi Bstan Bcos Chen Po Ngo Mtshar Gser Gyi Deb Ther," 481.

17. Blo bzang rta mgrin, "Byang Phyogs Chen Po Hor Gyi Rgyal Khams Kyi Rtogs Brjod Kyi Bstan Bcos Chen Po Ngo Mtshar Gser Gyi Deb Ther," 481.

18. Blo bzang rta mgrin, "Byang Phyogs Chen Po Hor Gyi Rgyal Khams Kyi Rtogs Brjod Kyi Bstan Bcos Chen Po Ngo Mtshar Gser Gyi Deb Ther," 481.

19. Blo bzang rta mgrin, "Chen Po Hor Gyi Yul Gru'i Sngon Rabs Kyi Brjed Byang Shāstra'i Zur Rgyan Du Sog Yig Las Bod Skad Du Bsgyur Te Bkod Pa," in *Rje Btsun Blo Bzang Rta Dbyangs Kyi Gsung 'Bum* (New Delhi: Mongolian Lama Guru Deva, 1975), vol. 2.

20. Blo bzang rta mgrin, "Gnas Brtan Bcu Drug Gi Lung Bstan Gsar Rnyed 'phros Dang Bcas Pa," in *Rje Btsun Blo Bzang Rta Dbyangs Kyi Gsung 'Bum*, 17 vols. (New Delhi: Mongolian Lama Guru Deva, 1975), 3:477–96.

21. Blo bzang rta mgrin, "Rgya Spar Gnas Brtan Bcu Drug Gi Zhal Byang Bod Skad Du Bsgyur Ba 'phros Bshad Dang Bcas Pa," in *Rje Btsun Blo Bzang Rta Dbyangs Kyi Gsung 'Bum*, 17 vols. (New Delhi: Mongolian Lama Guru Deva, 1975), 3:497–512.

22. Blo bzang rta mgrin, "Rnam Thar Gces Btus Bdud Rtsi'i Bsang Gtor," in *Rje Btsun Blo Bzang Rta Dbyangs Kyi Gsung 'Bum*, 17 vols. (New Delhi: Mongolian Lama Guru Deva, 1975), vol. 7; Blo bzang rta mgrin, "Rje Btsun Ce Tā Yan Gyi Rnam Thar Gces Btus Dran Thor Bsgyur Ba Chos Rnga'i Sgra Skad," in *Rje Btsun Blo Bzang Rta Dbyangs Kyi Gsung 'Bum*, 17 vols. (New Delhi: Mongolian Lama Guru Deva, 1975), 3:515–26; Blo bzang rta mgrin, "Ri Bo Rtse Lnga'i Bstod," in *Rje Btsun Blo Bzang Rta Dbyangs Kyi Gsung 'Bum*, 17 vols. (New Delhi: Mongolian Lama Guru Deva, 1975), 1:625–28; Blo bzang rta mgrin, "Rgya Spar Gnas Brtan Bcu Drug Gi Zhal Byang Bod Skad Du Bsgyur Ba 'phros Bshad Dang Bcas Pa"; Blo bzang rta mgrin, "Rgyal Sras Rtag Tu Ngu'i Rnam Thar Las Brtsams Pa'i Bstod Pa," in *Rje Btsun Blo Bzang Rta Dbyangs Kyi Gsung 'Bum*, 17 vols. (New Delhi: Mongolian Lama Guru Deva, 1975), 1:135–46; Blo bzang rta mgrin, "Rgyal Sras Gzhon Nu nor Bzang Gi Rnam Thar Las Brtsams Pa'i Bstod Pa," in *Rje Btsun Blo Bzang Rta Dbyangs Kyi Gsung 'Bum*, 17 vols. (New Delhi: Mongolian Lama Guru Deva, 1975), 1:119–34; Blo bzang rta mgrin, "Rgyal Chen Rdo Rje Shugs Ldan Rtsal Gyi Bskang 'phrin Mdor Bsdus Don Chen Myur Grub," in *Rje Btsun Blo Bzang Rta Dbyangs Kyi Gsung 'Bum*, 17 vols. (New Delhi: Mongolian Lama Guru Deva, 1975), 11:385–92; Blo bzang rta mgrin, "Rang Dgon Bstan Rtsis," in *Rje Btsun Blo Bzang Rta Dbyangs Kyi Gsung 'Bum*, 17 vols. (New Delhi: Mongolian Lama Guru Deva, 1975), 11:295–98; Blo bzang rta mgrin, "Bka' Drin Gsum Ldan Rtsa Ba'i Bla Ma Rdo Rje 'chang Mkhan Chen Sangs Rgyas Mtshan Can Gyi Rnam Thar Gsol 'Debs Dad Ldan Yid Kyi Mdzas Rgyan," in *Rje Btsun Blo Bzang Rta Dbyangs Kyi Gsung 'Bum*, 17 vols. (New Delhi: Mongolian Lama Guru Deva, 1975), 1:7–19; Blo bzang rta mgrin, " 'Jam Mgon Rgyal Ba Gnyis Pa'i Bstan Srung Thun Mong Ma Yin Pa Rgyal Chen Rdo Rje Shugs Ldan Rtsal Gyi Chos Skor Be Bum Du Bsgrigs Pa'i Dkar Chag Gnam Lcags 'Khor Lo'i Mu Khyud 'Phrin Las 'Od 'Bar," in *Rje Btsun Blo Bzang Rta Dbyangs Kyi Gsung 'Bum*, 17 vols. (New Delhi: Mongolian Lama

Guru Deva, 1975), 11:395–414; Blo bzang rta mgrin, "Gnas Brtan Bcu Drug Gi Lung Bstan Gsar Rnyed 'phros Dang Bcas Pa"; Blo bzang rta mgrin, "Gdan Sa Khu Re Chen Mo'i Chos Grwa Nub Ma'i 'byung Khungs Dang 'Brel Ba'i Gtam Gyi Phreng Ba," in *Rje Btsun Blo Bzang Rta Dbyangs Kyi Gsung 'Bum*, 17 vols. (New Delhi: Mongolian Lama Guru Deva, 1975), 1:503–40; Blo bzang rta mgrin, "Dpal Ldan 'bras Spungs Su Mchod Rten Gsar Du Bzhengs Pa'i Nang Gzhug Gi Dkar Chag," in *Rje Btsun Blo Bzang Rta Dbyangs Kyi Gsung 'Bum*, 17 vols. (New Delhi: Mongolian Lama Guru Deva, 1975), 6 (cha):443–48; Blo bzang rta mgrin, "Dpal Ldan Bla Ma Dam Pa Erteni Paṇḍita Sprul Sku'i Rnam Thar Gyi Sa Bon Dpag Bsam Myu Gu," in *Rje Btsun Blo Bzang Rta Dbyangs Kyi Gsung 'Bum*, 17 vols. (New Delhi: Mongolian Lama Guru Deva, 1975), vol. 7; Blo bzang rta mgrin, "Dga' Ldan Theg Chen Gling Gi Bsngags Pa Mdo Tsam Brjod Pa," in *Rje Btsun Blo Bzang Rta Dbyangs Kyi Gsung 'Bum*, 17 vols. (New Delhi: Mongolian Lama Guru Deva, 1975), 1:627–34; Blo bzang rta mgrin, "Dben Pa'i Bsti Gnas Gsar Rnying Gcig Tu 'dres Pa'i Lo Rgyus Ma Bu Cha 'Dzoms Kyi Gleng Mo," in *Rje Btsun Blo Bzang Rta Dbyangs Kyi Gsung 'Bum*, 17 vols. (New Delhi: Mongolian Lama Guru Deva, 1975), 1:607–16; Blo bzang rta mgrin, "Dam Can Chos Rgyal Dang Rgyal Chen Shugs Ldan Gnyis Kyi Nang Gzhug Dkar Chag Bdud Dpung Zil Gnon," in *Rje Btsun Blo Bzang Rta Dbyangs Kyi Gsung 'Bum*, 17 vols. (New Delhi: Mongolian Lama Guru Deva, 1975), 6:409–14; Blo bzang rta mgrin, "Byang Phyogs Hor Gyi Yul Grur Ston Pa'i Sku Tshab Tu Bzhugs Pa'i Rten Rnying Ertini Jo Bo'i Rnam Thar Dang 'brel Ba'i Dus Bstun Gsol 'Debs," in *Rje Btsun Blo Bzang Rta Dbyangs Kyi Gsung 'Bum*, 17 vols. (New Delhi: Mongolian Lama Guru Deva, 1975), 1:39–44; Blo bzang rta mgrin, "Bkra Shis Thos Bsam Gling Gi 'byung Khungs Tho Tsam," in *Rje Btsun Blo Bzang Rta Dbyangs Kyi Gsung 'Bum*, 17 vols. (New Delhi: Mongolian Lama Guru Deva, 1975), 1:597–606; Blo bzang rta mgrin, "Bkra Shis Gling Gi Gnas Bstod Khu Byug Skad Snyan," in *Rje Btsun Blo Bzang Rta Dbyangs Gyi Gsung 'Bum*, 17 vols. (New Delhi: Mongolian Lama Guru Deva, 1975), 1:637–40.

23. Blo bzang rta mgrin, "Chos Sde Chos Dbyings 'od Gsal Gling Gi 'Byung Khungs Mdo Tsam Brjod Pa," in *Rje Btsun Blo Bzang Rta Dbyangs Kyi Gsung 'Bum*, 17 vols. (New Delhi: Mongolian Lama Guru Deva, 1975), 1:541–85.

24. Blo bzang rta mgrin, "Bkra Shis Thos Bsam Gling Gi 'byung Khungs Tho Tsam."

25. Blo bzang rta mgrin, "Bkra Shis Gling Gi Gnas Bstod Khu Byug Skad Snyan."

26. Makoto Tachibana, "From Chronicle to National History: Mongolian Historiography in the Early Twentieth Century," paper presented at Association for Asian Studies 2017 Annual Conference, Toronto, March 19, 2017.

27. Lkhamsurengiin Khurelbaatar and G. Luvsantseren, *Ogtorguin tsagaan gardi* (Ulaanbaatar: Mongol Uls, Shinzhlekh Ukhaany Akademiin Khel Zokhiolyn Khureelen, 1996), II:239.

28. For examples of only some rich Mongolian scholarly treatments, see: Khurelbaatar and Luvsantseren, *Ogtorguin tsagaan gardi*; Sh. Soninbayar, *Lawain Egshig, 2* (Ulaanbaatar: Gadentegchenling Khiid, 1997). Two Soviet-era studies also stand out, which I reference elsewhere in this book: Byambyn Rinchen et al., *Travels of Fa Hsian Translated by Dordji Bansaroff* (Ulanbator: Corpus Scriptorum Mongolorum Instituti Linguae Litterarum Academiae Scientiarum Reipublicae Populi Mongolici, 1970); Sh Bira, *O "Zolotoi knige" Sh. Damdina [On Sh. Damdin's "Golden Book"]* (Ulan-Bator: Izd-vo Akademii nauk MNR, 1964). An exception to this lacuna in the European and North American academy is the body of work of Krisztina Teleki and Zsuzsa Majer, whose

ongoing projects to document the pre-purge past of Mongolian monasticism regularly reference Zava Damdin and his institutional "place." See, for example: Krisztina Teleki, "Mongólia Kolostorai Az Arany Krónika Jegyzéke Alapján," in *Bolor-un gerel: Kristályfény: Tanulmányok Kara György Professzor 70. Születésnapjának Tiszteletére*, ed. Ágnes Birtalan, 2 vols. (Budapest: Eötvös Lóránd Tudományegyetem, Belső-ázsiai Tanszék, 2005), 2:773–90; Krisztina Teleki, *Monasteries and Temples of Bogdiin Khuree* (Ulaanbaatar: Institute of History, Mongolian Academy of Sciences, 2011); Zsuzsa Majer, "Delgeriin Choir, the Monastery of Zawa Lam Damdin in the Gobi," in *Zentralasiatische Studien Des Seminars Für Sprach- Und Kulturwissenschaft Zentralasiens Der Universität Bonn* (International Institute for Tibetan and Buddhist Studies, 2012), 41:7–42.

29. M. M. Bakhtin and M. Holquist, *The Dialogic Imagination: Four Essays* (Austin: University of Texas Press, 1981), 253.

30. Katerina Clark and Michael Holquist, *Mikhail Bakhtin* (Cambridge, Mass.: Belknap Press of Harvard University Press, 1984), 278.

31. Bakhtin and Holquist, *The Dialogic Imagination*, 84.

32. In case there is any confusion, my use of Bakhtin's rubric of literary analysis is unconnected to Buddhist notions of "emptiness" as the ultimate nature of reality (Skt. *śūnyatā*; Tib. *stong pa nyid*; Mong. *kho γusun*) in Buddhist philosophy.

33. Bakhtin and Holquist, *The Dialogic Imagination*, 109.

34. Michael Holquist, *Dialogism: Bakhtin and His World* (New York: Routledge, 2003), 110.

35. Bakhtin and Holquist, *The Dialogic Imagination*, 94.

36. Bakhtin and Holquist, *The Dialogic Imagination*, 94.

37. Johan Elverskog, *Our Great Qing: The Mongols, Buddhism, and the State in Late Imperial China* (Honolulu: University of Hawai'i Press, 2006), 112.

38. Blo bzang rta mgrin, "Chen Po Hor Gyi Yul Gru'i Sngon Rabs Kyi Brjed Byang Shāstra'i Zur Rgyan Du Sog Yig Las Bod Skad Du Bsgyur Te Bkod Pa," 544.

39. Blo bzang rta mgrin, "Byang Phyogs Chen Po Hor Gyi Rgyal Khams Kyi Rtogs Brjod Kyi Bstan Bcos Chen Po Ngo Mtshar Gser Gyi Deb Ther," 321–25.

40. Blo bzang rta mgrin, "Byang Phyogs Chen Po Hor Gyi Rgyal Khams Kyi Rtogs Brjod Kyi Bstan Bcos Chen Po Ngo Mtshar Gser Gyi Deb Ther," 98.

41. Blo bzang rta mgrin, "Chen Po Hor Gyi Yul Gru'i Sngon Rabs Kyi Brjed Byang Shāstra'i Zur Rgyan Du Sog Yig Las Bod Skad Du Bsgyur Te Bkod Pa," 543.

42. According to the spatial conventions of these Tibeto-Mongolian sources, "upper" (*stod*) generally refers to west and "lower" (*smad*) to east.

43. Blo bzang rta mgrin, "Byang Phyogs Chen Po Hor Gyi Rgyal Khams Kyi Rtogs Brjod Kyi Bstan Bcos Chen Po Ngo Mtshar Gser Gyi Deb Ther," in *Rje Btsun Blo Bzang Rta Dbyangs Kyi Gsung 'Bum* (New Delhi: Mongolian Lama Guru Deva, 1975), 2:67.

44. Blo bzang rta mgrin, "Byang Phyogs Chen Po Hor Gyi Rgyal Khams Kyi Rtogs Brjod Kyi Bstan Bcos Chen Po Ngo Mtshar Gser Gyi Deb Ther," 54.

45. *Lho brag mkhan chen*. There are two incarnations to whom this may refer; both were thirteenth-century Sakya masters in the Géluk graduated path tradition (*lam rim*): Senggé Zangpo (Seng ge bzang po) and Namka Gyelpo (Nam mkha' rgyal po). Both of their biographies are included in Ye shes rgyal mtshan, *Lam Rim Bla Ma Brgyud Pa'i Rnam Thar*, 2 vols. (New Delhi: Grib Tshe Mchog Gling Grwa Tshang Gi Par Khang, 1970–1972).

46. Blo bzang rta mgrin, "Byang Phyogs Chen Po Hor Gyi Rgyal Khams Kyi Rtogs Brjod Kyi Bstan Bcos Chen Po Ngo Mtshar Gser Gyi Deb Ther," 68.

47. *'Od bag can.* I am unsure which bodhisattva this refers to. Perhaps this is an alternative (or mis-) spelling of Amitābha (Tib. *'Od dpag med*).

48. Skt. *Kaṁsadeśavyākaraṇa*; Tib. *Li yul lung bstan pa'i mdo.*

49. *Mutka la'i rigs.*

50. Blo bzang rta mgrin, "Byang Phyogs Hor Gyi Yul Du Dam Pa'i Chos Rin Po Che Byung Tshul Gyi Gtam Rgyud Bkra Shis Chos Dung Bzhad Pa'i Sgra Dbyangs," in *Rje Btsun Blo Bzang Rta Dbyangs Kyi Gsung 'Bum* (New Delhi: Mongolian Lama Guru Deva, 1975), 2:11–12.

51. Tib.: *Blo, Rdo, Kha khra, Kha sog, Gzha,' Kha sud, Dmar, Rtsa phung, Rdo bo ri, Bram tsha, Hu thug, Kha gling, Sprel slag, Khyi khyo, Dar slog, Zhang tsha bya.*

52. *Man tsi.*

53. *Yi wes.*

54. *Hwa sag.*

55. *Kho tsag.*

56. *Khir ki si.*

57. *Tsampa ka.*

58. *Rug ma.*

59. *Bu rasma.*

60. *Mi 'am ci.* "A class of wondrous celestial musicians in the court of KUBERA, ranking below the GANDHARVA" (Robert E. Buswell and Donald S. Lopez, *The Princeton Dictionary of Buddhism* [Princeton, N.J.: Princeton University Press, 2013], 436).

61. *Dri za.* Literally "smell eaters," these are understood to be the form samsaric beings take in the intermediate state, after death in one lifetime, but prior to the following rebirth. Their bodies are thought to be so subtle that they can only subsist on smell, not more solid substances. See Buswell and Lopez, *The Princeton Dictionary of Buddhism*, 3112.

62. *Snod sbyan.*

63. Blo bzang rta mgrin, "Byang Phyogs Chen Po Hor Gyi Rgyal Khams Kyi Rtogs Brjod Kyi Bstan Bcos Chen Po Ngo Mtshar Gser Gyi Deb Ther," 52–53.

64. *Su kha pān.*

65. Blo bzang rta mgrin, "Byang Phyogs Hor Gyi Yul Du Dam Pa'i Chos Rin Po Che Byung Tshul Gyi Gtam Rgyud Bkra Shis Chos Dung Bzhad Pa'i Sgra Dbyangs," 9–10.

66. Gray Tuttle, "Challenging Central Tibet's Dominance of History: The Oceanic Book, a Nineteenth-Century Politico-Religious Geographic History," in *Mapping the Modern in Tibet. PIATS 2006: Proceedings of the Eleventh Seminar of the International Association for Tibetan Studies. Königswinter 2006,* ed. Gray Tuttle ([Andiast, Switzerland]: IITBS, International Institute for Tibetan and Buddhist Studies GmbH, 2011), 135–72.

67. Blo bzang rta mgrin, "Byang Phyogs Hor Gyi Yul Du Dam Pa'i Chos Rin Po Che Byung Tshul Gyi Gtam Rgyud Bkra Shis Chos Dung Bzhad Pa'i Sgra Dbyangs," 9–10.

68. Blo bzang rta mgrin, "Byang Phyogs Hor Gyi Yul Du Dam Pa'i Chos Rin Po Che Byung Tshul Gyi Gtam Rgyud Bkra Shis Chos Dung Bzhad Pa'i Sgra Dbyangs," 12–13.

69. Blo bzang rta mgrin, "Byang Phyogs Hor Gyi Yul Du Dam Pa'i Chos Rin Po Che Byung Tshul Gyi Gtam Rgyud Bkra Shis Chos Dung Bzhad Pa'i Sgra Dbyangs," 175–77.

70. *K.wa li.*

71. *Phe ring dag gis a tsi ya'i gling zer.* Blo bzang rta mgrin, "Byang Phyogs Chen Po Hor Gyi Rgyal Khams Kyi Rtogs Brjod Kyi Bstan Bcos Chen Po Ngo Mtshar Gser Gyi Deb Ther," 53–54.

72. Blo bzang rta mgrin, "Chen Po Hor Gyi Yul Gru'i Sngon Rabs Kyi Brjed Byang Shāstra'i Zur Rgyan Du Sog Yig Las Bod Skad Du Bsgyur Te Bkod Pa," 545.

73. Rupen, "The Buriat Intelligentsia," 396 n. 34.

74. "A Short History of the Uyghurs" was written in 1912, but I am unsure when it was published in the *New Mirror* (Dittmar Schorkowitz, *Staat und national-itäten in Rußland: der Integrationsprozess der Burjaten und Kalmücken, 1822-1925* [Stuttgart: F. Steiner Verlag, 2001], 296 n. 79). Ramstedt wrote at least two major works on Mongolian writing and linguistics: G. J. Ramstedt, *Über die Konjugation des Khalkha-Mongolischen.* (Helsingfors: Finnischen Litteraturgesellschaft, 1902); G. J. Ramstedt and Suomalais-ugrilainen Seura, *Das Schriftmongolische und die Urgamundart, phonetisch verglichen* (Helsingfors: Druckerei der Finnischen Litteratur Gesellschaf, 1903). On Ramstedt's fascinating career, see Harry Halén and Suomalais-ugrilainen Seura, *Biliktu Bakshi, the Knowledgeable Teacher: G. J. Ramstedt's Career as a Scholar* (Helsinki: Finno-Ugrian Society, 1998); G. J. Ramstedt and John Richard Krueger, *Seven Journeys Eastward, 1898-1912: Among the Cheremis, Kalmyks, Mongols, and in Turkestan, and to Afghanistan* (Bloomington, Ind.: Mongolia Society, 1978).

75. Christopher Kaplonski, *Truth, History and Politics in Mongolia: The Memory of Heroes* (London; New York: RoutledgeCurzon, 2004), 101.

76. For an English translation and study, see Johan Elverskog, "G. J. Ramstedt's 'A Short History of the Uyghurs,'" in *Festschrift for Larry Clark on His 75th Birthday*, ed. Zsuzsanna Gulasci (Turnhout: Brepols, forthcoming).

77. Blo bzang rta mgrin, "Byang Phyogs Chen Po Hor Gyi Rgyal Khams Kyi Rtogs Brjod Kyi Bstan Bcos Chen Po Ngo Mtshar Gser Gyi Deb Ther," 78–83.

78. Léon Cahun, *La bannière bleue: Aventures d'un musulman, d'un chrétien et d'un païen, à l'époque des Croisades et de la conquête mongole* (Paris: Hachette, 1877).

79. Blo bzang rta mgrin, "Byang Phyogs Chen Po Hor Gyi Rgyal Khams Kyi Rtogs Brjod Kyi Bstan Bcos Chen Po Ngo Mtshar Gser Gyi Deb Ther," 54–55.

80. Khurelbaatar and Luvsantseren, *Ogtorguin tsagaan gardi*, II:228.

81. I.e., the famous Tibetan medical treatise *G.yu thog snying thig.*

82. Skt. *Nyāyabinduprakaraṇa*; Tib. *Rigs pa'i thig pa zhes bya ba'i rab tu byed pa.* One of Dharmakīrti's (circa) seventh-century "Seven Treatises on Valid Cognition" (Skt. *Pramanavartikadisapta-grantha-samgraha*; Tib. *Tshad ma sde bdun*). The quality of schol-arship on these sorts of Sanskrit treatises on logic and epistemology had made the Russian Buddhologists famous around the world. The strength of their work ensured a remarkably consistent trajectory of scholarly inquiry from tsarist Russia through the USSR period to today. It was Shcherbatsky who "organized a massive display in Petersburg of Buddhist exhibits, and leading buddhologists delivered lectures. Soviet as opposed to Russian study of Buddhism had begun" (James Thrower, *Marxist-Leninist "Scientific Atheism" and the Study of Religion and Atheism in the USSR* [Berlin; New York: Mouton, 1983], 421).

83. Blo bzang rta mgrin, "Rang Gi Byed Spyod Rags Bsdoms 'Di Snang Za Zi'i Rjes Gco," in *Rje Btsun Blo Bzang Rta Dbyangs Kyi Gsung 'Bum* (New Delhi: Mongolian Lama Guru Deva, 1975), 11:196.

84. Mikhael Tubyansky, "Nekotorye Problemy Mongol'skoi Literatury Dorevoly-Utsionnogo Perioda [Some Problems of Mongolian Literature of the Prerevolutionary Period]," *Sovremennaya Mongoliya* 5, no. 12 (1935): 7–30. Despite Tubyansky's presence in Zava Damdin's writing, I have been unable to find any writing by the former about his time with the Mongol monk.

85. Bira, *O "Zolotoi knige" Sh. Damdina*, 6.

86. Blo bzang rta mgrin, "Byang Phyogs Chen Po Hor Gyi Rgyal Khams Kyi Rtogs Brjod Kyi Bstan Bcos Chen Po Ngo Mtshar Gser Gyi Deb Ther," 84.

87. On very related topics, see: Munkh-Erdene Lhamsuren, "The Mongolian Nationality Lexicon: From the Chinggisid Lineage to Mongolian Nationality (From the Seventeenth to the Early Twentieth Century)," *Inner Asia* 8, no. 1 (2006): 51–98; Owen Lattimore, *Nationalism and Revolution in Mongolia: With a Translation from the Mongol of Sh. Nachukdorji's Life of Sukebatur* (New York: Oxford University Press, 1955); Uradyn Erden Bulag, *Nationalism and Hybridity in Mongolia* (Oxford; New York: Clarendon Press; Oxford University Press, 1998); David Sneath, "Political Mobilization and the Construction of Collective Identity in Mongolia," *Central Asian Survey* 29, no. 3 (2010): 251–67.

88. A. Amar, *Mongγol-Un Tobci Teüke [A Brief History of Mongolia]* (Bloomington, Ind.: The Mongolia Society, 1986), vol. 9.

89. Myriam Revault d'Allonnes, *La crise sans fin: essai sur l'expérience moderne du temps* (Paris: Seuil, 2012); Reinhart Koselleck, *Futures Past: On the Semantics of Historical Time* (New York: Columbia University Press, 2004); Paul Ricœur, *Memory, History, Forgetting*, trans. Kathleen Blamey and David Pellauer (Chicago: University of Chicago Press, 2010).

3. Milk

1. Svetlana Boym, *The Future of Nostalgia* (New York: Basic Books, 2001), xvi. I offer my deep thanks to Professor Johan Elverskog for suggesting Boym's work while responding to a presentation on material from this book on a panel about Qing nostalgia presented at the 2017 Annual Meeting of the Association for Asian Studies in Toronto.

2. Boym, *The Future of Nostalgia*, xvi.

3. Dipesh Chakrabarty, *Provincializing Europe: Postcolonial Thought and Historical Difference* (Princeton, N.J.: Princeton University Press, 2009); Robert A. Orsi, *History and Presence* (Cambridge, Mass.: Harvard University Press, 2016); Aisha M. Beliso-De Jesús, *Electric Santería: Racial and Sexual Assemblages of Transnational Religion* (New York: Columbia University Press, 2015); Michel de Certeau, *La Possession de Loudun* (Paris: Julliard, 1970).

4. Blo bzang rta mgrin, "Byang Phyogs Hor Gyi Yul Du Dam Pa'i Chos Rin Po Che Byung Tshul Gyi Gtam Rgyud Bkra Shis Chos Dung Bzhad Pa'i Sgra Dbyangs," in *Rje Btsun Blo Bzang Rta Dbyangs Kyi Gsung 'Bum* (New Delhi: Mongolian Lama Guru Deva, 1975), 2:34.

5. Blo bzang rta mgrin, "Chen Po Hor Gyi Yul Gru'i Sngon Rabs Kyi Brjed Byang Shāstra'i Zur Rgyan Du Sog Yig Las Bod Skad Du Bsgyur Te Bkod Pa," in *Rje Btsun Blo Bzang Rta Dbyangs Kyi Gsung 'Bum* (New Delhi: Mongolian Lama Guru Deva, 1975), 2:545.

6. Originally the name of the Dalai Lama's hereditary seat at Drépung monastery in Central Tibet (Tib. 'Bras spungs dgon), beginning with the Fifth Dalai Lama, his regent, Sanggyé Gyatso, and the Mongol forces of Güüshi Khaan, in the seventeenth century the Ganden Potrang became the de facto political authority in Central Tibet. For a fascinating discussion of the legal frameworks for the Ganden Potrang government, rooted firmly in the ideology of the Two Systems, see Rebecca R. French, "Tibetan Legal Literature: The Law Codes of the DGa' Ldan Pho Brang," in *Tibetan Literature: Studies in Genre*, ed. Lhundup Sopa, José Ignacio Cabezón, and Roger R. Jackson (Ithaca, N.Y.: Snow Lion, 1996), 438–57.

7. Nancy G. Lin, "Recounting the Fifth Dalai Lama's Rebirth Lineage," *Revue d'Etudes Tibétaines* 38 (Février 2017): 120.

8. Ishihama Yumiko, "The Notion of 'Buddhist Government' (chos srid) Shared by Tibet, Mongol, and Manchu in the Early 17th Century," in *The Relationship Between Religion and State (chos srid zung 'brel) in Traditional Tibet: Proceedings of a Seminar Held in Lumbini, Nepal, March 2000*, ed. Christoph Cüppers (Lumbini: Lumbini International Research Institute, 2004), 15–31; Peter Schwieger, *The Dalai Lama and the Emperor of China: A Political History of the Tibetan Institution of Reincarnation* (New York: Columbia University Press, 2015).

9. For a fascinating quantitative study of the growth of the *sprul sku* tradition out of Central Tibet during the Qing formation, see Gray Tuttle, "Pattern Recognition: Tracking the Spread of the Incarnation Institution Through Time and Across History," *Revue d'Etudes Tibétaines* 38 (Février 2017): 29–64.

10. Ishihama Yumiko, "The Notion of 'Buddhist Government' (chos srid) Shared by Tibet, Mongol, and Manchu in the Early 17th Century," 16.

11. Ishihama Yumiko, "The Notion of 'Buddhist Government' (chos srid) Shared by Tibet, Mongol, and Manchu in the Early 17th Century," 22.

12. Cited in Ishihama Yumiko, "The Notion of 'Buddhist Government' (chos srid) Shared by Tibet, Mongol, and Manchu in the Early 17th Century," 18.

13. Ishihama Yumiko, "The Notion of 'Buddhist Government' (chos srid) Shared by Tibet, Mongol, and Manchu in the Early 17th Century," 19.

14. See Carl Johan Elverskog, "Buddhism, History and Power: The Jewel Translucent Sutra and the Formation of Mongol Identity" (9993532, Indiana University, 2000), ProQuest Books & Theses (PQDT) (MSTAR_304600342); Johan Elverskog, "Mongol Time Enters a Qing World," in *Time, Temporality, and Imperial Transition: East Asia from Ming to Qing*, ed. Lynn A. Struve (Honolulu: Association for Asian Studies and University of Hawai'i Press, 2005); Johan Elverskog, *Our Great Qing: The Mongols, Buddhism, and the State in Late Imperial China* (Honolulu: University of Hawai'i Press, 2006).

15. Toni Huber, *The Holy Land Reborn: Pilgrimage and the Tibetan Reinvention of Buddhist India* (Chicago: University of Chicago Press, 2008); Toni Huber, *The Cult of Pure Crystal Mountain: Popular Pilgrimage and Visionary Landscape in Southeast Tibet* (New York: Oxford University Press, 1999); Charlene Makley, "Gendered Boundaries in Motion: Space and Identity on the Sino-Tibetan Frontier," *American Ethnologist: The*

Journal of the American Ethnological Society 30, no. 4 (2003): 597–619; Charlene E. Makley, *The Violence of Liberation: Gender and Tibetan Buddhist Revival in Post-Mao China* (Berkeley: University of California Press, 2007); Yael Bentor, *Consecration of Images and Stūpas in Indo-Tibetan Tantric Buddhism* (Leiden: Brill, 1996); Martin A. Mills, "Vajra Brother, Vajra Sister: Renunciation, Individualism, and the Household in Tibetan Buddhist Monasticism," unpublished ms., n.d.; Martin A. Mills, *Identity, Ritual and State in Tibetan Buddhism: The Foundations of Authority in Gelukpa Monasticism* (London; New York: RoutledgeCurzon, 2003); Vesna Wallace, "Texts as Deities: Mongols' Rituals of Worshipping Sutras and Rituals of Accomplishing Various Goals by Means of Sutras," in *Ritual in Tibetan Buddhism*, ed. José Cabezón (New York: Oxford University Press, 2009); Vesna Wallace, "Mongolian Livestock Rituals and Their Appropriations, Adaptations, and Permutations," in *Understanding Religious Rituals: Theoretical Approaches and Innovations.*, ed. John Hoffmann (London: Routledge, 2011); Vesna Wallace, "Diverse Aspects of the Mongolian Buddhist Manuscript Culture and Realms of Its Influence," in *Buddhist Manuscript Culture: Knowledge, Ritual, and Art*, ed. Steven Berkwitz, Juliane Schober, and Claudia Brown (London: Routledge, 2008).

16. Makley, "Gendered Boundaries in Motion"; Makley, *The Violence of Liberation*; Huber, *The Holy Land Reborn*; Huber, *The Cult of Pure Crystal Mountain*; Mills, *Identity, Ritual and State in Tibetan Buddhism*; Mills, "Vajra Brother, Vajra Sister."

17. Huber, *The Cult of Pure Crystal Mountain*, 16; Makley, *The Violence of Liberation*, 154.

18. Makley, *The Violence of Liberation*, 154–55.

19. Mills, *Identity, Ritual and State in Tibetan Buddhism*, 243.

20. Monastic residence or regional house: Tib. *khams tshan;* Mong. *ayimay.*

21. Blo bzang rta mgrin, "Bkra Shis Thos Bsam Gling Gi 'byung Khungs Tho Tsam," in *Rje Btsun Blo Bzang Rta Dbyangs Kyi Gsung 'Bum* (New Delhi: Mongolian Lama Guru Deva, 1975), 1:598–99.

22. Sources dating from relatively close to the events, such as the *Erdeni Tunumal Sudar,* suggest that these regional Mongolian rulers hardly "took up" the Géluk at the expense of other religious affiliations, as later monastic historians would have it. See: Johan Elverskog, *The Jewel Translucent Sūtra: Altan Khan and the Mongols in the Sixteenth Century*(Leiden; Boston: Brill, 2003); Elverskog, *Our Great Qing.*

23. Elverskog, *Our Great Qing.*

24. Blo bzang rta mgrin, "Byang Phyogs Chen Po Hor Gyi Rgyal Khams Kyi Rtogs Brjod Kyi Bstan Bcos Chen Po Ngo Mtshar Gser Gyi Deb Ther," in *Rje Btsun Blo Bzang Rta Dbyangs Kyi Gsung 'Bum* (New Delhi: Mongolian Lama Guru Deva, 1975), 2:108.

25. For example: Vladimir L. Uspenskij, "Ancient History of the Mongols According to Gombojab, an Eighteenth-Century Mongolian Historian," *Rocznik Orientalistyczny* (2005): 236–41; Elverskog, "Mongol Time Enters a Qing World"; Guilaine Mala, "A Mahāyānist Rewriting of the History of China by Mgon Po Skyabs in the Rgya Nag Chos 'Byung," in *Power, Politics, and the Reinvention of Tradition: Tibet in the Seventeenth and Eighteenth Centuries*, ed. Bryan J. Cuevas and Kurtis R. Schaeffer (Leiden: Brill, 2006), 145–70.

26. Blo bzang rta mgrin, "Byang Phyogs Chen Po Hor Gyi Rgyal Khams Kyi Rtogs Brjod Kyi Bstan Bcos Chen Po Ngo Mtshar Gser Gyi Deb Ther," 108.

27. Elverskog, "Mongol Time Enters a Qing World."

28. Blo bzang rta mgrin, "Byang Phyogs Chen Po Hor Gyi Rgyal Khams Kyi Rtogs Brjod Kyi Bstan Bcos Chen Po Ngo Mtshar Gser Gyi Deb Ther," 117–18.

29. Blo bzang rta mgrin, "Byang Phyogs Chen Po Hor Gyi Rgyal Khams Kyi Rtogs Brjod Kyi Bstan Bcos Chen Po Ngo Mtshar Gser Gyi Deb Ther," 123.

30. I have only been able to find Sanskrit and Tibetan versions of the *Prophecy of the Land of Li Sūtra*: Skt. *Kaṁsadeśavyākaraṇa*; Tib. *Li yul lung bstan pa'i mdo*. Versions of the *Oxhorn Prophecy Sūtra* are as follows: Skt. *Ārya-gośiṅgavyākaraṇa-nāma-mahāyāna-sūtra*; Tib. *'Phags pa glang ru lung bstan pa zhes bya ba'i theg pa chen po'i mdo*; Mong. *Khutuγ-tu üker aγulan-dur vivanggirid üjügülügsen neretü yeke kölgen sudur*.

31. I have been unable to identify which text this references.

32. Tib. *Glang ru lung bstan*. The *Ox-Horn Prophecy Sūtra* is a canonical source describing the Buddha's activities in "The Land of Li" (Tib. *Li yul*). Included in major Tibetan and Mongolian editions of the Kangyur, this work was often cited by Zava Damdin and other late-imperial Mongolian Buddhist historians as they sought "reliable sources" for their Buddhist history (Skt. *Ārya-gośiṅgavyākaraṇa-nāma-mahāyāna-sūtra*; Tib. *'Phags pa glang ru lung bstan pa zhes bya ba'i theg pa chen po'i mdo*; Mong. *Qutuγ-tu üker aγulan-dur vivanggirid üjügülügsen neretü yeke kölgen sudur*).

33. Tib. *yib ro phi pa dag.*

34. Tib. *thur khi.*

35. Tib. *Rgya mi'i gli.*

36. Blo bzang rta mgrin [Agvan Dorjiev], "Mtshan Zhabs Mkhan Chen Gyis Chos 'Byung Las Brtsams Te Bka' 'dri Gnang Ba'i Chab Shog," in *Rje Btsun Blo Bzang Rta Dbyangs Kyi Gsung 'Bum* (New Delhi: Mongolian Lama Guru Deva, 1975), 2:548.

37. Blo bzang rta mgrin, "Mtshan Zhabs Mkhan Chen Gyi Dogs Lan Tshangs Pa'i Drang Thig," 2:563.

38. *Blo sems 'tsho* and *Li the se.*

39. Bön (*bon*) is a non-Buddhist tradition that developed a distinct identity in Tibet alongside Buddhism in the "renaissance period" in the eleventh-twelfth century. Central to both religious formations at this time were contested memories of the Tibetan imperial collapse, the enlightened nature of Tibet's Buddhist kings, and the nature of Buddhist government. On their mutual constituency through the "mirror work" of interdependent historiography, see Zeff Bjerken, "The Mirrorwork of Tibetan Religious Historians: A Comparison of Buddhist and Bon Historiography" (Ph.D. diss., University of Michigan, 2001).

40. Blo bzang rta mgrin, "Byang Phyogs Chen Po Hor Gyi Rgyal Khams Kyi Rtogs Brjod Kyi Bstan Bcos Chen Po Ngo Mtshar Gser Gyi Deb Ther," 125.

41. *Tā zig.*

42. "Byang Phyogs Chen Po Hor Gyi Rgyal Khams Kyi Rtogs Brjod Kyi Bstan Bcos Chen Po Ngo Mtshar Gser Gyi Deb Ther," 125–26.

43. Blo bzang rta mgrin, "Byang Phyogs Chen Po Hor Gyi Rgyal Khams Kyi Rtogs Brjod Kyi Bstan Bcos Chen Po Ngo Mtshar Gser Gyi Deb Ther," 126.

44. *Bsam yas gtsug lag khang,* in Central Tibet.

45. Blo bzang rta mgrin, "Byang Phyogs Chen Po Hor Gyi Rgyal Khams Kyi Rtogs Brjod Kyi Bstan Bcos Chen Po Ngo Mtshar Gser Gyi Deb Ther," 126.

46. *Sog po dpal dbyangs can gzan gnya','* one of Padmasambhava's twenty-five disciples; and *Sog po ltag 'khrid.*

47. *Khri ral pa can*; alias Tri Tsuk Detsen, r.c. 815–838 CE.

48. I.e., if you respect them and take refuge in them.

49. One stage in the second of five "paths" (Skt. *mārga*; Tib. *lam*; Mong. *mör*) that describe a gradual maturation of a meditator's perception of ultimate truth (*don dam*).

50. Blo bzang rta mgrin, "Byang Phyogs Chen Po Hor Gyi Rgyal Khams Kyi Rtogs Brjod Kyi Bstan Bcos Chen Po Ngo Mtshar Gser Gyi Deb Ther," 214–15.

51. Blo bzang rta mgrin, "Byang Phyogs Chen Po Hor Gyi Rgyal Khams Kyi Rtogs Brjod Kyi Bstan Bcos Chen Po Ngo Mtshar Gser Gyi Deb Ther," 170.

52. For comprehensive studies on the anachronistic invention of Chinggis Khan as a devotee of Tibetan lamas, and more generally on the way that Vajrapāṇi was Mongolized, see: Vesna Wallace, "Envisioning a Mongolian Buddhist Identity Through Chinggis Khan," in *Buddhism in Mongolian History, Culture, and Society* (New York: Oxford University Press, 2015); Vesna Wallace, "How Vajrapāṇi Became a Mongol," in *Buddhism in Mongolian History, Culture, and Society* (New York: Oxford University Press, 2015), 179–201.

53. Zava Damdin writes that Dungkurpa of Tsang was a student of the famous Lama Zhang (*Bla ma zhang rin po che*).

54. Wallace, "How Vajrapāṇi Became a Mongol," 178.

55. Wallace, "How Vajrapāṇi Became a Mongol," 178.

56. Wallace, "How Vajrapāṇi Became a Mongol," 179.

57. Wallace, "How Vajrapāṇi Became a Mongol," 179.

58. D. Schuh, *Erlasse und Sendschreiben mongolischer Herrscher für tibetische Geistliche. Ein Beitrag zur Kenntnis der Urkunden des tibetischen Mittelalters und ihrer Diplomatik* (St. Augustin:, VGH-Wissenschaftsverlag, 1977).

59. Blo bzang rta mgrin, "Byang Phyogs Chen Po Hor Gyi Rgyal Khams Kyi Rtogs Brjod Kyi Bstan Bcos Chen Po Ngo Mtshar Gser Gyi Deb Ther," 180–81.

60. Blo bzang rta mgrin, "Byang Phyogs Chen Po Hor Gyi Rgyal Khams Kyi Rtogs Brjod Kyi Bstan Bcos Chen Po Ngo Mtshar Gser Gyi Deb Ther," 285–86.

61. Agata Bareja-Starzyńska, *The Biography of the First Khalkha Jetsundampa Zanabazar by Zaya Pandita Luvsanprinlei: Studies, Annotated Translation, Transliteration, and Facsimile* (Warsaw: Dom Wydawniczy ELIPSA, 2015); Agata Bareja-Starzynska, "The Mongolian Incarnation of Jo Nang Pa Taranatha Kun Dga' Snying Po: Ondor Gegeen Zanabazar Blo Bzang Bstan Pa'i Rgyal Mtshan (1635–1723): A Case Study of the Tibeto-Mongolian Relationship," *The Tibet Journal* 34, no. 3–4 (2009): 243+.

62. Blo bzang rta mgrin, "Byang Phyogs Chen Po Hor Gyi Rgyal Khams Kyi Rtogs Brjod Kyi Bstan Bcos Chen Po Ngo Mtshar Gser Gyi Deb Ther," 399–400.

63. Blo bzang rta mgrin, "Byang Phyogs Hor Gyi Yul Du Dam Pa'i Chos Rin Po Che Byung Tshul Gyi Gtam Rgyud Bkra Shis Chos Dung Bzhad Pa'i Sgra Dbyangs," 31–32.

4. Wandering in a Post-Qing World

1. Blo bzang rta mgrin, "Rang Gi Byed Spyod Rags Bsdoms 'Di Snang Za Zi'i Rjes Gco," in *Rje Btsun Blo Bzang Rta Dbyangs Kyi Gsung 'Bum* (New Delhi: Mongolian Lama

Guru Deva, 1975), 11:183. The Thirteenth Dalai Lama also went to Wutaishan. After leaving Urga and spending time in Amdo at Kumbüm monastery, the Dalai Lama stopped at the holy mountain in 1908 en route to Beijing. On its slopes he held court with devotees, bureaucrats, journalists, and adventurers from as far afield as Britain, America, and Russia.

2. Johan Elverskog, "Wutai Shan, Qing Cosmopolitanism, and the Mongols," *Journal of the International Association of Tibetan Studies* 6 (2011): 246.

3. Elverskog, "Wutai Shan, Qing Cosmopolitanism, and the Mongols"; Isabelle Charleux, *Nomads on Pilgrimage: Mongols on Wutaishan (China), 1800–1940* (Leiden: Brill, 2015).

4. See, for instance: Patricia Ann Berger, *Empire of Emptiness : Buddhist Art and Political Authority in Qing China* (Honolulu: University of Hawaii Press, 2003). Also of great interest is a special issue dedicated to Tibetan and Mongolian relations with Wutaishan during the Qing in *Journal of the International Association of Tibetan Studies* 6 (December 2011); Wen-Shing Lucia Chou, "The Visionary Landscape of Wutai Shan in Tibetan Buddhism from the Eighteenth to the Twentieth Century" (Ph.D. diss., University of California, Berkeley, 2011); Natalie Köhle, "Why Did the Kangxi Emperor Go to Wutai Shan?: Patronage, Pilgrimage, and the Place of Tibetan Buddhism at the Early Qing Court," *Late Imperial China* 29, no. 1 (2008): 73–119; Charleux, *Nomads on Pilgrimage.*

5. Tib. *Dga' ldan lnga mchod.* A ritual celebration commemorating the anniversary of the death of the Géluk founder, Tsong kha pa blo bzang grags pa, in 1419.

6. Blo bzang rta mgrin, "Rang Gi Byed Spyod Rags Bsdoms 'Di Snang Za Zi'i Rjes Gco," 184.

7. Blo bzang rta mgrin, "Byang Phyogs Chen Po Hor Gyi Rgyal Khams Kyi Rtogs Brjod Kyi Bstan Bcos Chen Po Ngo Mtshar Gser Gyi Deb Ther," in *Rje Btsun Blo Bzang Rta Dbyangs Kyi Gsung 'Bum* (New Delhi: Mongolian Lama Guru Deva, 1975), 2:187–88.

8. "Byang Phyogs Chen Po Hor Gyi Rgyal Khams Kyi Rtogs Brjod Kyi Bstan Bcos Chen Po Ngo Mtshar Gser Gyi Deb Ther," 184.

9. "Byang Phyogs Chen Po Hor Gyi Rgyal Khams Kyi Rtogs Brjod Kyi Bstan Bcos Chen Po Ngo Mtshar Gser Gyi Deb Ther," 184.

10. "Byang Phyogs Chen Po Hor Gyi Rgyal Khams Kyi Rtogs Brjod Kyi Bstan Bcos Chen Po Ngo Mtshar Gser Gyi Deb Ther," 184.

11. *dngul srang:* could refer either to an ounce measure eof silver (*dngul*), or an actual silver coin (*srang*). Blo bzang rta mgrin, "Rang Gi Byed Spyod Rags Bsdoms 'Di Snang Za Zi'i Rjes Gco," 184.

12. *Kun tu khyab pa'i lha khang.*

13. Gray Tuttle, "Tibetan Buddhism at Ri Bo Rtse Lnga/Wutai Shan in Modern Times," *Journal of the International Association of Tibetan Studies* 1, no. 2 (2006): 16.

14. "Changkya Rölpé Dorjé's guide to Wutai shan gives a brief description of this temple, including its Tibetan name: Küntu Khyappé Lhakhang. Rölpé Dorjé's guide says that this temple was the home of an 'Indian' by the name of 'Shri Ashraka' during the Yongle reign period (1403–1425) of the Ming dynasty. Hoong Teik Toh has argued that often those called Indians in Ming China were actually Tibetans. In any case, this siddha was apparently invited by the Chengzu emperor, and he is said to have given the emperor and his retinue many esoteric teachings. His reliquary stūpa

still exists within the courtyard of the prayer hall of this temple. At present, the hall behind the stūpa contains statues of the 'Three: Father and Sons' (*yapsé sum*), referring to Tsongkhapa and his two principle disciples. Although these images are almost certainly of fairly recent provenance, they clearly indicate the Buddhist tradition with which this temple has been aligned for many centuries" (Tuttle, "Tibetan Buddhism at Ri Bo Rtse Lnga/Wutai Shan in Modern Times"). The passage reads: *kun tu khyab pa'i lha khang tā ywon jo'u zi ni / ming gur gyi yung lo'i dus rgya gar gyi shri ā shraka zhes pa'i grub thob zhig gdan drangs te bzhugs pa'i gnas yin zhing des rgyal po 'khor bcas la gsang sngags kyi chos kyang mang du gnang / sku gdung mchod rten kyang lha khang 'di nyid na bzhugs so* (lCang skya rol pa'i rdo rje, *Zhing Mchog Ri Bo Dwangs Bsil Gyi Gnas Bshad Dad Pa'i Padmo Rgyas Byed Ngo Mtshar Nyi Ma'i Snang Ba* [Xining: mTsho sngon mi rigs dpe skrun khang, 1993], 39. Cited in Tuttle, "Tibetan Buddhism at Ri Bo Rtse Lnga/Wutai Shan in Modern Times," 16 n.42).

15. Such excavations reference the well-worn narratives of the "treasure" traditions (*gter ma*) common to some Tibeto-Mongolian Buddhist traditions (though not usually to the Géluk school, whose practitioners, including Zava Damdin, often derided such practices as superstitious or deceptive). For a relevant description of the tradition of the "treasure revealers" (Tib. *gter ston*) and a relatively ecumenical Géluk critique by a master embedded in the Qing cosmopolitan scene, see Tuken Chökyi Nyima's discussion: Thuken Losang Chökyi Nyima, *The Crystal Mirror of Philosophical Systems: A Tibetan Study of Asian Religious Thought*, trans. Geshé Lundub Sopa (Boston: Wisdom, 2009), 25:77–96. The last sections of both *The Dharma Conch* and *The Golden Book* argue that the Nyingma Buddhist tradition (proponents of the validity of the treasure tradition) is unsuitable for Mongolian territories.

16. *Rdo rams bak shi.*

17. These religious experiences on Mount Wutai inspired Zava Damdin to compose a short praise (*gnas stod*) to the five mountains. This text exists in his collected works under the title "A Flower Offering to Mañjuśrī: A Praise to the Sacred Place of the Superior Pure Realm Mount Wutai" (bLo bzang rta mgrin, "Ri Bo Rtse Lnga'i Bstod," in *Rje Btsun Blo Bzang Rta Dbyangs Kyi Gsung 'Bum*, 17 vols. [New Delhi: Mongolian Lama Guru Deva, 1975], 1:625–28). From scanning through the colophons to Zava Damdin's many works, it is clear that he wrote at least one other text while at Mount Wutai, though this is not mentioned in his autobiography: the *"Rosary of Pundarika Flowers*: A Praise Based on the Biography of the Victor's Child Gzhon nu nor bzang" (bLo bzang rta mgrin, "RGyal Sras Gzhon Nu nor Bzang Gi Rnam Thar Las Brtsams Pa'i Bstod Pa," in *Rje Btsun Blo Bzang Rta Dbyangs Kyi Gsung 'Bum*, 17 vols. [New Delhi: Mongolian Lama Guru Deva, 1975], 1:117–32).

18. Pusading was a major Géluk monastery at Wutai and the residence for both the Kangxi and Qianlong emperors while on pilgrimage at Wutaishan. Karl Debreczeny, "Wutai Shan: Pilgrimage to Five-Peak Mountain," *Journal of the International Association of Tibetan Studies* 6 (2011): 44.

19. Blo bzang rta mgrin, "Rang Gi Byed Spyod Rags Bsdoms 'Di Snang Za Zi'i Rjes Gco," 185.

20. Given that Zava Damdin writes obliquely that he left for Beijing from the fort (*mkhar*) of Tengju (*Teng ju*), this "fire chariot" may very well have been the Tianji-Lugouqiao Railway, the city's first railway built between 1895 and 1897 with financial

backing from the British. See: Linda Pomerantz-Zhang, *Wu Tingfang (1842-1922): Reform and Modernization in Modern Chinese History* (Hong Kong: Hong Kong University Press, 1992), 87.

21. Established under the supervision of Jangji-a Rolpé Dorjé during the Yong-zhen period (1722–1732 CE) and then granted imperial status following the latter's death in the middle of the eighteenth century under the Qianlong emperor, this complex was the central residence for visiting Tibetan and Mongolian monastics and devotees by the time Zava Damdin reached Beijing.

22. Pomerantz-Zhang, *Wu Tingfang (1842-1922)*, 87.

23. Blo bzang rta mgrin, "Rang Gi Byed Spyod Rags Bsdoms 'Di Snang Za Zi'i Rjes Gco," 185.

24. Blo bzang rta mgrin, "Rang Gi Byed Spyod Rags Bsdoms 'Di Snang Za Zi'i Rjes Gco," 185.

25. Johan Elverskog, *Our Great Qing: The Mongols, Buddhism, and the State in Late Imperial China* (Honolulu: University of Hawai'i Press, 2006), 185.

26. Blo bzang rta mgrin, "Chen Po Hor Gyi Yul Gru'i Sngon Rabs Kyi Brjed Byang Shāstra'i Zur Rgyan Du Sog Yig Las Bod Skad Du Bsgyur Te Bkod Pa," in *Rje Btsun Blo Bzang Rta Dbyangs Kyi Gsung 'Bum* (New Delhi: Mongolian Lama Guru Deva, 1975), 2:545.

27. Blo bzang rta mgrin (1975–1976), "Rang gi byed spyod rags bsdoms 'di snang za zi'i rjes gcod/." In gsung 'bum/_blo bzang rta mgrin 11: 169–203 (New Delhi: Mongolian Lama Gurudeva, 1975), 186.

28. Charles Roskelly Bawden, *A Contemporary Mongolian Account of the Period of Autonomy* (Bloomington, Ind.: The Mongolia Society, 1970), 4:9.

29. A. P. Okladnikov et al., *Istorija Mongolskoj Narodnoj Respubliki* (Moskva: Nauka, 1983), 265.

30. Charles R. Bawden, *The Modern History of Mongolia* (New York: Praeger, 1968), 56.

31. Blo bzang rta mgrin, "Rang Gi Byed Spyod Rags Bsdoms 'Di Snang Za Zi'i Rjes Gco," 187.

32. For a comparative study of grounds and paths analysis among the Géluk that includes a close look at Zava Damdin's text, see Jules Brooks Levinson, "The Metaphors of Liberation : A Study of Grounds and Paths According to the Middle Way Schools" (Ph.D. diss., University of Virginia, 1994).

33. Blo bzang rta mgrin, "Rang Gi Byed Spyod Rags Bsdoms 'Di Snang Za Zi'i Rjes Gco," 191–92.

34. Blo bzang rta mgrin, "Rang Gi Byed Spyod Rags Bsdoms 'Di Snang Za Zi'i Rjes Gco," 192–93.

35. Christopher Pratt Atwood, *Encyclopedia of Mongolia and the Mongolian Empire* (New York: Facts On File, 2004), 471.

36. Blo bzang rta mgrin, "Chen Po Hor Gyi Yul Gru'i Sngon Rabs Kyi Brjed Byang Shāstra'i Zur Rgyan Du Sog Yig Las Bod Skad Du Bsgyur Te Bkod Pa," 488.

37. Blo bzang rta mgrin, "Chen Po Hor Gyi Yul Gru'i Sngon Rabs Kyi Brjed Byang Shāstra'i Zur Rgyan Du Sog Yig Las Bod Skad Du Bsgyur Te Bkod Pa," 489.

38. "Three Jewels" of Buddhist refuge (Skt. *ratnatraya*; Tib. *dkon mchog gsum*; Mong. *ɣurban erdeni*): the Buddha as guide and example, the Dharma as path and realization, and the Saṃgha as enlightened colleagues and support.

39. Blo bzang rta mgrin, "Chen Po Hor Gyi Yul Gru'i Sngon Rabs Kyi Brjed Byang Shāstra'i Zur Rgyan Du Sog Yig Las Bod Skad Du Bsgyur Te Bkod Pa," 543–44.

40. Blo bzang rta mgrin, "Byang Phyogs Chen Po Hor Gyi Rgyal Khams Kyi Rtogs Brjod Kyi Bstan Bcos Chen Po Ngo Mtshar Gser Gyi Deb Ther," 477–78.

41. Blo bzang rta mgrin, "Dben Pa'i Bsti Gnas Gsar Rnying Gcig Tu 'dres Pa'i Lo Rgyus Ma Bu Cha 'Dzoms Kyi Gleng Mo," in *Rje Btsun Blo Bzang Rta Dbyangs Kyi Gsung 'Bum* (Delhi: Mongolian Lama Guru Deva, 1975), 1:615.

42. *Rga ba'i dus su dgon skyong gis g.yengs pa'i byed.*

43. *Rga ba'i dus su dgon skyong kyis kyi [sic.] g.yengs pa'i byed.*

44. Blo bzang rta mgrin, "Rang Gi Byed Spyod Rags Bsdoms 'Di Snang Za Zi'i Rjes Gco," 197.

45. Blo bzang rta mgrin, "Rang Gi Byed Spyod Rags Bsdoms 'Di Snang Za Zi'i Rjes Gco," 194.

46. Tib. *'Bras spungs sgo mang; 'Bras spungs blo gsal gling.*

47. I.e., the famous Tibetan medical treatise *G.yu thog snying thig.*

48. Blo bzang rta mgrin, "Rang Gi Byed Spyod Rags Bsdoms 'Di Snang Za Zi'i Rjes Gco," 196.

49. The Fourteenth Dalai Lama reputedly stopped using Zava Damdin's Kālacakra commentary and freely distributing Zava Damdin's *One Hundred and Eight Verses in Praise of Compassion* at the initiations because of the 1996 ban on the propitiation of Dorjé Shukden, with whom Zava Damdin is closely associated. For a wonderful relic of that period, see Lobsang Tayang and José Cabezón, *One Hundred and Eight Verses in Praise of Great Compassion: [A Precious Crystal Rosary]* (Mysore: Mysore Printing and Publishing House, 1984).

50. Emanuel Sarkisyanz, "Communism and Lamaist Utopianism in Central Asia," *The Review of Politics* 20, no. 4 (1958): 623–33.

51. For example: Blo bzang rta mgrin, "Dpal Dus Kyi 'khor Lo'i Sa Lam Gyi Ngos 'Dzin Rags Rim 'Phros Dang Bcas Pa," in *Rje Btsun Blo Bzang Rta Dbyangs Kyi Gsung 'Bum*, 17 vols. (New Delhi: Mongolian Lama Guru Deva, 1975), 9:9–80.

52. Perhaps by his student Gonchigdorj, in whose possession so many of Zava Damdin's writings survived the early part of the socialist period, according to Bira.

53. Blo bzang rta mgrin, "Rang Gi Byed Spyod Rags Bsdoms 'Di Snang Za Zi'i Rjes Gco," in *Rje Btsun Blo Bzang Rta Dbyangs Kyi Gsung 'Bum* (New Delhi: Mongolian Lama Guru Deva, 1975), 11:203.

54. Blo bzang rta mgrin, "Rang Gi Byed Spyod Rags Bsdoms 'Di Snang Za Zi'i Rjes Gco," 203.

55. Blo bzang rta mgrin, "Rang Gi Byed Spyod Rags Bsdoms 'Di Snang Za Zi'i Rjes Gco," 203.

56. G. Akim, "Zawa Bagshiin Sharilîg Kherkhen Khailuulsan Be?," *Unknown*, 1997, VI.I–VI.7, no. 22 (245) edition.

57. G. Akim, "Zawa Bagshiin Sharilîg Kherkhen Khailuulsan Be?," *Unknown*, 1997, VI.I–VI.7, no. 22 (245) edition.

58. G. Akim, "Zawa Bagshiin Sharilîg Kherkhen Khailuulsan Be?," *Unknown*, VI.I–VI.7, no. 22 (245) edition.

5. Vacant Thrones

1. José Ignacio Cabezón, *Buddhism and Language: A Study of Indo-Tibetan Scholasticism* (Albany, N.Y.: State University of New York Press, 1994), 20.

2. Cabezón, *Buddhism and Language*, 20.

3. Cabezón, *Buddhism and Language*, 20.

4. Cabezón, *Buddhism and Language*, 21.

5. Blo bzang rta mgrin, "Byang Phyogs Chen Po Hor Gyi Rgyal Khams Kyi Rtogs Brjod Kyi Bstan Bcos Chen Po Ngo Mtshar Gser Gyi Deb Ther," in *Rje Btsun Blo Bzang Rta Dbyangs Kyi Gsung 'Bum* (New Delhi: Mongolian Lama Guru Deva, 1975), 2:240–41.

6. Skt. *pañcakaṣāya*; Tib. *snyigs ma lnga*.

7. Skt. *kaliyuga*; Tib. *rtsod ldan gyi dus*.

8. The five degenerations are usually listed as: degeneration of life span, of views, of afflictions, of sentient beings (mentally and physically), and of the aeon (since the world and the environment are expected to deteriorate). See Robert E. Buswell and Donald S. Lopez, *The Princeton Dictionary of Buddhism* (Princeton, N.J.: Princeton University Press, 2013), 614.

9. See Jan Nattier, *Once Upon a Future Time: Studies in a Buddhist Prophecy of Decline* (Berkeley, Calif.: Asian Humanities Press, 1991).

10. Blo bzang rta mgrin, "Byang Phyogs Chen Po Hor Gyi Rgyal Khams Kyi Rtogs Brjod Kyi Bstan Bcos Chen Po Ngo Mtshar Gser Gyi Deb Ther," 443.

11. See, for example, Rebecca Empson, *Time, Causality and Prophecy in the Mongolian Cultural Region: Visions of the Future* (Folkestone: Global Oriental, 2006).

12. Christopher Kaplonski, *The Lama Question: Violence, Sovereignty, and Exception in Early Socialist Mongolia* (Honolulu: University of Hawai'i Press, 2014).

13. Kaplonski, *The Lama Question*.

14. Kaplonski, *The Lama Question*.

15. Blo bzang rta mgrin, "Byang Phyogs Chen Po Hor Gyi Rgyal Khams Kyi Rtogs Brjod Kyi Bstan Bcos Chen Po Ngo Mtshar Gser Gyi Deb Ther," 2:313.

16. Blo bzang rta mgrin, "Byang Phyogs Chen Po Hor Gyi Rgyal Khams Kyi Rtogs Brjod Kyi Bstan Bcos Chen Po Ngo Mtshar Gser Gyi Deb Ther," 314.

17. Blo bzang rta mgrin, "Byang Phyogs Chen Po Hor Gyi Rgyal Khams Kyi Rtogs Brjod Kyi Bstan Bcos Chen Po Ngo Mtshar Gser Gyi Deb Ther," 202.

18. Aleksej M. Pozdneev, *Mongolia and the Mongols* (Bloomington: Indiana University Press, 1971), 330–56.

19. Another key figure who bridged the fourth and fifth incarnations was Ngakwang Khédrup (Tib. Ngag dbang mkhas grub; Mong. Agwangkhaidub, 1779–1838), one of the most prominent scholastic figures in early nineteenth-century Khalkha who implemented the urban visions of the two Jebtsundambas he knew. Ngakwang Khédrup wrote prodigiously on the pilgrimage routes, new temples, special holy objects, and other material bases of the newly settled Urga with the aim not only to consolidate the authority of the Jebtsundambas but also to make all devotees fortunate enough to come into contact with this "second Bodhgaya to the north" and the enlightened presence it helped materialize into virtuous subjects of the Qing-Géluk formation. For some of Ngakwang Khédrup's fascinating prescriptions for

"using" Urga, see: Ngag dbang mkhas grub, "Rgyal Ba Byams Pa'i Sgrub Thabs Dang 'brel Ba'i Mchod Chog Dga' Ldan Pad Mtshor 'Jug Pa'i Gru Gzings," in *Collected Works of Kyai-Rdor Mkhan-Po Ngag-Dbang-Mkhas-Grub*, 5 vols. (Leh: S. W. Tashigangpa, 1972), 1:121–54; Ngag dbang mkhas grub, "Rgyal Ba Byams Mgon Gyi Gsol 'debs Byams Mgon Zhal Bzang Lta Ba'i Dga' Ston," in *Collected Works of Kyai-Rdor Mkhan-Po Ngag-Dbang-Mkhas-Grub*, vol. 1, 5 vols. (Leh: S.W. Tashigangpa, 1972), 155–66; Ngag dbang mkhas grub, "Rgyal Ba Byams Mgon Gyi 'dra Sku'i Nang Du 'Bul Rgyu'i 'Dod Gsol Dgos 'Dod Yid Bzhin 'Gugs Pa'i Lcags Kyu," in *Collected Works of Kyai-Rdor Mkhan-Po Ngag-Dbang-Mkhas-Grub*, vol. 1, 5 vols. (Leh: S.W. Tashigangpa, 1972), 275–80; Ngag dbang mkhas grub, "Khu Re Chen Mor Bzhengs Pa'i Byams Pa'i Sku Brnyan Gyi Dkar Chag Dad Pa'i Bzhin Ras Gsal Bar Byed Pa'i nor Bu'i Me Long," in *Collected Works of Kyai-Rdor Mkhan-Po Ngag-Dbang-Mkhas-Grub*, 5 vols. (Leh: S. W. Tashigangpa, 1972), 1:175–274; Ngag dbang mkhas grub, "Byams Pa'i Dam Bca'i Gzungs Bzla Tshul," in *Collected Works of Kyai-Rdor Mkhan-Po Ngag-Dbang-Mkhas-Grub*, 5 vols. (Leh: S. W. Tashigangpa, 1972), 1:281–86; Ngag dbang mkhas grub, " 'Bras Spungs Bkra Shis Tshe 'Phel Gling Gi Gnas Bstod," in *Collected Works of Kyai-Rdor Mkhan-Po Nag-Dban-Mkhas-Grub*, 5 vols. (Leh: S.W. Tashigangpa, 1972), 5 (ca): 399–404.

20. Kurtis Schaeffer, "New Scholarship in Tibet, 1650–1700," in *Forms of Knowledge in Early Modern Asia: Explorations in the Intellectual History of India and Tibet, 1500–1800*, ed. Sheldon Pollock (Durham, N.C.: Duke University Press, 2011), 291–310.

21. Michel de Certeau, "Walking in the City," in *The Practice of Everyday Life*, trans. Steven Rendall (Berkeley: University of California Press, 1988), 91–110.

22. Schaeffer, "New Scholarship in Tibet, 1650–1700," 390–391.

23. Schaeffer, "New Scholarship in Tibet, 1650–1700," 394.

24. Schaeffer, "New Scholarship in Tibet, 1650–1700," 400–401.

25. Schaeffer, "New Scholarship in Tibet, 1650–1700," 402.

26. Schaeffer, "New Scholarship in Tibet, 1650–1700," 403–404.

27. Blo bzang rta mgrin, "Byang Phyogs Chen Po Hor Gyi Rgyal Khams Kyi Rtogs Brjod Kyi Bstan Bcos Chen Po Ngo Mtshar Gser Gyi Deb Ther," 397.

28. Blo bzang rta mgrin, "Byang Phyogs Chen Po Hor Gyi Rgyal Khams Kyi Rtogs Brjod Kyi Bstan Bcos Chen Po Ngo Mtshar Gser Gyi Deb Ther," 409–10.

29. Blo bzang rta mgrin, "Byang Phyogs Chen Po Hor Gyi Rgyal Khams Kyi Rtogs Brjod Kyi Bstan Bcos Chen Po Ngo Mtshar Gser Gyi Deb Ther," 410.

6. Blood

1. See Jan Nattier, *Once Upon a Future Time: Studies in a Buddhist Prophecy of Decline* (Berkeley, Calif.: Asian Humanities Press, 1991). For a collection of papers that examine Mongolian language prophetic texts in circulation leading up to and during the Two Revolutions, see Rebecca Empson, *Time, Causality and Prophecy in the Mongolian Cultural Region: Visions of the Future* (Folkestone: Global Oriental, 2006).

2. *'Khor rnam bzhi*: i.e., the entire Buddhist community, divided according to gender and vows taken: nuns, monks, laywomen, and laymen.

3. Blo bzang rta mgrin, "Byang Phyogs Chen Po Hor Gyi Rgyal Khams Kyi Rtogs Brjod Kyi Bstan Bcos Chen Po Ngo Mtshar Gser Gyi Deb Ther," in *Rje Btsun Blo Bzang Rta Dbyangs Kyi Gsung 'Bum* (New Delhi: Mongolian Lama Guru Deva, 1975), 2:133–34.

4. Blo bzang rta mgrin, "Byang Phyogs Chen Po Hor Gyi Rgyal Khams Kyi Rtogs Brjod Kyi Bstan Bcos Chen Po Ngo Mtshar Gser Gyi Deb Ther," 202.

5. Dpal mang paṇḍita dkon mchog rgyal mtshan (1764–1853) was a prominent Géluk incarnate lama from eastern Tibet who became the twenty-fourth throne holder of Labrang (*Bla brang*). His *History of India, Tibet, and Mongolia* was widely circulated in nineteenth- and twentieth-century Inner Asia, and was an important secondary source for Zava Damdin. See Dkon mchog rgyal mtshan, *RGya Bod Hor Sog Gi Lo Rgyus Nyung Ngur Brjod Pa Byis Pa 'jug Pa'i Bab Stegs*, 11 vols. (New Delhi: Gyalten Gelek Namgyal, 1974), vol. 4.

6. Blo bzang rta mgrin, "Byang Phyogs Chen Po Hor Gyi Rgyal Khams Kyi Rtogs Brjod Kyi Bstan Bcos Chen Po Ngo Mtshar Gser Gyi Deb Ther," 241–42.

7. In the Buddhist cosmological schema of Zava Damdin's postimperial Géluk tradition (and most other Mahāyāna Buddhist schools in Central, Inner, and East Asia), ordinary beings are understood to be reborn in six realms of "cyclic existence" (Skt. *saṃsāra*; Tib. *'khor ba*; Mong. *sansar*): the three "higher realms" (with comparatively less suffering) are those of the divinities (Skt. *deva*; Tib. *lha*; Mong. *tngri*), demigods (Skt. *asura*; Tib. *lha min*; Mong. *tngri busu*), and humans (Skt. *manuṣya*; Tib. *mi*; Mong. *kumun*), and the three "lower realms" are those of animals (Skt. *tiryak*; Tib. *dud 'gro*; Mong. *adaγusu*), hungry ghosts (Skt. *preta*; Tib. *yid dwags*; Mong. *birid*), and hell beings (Skt. *nāraka*; Tib. *dmyal ba*; Mong. *tamu*).

8. I believe the *Transmission of the Vinaya* (Tib. *'Dul ba'i lung*) refers to a late fifteenth-century work by the Tibetan Sakya scholar Jamyang Kunga Chözang (1433–1503).

9. Skt. *Ārya-saddharmāsmṛtyupasthāna-sūtra*; Tib. *'Phags pa dam pa'i chos dran pa nye bar bzhag pa*; Mon. *Khutuγtu degedü-yin nom-i duradkhui oyir-a aγulkhui*.

10. Blo bzang rta mgrin, "Byang Phyogs Chen Po Hor Gyi Rgyal Khams Kyi Rtogs Brjod Kyi Bstan Bcos Chen Po Ngo Mtshar Gser Gyi Deb Ther," 324–25.

11. Blo bzang rta mgrin, "Byang Phyogs Chen Po Hor Gyi Rgyal Khams Kyi Rtogs Brjod Kyi Bstan Bcos Chen Po Ngo Mtshar Gser Gyi Deb Ther," 322.

12. Tib. *Lha btsun byang chub 'od*, 1186–1259. The king of Mnga' ris in the west of the Tibetan cultural region, he was partly responsible for inviting the Bengali master Atiśa Dīpaṃkara Śrījñāna (the founder of the Bka' gdams school) to Tibet and inaugurating the "later diffusion" (*phyi dar*) of the Dharma there. Unfortunately, I am unable to locate any bibliographic information about the "Letter That Reverses Mantra" (*Sngags log springs yig*) at this time.

13. The "Sixteen Pure Human Laws" (Tib. *mi chos gtsang ma bcu drug*) are commonly attributed to the seventh-century Buddhist king of imperial Tibet, Songtsen Gampo. Though their number and content often differ, Zava Damdin provides the following list in *The Golden Book*: Venerate the Three Jewels and Practice Holy Dharma; (Come to) Possess Merit and Respect (Your) Father and Mother; Respect Those of High Lineage and the Elderly; Maintain Friends and Government and Health for Your Countrymen; Be Straightforward of Mind as If (You Had) One Eye Only; Be

Competent in (Amassing) Food and Wealth Free of Deceit; Refrain from Envy, and Equalize (Yourself) with Everyone; Do Not Base Your Mind on Women; (Make Your) Great Vehicle Pleasant; and (practice) Wise Speech.

14. Blo bzang rta mgrin, "Byang Phyogs Chen Po Hor Gyi Rgyal Khams Kyi Rtogs Brjod Kyi Bstan Bcos Chen Po Ngo Mtshar Gser Gyi Deb Ther," 323–24.

15. Robert A. Rupen, "The Buriat Intelligentsia," *The Far Eastern Quarterly* 15, no. 3 (1956): 383–98.

16. Rupen, "The Buriat Intelligentsia," 385.

17. Anya Bernstein, "Pilgrims, Fieldworkers, and Secret Agents: Buryat Buddhologists and the History of an Eurasian Imaginary," *Inner Asia* 11, no. 1 (2009): 35.

18. Rupen, "The Buriat Intelligentsia," 385.

19. Rupen, "The Buriat Intelligentsia," 385.

20. Baabar, *History of Mongolia*, ed. Christopher Kaplonski (Ulaanbaatar: Monsudar Publishing, 2004), 164. Quoted in Jerzy Tulisow et al., eds., *In the Heart of Mongolia: 100th Anniversary of W. Kotwicz's Expedition to Mongolia in 1912: Studies and Selected Source Materials* (Crakow: Polish Academy of Arts and Sciences, 2012), 125.

21. Quoted in Shirin Akiner, *Mongolia Today* (London; New York: Kegan Paul International in association with the Central Asia Research Forum, London, 1991), 172.

22. Nikolay Tsyrempilov, "Modernizing Sangha: Buryat Buddhist Community in the Age of Revolution and Secularization, 1905–1940." Paper given at "Traditional Religions, Secularisms, and Revivals: Buddhism and Shamanism in Northern Eurasia" conference, Ruhr-Universität, Bochum, Germany, March 9, 2018.

23. Bernstein, "Pilgrims, Fieldworkers, and Secret Agents," 35.

24. Rupen, "The Buriat Intelligentsia," 398.

25. An early example of which was formed by Jamsrano, who in 1906 founded the Banner of the Buryat People (Buriyaad zonoi tug), described by Dugarova-Montgomery and Montgomery as "an illegal nationalist union consisting of about sixty Buriat teachers, mainly from Irkutsk Province, that agitated for the use of Buriat and Mongol in local schools." Yeshen-Khorlo Dugarava-Montgomery and Robert Montgomery, "The Buriat Alphabet of Agvan Dorzhiev," in *Mongolia in the Twentieth Century*, ed. Stephen and Bruce A. Elleman Kotkin (Armonk, N.Y.; London: M. E. Sharpe, 1999), 83.

26. Nikolay Tsyrempilov, "Samdan Tsydenov and His Buddhist Theocratic Project," in *Biographies of Eminent Mongol Buddhists*, ed. Johan Elverskog (Halle: IITBS, International Institute for Tibetan and Buddhist Studies, 2008), 117–38.

27. Kseniia Maksimovna Gerasimova, *Obnovlencheskoe dvizhenie buriatskogo lamaistskogo dukhovenstva* (Ulan-Ude: Buriatskoe knizhnoe izd-vo, 1964), 160–62. Quoted in Bernstein, "Pilgrims, Fieldworkers, and Secret Agents," 36.

28. An example is Jamsrano's work for the Polish Altaist scholar Wladyslaw Kotwicz's Mongolia expedition in 1912. See Tulisow et al., *In the Heart of Mongolia: 100th Anniversary of W. Kotwicz's Expedition to Mongolia in 1912*.

29. Blo bzang rta mgrin, "Mkhyen Ldan Lo Tsā Ba Tshe Dbang Gi Gros Lan Spos Shel Phreng Ba," in *Rje Btsun Blo Bzang Rta Dbyangs Kyi Gsung 'Bum*, 17 vols. (New Delhi: Mongolian Lama Guru Deva, 1975), 1:651–58.

30. Blo bzang rta mgrin, "Mkhyen Ldan Lo Tsā Ba Tshe Dbang Gi Gros Lan Spos Shel Phreng Ba," 652.

31. Blo bzang rta mgrin, "Mkhyen Ldan Lo Tsā Ba Tshe Dbang Gi Gros Lan Spos Shel Phreng Ba," 652.

32. Blo bzang rta mgrin, "Mkhyen Ldan Lo Tsā Ba Tshe Dbang Gi Gros Lan Spos Shel Phreng Ba," 652.

33. Lkhamsurengiin Khurelbaatar and G. Luvsantseren, *Ogtorguin tsagaan gardi*, vol. II (Ulaanbaatar: Mongol Uls, Shinzhlekh Ukhaany Akademiin Khel Zokhiolyn Khureelen, 1996), 245.

34. Blo bzang rta mgrin, "Mkhyen Ldan Lo Tsā Ba Tshe Dbang Gi Gros Lan Spos Shel Phreng Ba," 652–53.

35. Blo bzang rta mgrin, "Mkhyen Ldan Lo Tsā Ba Tshe Dbang Gi Gros Lan Spos Shel Phreng Ba," 653.

36. Blo bzang rta mgrin, "Mkhyen Ldan Lo Tsā Ba Tshe Dbang Gi Gros Lan Spos Shel Phreng Ba," 654.

37. Blo bzang rta mgrin, "Mkhyen Ldan Lo Tsā Ba Tshe Dbang Gi Gros Lan Spos Shel Phreng Ba," 654–55.

38. Blo bzang rta mgrin, "Mkhyen Ldan Lo Tsā Ba Tshe Dbang Gi Gros Lan Spos Shel Phreng Ba," 655.

39. Blo bzang rta mgrin, "Mkhyen Ldan Lo Tsā Ba Tshe Dbang Gi Gros Lan Spos Shel Phreng Ba," 655–56.

40. Blo bzang rta mgrin, "Mkhyen Ldan Lo Tsā Ba Tshe Dbang Gi Gros Lan Spos Shel Phreng Ba," 656.

41. Dugarava-Montgomery and Montgomery, "The Buriat Alphabet of Agvan Dorzhiev."

42. He wrote a versified autobiography in Mongolian in 1921, and as far as I am aware, the Tibetan version that I have access to and that Norbu and Martin translated in 1921 is simply a later translation of the Mongol original. The Mongol version is cited by Dugarova-Montgomery and Montgomery as "Vagindra [alias Agvan Dorjiev] (1921). *Dalai-yi ergijü bitügsen domog sonirqal-un bicig tedüi kemekü orosiba.* LOIVAN, Mongolia. S 531." Dugarava-Montgomery and Montgomery, "The Buriat Alphabet of Agvan Dorzhiev," 88.

43. Amended from Agvan Dorjiev, Thubten Jigme Norbu, and Dan Martin, *Dorjiev: Memoirs of a Tibetan Diplomat* (Tokyo: Hokke bunka kenkyū, 1991), 43. Ngag dbang blo bzang, "Ngag Dbang Blo Bzang Rang Gi Rnam Thar," in *Gsung Thor Bu/Ngag Dbang Blo Bzang Rdo Rje* (Mundgog, North Kanara, Karnataka: 'Bras blo gling gtsung lag gter mdzod 'phrul spar khang, n.d.), 1:61.

44. The Tibetan in the text reads *bon lugs*, i.e., the system of the Bon (the "indigenous" mirror tradition to Buddhism in Tibet). While "shamanism" as a descriptive term of any religious tradition is suspect, and the utility of the term itself is questionable, here it works because Agvan Dorjiev uses *bon lugs* as a gloss for local indigenous superstition and ritual (the very association that makes "shamanism" a suspect category in the academic study of religion).

45. Amended from Dorjiev, Thubten Jigme Norbu, and Martin, *Dorjiev: Memoirs of a Tibetan Diplomat*, 43. Ngag dbang blo bzang, "Ngag Dbang Blo Bzang Rang Gi Rnam Thar," 61.

46. Charles R. Bawden, *The Modern History of Mongolia* (New York: Praeger, 1968), 260–73. One example of this was the work of the prominent Mongolian incarnate

Darva Paṇḍita, whose life and work begs for a thorough academic treatment. According to Bawden and others, Darva Paṇḍita openly embraced and promoted a socialism authorized by means of what he saw as the egalitarian social program implicit in Buddhist tradition (269–71).

47. Skt. *pramāṇa*; Tib. *tshad ma*; Mon. *kemjiy-e*. *Pramāṇa* was a central area of scholastic inquiry in Agvan Dorjiev and Zava Damdin's shared Géluk network (just as it is today in the dispersed Tibetan scholastic world, including but not limited to the Géluk school). *Pramāṇa* in their authoritative sources usually defined technically as a consciousness that is not deceived with regard to its object.

48. There are usually three divisions of inference listed in Indo-Tibetan-Mongolian *pramāṇa* (Tib. *tshad ma*) literature as it was known to Agvan Dorjiev and Zava Damdin: inference through belief (*āpta-anumāna*), inference through renown (*prasiddha-anumāna*), and inference by the power of the fact (*vastu-bala-anumāna*).

49. Blo bzang rta mgrin [Agvan Dorjiev], "Mtshan Zhabs Mkhan Chen Gyis Chos 'Byung Las Brtsams Te Bka' 'dri Gnang Ba'i Chab Shog," in *Rje Btsun Blo Bzang Rta Dbyangs Kyi Gsung 'Bum* (New Delhi: Mongolian Lama Guru Deva, 1975), 2:554.

50. Blo bzang rta mgrin, "Mtshan Zhabs Mkhan Chen Gyi Dogs Lan Tshangs Pa'i Drang Thig," in *Rje Btsun Blo Bzang Rta Dbyangs Kyi Gsung 'Bum* (New Delhi: Mongolian Lama Guru Deva, 1975), 2:567–68.

51. Skt. *Pramāṇavārttika*; Tib. *Tshad ma rnam 'grel*.

52. Blo bzang rta mgrin, "Byang Phyogs Chen Po Hor Gyi Rgyal Khams Kyi Rtogs Brjod Kyi Bstan Bcos Chen Po Ngo Mtshar Gser Gyi Deb Ther," 428–29.

53. The four chapters of the *Pramāṇavārttika* are: Inference (*rang don rjes su dpag pa*); Valid Cognition (*tshad ma grub pa*); Direct Perception (*mngon sum*); and Logic (*gzhan gyi don*).

54. *Spyir 'jig rten du chos ji ltar byng tshul*. Dharmatāla provides a fascinating general account of the Mongols later in the text, but does not devote such attention to establishing a "valid" account of the physical distribution of the universe and its beings as the first order of business. See Dharmatāla, "Classification of the Mongols" (*Hor Sog gi rnam gzhag*), in *Dharmatala's Annals of Buddhism* (New Delhi: Smt. Sharada Rani, 1975 [1889]), 42–60.

55. Skt. *Buddha-avataṃsaka-nāma-mahāvaipulya-sūtra*; Tib. *Sangs rgyas phal po che zhes bya ba shin tu rgyas pa chen po'i mdo*; Mon. *Olangki burkhan neretü masida delgeregsen yeke sudar*. Zava Damdin composed a praise text based on one of the most famous characters in this sutra, the bodhisattva Gzhon nu nor bzang (Skt. Sudhanakumāra), who is one of the archetypes of the perfect Buddhist disciple in Mahāyāna literature. See Blo bzang rta mgrin, "Rgyal Sras Gzhon Nu nor Bzang Gi Rnam Thar Las Brtsams Pa'i Bstod Pa," in *Rje Btsun Blo Bzang Rta Dbyangs Kyi Gsung 'Bum*, 17 vols. (New Delhi: Mongolian Lama Guru Deva, 1975), 1:117–32.

56. For a longer study of this extended passage in the broader context of Qing-era scholasticism, see Matthew W. King, "Modernities, Sense-Making, and the Inscription of Mongolian Buddhist Place," in *Buddhism in Mongolian History, Culture and Society*, ed. Vesna Wallace (Oxford: Oxford University Press, 2015), 53–69.

57. Blo bzang rta mgrin, "Byang Phyogs Chen Po Hor Gyi Rgyal Khams Kyi Rtogs Brjod Kyi Bstan Bcos Chen Po Ngo Mtshar Gser Gyi Deb Ther," 44.

58. Here, the "Upper Abhidharma" is that of the Mahāyāna school (Tib. *theg pa chen po*), and the "Lower Abhidharma" is that of the Śrāvakayāna (Tib. *snyan thos kyi theg pa*). Both of these were studied extensively in the Géluk scholastic institutions of Tibet and Mongolia. The Abhidharma is one of the "Three Baskets" of the Buddhist canon (Skt. *tripiṭaka*; Tib. *sde snod gsum*), and is a term that is notoriously difficult to translate. It has been rendered into English variously as "phenomenology," "higher knowledge," "manifest knowledge," and so forth. Anbhidharma is, in general, concerned with classifying experience, and systematizes many of the topics mentioned in the sutras (the "Sayings of the Buddha," another of the canonical *tripiṭaka*). Topics include: the five psycho-physical aggregates (Skt. *pañcaskandha*; Tib. *phung po lnga*), which are the basis for inputing the "self"; the six sense faculties and their six sense objects (Skt. *dvadaśa āyatana*; Tib. *skye mched bcu gnyis*); and the eighteen classifications of all knowable things (Skt. *aṣṭadaśa dhātu*; Tib. *khams bco brgyad*). One such classification, which Zava Damdin evokes here, concerns the physical structure and genesis of the universe. These are generally divided up into the physical world, understood as a "vessel" (*nod*) and the beings who inhabit it, known as the "contents" (*bcud*). Famous commentaries to the Abhidharma include Asaṅga's fourth-century *Compendium of Abhidharma* (Skt. *Abhidharmasamuccaya*; Tib. *mngon pa kun btus*), and his younger brother Vasubandhu's *Treasury of Abhidharma* (Skt. *Abhidharmakośa*; Tib. *chos mngon pa'i mdzod*) and *Auto-Commentary on the* Treasury of Abhidharma (Skt. *Abhidharmakośa-Bhāṣya*; Tib. *chos mngon pa mdzod kyi bshad pa*).

59. Blo bzang rta mgrin, "Byang Phyogs Chen Po Hor Gyi Rgyal Khams Kyi Rtogs Brjod Kyi Bstan Bcos Chen Po Ngo Mtshar Gser Gyi Deb Ther," 44. Emphasis mine.

60. Blo bzang rta mgrin, "Byang Phyogs Chen Po Hor Gyi Rgyal Khams Kyi Rtogs Brjod Kyi Bstan Bcos Chen Po Ngo Mtshar Gser Gyi Deb Ther," 44.

61. Blo bzang rta mgrin, "Byang Phyogs Chen Po Hor Gyi Rgyal Khams Kyi Rtogs Brjod Kyi Bstan Bcos Chen Po Ngo Mtshar Gser Gyi Deb Ther," 45. This latter reference is to a composition by Asaṅga (Skt. *Mahāyāasaṃgraha*; Tib. *Theg pa chen po bsdus pa*). The story, familiar in many global literary traditions, describes the partial, inaccurate descriptions of an elephant by eighteen blind people who each can only access one feature (a tail, a foot, etc.). The analogy is to the Buddhist doctrinal understanding of the limited experience of the world by those "blinded" by karma and delusions.

Conclusion

1. Today it is known as Delgeriin Choir, in Dungov Aimag (Central Gob province), known in the early twentieth century as Chöying Ösel Ling (Tib. *Chos dbying 'od gsal gling*).

2. Two fairly recent studies explore Zava Rinpoché's Buddhist revivalist projects: Zsuzsa Majer, "Delgeriin Choir, the Monastery of Zava Lam Damdin in the Gobi," in *Zentralasiatische Studien: Des Seminars Für Sprach- Und Kulturwissenschaft Zentralasiens Der Universität Bonn*, vol. 41 (Bonn: International Institute for Tibetan and Buddhist

Studies, 2012), 7–42; Lkhagvademchig Jadamba and Bernhard Schittich, "Negotiating Self and Other: Transnational Cultural Flows and the Reinvention of Mongolian Buddhism," *Internationales Asienforum* 10, no. 1–2 (2010): 83–102.

3. "Zava Damdin," https://www.youtube.com/channel/UC3ZxPBYGcK_0e5Oqy subwgg/videos (accessed June 27, 2017).

4. Carlo Ginzburg, *The Cheese and the Worms: The Cosmos of a Sixteenth-Century Miller* (Baltimore: Johns Hopkins University Press, 1980), xxvi.

5. Blo bzang rta mgrin, "Byang Phyogs Chen Po Hor Gyi Rgyal Khams Kyi Rtogs Brjod Kyi Bstan Bcos Chen Po Ngo Mtshar Gser Gyi Deb Ther," in *Rje Btsun Blo Bzang Rta Dbyangs Kyi Gsung 'Bum* (New Delhi: Mongolian Lama Guru Deva, 1975), 2:479.

6. Brian Keith Axel, "Historical Anthropology and Its Vicissitudes," in *From the Margins: Historical Anthropology and Its Futures*, ed. Brian Keith Axel (Durham, N.C. and London: Duke University Press, 2002), 3.

7. Ngag dbang nyi ma, *Chos 'byung Lung Rigs Sgron Me* (Varanasi, India: N.p., 1965).

8. Jam dpal shes rab, *Chen po Hor gyi rgyal khams su dam pai chos rin po che lan gsum du dar bai tshul las brtsams pai gtam dwangs gsal me lon* (Mundgod, North Kanara, K.S., India: Drepung Gomang Dratsang College, 1991).

9. Jam dpal shes rab, *Chen po Hor gyi rgyal khams su dam pai chos rin po che lan gsum du dar bai tshul las brtsams pai gtam dwangs gsal me lon*, 4–7; Ngag dbang nyi ma, *Chos 'byung Lung Rigs Sgron Me*, 257–64.

10. Jeffrey Hopkins, "A Tibetan Perspective on the Nature of Spiritual Experience," in *Paths to Liberation: The Mārga and Its Transformations in Buddhist Thought*, ed. Robert E. Buswell and Robert M. Gimello (Honolulu: University of Hawaii Press, 1992); Tupden Kensur Yeshey et al., *Path to the Middle: Oral Madhyamika Philosophy in Tibet: The Spoken Scholarship of Kensur Yeshey Tupden Commenting on Tsong-Kha-Pa's Illumination of the Thought, Extensive Explanation of (Candrakirti's) "Entrance to (Nāgārjuna's) 'Treatise on the Middle Way'": (dbu Ma Dgongs Pa Rab Gsal), the Sixth Chapter, "Perfection of Wisdom" Verses 1-7* (Albany: State University of New York Press, 1994); Elizabeth Napper, *Dependent-Arising and Emptiness: A Tibetan Buddhist Interpretation of Madhyamika Philosophy Emphasizing the Compatibility of Emptiness and Conventional Phenomena* (Boston: Wisdom, 1989); Jules Levinson, "Metaphors of Liberation: Tibetan Treatises on Grounds and Paths," in *Tibetan Literature: Studies in Genre: Essays in Honor of Geshe Lhundrup Sopa*, ed. José Ignacio Cabezón, Roger Jackson, and Lundup Sopa (Ithaca, N.Y.: Snow Lion, 1996), 261–74; Jules Brooks Levinson, "The Metaphors of Liberation : A Study of Grounds and Paths According to the Middle Way Schools" (Ph.D. diss., University of Virginia, 1994).

11. L. W. J. van der Kuijp, "Tibetan Contributions to the 'Apoha' Theory: The Fourth Chapter of the Tshad-Ma Rigs-Pa'i Gter," *Journal of the American Oriental Society* 99, no. 3 (1979): 408–22; L. W. J. van der Kuijp, "Phya-Pa Chos-Kyi Seng-Ge's Impact on Tibetan Epistemological Theory," *Journal of Indian Philosophy* 5, no. 4 (1978): 355–69.

12. Vladimir Uspensky, "The Previous Incarnations of the Qianlong Emperor According to the Panchen Lama Blo Bzang Dpal Ldan Ye Shes," in *Tibet, Past and Present: Tibetan Studies I. PIATS 2000: Tibetan Studies: Proceedings of the Ninth Seminar of the International Association for Tibetan Studies*, ed. Henk McKay Blezer (Leiden; Boston; Köln: Brill, 2002), 215–28; E. Gene Smith and Kurtis R. Schaeffer, *Among Tibetan Texts: History and Literature of the Himalayan Plateau* (Boston: Wisdom, 2001), 426 n. 305; Dieter Schuh, "Erlasse und Sendschreiben mongolischer Herrscher für

tibetische Geistliche. Ein Beitrag zur Kenntnis der Urkunden des tibetischen Mittelalters und ihrer Diplomatik" (VGH-Wissenschaftsverlag, 1977), xvii, 18, 51f, 76, 125; Toni Huber, *The Holy Land Reborn: Pilgrimage and the Tibetan Reinvention of Buddhist India* (Chicago: University of Chicago Press, 2008).

13. Lobsang Tayang and José Cabezón, *One Hundred and Eight Verses in Praise of Great Compassion: [A Precious Crystal Rosary]* (Mysore: Mysore Printing and Publishing House, 1984).

14. Lhundup Sopa, Michael J. Sweet, and Leonard Zwilling, *Peacock in the Poison Grove: Two Buddhist Texts on Training the Mind; the Wheel Weapon (Mtshon Cha'khor Lo) and the Poison-Destroying Peacock (Rma Bya Dug 'joms) Attributed to Dharmarakṣita* (BostonA: Wisdom, 2001).

15. The result was: bLo bzang rta mgrin, " 'Jam Mgon Rgyal Ba Gnyis Pa'i Bstan Srung Thun Mong Ma Yin Pa Rgyal Chen Rdo Rje Shugs Ldan Rtsal Gyi Chos Skor Be Bum Du Bsgrigs Pa'i Dkar Chag Gnam Lcags 'Khor Lo'i Mu Khyud 'phrin Las 'Od 'Bar," in *Rje Btsun Blo Bzang Rta Dbyangs Kyi Gsung 'Bum*, 17 vols. (New Delhi: Mongolian Lama Guru Deva, 1975), 11:395–414.

16. Blo bzang rta mgrin, "Rang Gi Byed Spyod Rags Bsdoms 'Di Snang Za Zi'i Rjes Gco," in *Rje Btsun Blo Bzang Rta Dbyangs Kyi Gsung 'Bum* (New Delhi: Mongolian Lama Guru Deva, 1975), 11:192.

17. Georges Dreyfus, *The Shuk-Den Affair: Origins of a Controversy; Nachdruck Eines Artikels Aus: Journal of the International Association of Buddhist Studies, Vol. 21, Number 2, 1998* (Dharamsala: Narthang Publ., 1999).

18. For example: David L. McMahan, *The Making of Buddhist Modernism* (New York: Oxford University Press, 2008); Donald S. Lopez, *Prisoners of Shangri-La: Tibetan Buddhism and the West* (Chicago: University of Chicago Press, 1998); Gendun Chopel, Donald Lopez, and Thupten Jinpa, *Grains of Gold: Tales of a Cosmopolitan Traveler* (Chicago: University of Chicago Press, 2014); Donald S. Lopez, *A Modern Buddhist Bible: Essential Readings from East and West* (Boston: Beacon Press, 2002); Jason Ananda Josephson, *Invention of Religion in Japan* (Chicago: University of Chicago Press, 2012); Jin Y. Park, *Makers of Modern Korean Buddhism* (Albany: State University of New York Press, 2010); Erik Braun, *The Birth of Insight: Meditation, Modern Buddhism, and the Burmese Monk Ledi Sayadaw* (Chicago: University of Chicago Press, 2015); Jan Kiely, *Recovering Buddhism in Modern China* (New York: Columbia University Press, 2016); Richard S. Cohen, *Beyond Enlightenment: Buddhism, Religion, Modernity* (London; New York: Routledge, 2009); Steven Heine, *Buddhism in the Modern World: Adaptations of an Ancient Tradition* (New York: Oxford University Press, 2011); Brian Bocking et al., *Buddhist Crossroads Pioneer Western Buddhists and Asian Networks 1860-1960*, (London: Routledge, 2015).

19. Talal Asad, *Formations of the Secular: Christianity, Islam, Modernity* (Stanford, Calif.: Stanford University Press, 2003).

20. McMahan, *The Making of Buddhist Modernism*, 8–9.

21. Saba Mahmood, *Politics of Piety: The Islamic Revival and the Feminist Subject* (Princeton, N.J.: Princeton University Press, 2005), 115–16.

22. Reinhart Koselleck, *Futures Past: On the Semantics of Historical Time* (New York: Columbia University Press, 2004).

Bibliography

Primary Sources

Akim. "Zawa Bagshiin Sharilîg Kherkhen Khailuulsan Be?" Unknown newspaper, 1997, VI.I–VI.7, no. 22 (245) edition.

Amar, A. *Monggol-Un Tobci Teüke* [*A Brief History of Mongolia*]. The Mongolia Society Papers, vol. 9. Bloomington, Ind.: The Mongolia Society, 1986.

Blo bzang 'phrin las. *Shākya'i Btsun Pa Blo Bzang 'phrin Las Kyi Zab Pa Dang Rgya Che Ba'i Dam Pa'i Chos Kyi Thob Yig Gsal Ba'i Me Long*. 4 vols. New Delhi: International Academy of Indian Culture, 1981.

Blo bzang rta mgrin. "Bka' Drin Gsum Ldan Rtsa Ba'i Bla Ma Rdo Rje 'chang Mkhan Chen Sangs Rgyas Mtshan Can Gyi Rnam Thar Gsol 'Debs Dad Ldan Yid Kyi Mdzas Rgyan." In *Rje Btsun Blo Bzang Rta Dbyangs Kyi Gsung 'Bum*, 1:7–19. New Delhi: Mongolian Lama Guru Deva, 1975.

——. "Bkra Shis Gling Gi Gnas Bstod Khu Byug Skad Snyan." In *Rje Btsun Blo Bzang Rta Dbyangs Gyi Gsung 'Bum*, 1:637–40. New Delhi: Mongolian Lama Guru Deva, 1975.

——. "Bkra Shis Thos Bsam Gling Gi 'byung Khungs Tho Tsam." In *Rje Btsun Blo Bzang Rta Dbyangs Kyi Gsung 'Bum*, 1:597–606. New Delhi: Mongolian Lama Guru Deva, 1975.

——. "Btsun Pa Phā Hyin Gyis 'phags Pa'i Yul Du 'Grims Pa'i Rnam Thar Rje Nyid Kyis Gsar 'Gyur Mchan Dang Bcas Pa." In *Rje Btsun Blo Bzang Rta Dbyangs Kyi Gsung 'Bum*, 1:147–246. New Delhi: Mongolian Lama Guru Deva, 1975.

——. "Byang Phyogs Bstan 'gro'i Rtsa Lag Mchog Sprul Rin Po Che Dar Ba Paṇḍita'i 'Khrungs Rabs Gsol 'Debs Dad Ldan Dga' Bskyed." In *Rje Btsun Blo Bzang Rta Dbyangs Kyi Gsung 'Bum*, 6:259–64. New Delhi: Mongolian Lama Guru Deva, 1975.

——. "Byang Phyogs Chen Po Hor Gyi Rgyal Khams Kyi Rtogs Brjod Kyi Bstan Bcos Chen Po Ngo Mtshar Gser Gyi Deb Ther." In *Rje Btsun Blo Bzang Rta Dbyangs Kyi Gsung 'Bum*, 2:43–490. New Delhi: Mongolian Lama Guru Deva, 1975.

——. "Byang Phyogs Hor Gyi Yul Du Dam Pa'i Chos Rin Po Che Byung Tshul Gyi Gtam Rgyud Bkra Shis Chos Dung Bzhad Pa'i Sgra Dbyangs." In *Rje Btsun Blo Bzang Rta Dbyangs Kyi Gsung 'Bum*, 2:9–42. New Delhi: Mongolian Lama Guru Deva, 1975.

——. "Byang Phyogs Hor Gyi Yul Grur Ston Pa'i Sku Tshab Tu Bzhugs Pa'i Rten Rnying Ertini Jo Bo'i Rnam Thar Dang 'brel Ba'i Dus Bstun Gsol 'Debs." In *Rje Btsun Blo Bzang Rta Dbyangs Kyi Gsung 'Bum*, 1:39–44. New Delhi: Mongolian Lama Guru Deva, 1975.

——. "Chen Po Hor Gyi Yul Gru'i Sngon Rabs Kyi Brjed Byang Shāstra'i Zur Rgyan Du Sog Yig Las Bod Skad Du Bsgyur Te Bkod Pa." In *Rje Btsun Blo Bzang Rta Dbyangs Kyi Gsung 'Bum*, 2:487–546. New Delhi: Mongolian Lama Guru Deva, 1975.

——. "Chos Sde Chos Dbyings 'od Gsal Gling Gi 'Byung Khungs Mdo Tsam Brjod Pa." In *Rje Btsun Blo Bzang Rta Dbyangs Kyi Gsung 'Bum*, 1:541–85. New Delhi: Mongolian Lama Guru Deva, 1975.

——. "Dam Can Chos Rgyal Dang Rgyal Chen Shugs Ldan Gnyis Kyi Nang Gzhug Dkar Chag Bdud Dpung Zil Gnon." In *Rje Btsun Blo Bzang Rta Dbyangs Kyi Gsung 'Bum*, 6:409–14. New Delhi: Mongolian Lama Guru Deva, 1975.

——. "Dam Pa Gong Ma'i Gsang Ba'i Lung Bstan 'ga' Zhig Gi Don Mchan Bus Gsal Bar Byas Pa." In *Rje Btsun Blo Bzang Rta Dbyangs Kyi Gsung 'Bum*, 14:359–66. New Delhi: Mongolian Lama Guru Deva, 1975.

——. "Dben Pa'i Bsti Gnas Gsar Rnying Gcig Tu 'dres Pa'i Lo Rgyus Ma Bu Cha 'Dzoms Kyi Gleng Mo." In *Rje Btsun Blo Bzang Rta Dbyangs Kyi Gsung 'Bum*, 1:607–16. New Delhi: Mongolian Lama Guru Deva, 1975.

——. "Dga' Ldan Theg Chen Gling Gi Bsngags Pa Mdo Tsam Brjod Pa." In *Rje Btsun Blo Bzang Rta Dbyangs Kyi Gsung 'Bum*, 1:627–34. New Delhi: Mongolian Lama Guru Deva, 1975.

——. "Dpal Dus Kyi 'khor Lo'i Sa Lam Gyi Ngos 'Dzin Rags Rim 'Phros Dang Bcas Pa." In *Rje Btsun Blo Bzang Rta Dbyangs Kyi Gsung 'Bum*, 9:9–80. New Delhi: Mongolian Lama Guru Deva, 1975.

——. "Dpal Ldan Bla Ma Dam Pa Erteni Paṇḍita Sprul Sku'i Rnam Thar Gyi Sa Bon Dpag Bsam Myu Gu." In *Rje Btsun Blo Bzang Rta Dbyangs Kyi Gsung 'Bum*, vol. 7. New Delhi: Mongolian Lama Guru Deva, 1975.

——. "Dpal Ldan 'bras Spungs Su Mchod Rten Gsar Du Bzhengs Pa'i Nang Gzhug Gi Dkar Chag." In *Rje Btsun Blo Bzang Rta Dbyangs Kyi Gsung 'Bum*, 6 (cha):443–48. New Delhi: Mongolian Lama Guru Deva, 1975.

——. "Gdan Sa Khu Re Chen Mo'i Chos Grwa Nub Ma'i 'byung Khungs Dang 'Brel Ba'i Gtam Gyi Phreng Ba." In *Rje Btsun Blo Bzang Rta Dbyangs Kyi Gsung 'Bum*, 1:503–40. New Delhi: Mongolian Lama Guru Deva, 1975.

——. "Gnas Brtan Bcu Drug Gi Lung Bstan Gsar Rnyed 'phros Dang Bcas Pa." In *Rje Btsun Blo Bzang Rta Dbyangs Kyi Gsung 'Bum*, 3:477–96. New Delhi: Mongolian Lama Guru Deva, 1975.

——. "'Jam Mgon Rgyal Ba Gnyis Pa'i Bstan Srung Thun Mong Ma Yin Pa Rgyal Chen Rdo Rje Shugs Ldan Rtsal Gyi Chos Skor Be Bum Du Bsgrigs Pa'i Dkar Chag Gnam Lcags 'Khor Lo'i Mu Khyud 'Phrin Las 'Od 'Bar." In *Rje Btsun Blo Bzang Rta Dbyangs Kyi Gsung 'Bum*, 11:395–414. New Delhi: Mongolian Lama Guru Deva, 1975.

——. "Mkhyen Ldan Lo Tsā Ba Tshe Dbang Gi Gros Lan Spos Shel Phreng Ba." In *Rje Btsun Blo Bzang Rta Dbyangs Kyi Gsung 'Bum*, 1:651–58. New Delhi: Mongolian Lama Guru Deva, 1975.

——. "Mtshan Zhabs Mkhan Chen Gyi Dogs Lan Tshangs Pa'i Drang Thig." In *Rje Btsun Blo Bzang Rta Dbyangs Kyi Gsung 'Bum*, 2:561–72. New Delhi: Mongolian Lama Guru Deva, 1975.

——. "Mtshan Zhabs Mkhan Chen Gyis Chos 'Byung Las Brtsams Te Bka' 'dri Gnang Ba'i Chab Shog." In *Rje Btsun Blo Bzang Rta Dbyangs Kyi Gsung 'Bum*, 2:551–54. New Delhi: Mongolian Lama Guru Deva, 1975.

——. "Rang Dgon Bstan Rtsis." In *Rje Btsun Blo Bzang Rta Dbyangs Kyi Gsung 'Bum*, 11:295–98. New Delhi: Mongolian Lama Guru Deva, 1975.

——. "Rang Gi Byed Spyod Rags Bsdoms 'Di Snang Za Zi'i Rjes Gco." In *Rje Btsun Blo Bzang Rta Dbyangs Kyi Gsung 'Bum*, 11:169–204. New Delhi: Mongolian Lama Guru Deva, 1975.

——. "Rgya Bod Hor Gsum Gyi Bstan Rtsis Rags Bsdus Legs Bshad Bdud Rtsi'i Thig Pa." In *Rje Btsun Blo Bzang Rta Dbyangs Gyi Gsung 'Bum*, vol. 1. New Delhi: Mongolian Lama Guru Deva, 1975.

——. "Rgya Spar Gnas Brtan Bcu Drug Gi Zhal Byang Bod Skad Du Bsgyur Ba 'phros Bshad Dang Bcas Pa." In *Rje Btsun Blo Bzang Rta Dbyangs Kyi Gsung 'Bum*, 3:497–512. New Delhi: Mongolian Lama Guru Deva, 1975.

——. "Rgyal Chen Rdo Rje Shugs Ldan Rtsal Gyi Bskang 'phrin Mdor Bsdus Don Chen Myur Grub." In *Rje Btsun Blo Bzang Rta Dbyangs Kyi Gsung 'Bum*, 11:385–92. New Delhi: Mongolian Lama Guru Deva, 1975.

——. "Rgyal Sras Gzhon Nu nor Bzang Gi Rnam Thar Las Brtsams Pa'i Bstod Pa." In *Rje Btsun Blo Bzang Rta Dbyangs Kyi Gsung 'Bum*, 1:119–34. New Delhi: Mongolian Lama Guru Deva, 1975.

——. "Rgyal Sras Gzhon Nu nor Bzang Gi Rnam Thar Las Brtsams Pa'i Bstod Pa." In *Rje Btsun Blo Bzang Rta Dbyangs Kyi Gsung 'Bum*, 1:117–32. New Delhi: Mongolian Lama Guru Deva, 1975.

——. "Rgyal Sras Rtag Tu Ngu'i Rnam Thar Las Brtsams Pa'i Bstod Pa." In *Rje Btsun Blo Bzang Rta Dbyangs Kyi Gsung 'Bum*, 1:135–46. New Delhi: Mongolian Lama Guru Deva, 1975.

——. "Ri Bo Rtse Lnga'i Bstod." In *Rje Btsun Blo Bzang Rta Dbyangs Kyi Gsung 'Bum*, 1:625–28. New Delhi: Mongolian Lama Guru Deva, 1975.

——. "Rje Btsun Ce Tā Yan Gyi Rnam Thar Gces Btus Dran Thor Bsgyur Ba Chos Rnga'i Sgra Skad." In *Rje Btsun Blo Bzang Rta Dbyangs Kyi Gsung 'Bum*, 3:515–26. New Delhi: Mongolian Lama Guru Deva, 1975.

——. "Rnam Thar Gces Btus Bdud Rtsi'i Bsang Gtor." In *Rje Btsun Blo Bzang Rta Dbyangs Kyi Gsung 'Bum*, vol. 7. New Delhi: Mongolian Lama Guru Deva, 1975.

——. "Sprul Pa'i Chos Skyong Chen Po'i Sger Gyi Lung Bstan Snga Phyir Phebs Pa Gnyis." In *Rje Btsun Blo Bzang Rta Dbyangs Kyi Gsung 'Bum*, 14:368–74. New Delhi: Mongolian Lama Guru Deva, 1975.

——. "Thog Mtha' Bar Du Dge Ba Dam Chos Bdud Rtsi'i Zil Mngar Cung Zhig Myang Ba'i Thob Yig Zab Rgyas Gsang Ba'i Gdams Pa Rin Chen Gter Gyi Kha Byang." In *Rje Btsun Blo Bzang Rta Dbyangs Kyi Gsung 'Bum*, 15–17:7–502 (pod dang po), 7–508 (pod gnyis pa), 7–560 (pod gsum pa). New Delhi: Mongolian Lama Guru Deva, 1975.

Blo-bzaṅ-rta-mgrin. *The Golden Annals of Lamaism Being the Original Tibetan Text of the Hor-Chos-Ḥbyuṅ of Blo-Bzaṅ-Rta-Mgrin Entitled 'Jam Gliṅ Byaṅ Phyogs Chen Po Hor Gyi Rgyal Khams Kyi Rtogs Pa Brjod Pa'i Bstan Bcos Chen Po Dpyod Ldan Mgu Byed Ṅo Mćhar Gser Gyi Deb Ther.* Ed. Lokesh Chandra. Śata-Piṭaka 34. New Delhi: International Academy of Indian Culture, 1964.

Byambaa, ed. "Khyab Bdag Rdo Rje 'chang Dang Ngo Bo Dbyer Ma Mchis Ba'i Dpal Ldan Bla Ma Dam Pa 'Dar Pa Paṇḍita Rin Po Che Rje Btsun Ngag Dbang Chos 'Byor Don Grub Dpal Bzang Po'i Skyes Rabs Rnam Thar Rgyal Bstan Mdzes Byed Rin Chen 'Phrin Ba." In *Khyab Bdag Rdo Rje 'chang 'Dar Pa Paṇḍita Ngag Dbang Chos 'Byor Don Grub Dpal Bzang Po'i Skyes Rabs Rnam Thar Dang Gsung Thor Bu*, 1–395. Mongol Bilig: Mongolchuudin Töwd Khelt Büteeliïg Sudlakh Tsuwral. Ulaanbaatar, Mongolia: R. Byambaa, 2011.

Dkon mchog rgyal mtshan. *RGya Bod Hor Sog Gi Lo Rgyus Nyung Ngur Brjod Pa Byis Pa 'jug Pa'i Bab Stegs.* Vol. 4. 11 vols. New Delhi: Gyalten Gelek Namgyal, 1974.

"Grand Abbot of Mongolia, One of Three Living Buddhas, May Soon Lose Throne Through the Diplomacy of Russia." *The Washington Post*, April 5, 1914.

Jam dpal shes rab. *Chen po Hor gyi rgyal khams su dam pai chos rin po che lan gsum du dar bai tshul las brtsams pai gtam dwangs gsal me lon.* Mundgod, North Kanara, K.S., India: Drepung Gomang Dratsang College, 1991.

Khurelbaatar, Lkhamsurengiin, and G. Luvsantseren. *Ogtorguin tsagaan gardi.* Vol. II. Ulaanbaatar: Mongol Uls, Shinzhlekh Ukhaany Akademiin Khel Zokhiolyn Khureelen, 1996.

Lcang skya rol pa'i rdo rje. *Zhing Mchog Ri Bo Dwangs Bsil Gyi Gnas Bshad Dad Pa'i Padmo Rgyas Byed Ngo Mtshar Nyi Ma'i Snang Ba.* Xining: mTsho sngon mi rigs dpe skrun khang, 1993.

Lenin, Vladimir Il'ich. *Collected Works.* Vol. 42. 45 vols. Moscow: Progress Publishers, 1972.

Maiskii, I. *Sovremennaya Mongoliya.* Irkutsk, R.S.F.S.R.: Gosudarstvennoe Izdatel'stvo, Irkutskoe Otdeleniye, 1921.

Ngag dbang blo bzang. "Ngag Dbang Blo Bzang Rang Gi Rnam Thar." In *Gsung Thor Bu/Ngag Dbang Blo Bzang Rdo Rje*, Vol. 1. Mundgog, North Kanara, Karnataka: 'Bras blo gling gtsung lag gter mdzod 'phrul spar khang, n.d.

Ngag dbang chos 'byor don grub. *Khyab Bdag Rdo Rje'i 'chang 'Dar Pa Paṇḍita Nga Dbang Chos 'Byor Don Grub Dpal Bzang Po'i Skyes Rabs Rnam Thar Dang Gsung Thor.* Mongol Bilig: Mongolchuudin Tövd Khelt Büteeliïg Sudlakh Tsuvral. Ulaanbaatar, Mongolia: R. Byambaa, 2011.

Ngag dbang mkhas grub. " 'Bras Spungs Bkra Shis Tshe 'Phel Gling Gi Gnas Bstod." In *Collected Works of Kyai-Rdor Mkhan-Po Nag-Dban-Mkhas-Grub*, 5 (ca):399–404. Leh: S. W. Tashigangpa, 1972.

——. "Byams Pa'i Dam Bca'i Gzungs Bzla Tshul." In *Collected Works of Kyai-Rdor Mkhan-Po Ngag-Dbang-Mkhas-Grub*, 1:281–86. Leh: S. W. Tashigangpa, 1972.

——. "Khu Re Chen Mor Bzhengs Pa'i Byams Pa'i Sku Brnyan Gyi Dkar Chag Dad Pa'i Bzhin Ras Gsal Bar Byed Pa'i nor Bu'i Me Long." In *Collected Works of Kyai-Rdor Mkhan-Po Ngag-Dbang-Mkhas-Grub*, 1:175–274. Leh: S. W. Tashigangpa, 1972.

——. "Rgyal Ba Byams Mgon Gyi 'dra Sku'i Nang Du 'Bul Rgyu'i 'Dod Gsol Dgos 'Dod Yid Bzhin 'Gugs Pa'i Lcags Kyu." In *Collected Works of Kyai-Rdor Mkhan-Po Ngag-Dbang-Mkhas-Grub*, 1:275–80. Leh: S. W. Tashigangpa, 1972.

——. "Rgyal Ba Byams Mgon Gyi Gsol 'debs Byams Mgon Zhal Bzang Lta Ba'i Dga' Ston." In *Collected Works of Kyai-Rdor Mkhan-Po Ngag-Dbang-Mkhas-Grub*, 1:155–66. Leh: S. W. Tashigangpa, 1972.

——. "Rgyal Ba Byams Pa'i Sgrub Thabs Dang 'brel Ba'i Mchod Chog Dga' Ldan Pad Mtshor 'Jug Pa'i Gru Gzings." In *Collected Works of Kyai-Rdor Mkhan-Po Ngag-Dbang-Mkhas-Grub*, 1:121–54. Leh: S. W. Tashigangpa, 1972.

Ngag dbang nyi ma. *Chos 'byung Lung Rigs Sgron Me*. Varanasi, India: unknown, 1965.

Okladnikov, A. P., S. Bira, Sssr Akademia nauk, and M. N. R. Akademija nauk. *Istorija Mongolskoj Narodnoj Respubliki*. Moskva: Nauka, 1983.

Rinchen. *Mongol Ard Ulsyn Ugsaatny Sudlal, Khelnïĭ Shinzhleliïn Atlas =: Atlas Ethnologique et Linguistique de La République Populaire de Mongolie*. Ulaanbaatar: BNMAU Shinzhlekh ukhaany akademi, 1979.

Rinchen, Byambyn, Faxian, Luwsandamdin, and Dorji Banzarov. *Travels of Fa Hsian Trans. Dordji Bansaroff*. Ulanbator: Corpus Scriptorum Mongolorum Instituti Linguae Litterarum Academiae Scientiarum Reipublicae Populi Mongolici, 1970.

Ye shes rgyal mtshan. *Lam Rim Bla Ma Brgyud Pa'i Rnam Thar*. 2 vols. 'Bar khams: rNga khul bod yig rtsom sgyur cus. New Delhi: Grib tshe mchog gling grwa tshang gi par khang, 1970–1972.

Secondary Sources

Akiner, Shirin. *Mongolia Today*. London; New York: Kegan Paul International in association with the Central Asia Research Forum, London.

Amar, A. *Monggol-Un Tobci Teüke [A Brief History of Mongolia]*. Vol. 9. The Mongolia Society Papers. Bloomington, Ind.: The Mongolia Society, 1986.

Amar, A., Š. Ajuudajn Očir Čojmaa, Ḥarnuud Z. Lonžid, and C. Törbat. *Mongolyn tovč tüüh*. Ulaanbaatar: So·embo Printing, 2006.

Ary, Elijah S. *Authorized Lives: Biography and the Early Formation of Geluk Identity*. Somerville, Mass.: Wisdom, 2015.

Asad, Talal. *Formations of the Secular: Christianity, Islam, Modernity*. Stanford, Calif.: Stanford University Press, 2003.

Atwood, Christopher P. "Buddhism and Popular Ritual in Mongolian Religion: A Reexamination of the Fire Cult." *History of Religions* 36, no. 2 (1996): 112–39.

——. *Encyclopedia of Mongolia and the Mongolian Empire*. New York: Facts On File, 2004.

——. *Young Mongols and Vigilantes in Inner Mongolia's Interregnum Decades, 1911–1931*. Leiden: Brill, 2002.

Axel, Brian Keith. "Historical Anthropology and Its Vicissitudes." In *From the Margins: Historical Anthropology and Its Futures*, ed. Brian Keith Axel, 1–44. Durham, N.C., and London: Duke University Press, 2002.

Baabar. *History of Mongolia*. Ed. Christopher Kaplonski. Ulaanbaatar: Monsudar Publishing, 2004.

Bakhtin, M. M., and Michael Holquist. *The Dialogic Imagination: Four Essays.* Austin: University of Texas Press, 1981.

Bareja-Starzyńska, Agata. *The Biography of the First Khalkha Jetsundampa Zanabazar by Zaya Pandita Luvsanprinlei: Studies, Annotated Translation, Transliteration and Facsimile.* Warsaw: Dom Wydawniczy ELIPSA, 2015.

——. "The Mongolian Incarnation of Jo Nang Pa Taranatha Kun Dga' Snying Po: Ondor Gegeen Zanabazar Blo Bzang Bstan Pa'i Rgyal Mtshan (1635–1723): A Case Study of the Tibeto-Mongolian Relationship." *The Tibet Journal* 34, no. 3–4 (2009): 243+.

Batsaikhan, Emget Ookhnoi. *Bogd Jebtsundamba Khutuktu, The Last King of Mongolia.* Ulaanbaatar: Admon, 2009.

Batsaĭkhan, Ookhnoĭn, Zorigtyn Lonzhid, and Olon Uls Sudlalyn Khŭrėėlėn (Mongolyn Shinzhlėkh Ukhaany Akademi). *Bogdo Jebtsundamba Khutuktu, the Last King of Mongolia: Mongolia's National Revolution of 1911: Research Work.* Ulaanbaatar: Admon, 2009.

Bawden, Charles R. *The Modern History of Mongolia.* New York: Praeger, 1968.

——. *A Contemporary Mongolian Account of the Period of Autonomy.* 1st ed. Vol. 4. Bloomington, Ind.: The Mongolia Society, 1970.

Beliso-De Jesús, Aisha M. *Electric Santería: Racial and Sexual Assemblages of Transnational Religion.* New York: Columbia University Press, 2015.

Bell, Charles Alfred. *Portrait of a Dalai Lama: The Life and Times of the Great Thirteenth.* London: Wisdom, 1987.

Bentor, Yael. *Consecration of Images and Stūpas in Indo-Tibetan Tantric Buddhism.* Leiden: Brill, 1996.

Berger, Patricia Ann. *Empire of Emptiness: Buddhist Art and Political Authority in Qing China.* Honolulu: University of Hawaii Press, 2003.

Bernstein, Anya. "Pilgrims, Fieldworkers, and Secret Agents: Buryat Buddhologists and the History of an Eurasian Imaginary." *Inner Asia* 11, no. 1 (2009): 23–45.

Bhabha, Homi K. *The Location of Culture.* London; New York: Routledge Classics, 1994.

Bira, Sh. *O "Zolotoi knige" Sh. Damdina [On Sh. Damdin's "Golden Book"].* Ulan-Bator: Izdvo Akademii nauk MNR, 1964.

Bjerken, Zeff. "The Mirrorwork of Tibetan Religious Historians: A Comparison of Buddhist and Bon Historiography." Ph.D. diss., University of Michigan, 2001. ProQuest Dissertations & Theses (PQDT). http://ezproxy.qa.proquest.com/docview /230863771?accountid=14771.

Bla-ma, bTsan-po, and Turrell V. Wylie. *The Geography of Tibet According to the 'dZam-Gling-RGyas-BShad.* Roma: Istituto italiano per il Medio ed Estremo Oriente, 1962.

Blo-bzaṅ-tshul-khrims and Rudolf Kaschewsky. *Das Leben Des Lamaistischen Heiligen Tsongkhapa Blo-Bzan-Grags-Pa (1357–1419): Dargestellt Und Erlautert Anhand Seiner Vita "Quellort Allen Gluckes.* Wiesbaden: O. Harrassowitz, 1917.

Bocking, Brian.. *Buddhist Crossroads: Pioneer Western Buddhists and Asian Networks 1860-1960.* London: Routledge, 2015.

Boym, Svetlana. *The Future of Nostalgia.* New York: Basic Books, 2001.

Braun, Erik. *The Birth of Insight: Meditation, Modern Buddhism, and the Burmese Monk Ledi Sayadaw.* Chicago: University of Chicago Press, 2015.

Brown, William A., Urgunge Onon, and B. Shirėndėv. *History of the Mongolian People's Republic*. Cambridge, Mass.: East Asian Research Center, Harvard University, 1976.

Bstan-'dzin-nor-bu, Benjamin Bogin, and Bstan-'dzin-nor-bu. *The Illuminated Life of the Great Yolmowa*. Chicago: Serindia Contemporary, 2013.

Bulag, Uradyn Erden. *Nationalism and Hybridity in Mongolia*. Oxford; New York: Clarendon Press; Oxford University Press, 1998.

Buswell, Robert E., and Donald S. Lopez. *The Princeton Dictionary of Buddhism*. Princeton, N.J.: Princeton University Press, 2013.

Cabezón, José Ignacio. *Buddhism and Language : A Study of Indo-Tibetan Scholasticism*. Albany: State University of New York Press, 1994.

Carmona, Bernard, Gaston Pineau, Université François-Rabelais (Tours), École doctorale Sciences de l'homme et de la société (Tours), and représentations Plurilinguismes expressions francophones, informations, communication, sociolinguistique-Dynamiques et enjeux de la diversité (Tours). "Formation transdisciplinaire, trajet anthropologique et tradition tibétaine: Recherche sur l'ingenium de la pratique du débat dans l'Ecole Gelugpa." SCD de l'université de Tours, 2012.

de Certeau, Michel. *Heterologies: Discourse on the Other*. Minneapolis: University of Minnesota Press, 1986.

——. *Histoire et Psychanalyse Entre Science et Fiction*. Paris: Gallimard, 1987.

——. "The Historiographic Operation." In *The Writing of History*, 56–113. New York: Columbia University Press, 1988.

——. *La Possession de Loudun*. Paris: Julliard, 1970.

——. *L'absent de l'histoire*. Tours: Mame, 1973.

——. *L'écriture de l'histoire*. Paris: Gallimard, 1975.

——. "Walking in the City." In *The Practice of Everyday Life*, trans. Steven Rendall, 91–110. Berkeley: University of California Press, 1988.

——. *The Writing of History*. Trans. Tom Conley. New York: Columbia University Press, 1988.

de Certeau, Michel, and Luce Giard. *Culture in the Plural*. Minneapolis: University of Minnesota Press, 1997.

Chakrabarty, Dipesh. *Provincializing Europe: Postcolonial Thought and Historical Difference*. Princeton, N.J.: Princeton University Press, 2009.

Chaloupkova, L., and D. Dashbadrakh. "About the Biography of Darpa Pandita Called The Beautiful Jewel Rosary of Victorious Teaching." *Archiv Orientalni* 71 (2003): 285–92.

Chapman, Frederick Spencer. *Lhasa, the Holy City*. New York; London: Harper & Bros., 1939.

Charleux, Isabelle. "Buddhist Monasteries in Southern Mongolia." In *The Buddhist Monastery: A Cross-Cultural Survey*, ed. Pierre Pichard and F. Lagirarde, 351–90. Paris: École française d'extrême-orient, 2003.

——. "Mongol Pilgrimages to Wutai Shan in the Late Qing Dynasty." *Journal of the International Association of Tibetan Studies* 6 (December 2011): 275–326.

——. *Nomads on Pilgrimage: Mongols on Wutaishan (China), 1800-1940*. Leiden: Brill, 2015.

Chartier, Roger, and Lydia G. Cochrane. *Cultural History: Between Practices and Representations*. Ithaca, N.Y.: Cornell University Press, 1988.

Choijamts, D., and Sh. Choimaa, eds. *Mongolîn Burkhanî Shashanî Tüükhen Surwalj: Töwd Khelt Surwaljiin Orchuulga, Mailbar, Müükhiin On Tsagiin Khelkhees*. Trans. D. Bürnee and D. Enkhtör. Ulaanbaatar: N.p., 2004.

Chopel, Gendun, Donald Lopez, and Thupten Jinpa. *Grains of Gold: Tales of a Cosmopolitan Traveler*. Chicago: University of Chicago Press, 2014.

Chou, Wen-Shing Lucia. "The Visionary Landscape of Wutai Shan in Tibetan Buddhism from the Eighteenth to the Twentieth Century." Ph.D. diss., University of California, Berkeley, 2011.

Chuluun, Sampildondov, and Uradyn E. Bulag. *The Thirteenth Dalai Lama on the Run (1904-1906): Archival Documents from Mongolia*. Leiden: Brill, 2013.

Clark, Katerina, and Michael Holquist. *Mikhail Bakhtin*. Cambridge, Mass.: Belknap Press of Harvard University Press, 1984.

Cohn, Bernard S. *An Anthropologist Among the Historians and Other Essays*. Delhi: Oxford University Press, 1987.

——. *Beyond Enlightenment: Buddhism, Religion, Modernity*. London; New York: Routledge, 2009.

——. *Colonialism and Its Forms of Knowledge: The British in India*. 1996.

——. "India as a Racial, Linguistic, and Cultural Area." In *Introducing India in Liberal Education*, ed. Milton Singer. Chicago: University of Chicago Press, 1957.

Cowan, Benjamin A. "Sexing Empire." *Sexing Empire* 123 (2015): 1–123.

Crossley, Pamela Kyle. *A Translucent Mirror: History and Identity in Qing Imperial Ideology*. Berkeley: University of California Press, 1999.

Crossley, Pamela Kyle, Helen F. Siu, and Donald S. Sutton. *Empire at the Margins: Culture, Ethnicity, and Frontier in Early Modern China*. Berkeley: University of California Press, 2006.

Debreczeny, Karl. "Wutai Shan: Pilgrimage to Five-Peak Mountain." *Journal of the International Association of Tibetan Studies* 6 (2011): 1–133.

Diemberger, Hildegard, and Uradyn Bulag. "Towards Critical Studies of the Mongolian-Tibet Interface." In *The Mongolia-Tibet Interface: Opening New Research Terrains in Inner Asia: PIATS 2003: Tibetan Studies: Proceedings of the Tenth Seminar of the International Association for Tibetan Studies, Oxford, 2003*. Leiden; Boston: Brill, 2007.

Dindub, and John G. Hangin. *A Brief History of Mongolia in the Autonomous Period*. Bloomington, Ind.: The Mongolia Society, 1977.

Dorjiev, Agvan, Thubten Jigme Norbu, and Dan Martin. *Dorjiev: Memoirs of a Tibetan Diplomat*. Tokyo: Hokke bunka kenkyū, 1991.

Dreyfus, Georges. *The Shuk-Den Affair: Origins of a Controversy; Nachdruck Eines Artikels Aus: Journal of the International Association of Buddhist Studies, Vol. 21, Number 2, 1998*. Dharamsala: Narthang Publ., 1999.

——. *The Sound of Two Hands Clapping: The Education of a Tibetan Buddhist Monk*. Berkeley: University of California Press, 2008.

Duara, Prasenjit. *Rescuing History from the Nation: Questioning Narratives of Modern China*. Chicago: University of Chicago Press, 1996.

Dugarava-Montgomery, Yeshen-Khorlo, and Robert Montgomery. "The Buriat Alphabet of Agvan Dorzhiev." In *Mongolia in the Twentieth Century*, ed. Stephen and Bruce A. Elleman Kotkin, 79–97. Armonk, N.Y.; London: M. E. Sharpe, 1999.

Elliott, Mark C. *The Manchu Way: The Eight Banners and Ethnic Identity in Late Imperial China*. Stanford, Calif.: Stanford University Press, 2001.

Elverskog, Carl Johan. "Buddhism, History and Power: The Jewel Translucent Sutra and the Formation of Mongol Identity." Ph.D. diss., Indiana University, 2000. Pro-Quest Dissertations & Theses (PQDT) (MSTAR_304600342).

Elverskog, Johan, ed. *Biographies of Eminent Mongol Buddhists*. Halle: IITBS, International Institute for Tibetan and Buddhist Studies, 2008.

——. "G. J. Ramstedt's 'A Short History of the Uyghurs.'" In *Festschrift for Larry Clark on His 75th Birthday*, ed. Zsuzsanna Gulasci. Turnhout: Brepols, forthcoming.

——. *The Jewel Translucent Sūtra: Altan Khan and the Mongols in the Sixteenth Century*. Leiden; Boston: Brill, 2003.

——. "Mongol Time Enters a Qing World." In *Time, Temporality, and Imperial Transition: East Asia from Ming to Qing*, ed. Lynn A. Struve. Honolulu: Association for Asian Studies and University of Hawai'i Press, 2005.

——. *Our Great Qing: The Mongols, Buddhism and the State in Late Imperial China*. Honolulu: University of Hawai'i Press, 2006.

——. "Tibetocentrism, Religious Conversion and the Study of Mongolian Buddhism." In *The Mongolia-Tibet Interface: Opening New Research Terrains in Inner Asia: PIATS 2003: Tibetan Studies: Proceedings of the Tenth Seminar of the International Association for Tibetan Studies, Oxford, 2003*, ed. Uradyn E. Bulag and Hildegard G.M. Diemberger. Leiden; Boston: Brill, 2007.

——. "Wutai Shan, Qing Cosmopolitanism, and the Mongols." *Journal of the International Association of Tibetan Studies* 6 (2011): 243–74.

Empson, Rebecca. *Time, Causality and Prophecy in the Mongolian Cultural Region: Visions of the Future*. Folkestone: Global Oriental, 2006.

Even, Marie-Dominique. "Ritual Efficacy or Spiritual Quest? Buddhism and Modernity in Post-Communist Mongolia." In *Revisiting Rituals in a Changing Tibetan World*, ed. Katia Buffetrille, 241–72. Leiden: Brill, 2012.

Ewing, Thomas E. *Between the Hammer and the Anvil?: Chinese and Russian Policies in Outer Mongolia, 1911–1921*. Bloomington: Research Institute for Inner Asian Studies, Indiana University, 1980.

——. "Russia, China, and the Origins of the Mongolian People's Republic, 1911–1921: A Reappraisal." *The Slavonic and East European Review* 58, no. 3 (1980): 399–421.

Farquhar, David M. "Emperor as Bodhisattva in the Governance of Ch'ing Empire." *Harvard Journal of Asiatic Studies* 38, no. 1 (1978).

French, Rebecca R. "Tibetan Legal Literature: The Law Codes of the DGa' Ldan Pho Brang." In *Tibetan Literature: Studies in Genre*, ed. Lhundup Sopa, José Ignacio Cabezón, and Roger R. Jackson, 438–57. Ithaca, N.Y.: Snow Lion, 1996.

Gayley, Holly. *Love Letters from Golok: A Tantric Couple in Modern Tibet*. New York: Columbia University Press, 2016.

Gerasimova, Kseniia Maksimovna. *Obnovlencheskoe dvizhenie buriatskogo lamaistskogo dukhovenstva*. Ulan-Ude: Buriatskoe knizhnoe izd-vo, 1964.

Gerasimovich, L. *History of Modern Mongolian Literature, 1921–1964 [Literatura Mongol'skoj Narodnoj Respubliki 1921–1964 Godov]*. Bloomington, Ind.: The Mongolia Society, 1970.

Ginzburg, Carlo. *The Cheese and the Worms: The Cosmos of a Sixteenth-Century Miller*. Baltimore: Johns Hopkins University Press, 1980.

Goldstein, Melvyn C. *A History of Modern Tibet, 1913–1951: The Demise of the Lamaist State*. Berkeley: University of California Press, 1989.

Ġoncuġjab, and Johan Elverskog. *The Pearl Rosary: Mongol Historiography in Early Nineteenth-Century Ordos*. Bloomington, Ind.: The Mongolia Society, 2007.

Goodyear, Sara Suleri. *The Rhetoric of English India*. Chicago: University of Chicago Press, 1992.

Grönbold, Günter. "Materialen Zur Geschichte Des Ṣaḍaṅga-Yoga: III. Die Guru-Reihen Im Buddhistischen Ṣaḍaṅga-Yoga." *Zentralasiatische Studien* 16 (1982): 337–47.

Gyatso, Janet. *Apparitions of the Self: The Secret Autobiographies of a Tibetan Visionary: A Translation and Study of Jigme Lingpa's Dancing Moon in the Water and Ḍākki's Grand Secret-Talk*. Princeton, N.J.: Princeton University Press, 1998.

——. *Being Human in a Buddhist World: An Intellectual History of Medicine in Early Modern Tibet*. New York: Columbia University Press, 2015.

——. "Experience, Empiricism, and the Fortunes of Authority: Tibetan Medicine and Buddhism on the Eve of Modernity." In *Forms of Knowledge in Early Modern Asia: Explorations in the Intellectual History of India and Tibet, 1500–1800*, ed. Sheldon Pollock, 311–35. Durham, N.C.: Duke University Press, 2011.

——. "From the Autobiography of a Visionary." In *Religions of Tibet in Practice*, ed. Donald S. Lopez, 369–75. Princeton, N.J.: Princeton University Press, 1997.

——. "Turning Personal: Recent Work on Autobiography in Tibetan Studies." *The Journal of Asian Studies* 75, no. 1 (2016): 229–35.

Halén, Harry, and Suomalais-ugrilainen Seura. *Biliktu Bakshi, the Knowledgeable Teacher: G. J. Ramstedt's Career as a Scholar*. Helsinki: Finno-Ugrian Society, 1998.

Hegel, Georg Wilhelm Friedrich, Hugh Barr Nisbet, and Duncan Forbes. *Lectures on the Philosophy of World History*. Cambridge: Cambridge University Press, 1975.

Heine, Steven. *Buddhism in the Modern World: Adaptations of an Ancient Tradition*. New York: Oxford University Press, 2011.

Ho, Engseng. "Inter-Asian Concepts for Mobile Societies." *The Journal of Asian Studies* 76, no. 4 (2017): 907–28.

Holquist, Michael. *Dialogism: Bakhtin and His World*. New York: Routledge, 2003.

Hopkins, Jeffrey. "A Tibetan Perspective on the Nature of Spiritual Experience." In *Paths to Liberation: The Mārga and Its Transformations in Buddhist Thought*, ed. Robert E. Buswell and Robert M. Gimello. Honolulu: University of Hawaii Press, 1992.

Huber, Toni. *The Cult of Pure Crystal Mountain: Popular Pilgrimage and Visionary Landscape in Southeast Tibet*. New York: Oxford University Press, 1999.

——. *The Holy Land Reborn: Pilgrimage and the Tibetan Reinvention of Buddhist India*. Chicago: University of Chicago Press, 2008.

Humphrey, Caroline. "Remembering an Enemy: The Bogd Khaan in Twentieth-Century Mongolia." In *Memory, History, and Opposition Under State Socialism*, ed. Rubie S. Watson, 21–44. Sante Fe, N.M.: School of American Research Press, 1994.

Hyer, Paul, and Sechin Jagchid. *A Mongolian Living Buddha: Biography of the Kanjurwa Khutughtu*. Albany: State University of New York Press, 1983.

International Association for Tibetan Studies, Seminar, and Johan Elverskog. *Biographies of Eminent Mongol Buddhists: PIATS 2006, Tibetan Studies, Proceedings of the*

Eleventh Seminar of the International Association for Tibetan Studies, Königswinter 2006. Halle: IITBS, International Institute for Tibetan and Buddhist Studies, 2008.

Ishihama Yumiko. "The Notion of 'Buddhist Government' (chos srid) Shared by Tibet, Mongol, and Manchu in the Early 17th Century." In *The Relationship Between Religion and State (chos srid zung 'brel) in Traditional Tibet: Proceedings of a Seminar Held in Lumbini, Nepal, March 2000*, ed. Christoph Cüppers, 15–31. Lumbini: Lumbini International Research Institute, 2004.

Jackson, David P. "Enlightenment by a Single Means: Tibetan Controversies on the 'Self-Sufficient White Remedy' (Dkar Po Chig Thub)." In *Beiträge Zur Kultur- Und Geistesgeschichte Asiens*, vol. 12. Wien: Verlag der Österreichischen Akademie der Wissenschaften, n.d.

——. *A History of Tibetan Painting: The Great Tibetan Painters and Their Traditions.* Wien: Verlag der Österreichischen Akademie der Wissenschaften, 1996.

Jackson, David Paul, and Sa-skya Paṇḍi-ta Kun-dga'-rgyal-mtshan. *The Entrance Gate for the Wise (Section III): Sa-Skya Paṇḍita on Indian and Tibetan Traditions of Pramāṇa and Philosophical Debate.* Wien: Arbeitskreis für Tibetische und Buddhistische Studien, Universität Wien, 1987.

Jacoby, Sarah. *Love and Liberation: Autobiographical Writings of the Tibetan Buddhist Visionary Sera Khandro.* New York: Columbia University Press, 2014.

Jadamba, Lkhagvademchig, and Bernhard Schittich. "Negotiating Self and Other: Transnational Cultural Flows and the Reinvention of Mongolian Buddhism." *Internationales Asienforum* 10, no. 1–2 (2010): 83–102.

Josephson, Jason Ananda. *Invention of Religion in Japan.* Chicago: University of Chicago Press, 2012.

Kaplonski, Christopher. *The Lama Question: Violence, Sovereignty, and Exception in Early Socialist Mongolia.* Honolulu: University of Hawai'i Press, 2014.

——. *Truth, History and Politics in Mongolia: The Memory of Heroes.* London; New York: RoutledgeCurzon, 2004.

Kapstein, Matthew. *Buddhism Between Tibet and China.* Boston: Wisdom, 2009.

——. "Just Where on Jambudvīpa Are We? New Geographical Knowledge and Old Cosmological Schemes in Eighteenth-Century Tibet." In *Forms of Knowledge in Early Modern Asia: Explorations in the Intellectual History of India and Tibet, 1500-1800*, ed. S. Pollock, 336–64. Durham, N.C.: Duke University Press, 2011.

Kensur Yeshey, Tupden, Anne C. Klein, Jeffrey Hopkins, and Blo-bzan-grags-pa Tson-kha-pa. *Path to the Middle: Oral Madhyamika Philosophy in Tibet: The Spoken Scholarship of Kensur Yeshey Tupden Commenting on Tsong-Kha-Pa's Illumination of the Thought, Extensive Explanation of (Candrakirti's) "Entrance to (Nagarjuna's) 'Treatise on the Middle Way' ": (Dbu Ma Dgongs Pa Rab Gsal), the Sixth Chapter, "Perfection of Wisdom" Verses 1-7.* Albany: State University of New York Press, 1994.

Kiely, Jan. *Recovering Buddhism in Modern China.* New York: Columbia University Press, 2016.

King, Matthew W. "A 1931 Survey of Mongolian Monastic Colleges from the Golden Book (Altan Devter)." In *Sources of Mongolian Buddhism*, ed. Vesna Wallace. New York: Oxford University Press, forthcoming.

——. "Fragments from Gesar's Iron Chain: Biography as Aesthetics of Empire in the Minor Works of the Chahar Gewsh Lubsantsültim (1747–1810)." In *The Many Faces of Ling Gesar: Contributions in Honour of the Late R. A. Stein*, ed. Matthew Kapstein and Charles Ramble. Leiden: Brill, forthcoming.

——. "Modernities, Sense-Making, and the Inscription of Mongolian Buddhist Place." In *Buddhism in Mongolian History, Culture and Society*, ed. Vesna Wallace, 53–69. Oxford: Oxford University Press, 2015.

King, Matthew W., and Pamela E. Klassen. "Suppressing the Mad Elephant: Missionaries, Lamas, and the Mediation of Sacred Historiographies in the Tibetan Borderlands." *History and Anthropology* 26, no. 5 (2015): 529–52.

Köhle, Natalie. "Why Did the Kangxi Emperor Go to Wutai Shan?: Patronage, Pilgrimage, and the Place of Tibetan Buddhism at the Early Qing Court." *Late Imperial China* 29, no. 1 (2008): 73–119.

Korostovets, Ivan IAkovlevich, and Erich Hauer. *Von Cinggis Khan zur Sowjetrepublik; eine kurze Geschichte der Mongolei unter besonderer Ber̦cksichtigung der neuesten Zeit.* Berlin; Leipzig: W. de Gruyter & Co., 1926.

Koselleck, Reinhart. *Futures Past: On the Semantics of Historical Time.* New York: Columbia University Press, 2004..

Kotkin, Stephen, and Bruce A. Elleman. *Mongolia in the Twentieth Century: Landlocked Cosmopolitan.* Armonk, N.Y.: M. E. Sharpe, 1999.

van der Kuijp, Leonard W.J. "On the Life and Political Career of T'ai Si Tu Byang Chub Rgyal Mtshan." In *Tibetan History and Language: Studies Dedicated to Uray Gèza on His Seventieth Birthday*, ed. E. Steinkellner. Wiener Studien Zur Tibetologie Und Buddhismuskunde 26. Wien: Arbeitskreis für Tibetische und Buddhistische Studien, 1992.

——. "Phya-Pa Chos-Kyi Seng-Ge's Impact on Tibetan Epistemological Theory." *Journal of Indian Philosophy* 5, no. 4 (1978): 355–69.

——. "Tibetan Contributions to the 'Apoha' Theory: The Fourth Chapter of the Tshad-Ma Rigs-Pa'i Gter." *Journal of the American Oriental Society* 99, no. 3 (1979): 408–22.

Kuleshov, Nikolai. "Agvan Dorjiev, the Dalai Lama's Ambassador." *Asian Affairs* 23, no. 1 (1992): 20–33.

Lattimore, Owen. *Nationalism and Revolution in Mongolia: With a Translation from the Mongol of Sh. Nachukdorji's Life of Sukebatur.* New York: Oxford University Press, 1955.

——. *Nomads and Commissars: Mongolia Revisited.* New York: Oxford University Press, 1962.

Lattimore, Owen, Fujiko Isono, and Diluv Khutagt. *The Diluv Khutagt: Memoirs and Autobiography of a Mongol Buddhist Reincarnation in Religion and Revolution.* Wiesbaden: O. Harrassowitz, 1982.

Lattimore, Owen, Sh. Natsagdorj, I. Ya Zlatkin, J. Sambuu, S. P̦revjav, Damdinșren Ts, D. Tsedev, and D. Dashjamts. "Religion and Revolution in Mongolia." *Modern Asian Studies* 1, no. 1 (1967): 81–94.

Lempert, Michael. *Discipline and Debate: The Language of Violence in a Tibetan Buddhist Monastery.* Berkeley: University of California Press, 2012.

Levinson, Jules. "Metaphors of Liberation: Tibetan Treatises on Grounds and Paths." In *Tibetan Literature: Studies in Genre: Essays in Honor of Geshe Lhundrup Sopa*, ed. José

Ignacio Cabezón, Roger Jackson, and Lundup Sopa, 261–74. Ithaca, N.Y.: Snow Lion, 1996.

——. "The Metaphors of Liberation: A Study of Grounds and Paths According to the Middle Way Schools." Ph.D. diss., University of Virginia, 1994.

Lévi-Strauss, Claude. *Structural Anthropology*. Trans. Claire Jacobson and Brooke Grundfest Schoepf. New York: Basic Books, 1963.

Lhamsuren, Munkh-Erdene. "The Mongolian Nationality Lexicon: From the Chinggisid Lineage to Mongolian Nationality (From the Seventeenth to the Early Twentieth Century)." *Inner Asia* 8, no. 1 (2006): 51–98.

Lhundup Sopa, Michael J. Sweet, and Leonard Zwilling. *Peacock in the Poison Grove: Two Buddhist Texts on Training the Mind; the Wheel Weapon (Mtshon Cha'khor Lo and the Poison-Destroying Peacock (Rma Bya Dug 'joms) Attributed to Dharmarakṣita*. Boston: Wisdom, 2001.

Lin, Nancy G. "Recounting the Fifth Dalai Lama's Rebirth Lineage." *Revue d'Etudes Tibétaines* 38 (Février 2017): 119–56.

Lobsang Tayang and José Cabezón. *One Hundred and Eight Verses in Praise of Great Compassion: [A Precious Crystal Rosary]*. Mysore: Mysore Printing and Publishing House, 1984.

Lopez, Donald S. *A Modern Buddhist Bible: Essential Readings from East and West*. Boston: Beacon Press, 2002.

——. *Prisoners of Shangri-La: Tibetan Buddhism and the West*. Chicago: University of Chicago Press, 1998.

——. *Strange Tales of an Oriental Idol: An Anthology of Early European Portrayals of the Buddha*. Chicago: University of Chicago Press, 2016.

Mahmood, Saba. *Politics of Piety: The Islamic Revival and the Feminist Subject*. Princeton, N.J.: Princeton University Press, 2005.

Majer, Zsuzsa. "Delgeriin Choir, the Monastery of Zawa Lam Damdin in the Gobi." In *Zentralasiatische Studien Des Seminars Für Sprach- Und Kulturwissenschaft Zentralasiens Der Universität Bonn*, 41:7–42. Bonn: International Institute for Tibetan and Buddhist Studies, 2012.

Makley, Charlene. "Gendered Boundaries in Motion: Space and Identity on the Sino-Tibetan Frontier." *American Ethnologist : The Journal of the American Ethnological Society* 30, no. 4 (2003): 597–619.

——. *The Violence of Liberation: Gender and Tibetan Buddhist Revival in Post-Mao China*. Berkeley: University of California Press, 2007.

Mala, Guilaine. "A Mahāyānist Rewriting of the History of China by Mgon Po Skyabs in the Rgya Nag Chos 'Byung." In *Power, Politics, and the Reinvention of Tradition: Tibet in the Seventeenth and Eighteenth Centuries*, ed. Bryan J. Cuevas and Kurtis R. Schaeffer, 145–70. Leiden: Brill, 2006.

Marshall, Peter. *Demanding the Impossible: A History of Anarchism*. Oakland, Calif.: PM Press, 2010.

Martin, Dan, and Yael Bentor. *Tibetan Histories: A Bibliography of Tibetan-Language Historical Works*. London: Serindia, 1997.

Mayskiy, I. M. *Mongoliya Nakanune Revolyutsii (Mongolia on the Eve of Revolution)*. Ulaanbaatar, Mongolia: Oriental Literature Press, 1959.

McMahan, David L. *The Making of Buddhist Modernism*. New York: Oxford University Press, 2008.

Mills, Martin A. *Identity, Ritual and State in Tibetan Buddhism: The Foundations of Authority in Gelukpa Monasticism*. London; New York: RoutledgeCurzon, 2003.

——. "*Vajra* Brother, *Vajra* Sister: Renunciation, Individualism and the Household in Tibetan Buddhist Monasticism." *Journal of the Royal Anthropological Institute* 6, no. 1 (2003): 17–34.

Morozova, Irina Y. *Socialist Revolutions in Asia: The Social History of Mongolia in the 20th Century*. Abingdon, Oxon; New York: Routledge, 2009.

Moses, Larry William. *Introduction to Mongolian History and Culture*. Bloomington: Research Institute for Inner Asian Studies, Indiana University, 1985.

——. *The Political Role of Mongol Buddhism*. Bloomington: Asian Studies Research Institute, Indiana University, 1977.

Murphy, George G. S. *Soviet Mongolia: A Study of the Oldest Political Satellite*. Berkeley: University of California Press, 1966.

Napper, Elizabeth. *Dependent-Arising and Emptiness: A Tibetan Buddhist Interpretation of Madhyamika Philosophy Emphasizing the Compatibility of Emptiness and Conventional Phenomena*. Boston: Wisdom, 1989.

Natsagdorzh, Sh., Kh. Perlee, and Khureelen Tuukhiin. *Khalkhyn tuukh*. Ulaanbaatar: ["Bembi San" KhKhK], 2008.

Nattier, Jan. *Once Upon a Future Time: Studies in a Buddhist Prophecy of Decline*. Berkeley, Calif.: Asian Humanities Press, 1991.

Newland, Guy. "Debate Manuals (Yig Cha) in DGe Lugs Monastic Colleges." In *Tibetan Literature: Studies in Genre*, ed. José Ignacio Cabezón and Roger R Jackson, 202–16. Ithaca, N.Y.: Snow Lion, 1996.

Onon, Urgunge, and Derrick Pritchatt. *Asia's First Modern Revolution: Mongolia Proclaims Its Independence in 1911*. Leiden; New York: E. J. Brill, 1989.

Orsi, Robert A. *History and Presence*. Cambridge, Mass.: Harvard University Press, 2016.

Park, Jin Y. *Makers of Modern Korean Buddhism*. Albany: State University of New York Press, 2010.

Perdue, Daniel. *The Course in Buddhist Reasoning and Debate: An Asian Approach to Analytical Thinking Drawn from Indian and Tibetan Sources*. Boston: Snow Lion, 2013.

Perdue, Daniel, and Phur-bu-lcog Byams-pa-rgya-mtsho. *Debate in Tibetan Buddhism*. Ithaca, N.Y.: Snow Lion, 1992.

Perdue, Peter C. *China Marches West: The Qing Conquest of Central Eurasia*. Cambridge, Mass.: Belknap Press of Harvard University Press, 2005.

Pomerantz-Zhang, Linda. *Wu Tingfang (1842-1922): Reform and Modernization in Modern Chinese History*. Hong Kong: Hong Kong University Press, 1992.

Pozdneev, Aleksej M. *Mongolia and the Mongols*. Bloomington: Indiana University Press, 1971.

Pozdneev, Alekseĭ Matveevich, and John Richard Krueger. *Religion and Ritual in Society: Lamaist Buddhism in Late 19th-Century Mongolia*. Bloomington, Ind.: The Mongolia Society, 1978.

Purevzhav, S. *BNMAU-D sum khiid, lam naryn asuudlyg shiidverlesen ní : 1921-1940 on*. Ulaanbaatar: Ulsyn khevleliin khereg erkhlekh khoroo, 1965.

Quintman, Andrew. "Between History and Biography: Notes on Zhi Byed Ri Pa's 'Illuminating Lamp of Sun and Moon Beams,' a Fourteenth-Century Biographical State of the Field." *Revue d'Etudes Tibétaines* 23 (Avril 2012): 5–41.

——. *The Yogin and the Madman: Reading the Biographical Corpus of Tibet's Great Saint Milarepa.* New York: Columbia University Press, 2013.

Raldin, Kh. Ts. "Great October and the Affirmation of the Socialist Mongolian Nation." *Studia Historica* 7, no. 3 (1968).

Ramstedt, G. J. *Über die Konjugation des Khalkha-Mongolischen.* Helsingfors: Finnischen Litteraturgesellschaft, 1903.

Ramstedt, G. J., and John Richard Krueger. *Seven Journeys Eastward, 1898-1912: Among the Cheremis, Kalmyks, Mongols, and in Turkestan, and to Afghanistan.* Bloomington, Ind.: The Mongolia Society, 1978.

Ramstedt, G. J., and Suomalais-ugrilainen Seura. *Das Schriftmongolische und die Urgamundart, phonetisch verglichen.* Helsingfors: Druckerei der Finnischen Litteratur Gesellschaft, 1902.

Revault d'Allonnes, Myriam. *La crise sans fin: essai sur l'expérience moderne du temps.* Paris: Seuil, 2012.

Rupen, Robert A. "The Buriat Intelligentsia." *The Far Eastern Quarterly* 15, no. 3 (1956): 383–98.

——. *How Mongolia Is Really Ruled: A Political History of the Mongolian People's Republic, 1900-1978.* Stanford, Calif.: Hoover Institution Press, Stanford University, 1979.

——. *Mongols of the Twentieth Century.* Bloomington: Indiana University Press, 1964.

Sablin, Ivan. *Governing Post-Imperial Siberia and Mongolia, 1911-1924: Buddhism, Socialism, and Nationalism in State and Autonomy Building.* London; New York: Routledge, 2017.

Sandag, Sh., Harry H. Kendall, and Frederic E. Wakeman. *Poisoned Arrows: The Stalin-Choibalsan Mongolian Massacres, 1921-1941.* Boulder, Colo.: Westview Press, 2000.

Sanders, Alan J. K. *Mongolia: Politics, Economics and Society.* London; Boulder: F. Pinter; L. Rienner, 1987.

——. *The People's Republic of Mongolia: A General Reference Guide.* London; New York: Oxford University Press, 1968.

Sarkisyanz, Emanuel. "Communism and Lamaist Utopianism in Central Asia." *The Review of Politics* 20, no. 4 (1958): 623–33.

Schaeffer, Kurtis R. *Himalayan Hermitess: The Life of a Tibetan Buddhist Nun.* New York: Oxford University Press, 2004.

——. "New Scholarship in Tibet, 1650–1700." In *Forms of Knowledge in Early Modern Asia: Explorations in the Intellectual History of India and Tibet, 1500-1800*, ed. Sheldon Pollock, 291–310. Durham, N.C.: Duke University Press, 2011.

——. "Tibetan Biography: Growth and Criticism." In *Editions, Éditions: L'Écrit Au Tibet, Évolution et Devenir.* München: Indus Verlag, 2010.

Schorkowitz, Dittmar. *Staat und nationalitäten in Rußland: der Integrationsprozess der Burjaten und Kalmücken, 1822-1925.* Stuttgart: F. Steiner Verlag, 2001.

Schuh, Dieter. *Erlasse und Sendschreiben mongolischer Herrscher für tibetische Geistliche. Ein Beitrag zur Kenntnis der Urkunden des tibetischen Mittelalters und ihrer Diplomatik.* St. Augustin: VGH-Wissenschaftsverlag, 1977.

Schwieger, Peter. *The Dalai Lama and the Emperor of China: A Political History of the Tibetan Institution of Reincarnation*. New York: Columbia University Press, 2015.

Shirendyb, B. *By-Passing Capitalism*. Ulaanbaatar: Mongolian People's Republic State Press, 1968.

——. *V. I. Lenin I Mongolyskiy Narod (V. I. Lenin and the Mongolian People)*, n.d.

Smith, E. Gene, and Kurtis R. Schaeffer. *Among Tibetan Texts: History and Literature of the Himalayan Plateau*. Boston: Wisdom, 2001.

Sneath, David. "Political Mobilization and the Construction of Collective Identity in Mongolia." *Central Asian Survey Central Asian Survey* 29, no. 3 (2010): 251–67.

Snelling, John. *Buddhism in Russia: The Story of Agvan Dorzhiev, Lhasa's Emissary to the Tzar*. Shaftesbury, Dorset; Rockport, Mass.: Element, 1993.

Sobisch, Jan-Ulrich. "The 'Records of Teachings Received' in the Collected Works of A Mes Zhabs: An Untapped Source for the Study of Sa Skya Pa Biographies." In *Tibet, Past and Present: Tibetan Studies I. PIATS 2000: Tibetan Studies: Proceedings of the Ninth Seminar of the International Association Fro Tibetan Studies, Leiden 2000*, 1:161–81. Leiden; Boston; Köln: Brill, 2002.

Soninbayar, Sh. *Lawain Egshig*. 2. Ulaanbaatar: Gadentegchenling Khiid, 1997.

Stenmark, Lisa L. "Going Public: Feminist Epistemologies, Hannah Arendt, and the Science-and-Religion Discourse." In *The Oxford Handbook of Religion and Science*, ed. Philip Clayton, 821–35. New York: Oxford University Press, 2008.

Stoler, Ann Laura. *Imperial Debris: On Ruins and Ruination*. Durham, N.C.: Duke University Press, 2013.

Stoler, Ann Laura, and Carole McGranahan. "Refiguring Imperial Terrains." In *Imperial Formations*, ed. Ann Laura Stoler, Carole McGranahan, and Peter C. Perdue, 3–42. Santa Fe, N.M. : School for Advanced Research Press, 2007.

Tachibana, Makoto. "From Chronicle to National History: Mongolian Historiography in the Early Twentieth Century." Paper presented at the Association for Asian Studies 2017 Annual Conference, Toronto, March 19, 2017.

Taube, Manfred. "Die Bedeutung Eiheimischer Bibliographien Für Die Erforschung Der Tibetischen Literatur." *Studia Asiae, Festschrift Zum 70. Geburtstag von Johannes Schubert*, 277–99. Halle: Buddhist Centre Halle, 1968.

Teleki, Krisztina. "Bogdiin Khüree: Monasteries and Temples of the Mongolian Capital (1651–1938)." *Études Mongoles, Sibériennes, Centralasiatiques et Tibétaines* 40 (2009).

——. *Monasteries and Temples of Bogdiin Khuree*. Ulaanbaatar: Institute of History, Mongolian Academy of Sciences, 2011.

——. "Mongólia Kolostorai Az Arany Krónika Jegyzéke Alapján." In *Bolor-un gerel: Kristályfény : Tanulmányok Kara György Professzor 70. Születésnapjának Tiszteletére*, ed. Ágnes Birtalan, 2:773–90. Budapest: Eötvös Lóránd Tudományegyetem, Belső-ázsiai Tanszék, 2005.

Tenpa, Lobsang. "The 1913 Mongol-Tibet Treaty and the Dalai Lama's Proclamation of Independence." *The Tibet Journal* 37, no. 2 (2012): 3–29.

The History of Mongolia 3, The Qing Period Twentieth-Century Mongolia. S.l.: s.n., 2010.

Thrower, James. *Marxist-Leninist "Scientific Atheism" and the Study of Religion and Atheism in the USSR*. Berlin; New York: Mouton, 1983.

Thuken Losang Chökyi Nyima. *The Crystal Mirror of Philosophical Systems: A Tibetan Study of Asian Religious Thought*. Trans. Geshé Lundub Sopa. Boston: Wisdom, 2009.

Tillemans, Tom J. F. "Formal and Semantic Aspects of Tibetan Buddhist Debate Logic." *Journal of Indian Philosophy* 17 (1989).

Tsultemin, Uranchimeg. "Cartographic Anxieties in Mongolia: The Bogd Khan's Picture-Map." *Cross-Currents: East Asian History and Cultural Review* 21 (2016): 66–87.

——. "Ikh Khüree: A Nomadic Monastery and the Later Buddhist Art of Mongolia." PhD. diss., University of California, Berkeley, 2009.

Tsyrempilov, Nikolay. "Modernizing Sangha: Buryat Buddhist Community in the Age of Revolution and Secularization, 1905–1940." Paper presented at the conference onTraditional Religions, Secularisms, and Revivals: Buddhism and Shamanism in Northern Eurasia, Käte Hamburger Kolleg Dynamics in the History of Religions between Asia and Europe, Ruhr University Bochum, March 9, 2018.

——. "The Open and Secret Diplomacy of Tsarist and Soviet Russia in Tibet: The Role of Agvan Dorzhiev (1912–1925)." In *Asiatic Russia: Imperial Power in Regional and International Contexts*, ed. Tomochiko Uyama. London and New York: Routledge, 2012.

——. "Samdan Tsydenov and His Buddhist Theocratic Project." In *Biographies of Eminent Mongol Buddhists*, ed. Johan Elverskog, 117–38. Halle: IITBS, International Institute for Tibetan and Buddhist Studies, 2008.

Tubyansky, Mikhael. "Nekotorye Problemy Mongol'skoi Literatury Dorevoly-Utsionnogo Perioda [Some Problems of Mongolian Literature of the Pre-Revolutionary Period]." *Sovremennaya Mongoliya* 5, no. 12 (1935): 7–30.

Tulisow, Jerzy, Osamu Inoue, Agata Bareja-Starzynska, and Ewa Dziurzyńska, eds. *In the Heart of Mongolia: 100th Anniversary of W. Kotwicz's Expedition to Mongolia in 1912: Studies and Selected Source Materials.* Crakow: Polish Academy of Arts and Sciences, 2012.

Tuttle, Gray. "Challenging Central Tibet's Dominance of History: The Oceanic Book, a Nineteenth-Century Politico-Religious Geographic History." In *Mapping the Modern in Tibet. PIATS 2006: Proceedings of the Eleventh Seminar of the International Association for Tibetan Studies. Königswinter 2006*, ed. Gray Tuttle, 135–72. Andiast, Switzerland: IITBS, International Institute for Tibetan and Buddhist Studies GmbH, 2011.

——. *Mapping the Modern in Tibet. PIATS 2006: Tibetan Studies: Proceedings of the Eleventh Seminar of the International Association for Tibetan Studies.* Königswinter: International Institute for Tibetan and Buddhist Studies GmbH, 2011.

——. "Pattern Recognition: Tracking the Spread of the Incarnation Institution Through Time and Across History." *Revue d'Etudes Tibétaines* 38 (Février 2017): 29–64.

——. "Tibetan Buddhism at Ri Bo Rtse Lnga/Wutai Shan in Modern Times." *Journal of the International Association of Tibetan Studies* 1, no. 2 (2006).

——. *Tibetan Buddhists in the Making of Modern China.* New York: Columbia University Press, 2007.

Ujeed, Sangseraima. "The Thob Yig Gsal Ba'i Me Long by Dza-Ya Paṇḍita Blo-Bzang 'phin-Las (1642–1715): An Enquiry into Biographies as Lineage History." Ph.D. thesis, University of Oxford, 2017.

Uspenskij, Vladimir L. "Ancient History of the Mongols According to Gombojab, an Eighteenth-Century Mongolian Historian." *Rocznik Orientalistyczny* (2005):236–41.

——. "The Previous Incarnations of the Qianlong Emperor According to the Panchen Lama Blo Bzang Dpal Ldan Ye Shes." In *Tibet, Past and Present: Tibetan Studies I.*

PIATS 2000: Tibetan Studies: Proceedings of the Ninth Seminar of the International Association for Tibetan Studies, ed. Henk McKay Blezer, 215–28. Leiden; Boston; Köln: Brill, 2002.

Van Vleet, Stacey. "Medicine, Monasteries and Empire: Rethinking Tibetan Buddhism in Qing China." Ph.D. diss., Columbia University, 2015.

Vassilijev, V. P. "Die Auf Den Buddhismus Bezüglichen Werke Der Universitätsbibliothek Zu Kasan." *Melanges Asiatiques* 2 (1856): 347–86.

Vostrikov, A. I. *Tibetan Historical Literature.* Richmond, Surrey: Curzon Press, 1994.

Wallace, Vesna. "Diverse Aspects of the Mongolian Buddhist Manuscript Culture and Realms of Its Influence." In *Buddhist Manuscript Culture: Knowledge, Ritual, and Art*, ed. Steven Berkwitz, Juliane Schober, and Claudia Brown. London: Routledge, 2008.

——. "Envisioning a Mongolian Buddhist Identity Through Chinggis Khan." In *Buddhism in Mongolian History, Culture, and Society.* New York: Oxford University Press, 2015.

——. "How Vajrapāṇi Became a Mongol." In *Buddhism in Mongolian History, Culture, and Society*, 179–201. New York: Oxford University Press, 2015.

——. "Mongolian Livestock Rituals and Their Appropriations, Adaptations, and Permutations." In *Understanding Religious Rituals: Theoretical Approaches and Innovations*, ed. John Hoffmann. London: Routledge, 2011.

——. "Texts as Deities: Mongols' Rituals of Worshipping Sutras and Rituals of Accomplishing Various Goals by Means of Sutras." In *Ritual in Tibetan Buddhism*, ed. José Cabezón. New York: Oxford University Press, 2009.

Wang, Xiangyun. *Tibetan Buddhism at the Court of Qing: The Life and Work of LCang-Skya Rol-Pa'i-Rdo-Rje, 1717–86.* Ph.D. thesis, Harvard University, 1995.

Watt, John R. "The Yamen and Urban Administration." In *The City in Late Imperial China*, ed. George William Skinner, 353–90. Stanford, Calif.: Stanford University Press, 1977.

White, Hayden V. *Metahistory: The Historical Imagination in Nineteenth-Century Europe.* Baltimore: Johns Hopkins University Press, 1973.

Willis, Janice Dean. *Enlightened Beings: Life Stories from the Ganden Oral Tradition.* Boston: Wisdom, 1995.

Ye-śes-mtsho-rgyal, Tarthang Tulku, and gter-ston O-rgyan-glin-pa. *The Life and Liberation of Padmasambhava, Padma Bka' Thaṅ.* Berkeley, Calif.: Dharma Publications, 2007.

Yongdan, Lobsang. "Tibet Charts the World: The Btsan Po No Mon Han's Detailed Description of the World, an Early Major Scientific Work in Tibet." In *Mapping the Modern in Tibet*, ed. Gray Tuttle. Königswinter: IITBS, International Institute for Tibetan and Buddhist Studies GmbH, 2011.

Zhambal, Boryn, Charles R. Bawden, Ts. Damdinsüren, and England Institute of Buddhist Studies. *Tales of an Old Lama.* Tring: Institute of Buddhist Studies, 1997.

Index

Abahai, 113–14

Abél-Remussat, Jean-Pierre, 67–68

Abhidharma, the, 48, 72, 77, 170, 192, 245n58

An Account of Bringing Together Mother and Son (Zava Damdin), 138

Agamben, Giorgio, 153–54

Akim, G., 145

Alashan monastery, 49

All-Illuminating Emanated Mirror That Reflects the Source of the Victor's Teachings. See *The Mirror*

Altan Khan, 63, 69

The Amber Rosary (Jamsrano letter to Zava Damdin), 182–83

Amdo, Zava Damdin's journey to (1899), 48–53

Americas: Euro-American narratives and scholarship, 22, 154, 199, 200, 205; Mongol peoples in, 76

Amitābha, 115

Anandin Amar, 88

Angi Shagdar, 57

archaeology, 72, 88, 92, 104, 126–27, 129, 148

An Arrangement of Translations from Mongol Into Tibetan as an Appendix to the Memoranda Explanations of Great Mongolia's Ancient History. See *The Memoranda*

Asad, Talal, 205

Atwood, Christopher, 68

autobiographical genres, 32–34, 37–40, 43, 123, 125, 218nn 37–39

autobiographical writing of Zava Damdin, 29–58, 123–46; accounts of activities during the socialist period (1921–1937), 139–43; accounts of childhood and youth, 40–45; accounts of education and teaching, 46–48; accounts of journey to eastern Tibet (Amdo; 1899), 48–53; accounts of late life, 143–46; accounts of middle age, 130–32; accounts of mystical experiences, 40, 49–51, 123–30; accounts of travels to Mount Wutai and Beijing (1906), 37, 124–30; autobiography of 1936 (see *Summary of This Life's Activities*); explicit political and ethnographic details absent from, 49, 55, 130, 133–34, 136; and "inner" biography, 23, 40, 49, 123, 125; and "outer" biography, 23, 40, 49, 125;

d'Allonned, Myriam Revault, 88–89
Darva Paṇḍita, 38, 52, 56, 223n89,
    244n46
Dashichoijurling monastic college, 1–5,
    8, 11, 35, 46–48
debates/dialectical contests, 44, 46–48,
    56–57, 127, 141
de Certeau, Michel, 7–8, 35, 92, 161
degeneracy, 151–67, 171–72, 239n8
Delgeriin Choira monastery, 41, 195–96.
    See also Chöying Ösel Ling
    monastery
Delgertsogt, 41, 195
Deva Rinpoché, 201–2
The Dharma Conch (Zava Damdin; c.
    1910), 60–61, 64, 69; and Buddhism
    and early Mongol agency in Tibet
    and China, 108; and cosmology,
    191–92; and ethnopolitical units of
    Mongolian peoples, 82–83; and the
    First Jebtsundamba and the origins
    of the Qing-Géluk formation, 117–19;
    and history of the Dharma in
    Mongolia, 102–4, 108, 110, 111; and
    Khotan, 104; and the Two Systems,
    92–93
Dharmakīrti, 190–91
Dharmatāla Damchö Gyatso, 102, 191,
    244n54
diaspora and refugee communities, 6,
    25, 66, 72, 88, 194, 198–203
disenchantment, 92, 169; and post-Qing
    situation, 168–93; Zava Damdin's
    theorization of the causes and
    directions of disenchantment of
    Eurasia, 24, 150–67, 171–74
Dorjé Shukden lineage, 160
Dorjé Shukden ritual collections, 143,
    201
Dorjé Shukden schism, 25, 170, 201–3,
    238n49
Dorjé Tenpa monastery, 44
Dorjiev, Agvan, 25, 63, 179, 199, 243nn
    42,43,44; arrests and death of, 186;
    background and career, 59, 186–87;
    and Buddhism and socialism,

186–87; Dalai Lama and, 15, 53, 59,
    186; and location of the Land of Li,
    105–6; as member or the Buryat
    Intelligentsia, 176; and moderniza-
    tion of Buddhist scholasticism,
    180–81; and questions for Zava
    Damdin, 59–61, 188–90; and Russian
    Revolution and Kālacakra imagery,
    141–42
doro shajin, 96
Drakgön Zhapdrung Könchok Tengpa
    Rapgyé, 82
Drapka Gyeltsen, 150, 168, 170, 172–73
Drépung monastery, 44, 46, 50, 219n54
Dreyfus, Georges, 202
Drop of Amṛta (Zava Damdin; 1900), 52,
    63–64, 92–93
Drotsang, 51
Duara, Prasenjit, 7
Dungkurpa, 110–11, 243n53

earth, roundness of, 72, 191
education: Buddhist reform movement
    and reformation of monastic
    education, 180–88; and debates/
    dialectical contests, 44, 46–48,
    56–57, 127; Dharmakīrti and, 190–91;
    education of Zava Damdin, 43–44,
    46–53, 58; and mixing of social
    categories, 183–85; monastic
    colleges as centers of intellectual
    activity, 35–36; Zava Damdin's
    expansion of monastic curricula
    and colleges, 140–41
Elverskog, Johan, 13, 75, 127
empiricism, 25, 37, 169, 171, 175, 188–93.
    See also science
"empty" time. See "real" and "empty"
    time
enchantment, 91; and autobiographical
    writing, 37; and histories of Qing
    time, space, communities, and
    religiosity, 58; and "real" and
    "empty" time, 24; and three
    dispensations story of the Dharma
    in Mongol lands, 100–119; and the

The Golden Book (cont.)
Qing, 158–67; and prophecies
warning about degeneracy, 171–74;
and the "Sixteen Pure Human
Laws," 175, 241–42n13; structure and
contents, 69–70; Tubyansky and, 88;
and the Two Systems, 92–93; and
Zava Damdin's objections to social
mobility/mixing of social catego-
ries, 174–75; and Zava Damdin's
travels to Mount Wutai, 125
Gomboev, Galsan, 176
Gombojab, 39, 75, 102, 103
Gönlung monastery, 51
Goodyear, Sara Suleri, 22–23
Great, Amazing Golden Book. See *The
Golden Book*
Great Britain, 17, 24, 53–54
Great Tang Records (Xuanzang),
66–67
Guangji Temple, 129
Guangxu, Emperor, 55
Gündinjal, 145
Gungachoiling monastic college, 46–48,
54. *See also* Dashichoijurling
monastic college
Güng Gombojab, 67
Gungtang Könchok Tenpé Drönmé, 158,
166
Gungtangpa, 111–12
Gushri Tsépel, 191
Güüshi Khan, 94, 116, 231n6
Güyük, 112
Gyatso, Janet, 39, 218n37
Gyayak Trülku, 51

historical works of Zava Damdin, 23–24,
59–89, 147–67; *An Account of Bringing
Together Mother and Son*, 138; and
archaeology, 72, 88, 92, 104, 148;
arguments about Buddhism and
early Mongol agency in Tibet and
China, 24, 68, 72, 100–108, 199; Bira
on, 8–9; Boγda Khaγanate's state
history project, 64–66; and the
British invasion of Tibet and the

flight of the Dalai Lama, 54–55; and
catalogue of monastic colleges, 36;
and the causes and consequences of
the Qing collapse, 60, 150–67; and
the challenges of writing, 137–38;
Chandra and, 11; and Chinggis Khan
and the Mongol Empire, 108–13; and
collapse of the Qing Empire, 60,
149–67; cosmopolitan sources (old
and new) and synthetic nature of
works, 60, 61, 66–68, 71, 75, 82–89, 92,
102–5, 147, 166, 203–4; and the deep
history of Mongolian peoples, 60, 63,
75–89, 137–38, 199; *The Dharma Conch*
(see *The Dharma Conch*); and diaspora
and refugee communities, 198–203;
Drop of Amṛta, 52, 63–64, 92–93; and
enlightened beings, 157–67; *Excellent
Gift to Please Scholars*, 70; and the Fifth
Jebtsundamba Khutuγtu and
following fraudulent Jebtsundamba
Khutuγtus, 158–67; and Géluk
scholastic tradition, 70–71, 80, 89,
148–49; and geography of Asia,
80–82, 84; *The Golden Book* (see *The
Golden Book*); histories of material
objects, 70; histories of monastic
institutions, 70; history of Buddhism
in Mongol lands, 36, 62–64, 75, 83–84,
100–119, 199; identification of
additional early nomadic peoples as
"Mongols," 75–89, 102–3; identification of the Land of Li, 103–5; major
historical works, 63, 69 (see also *The
Golden Book*); *The Memoranda* (see *The
Memoranda*); middle-length historical works, 63, 66; minor historical
studies, 63, 70; *The Mirror* (annotated
translation of Faxian's *Fuguoji*; 1917),
66–68; motivations for writing,
64–66, 69, 88, 136, 138; overview of
works, 62–72; and paleography, 72,
147, 148; and philology, 72, 75, 80,
84–86, 92, 108, 147; polemical letters,
63; prophetic sources (*see* prophecy);
and Qing-Géluk formation, 113–19;

radical claims and extensions of narratives in, 60, 61, 64, 66, 68, 71, 75–89, 101–13, 199–200 (*see also specific topics under this heading*); and "real" and "empty" time, 24, 72–75, 77, 81, 84, 89, 91–92, 111, 149, 164, 199; and *ten-tsi* genre, 52; and three dispensations story of the Dharma in Mongol lands, 64, 100–119; *Tibetan Translation of the Inscriptions for the Chinese Sixteen Arhats Together with Supplementary Explanations*, 70; and the Two Systems, 92–94; writing style and structure of works, 63, 68–71

History of Buddhism in China (Gombojab), 75, 102

History of Buddhism in Mongolia (Gushri Tsépel), 191

History of the Dharma, a Lamp on Scripture and Reasoning (Ngakwang Nyima), 199

Ho, Engseng, 7

homo sacer, 154

Huber, Toni, 97

Humphrey, Caroline, 18

incarnation lineages: courtly and monastic incarnations in Qing imperial order, 2, 13–14; current incarnation of Zava Damdin, 41, 194–97, 201–2; Dalai Lamas as incarnations of Avalokiteśvara, 74, 94, 95, 115; Jebtsundamba Khutuγtus as incarnations of Vajrapāṇi, 115, 116; "lama problem" of revolutionary factions, 16–18; Manchu emperors as incarnations of Mañjuśrī, 1–4, 95, 97, 114–16; and origins of the Two Systems, 13–14; Panchen Lamas as incarnations of Amitābha, 115; recognition of incarnations forbidden in Mongolian People's Republic, 6; and the "state of exception" and making lamas

killable, 153–56; and Tibetan themes of presence of enlightened beings in the material world, 13–14 (*see also* enlightened beings); tsars and tsarinas as incarnations of White Tārā, 115; Zava Damdin's past and future lives, 30–31

India, 2, 8, 11; diaspora and refugee communities, 199–200; Faxian's *Fuguoji* and, 66–68; and history of the Dharma in Mongolia, 33, 100–106, 109–10; and history of the Dharma in Tibet, 108; and monastic education, 183–84; and Mongol peoples, 80–81, 87; and previous incarnations of Zava Damdin, 30, 31

"inner" biography, 39–40, 49, 123, 125, 218n39

Jambudvīpa, 2

Jamsrano, Tseveen, 25, 61, 63, 85, 88, 176–87, 242n25

Jamyang Chöjé, 116

Jamyang Lama Tendar, 54

Jamyang Zhépa, incarnation of, 49

Jangji-a Khutuγtu Rölpe Dorjé, 39, 51, 71, 127, 156–57

Japan, 8, 12, 17, 76

Jebtsundamba Khutuγtus, 158–67; First Jebtsundamba (Zanabazar), 116–19, 158–59; Fourth Jebtsundamba (Lubsangtübdanwangchug), 160–61; Fifth Jebtsundamba (Tsültimjigmidambajaltsan), 158–64; Eighth Jebtsundamba (Boγda Gegegen Khaγan), 14–15, 53–54, 64, 132, 158, 164 (*see also* Boγda Khaγanate); fraudulent later Jebtsundama Khutūtus, 164–67; as incarnations of Vajrapāṇi, 115, 116; and prophecy, 161–64; and Qing-Gélук formation, 117–19, 158–67; and the Thirteenth Dalai Lama, 53–54

jel, 49

Jigjid ("Lord of Exposition"), 46

and Jebtsundamba Khutuɣtus,
158–67; and prophecy, 1–5, 159,
161–64; and three dispensations
story of the Dharma in Mongol
lands, 100–119; Zava Damdin's
history of/praise for, 1–4, 91–94,
113–19, 200; and Zava Damdin's
pilgrimage to Mount Wutai and
Beijing, 124; and Zava Damdin's
vision of deep history, 76–77 (*see also*
historical works of Zava Damdin).
See also Two Systems, the

Rabjamjamyan, 87
Ramstedt, Gustaf John, 86, 181, 229n74
rang-nam, 39–40
Rashipunsuɣ, 75, 100, 102
"real" and "empty" time, 24, 72–75, 89,
149, 199; and Chinggis Khan and the
Mongol Empire, 111; and collapse of
the Qing Empire, 91, 164; and death
of the Fifth Jebtsundamba
Khutuɣtu, 164; and deep history of
Mongol lands and peoples, 84;
defined/described, 73–74; and First
Jebsundamba Khutuɣtu, 116; and
geography of Asia, 81; intersection
of the real and the empty ("enchant-
ment"), 92, 98; and Zava Damdin's
travels to Mount Wutai, 125. *See also*
Qing-Géluk formation
*The Record of Teachings Received That
Tastes Some of the Ambrosial Nectar of
the Virtuous, Holy Dharma in the
Beginning, End, and Middle. See The
Catalogue*
Réla Trülku, 166
Ricoeur, Paul, 88
Rinchen, B., 67
Rinchino, Elbekdorji, 176
The Root Tantra of Mañjuśrī, 150–51, 170
*Root Verses of the History of the Dharma in
Mongolia. See The Dharma Conch*
Rosary of White Lotuses (Dharmatāla),
191
Rupen, Robert, 176

Russia/Soviet Union: activities and
influence in post-Qing Mongolia,
15–17, 36–37, 54, 67–68, 176–88; and
Buryat Intelligentsia, 176–83; Géluk
monks as intermediaries for Qing
and tsarist powers, 12–14; intellectual institutions, 36–37, 67, 242n25;
and Kālacakra Tantra, 141–42; and
nostalgia, 91; scholarship on Zava
Damdin, 8–9; tsars and tsarinas as
incarnations of White Tārā, 115;
White Russian occupation of
Mongolia (1920), 69, 134, 177. *See also
specific scholars*

Sakya Paṇḍita, 112–13, 125, 170, 200
Śambhala, kingdom of, 17, 80, 81, 142
Sāmudra, 48
Samyé monastery, 108
Sando, 131
Sanggyé Gyatso, 94, 116, 161
Sangjai (Ācārya Sangai), 42, 43, 44, 46
Sarkisyanz, Emanuel, 16–17
Śata-Piṭaka Series in Indo-Asian Literatures
(Chandra), 11
Sayin Noyan, 55
Schaeffer, Kurtis, 39
scholar tours, 53, 141, 143
Schuh, Dieter, 112
science: and Buddhist reform movement and reformation of monastic
education, 180–88; and cosmology,
191–92; European knowledge and
scholarship disseminated via the
New Mirror newspaper, 85, 192; and
"karmic relativity," 191–92; scientific associations in Urga formed by
Jamsrano, 181–82; and Zava Damdin's affiliation with post-Qing
intellectual institutions, 36–37, 182;
Zava Damdin's rejection of the
authority of scientific knowledge/
empiricism, 25, 37, 169, 171, 175,
188–93
"secret" biography, 40, 49, 123, 125,
218n39

historical works of Zava Damdin);
Ramstedt and, 86; return to Gobi
homeland for last visit with parents,
51–52; and scholar tours, 53, 141, 143;
scholastic career in Urga, 45–48, 51;
and self-censorship, 55, 132, 170; as
senior monastic figure in Gobi
homeland, 140; as senior monastic
figure in Urga, 23, 52, 129–30, 140;
Shcherbatsky and, 58; tantric
initiation, 51; as tantric practitioner,
52, 141–43 (see also Kālacakra
Tantra); as teacher, 48, 52, 133, 135,
140; teachers, 42–44, 46, 48, 49, 51;
theorization of the causes and
directions of disenchantment of
Eurasia, 24, 150–67, 171–74; as "the

spiritual friend who pleases
Mañjughoṣa" (address at Dashichoijurling monastic college, 1924), 1–4,
37, 140; translation of materials into
Tibetan, 66–70, 85, 86, 181 (see also
The Memoranda); travels to Mount
Wutai and Beijing, 37, 124–30, 236nn
17,20, 237n21; and Tsakhiurtiin
khiid banner monastery, 42, 44;
Tubyansky and, 87–88; and writing
about the post-Qing situation,
168–93; writing style and structure
of works, 32–34, 40, 63, 68–71, 169–70
Zava Damdin Rebüchi Luwsandarjaa,
195–97
Zaya Paṇḍita Lubsangperinlei, 33, 34,
38, 54, 95